The Lessons
of Wage and Price Controls—
The Food Sector

The Lessons
of Wage and Price Controls—
The Food Sector

Edited by John T. Dunlop and Kenneth J. Fedor

John T. Dunlop   Ray A. Goldberg   Reginald J. Brown

Glenn L. Nelson   Kenneth J. Fedor   William M. Vaughn, III

DIVISION OF RESEARCH
GRADUATE SCHOOL OF BUSINESS ADMINISTRATION
HARVARD UNIVERSITY
BOSTON   ●   1977

Distributed by Harvard University Press, Cambridge, Mass.   ●   *London, England*

© Copyright 1977

by the President and Fellows of Harvard College

Library of Congress Catalog Card No. 77-86591
ISBN 0-87584-117-1

Faculty research at the Harvard Business School is undertaken with the expectation of publication. In such publication the Faculty member responsible for the research project is also responsible for statements of fact, opinions, and conclusions expressed. Neither the Harvard Business School, its Faculty as a whole, nor the President and Fellows of Harvard College reach conclusions or make recommendations as results of Faculty research.

Printed in the United States of America by
DEKR Corporation and The Book Press

Contents

Tables

Appendix Tables

Illustrations

INTRODUCTION

JOHN T. DUNLOP

Introduction

John T. Dunlop

AN UNDERLYING RATE *of inflation of 5% or 6% a year in 1976 and 1977 continues to focus attention on public policy measures to constrain price and wage increases. These rates are more than double the average of the 20 years before 1973 in this country. The standard economic forecasts out to 1980 envisage no diminution in this rate of inflation. The risks in the forecast, moreover, appear to lie on the side of an acceleration.*

President Carter stated on February 23, 1977, in response to a news conference question: "I announced earlier my firm commitment not to have mandatory wage and price laws or authority, not to have standby wage and price authority. . . . But I will retain the option in the future of assessing what we need to do to control inflation." But earlier presidents have made comparable disavowal statements and then found it imperative or convenient to resort to direct wage and price controls. The specter of controls is not easy to dissipate with its inflationary effects arising from precautionary increases. Moreover, public opinion polls in December 1976 reflected that the American public is almost equally divided between favoring and opposing controls, and a higher rate of inflation develops public support for controls.

There is a considerable body of economic and editorial opinion which advocates measures to constrain inflation short of controls by guidelines, guideposts, jawboning, prenotification, and various forms of "incomes policies" involving more or less elements of coercion. The use of these approaches has the defect that they tend to create a demand for more stringent forms of direct controls. Devices that are less than full controls will appear to be unsuccessful; private parties are likely to resist public preachments, and the resort to direct controls that appear to be more powerful will be widely urged with accelerating inflation. Government intervention tends to escalate.

In this setting, an informed account of the operations, problems, and issues of controls in one of the most sensitive and vital sectors of the economy—food and processed agriculture—is designed to provide both a realistic view of the controls alternative, its international repercussions, and a statement of the hard lessons of the past should that alternative be selected again by a president and congress. This analysis of controls should encourage in times of severe price pressures a closer consideration of other alternatives to direct restraint of prices and wages in the food manufacturing, wholesale, and retail sectors, including production stimulus, export restraints, and subsidies.

Within each era of wage and price controls in our history there have been changes in policies, institutions, and administrators with changing economic conditions, political strains and necessities, and administrative styles. The stabilization programs of 1971–1974 were no exception; indeed, these changes were probably more sharply delineated and labeled in phases and stages than in the Korean War period or during the World War II era and its immediate aftermath.

From August 15, 1971, to April 30, 1974, there were two periods of freeze, the first applied to wages and prices and the second only to prices. The controls period involved four phases, and the fourth had two stages relating to food prices. There were a number of major changes in administrative organizations, in substantive rules and regulations, and a major change in administrators was made on January 11, 1973, the dividing point between Phase II and Phase III. There were, of course, certain continuities in policies, procedures, and forms throughout the period.

In order to assist the reader in following these changes and to facilitate familiarity with the specialized vocabulary, the following tabulation for ready reference is designed to show the major changes in organization in chronological order.

ECONOMIC STABILIZATION PROGRAM, 1971–1974

PHASE I (FREEZE I)—*90-day wage and price freeze, August 15 to November 13, 1971.*

> Administered directly by the Cost of Living Council. John B. Connally, Secretary of the Treasury, Chairman, and Arnold R. Weber, Executive Director.

PHASE II—*November 14, 1971, to January 10, 1973.*

> The Cost of Living Council provided general supervision of the program, John B. Connally, Secretary of the Treasury, Chairman, and Donald Rumsfeld, Director.

> The Price Commission was comprised of seven members, C. Jackson Grayson, Chairman.

> The Pay Board, originally tripartite, had Judge George H. Bolt as Chairman.

PHASE III—*January 11, 1973 to June 12, 1973.*

> The Cost of Living Council was under the chairmanship of George P. Shultz, Secretary of the Treasury, John T. Dunlop, Director. The Price Commission and Pay Board were abolished and the Director directly administered wage and price controls, including decontrol, until authority for controls expired on April 30, 1974.

> A Food Committee of the Cost of Living Council was chaired by the Chairman of the Cost of Living Council and included the Secretary of Agriculture, the Director, the Chairman of the Council of Economic Advisers, and the Director of Office of Management and Budget.

> A labor-management advisory committee to the Chairman and Director of the Cost of Living Council was established. A Tripartite Food Industry Wage and Salary Committee was established to administer wage controls. A Cost of Living Council Food Advisory Committee was comprised of members from various enterprises in the food and agricultural sector, from consumer groups, academic specialists and from labor organizations.

Freeze II—*June 13, 1973, for a period up to 60 days; depending on sector.*

Phase IV—*August 12, 1973, to April 30, 1974.*

There were two stages of implementation for food:

Stage A—Transition from freeze to margin control, August 12 to September 8, 1973.

Stage B—Food margin control, September 9, 1973, to end of controls.

Wage and price controls, initiated with the freeze of August 15, 1971, expired on April 30, 1974, and the Cost of Living Council that had responsibility for their administration lapsed two months later. A stabilization unit placed in the Treasury was concerned for six months thereafter with wind-down operations and the preparation of historical records and studies.

In the fall of 1974 discussion with former colleagues in the Cost of Living Council, all of us then in the private sector, suggested a cooperative venture to review the experience with controls in the food and agricultural sector and to attempt to state succinctly the lessons for future periods of public policy concern with inflation, and particularly with food and agricultural inflation. We were all acutely aware of the pivotal role of food and agricultural prices to all stabilization programs and particularly to the 1971–1974 experience.

On January 16 and 27, 1975, two discussion sessions were held at the Harvard University Graduate School of Business Administration with a dozen or more specialists familiar with the program including Donald S. Perkins, Chairman of the Board, Jewel Companies, Inc., who had been chairman of the Cost of Living Council Food Advisory Committee that had made an outstanding contribution to the formulation and critique of the stabilization program as it changed in the difficult circumstances of 1973–1974. These discussions considered early drafts of Chapters I and V and centered upon general lessons of the period.

The authors of the first five chapters continued to develop their materials and conclusions in 1975 and early 1976 when my return to the University again, after a lapse of almost another year in the government, permitted a resumption of responsibilities for this volume.

Five of the six authors worked for the Cost of Living Council. All of the authors have at one time or another been associated with teaching and research in universities. Two of the six authors are currently working for businesses in the food sector and one has returned to work for the government; the other three are associated with universities. Thus, the authors as a group have had a wide degree of experience in government and business as well as research in the academic world.

When Dean Lawrence E. Fouraker of the Harvard Graduate School of Business Administration heard of the proposed volume in the fall of 1974, he suggested that the project become a research activity of the Business School. An allocation from the funds contributed by The Associates of the Harvard Business School was made to defray the expenses of the project, editorial work, and publication costs. We are indebted to Dean Fouraker and the Business School for this support and to Ruth Norton and Nancy Hansen for editorial and publication guidance.

Soldiers Field
Boston, Massachusetts
June 1977

CHAPTER I

Agricultural Developments

GLENN L. NELSON

GLENN L. NELSON

Glenn L. Nelson is associate professor in the Department of Agricultural and Applied Economics, University of Minnesota. He was formerly assistant professor in the Department of Agricultural Economics, Purdue University. He served with the Cost of Living Council as branch chief of the Analytic Branch, Policy Analysis Division, Office of Food where his duties included supervising economic and statistical analyses related to food and agricultural policy. His governmental experience also includes positions as economist of the Policy Research Division, Office of Economic Opportunity, and as a consultant for higher education with the Bureau of Higher Education, Michigan Department of Education.

Professor Nelson is the author of two reports on the impact of price controls, prepared under contract with the U.S. Department of the Treasury; he was also a consultant for a study of shortages in the livestock-feed grain sector which was funded by the National Commission on Supplies and Shortages.

He was a member of a task force jointly sponsored by the Economic Statistics Committee of the American Agricultural Economics Association and by the Economic Research Service of the U.S. Department of Agriculture which reported in January 1976 on Review and Evaluation of Price Spread Data for Foods.

CHAPTER I

Agricultural Developments

THE NARRATIVE of developments in the food and agricultural sector of the U.S. economy during the Economic Stabilization Program is examined in this chapter.[1] The emphasis is on the interplay between economic events and governmental policy. Even though the proximate cause for government action was often public pressure, in most cases there were important underlying economic events behind this pressure. The broad range of federal agricultural and food policy is included, rather than limiting the discussion to stabilization activities, for the parts take on meaning only in their relationship to the whole.

The general order of presentation is chronological, beginning with a brief description of the circumstances just prior to the first freeze on wages and prices on August 15, 1971.

ENVIRONMENT PRIOR TO THE ECONOMIC STABILIZATION PROGRAM

Three sets of economic variables were particularly important in conditioning thinking in mid-1971 as policy makers made decisions affecting food and agriculture. First, the general economy was suffering from continued inflation despite sluggish performance in terms of output and employment. Second, the feed grain-livestock sector of the economy was absorbing the shock of a small crop caused by corn blight. Third, the "green revolution" in developing countries was showing signs of success.

General Economy

Total real output of the economy was growing slowly in mid-1971 after declining in the 1969–1970 recession. The sluggishness was reflected in an unemployment rate of 5.8% to 6.0% in the first six months of 1971. This represented a considerable increase from the 3.5% to 3.8% range for the annual averages in 1966–1969, or even from the 1970 average of 4.9% unemployed.

Inflation did not subside as quickly as policy makers hoped or expected. Their impatience was heightened by the upcoming presidential election in 1972. The Consumer Price Index (CPI) was rising at a rate of slightly more than 4% in the first half of 1971. The food component of the CPI, always a particularly sensitive barometer in the public eye, rose at an annual rate of 7.6% from January to July. Although these rates of inflation would seem very modest only 18 months later, in mid-1971 they were viewed as major problems. Average hourly earnings in manufacturing (excluding overtime) in the first six months of 1971 were about 7% above year earlier levels. Despite high unemployment, wages were increasing faster than the 6.3% rate from 1969 to 1970 and the 6.0% rate from 1968 to 1969. A wage-price spiral or cost-push inflation appeared to threaten further progress in the battle against inflation.

Adding to these woes was a rapidly deteriorating balance of payments position. The balance moved from a surplus of $2.7 billion in 1969 to deficits of $9.8 billion in 1970, $5.6 billion in the first quarter of 1970 and $6.3 billion in the second quarter of 1971 (official reserve transactions balance).

Feed Grain-Livestock Sector

The U.S. corn crop harvested in 1970 was damaged severely by blight, which contributed to a chain of events which has taken years to unfold. Production of corn in 1970 was 11% below the year earlier level (Appendix Table I-1). The 1970–1971 season's average corn price rose 15% despite the availability of substantial stocks which were drawn upon. The federal government's reaction was to reduce set-aside acres by nearly one-half in 1971 in order to encourage greater production. This policy, in conjunction with favorable weather and no recurrence of blight, led to a record corn crop in the fall of 1971.

Hog producers entered a liquidation phase of the production cycle in 1971 (Appendix Table I-2). High net returns in 1969 and early 1970 had encouraged a major expansion in numbers of hogs (see Figure I-1). The resulting increase in supplies in combination with the stagnating economy led to sharply lower hog prices in late 1970 and the first half of 1971. The high corn price in 1970–1971 reinforced the trend toward liquidation; net returns fell to very low levels, probably negative for most producers. In the short term the slaughter of breeding stock led to a larger pork supply, but the longer term effect was to reduce pork production. In summary, pork production was at a cyclical peak in 1971, but the seeds of a large decline in future production were firmly embedded.

FIGURE I-1.   ESTIMATED NET RETURNS FOR HOG PRODUCTION,
JANUARY 1970–MAY 1974

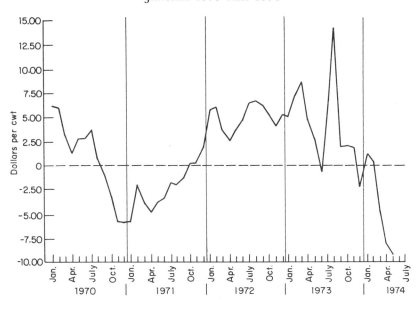

SOURCE: Cost of Living Council.

The beef cow herd was expanding rapidly in 1970 and 1971 (Appendix Table I-3). Feeder cattle prices had been generally trending upward since a low in 1964 and 1965. Ranchers were optimistic and were both keeping cows longer and holding more heifers back from slaughter. While this expansion phase promised larger beef supplies at some future date, its short-term effect was to slow the growth of beef supplies at the consumer level.

"Green Revolution"

The efforts to develop and transfer new, productive technology to agriculture in the lesser developed countries (LDC's) seemed to be bearing fruit by 1971. Hybrid varieties were available which could increase yields greatly if combined with water, fertilizer, and improved management practices. Observed yields of wheat in the LDC's showed significant gains of 4% and 2% in 1969 and 1970 respectively; rice yields increased by a remarkable 7% in 1970 after a small gain of 1% in 1969.

These successes encouraged hope that the specter of famine on a large scale, which seemed very real and close in the mid-1960's, could be banished from the earth. Production of food in the LDC's was expected by many to equal, or possibly exceed, population growth rates in the coming years. An important corollary was that the need for concessionary sales from U.S. sources would be less; some people speculated that there might even be a dampening effect on commercial sales.

FREEZE I: AUGUST 15, 1971—NOVEMBER 13, 1971

The President announced the New Economic Policy on August 15, 1971. This marked the beginning of direct controls on prices, wages, and other economic variables which would not end until April 30, 1974, a period of almost three years. Although the direct impact of the freeze on food and agriculture proved to be small, events of this period added to the strain on U.S. agricultural supplies.

Announced Policy

The measures announced on August 15, 1971, constituted a three-pronged attack on three major problems.[2] The problems, as noted above, were (1) rapid inflation, (2) balance of payments deficit, and (3) high unemployment.

One component of the policy was a 90-day freeze on wages, rents, and nearly all prices. The stipulation that "the provisions [freezing prices and wages] shall not apply to the prices charged for raw agricultural products" was made by decision in an executive order rather than by statute.[3] Raw, unprocessed agricultural commodities were exempt primarily because of the extreme difficulty of enforcement at the farm level where there are about 1.7 million individual farm units.[4] Retail food prices were frozen, creating the potential for a squeeze on food processors and retailers if raw product prices rose. The food price and wage regulations are described and analyzed in detail in Chapters III and IV.

A second element of the program consisted of suspending the convertibility of the dollar into gold and imposing a surcharge, 10% in most cases, on imports. The suspension of convertibility had an immediate effect of devaluing the dollar.

Finally, the announcement included proposals for tax reductions designed to stimulate output and employment. The principal tax items were a one-year investment tax credit of 10% and a 5% investment credit thereafter, repeal of the 7% excise tax on automobiles, and acceleration of the effective date of individual income tax cuts that had been previously legislated.

Impact on Agriculture and Food

Despite the potential squeeze on food processors and retailers, the Freeze did not lead to major disruptions or problems. In fact, the Freeze probably had little or no effect on food prices, and the stability in food prices during this period should not be attributed to the

Freeze. The primary reason is that the farm, or raw material, component of retail prices declined for a brief period after peaking in July or August (Figure I-2).[5] Aggregate retail food prices were actually lower in each of September, October, and November than in August—rather than remaining pressed against ceiling levels.

Seasonal factors were partly responsible for the lack of problems during the Freeze. The peak seasonal price for most, but not all, commodities comes in the June-August summer period. Late summer and fall harvests typically lead to declining prices for many products. Seasonal adjustment factors for some of the more seasonable products, as well as meats and total food, are presented in Table I-1. In addition to normal seasonal factors, Figure I-3 shows that supplies of meats, poultry, and fish were considerably higher during the Freeze months compared with both earlier and later periods, particularly during the second Freeze.

This combination of supply factors, then, provides evidence that food prices would have remained stable during the Freeze months

FIGURE I-2. MARKET BASKET OF FARM FOOD: RETAIL COST, FARM VALUE, AND FARM-RETAIL SPREAD, JANUARY 1970–DECEMBER 1974

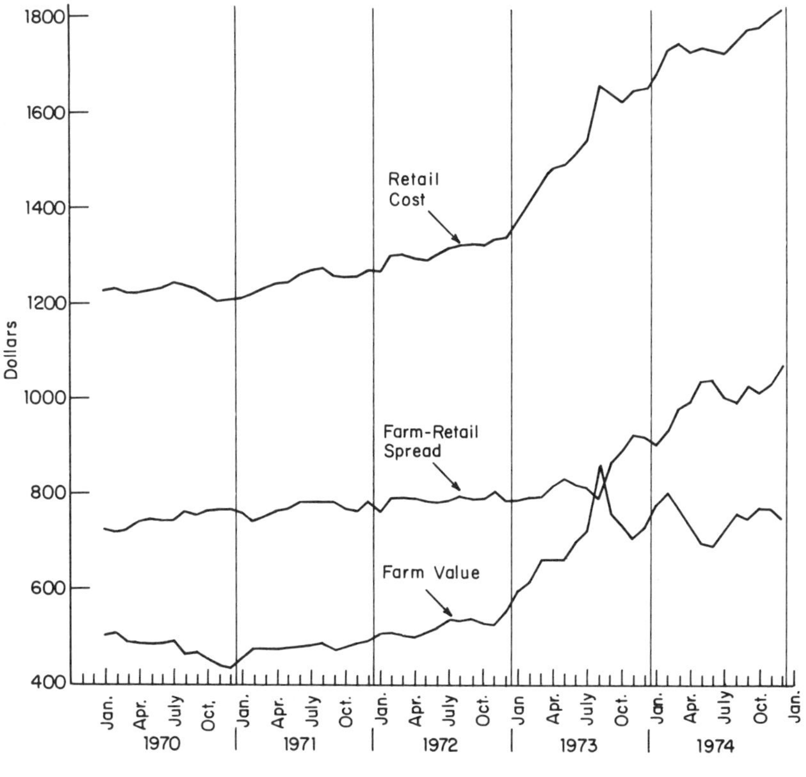

SOURCE: USDA, Economic Research Service.

TABLE I-1. SEASONAL ADJUSTMENT FACTORS FOR RETAIL PRICES OF SELECTED FOODS AND FOOD GROUPS^a (IN PERCENTAGES)

Month	Food at Home	Meats, Poultry and Fish	Eggs	Fresh Fruits			Fresh Vegetables		
				Total[b]	Apples	Oranges	Total[c]	Potatoes	Tomatoes
January	99.7	99.1	110.5	92.9	91.2	94.4	102.6	94.7	105.9
February	99.8	99.2	104.2	95.0	93.4	95.5	100.3	96.0	102.3
March	99.9	100.2	101.6	96.0	96.0	95.9	103.3	96.8	101.3
April	100.2	100.4	99.6	98.8	98.1	94.2	103.9	98.0	109.6
May	100.0	99.8	92.7	99.5	102.5	95.5	106.7	100.1	109.6
June	100.5	100.3	86.9	107.5	111.3	98.3	105.3	106.6	112.8
July	101.0	101.3	92.9	110.1	118.4	101.4	103.3	116.2	100.0
August	100.7	101.5	99.0	109.3	119.9	106.0	97.8	111.5	86.7
September	100.1	101.0	102.4	104.4	108.4	106.7	92.0	98.3	73.2
October	99.4	99.9	101.9	99.0	87.8	108.6	90.4	93.4	82.2
November	99.0	98.9	99.4	94.7	85.2	104.7	95.6	94.0	97.1
December	99.7	98.5	109.0	92.8	87.8	98.8	98.8	94.5	119.3

^a Revised 1972 factors intended for use with 1973 indexes; calculated from data for January 1956 through March 1973.
^b Includes fresh fruits other than apples and oranges.
^c Includes fresh vegetables other than potatoes and tomatoes.
SOURCE: USDA, *Food Consumption, Prices, Expenditures*, 1972 supplement to Agricultural Economic Report No. 138.

FIGURE I-3. PRICE OF MEATS, POULTRY, AND FISH, WITH SUPPLY AND
INCOME FACTORS, JANUARY 1970–DECEMBER 1974

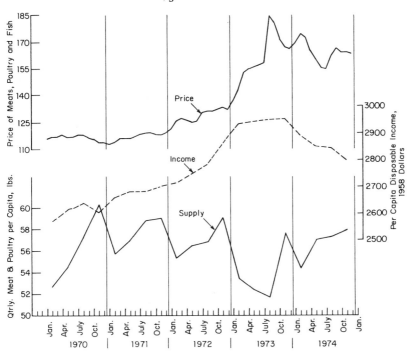

SOURCES: Consumer Price Index, U.S. Department of Labor, *Monthly Labor Review*
and *Handbook of Labor Statistics, 1973*. Income, U.S. Department of Commerce, *Survey of
Current Business*. Supply, USDA, *Livestock and Meat Statistics*, and U.S. Bureau of the
Census, *Current Population Reports*, Series P-25, "Population Estimates and Projections."

even if the Freeze had not been implemented. It is interesting to note,
however, that a large portion of the popular perception of the success
of the Freeze is probably attributable to this very stability of food
prices.

The dollar devaluation and the tax measures had longer-range
effects which will not be discussed here but left to later sections.

PHASE II: NOVEMBER 14, 1971—JANUARY 10, 1973

Phase II was perceived as a general success, except for a persistent
frustration with food prices. The tax reductions requested in August
were signed into law on December 10, 1971, with some revisions. On
December 18, 1971, the Smithsonian Accord was concluded; the
major features were a recognition of new exchange rates and a removal by the United States of the temporary surcharge on imports.
The exchange value of the dollar relative to currencies of major U.S.

agricultural customers had fallen about 6% from the July value; devaluation and its impact are discussed in more detail in Chapter V on International Food Policy Issues. Real GNP rose at a rapid rate of 7.2% from the fourth quarter of 1971 to the same quarter of 1972. The unemployment rate (seasonally adjusted) fell from 6.0% in November 1971 to 5.0% in January 1973. The deficit in the balance of payments declined to $10 billion in 1972 from $30 billion in 1971, a significant improvement even though the sizable deficit continued to be a problem. And finally, the Consumer Price Index for all items less food increased at an annual rate of only 2.6% from November 1971 through January 1973—well within Administration goals and public tolerance (Appendix Table I-7).

Phase II price and wage controls focused on limiting margins of firms rather than on maintaining prices at or below some specified level. Firms were allowed to pass through material and labor cost increases with the latter being offset by average productivity gains for the particular industry, so long as there was no increase above a base period in the pretax profit margin as a percentage of sales. Raw agricultural products remained exempt from controls, and price increases at the farm level tended to be quickly reflected at wholesale and retail levels. Monitoring and reporting requirements were stricter for larger firms and labor groups.

Food prices rose at an annual rate of 6.9% during Phase II, nearly double the rate in the preceding 12 months. This relatively poor performance threatened to destroy the credibility of the controls program, for food seemed a particularly important factor in people's perception of inflation.

Rising farm prices were the underlying problem (Figure I-2). The farm component of the USDA's market basket increased at an annual rate of 18.7% from November 1971 to January 1973, while the farm-retail spread rose at an annual rate of only 1.3% over the same period.

Feed Grain-Livestock Sector

The large corn crop in the fall of 1971, caused by a relaxation of federal acreage controls, good weather, and a failure of the corn blight to reappear, led to a major decline in prices. In October and November corn prices received by farmers averaged $0.974 to $1.00 per bushel, 25% below the 1970 blight year levels; perhaps more significant, prices were 10% below 1969 levels. Corn producers were unhappy, and government-held stocks seemed certain to increase dramatically.* The Administration was facing an election in November 1972, and the memory of losing the 1960 election by a few thousand votes in Illinois may have persisted in policy circles.

---

* This forecast proved correct, and government stocks grew by 118%.

Secretary of Agriculture Clifford Hardin resigned in November 1971 under a storm of protest from Corn Belt farmers and their representatives as a result of low prices and incomes. His successor, Earl L. Butz, was confirmed in December by the narrow margin of 51 to 44 after both Democratic and Republican Senators sought and gained pledges from Butz that he would take quick action to raise farm prices.[6]

All factors seemed to point to the need for less production in 1972, and a more restrictive 1972 feed grain program was announced in October 1971.[7] The general goals of the program were to reduce carry-over stocks and increase farm income through higher feed grain prices. The specific goal was to attain a feed grain set-aside of at least 38 million acres, more than double the 18.2 million acres of 1971. A survey of planting intentions as of January 1, 1972, showed that the desired set-aside was not likely to be reached under the program as announced. On February 2, 1972, a new option was extended to farmers which succeeded in reducing acreage by the desired amount.[8]

Although in retrospect it is clear that a less restrictive 1972 feed grain program would have been desirable because of the unexpected surge in foreign demand, the decisions of late 1971 and early 1972 are difficult to fault. Farm prices were low, and surpluses were a heavy burden on U.S. taxpayers. In 1971 farmers had demonstrated a seeming ability to inundate markets with huge crops in response to a relaxation of acreage controls. These events serve as one among many examples of the difficulties of formulating accurate forecasts and devising effective policies for the agricultural sector.

Meat prices were a major problem in late 1971 and early 1972 despite the low cost of feed. From November to February the Consumer Price Index for meats, poultry, and fish rose 6.9%—an annual rate of increase of 30.8%. Most of the increase occurred in a single, phenomenal jump of 4.6% from January to February.

The underlying causes of the meat price surge were reduced supplies and rising incomes of consumers (Figure I-3). December and January per capita production totals were 4% and 5% respectively, below year earlier figures. Although beef production was down, the single most important development was a 13% decline in January 1972 pork production compared with year earlier levels. Throughout 1972 and 1973 pork production tended to lag behind year earlier levels. Real per capita disposable personal income rose 2.2% from the first quarter of 1971 to the first quarter of 1972.

A contributing factor to the retail price rise was a significant expansion of the farm-retail spread for beef as computed by USDA. From November 1971 to February 1972 the spread increased 13%; this accounted for about half of the advance in retail beef prices (Figure I-4). The widening spread was not only particularly irritable to con-

FIGURE I-4.   CHOICE BEEF: RETAIL PRICE, FARM VALUE, AND FARM-RETAIL
SPREAD, JANUARY 1970–DECEMBER 1974

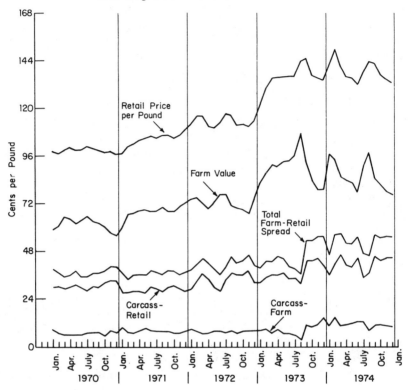

SOURCE: USDA, *Marketing and Transportation Situation* and *Agricultural Outlook.*

sumers and government officials at a time of rising farm prices, but it
was also quite unusual. The typical pattern was for the spread to
narrow as farm prices rose and widen as farm prices declined, thus
dampening retail price fluctuations relative to farm price variation.
Some government response seemed advisable for both fundamental
and political reasons.

On March 29 John Connally, Chairman of the Cost of Living
Council and Secretary of the Treasury, held a widely publicized
meeting with the heads of the major supermarket chains. (The February CPI was, of course, not released until late March.) Just a few
days earlier President Nixon had noted that the farm-retail spread
was "too great."[9] Connally reinforced the President's remarks, warn-
ing that retailers' prices and profits were receiving careful attention.
The result of the meeting was a statement that Connally and the
retailers expected meat prices to ease somewhat in the coming months
as the result of natural market forces.[10]

The price of meats, poultry, and fish was lower in April-June than

FIGURE I-4.   CHOICE BEEF: RETAIL PRICE, FARM VALUE, AND FARM-RETAIL
SPREAD, JANUARY 1970–DECEMBER 1974

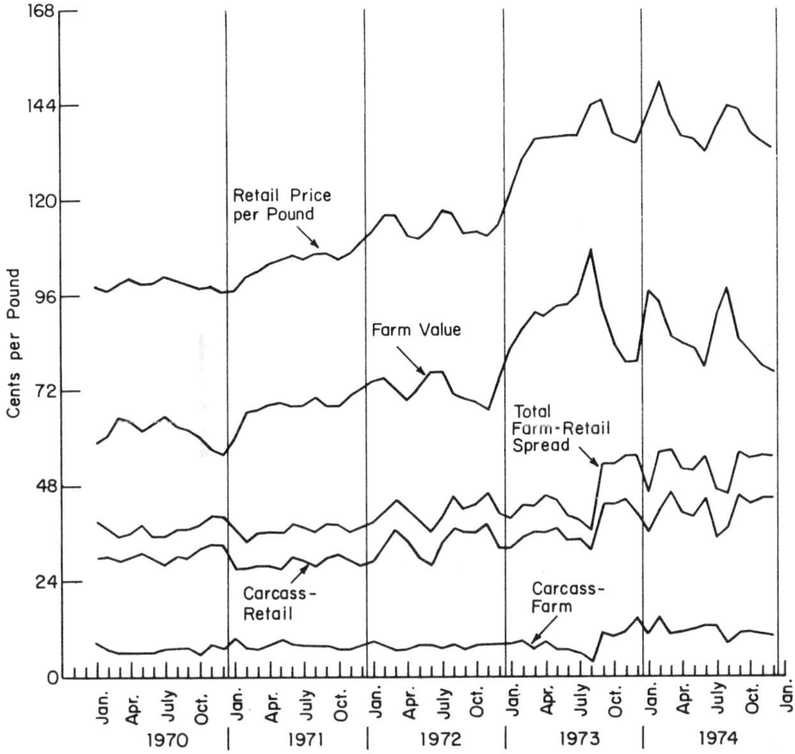

SOURCE: USDA, *Marketing and Transportation Situation* and *Agricultural Outlook.*

sumers and government officials at a time of rising farm prices, but it
was also quite unusual. The typical pattern was for the spread to
narrow as farm prices rose and widen as farm prices declined, thus
dampening retail price fluctuations relative to farm price variation.
Some government response seemed advisable for both fundamental
and political reasons.

On March 29 John Connally, Chairman of the Cost of Living
Council and Secretary of the Treasury, held a widely publicized
meeting with the heads of the major supermarket chains. (The February CPI was, of course, not released until late March.) Just a few
days earlier President Nixon had noted that the farm-retail spread
was "too great."[9] Connally reinforced the President's remarks, warn-
ing that retailers' prices and profits were receiving careful attention.
The result of the meeting was a statement that Connally and the
retailers expected meat prices to ease somewhat in the coming months
as the result of natural market forces.[10]

The price of meats, poultry, and fish was lower in April–June than

Secretary of Agriculture Clifford Hardin resigned in November 1971 under a storm of protest from Corn Belt farmers and their representatives as a result of low prices and incomes. His successor, Earl L. Butz, was confirmed in December by the narrow margin of 51 to 44 after both Democratic and Republican Senators sought and gained pledges from Butz that he would take quick action to raise farm prices.[6]

All factors seemed to point to the need for less production in 1972, and a more restrictive 1972 feed grain program was announced in October 1971.[7] The general goals of the program were to reduce carry-over stocks and increase farm income through higher feed grain prices. The specific goal was to attain a feed grain set-aside of at least 38 million acres, more than double the 18.2 million acres of 1971. A survey of planting intentions as of January 1, 1972, showed that the desired set-aside was not likely to be reached under the program as announced. On February 2, 1972, a new option was extended to farmers which succeeded in reducing acreage by the desired amount.[8]

Although in retrospect it is clear that a less restrictive 1972 feed grain program would have been desirable because of the unexpected surge in foreign demand, the decisions of late 1971 and early 1972 are difficult to fault. Farm prices were low, and surpluses were a heavy burden on U.S. taxpayers. In 1971 farmers had demonstrated a seeming ability to inundate markets with huge crops in response to a relaxation of acreage controls. These events serve as one among many examples of the difficulties of formulating accurate forecasts and devising effective policies for the agricultural sector.

Meat prices were a major problem in late 1971 and early 1972 despite the low cost of feed. From November to February the Consumer Price Index for meats, poultry, and fish rose 6.9%—an annual rate of increase of 30.8%. Most of the increase occurred in a single, phenomenal jump of 4.6% from January to February.

The underlying causes of the meat price surge were reduced supplies and rising incomes of consumers (Figure I-3). December and January per capita production totals were 4% and 5% respectively, below year earlier figures. Although beef production was down, the single most important development was a 13% decline in January 1972 pork production compared with year earlier levels. Throughout 1972 and 1973 pork production tended to lag behind year earlier levels. Real per capita disposable personal income rose 2.2% from the first quarter of 1971 to the first quarter of 1972.

A contributing factor to the retail price rise was a significant expansion of the farm-retail spread for beef as computed by USDA. From November 1971 to February 1972 the spread increased 13%; this accounted for about half of the advance in retail beef prices (Figure I-4). The widening spread was not only particularly irritable to con-

fell 33 million tons* from 1971–1972 (Table I-2). The United States accounted for 10 million tons, or nearly one-third, of the drop in production, mostly due to restrictive government policies. Although production had previously declined twice after 1960–1961, neither of these instances approached the scale of the 1972–1973 decrease. Adding to the problem was a low *world* stock level relative to the preceding decade. Known ending stocks of wheat and coarse grains, the primary reserves, equaled only 12.2% of world grains and rice consumption in 1971–1972 (Table I-2). Known stocks as a percentage of consumption were lower in only two years following 1960–1961

TABLE I-2. WORLD GRAINS AND RICE SUPPLY AND CONSUMPTION, MARKETING YEARS 1960–1961 THROUGH 1975–1976[a] (IN MILLIONS OF METRIC TONS)

Year	Production	Consumption[b]	Ending Stocks (Omitting Rice)[c]	Stocks (Omitting Rice) as Percentage of Consumption
1960–1961	883.4	870.7	176.7	20.3
1961–1962	861.7	888.4	150.0	16.9
1962–1963	908.4	905.2	153.2	16.9
1963–1964	914.4	919.6	148.0	16.1
1964–1965	967.8	964.5	151.3	15.7
1965–1966	966.0	1001.7	115.6	11.5
1966–1967	1041.2	1012.2	144.6	14.3
1967–1968	1074.3	1059.5	159.4	15.0
1968–1969	1113.6	1084.9	188.1	17.3
1969–1970	1127.2	1147.1	168.2	14.7
1970–1971	1137.9	1175.6	130.5	11.1
1971–1972	1230.5	1213.3	147.7	12.2
1972–1973	1197.5	1237.1	108.1	8.7
1973–1974	1301.1	1299.2	110.0	8.5
1974–1975[d]	1248.8	1258.7	100.1	8.0
1975–1976[e]	1292.4	1292.4	100.1	7.7

[a] Data are based on an aggregate of differing local marketing years.

[b] For countries for which stocks data are not available, or for which no adjustments have been made for year-to-year changes, consumption estimates assume a constant stocks level. Rice consumption is assumed to be equal to rice production.

[c] Stocks data are only for selected countries and exclude such important countries as the USSR, the People's Republic of China, and part of Eastern Europe for which stocks data are not available; the aggregate stocks level have, however, been adjusted for estimated year-to-year changes in USSR grain stocks. Few countries maintain appreciable stocks of rice.

[d] Preliminary.

[e] Projection.

SOURCES: USDA, *Foreign Agriculture Circular*, FG 12-75, October 7, 1975. Personal communication with FAS, USDA.

---

* Metric tons will be used throughout this discussion.

(11.5% and 11.1% in 1965–1966 and 1970–1971, respectively); in both cases good crops were harvested in the following years and stock rebuilding occurred.

Production in all three major categories—rice, wheat, and coarse grains—declined from 1971–1972 to 1972–1973 (Tables I-3, I-4, and I-5). This was unprecedented in the period examined here, beginning with 1960–1961. Coarse grain production was down 14.4 million tons, rice down 12.3 million tons, and wheat down 6.3 million tons. Known stocks of wheat at the end of 1971–1972 were only 11.2% of total wheat and rice production, a low level relative to the 1960's

TABLE I-3. WORLD RICE AND WHEAT SUPPLY AND CONSUMPTION, MARKETING YEARS 1960–1961 THROUGH 1975–1976[a] (IN MILLIONS OF METRIC TONS)

		Wheat			
Year	Rice Production[b]	Production	Consumption[c]	Ending Stocks[d]	Stocks as Percentage of Consumption
1960–1961	226.9	240.5	237.4	76.9	32.4
1961–1962	238.0	226.6	238.4	65.1	27.3
1962–1963	234.7	256.5	251.1	70.5	28.1
1963–1964	250.3	238.3	246.8	62.0	25.1
1964–1965	264.3	275.6	265.5	72.1	27.2
1965–1966	256.8	265.8	284.6	53.3	18.7
1966–1967	259.1	307.5	282.7	78.1	27.6
1967–1968	282.8	295.8	292.0	81.9	28.0
1968–1969	284.1	328.4	303.2	107.1	35.3
1969–1970	295.1	309.5	322.8	93.8	29.1
1970–1971	305.2	313.8	335.3	72.3	21.6
1971–1972	310.5	346.2	345.1	73.4	21.3
1972–1973	298.2	339.9	361.8	51.5	14.2
1973–1974	324.5	368.4	363.2	56.7	15.6
1974–1975[e]	327.9	350.3	352.6	54.4	15.4
1975–1976[f]	341.0	359.0	361.0	52.4	14.5

[a] Data are based on an aggregate of differing local marketing years.

[b] Rice consumption is assumed to be approximately equal to rice production, and few countries maintain appreciable stocks.

[c] For countries for which stock data are not available, or for which no adjustments have been made for year-to-year changes, consumption estimates assume a constant stock level.

[d] Stocks data are only for selected countries and exclude such important countries as the USSR, the People's Republic of China and part of Eastern Europe for which stocks data are not available; the aggregate stocks level have, however, been adjusted for estimated year-to-year changes in USSR grain stocks.

[e] Preliminary.

[f] Projections.

SOURCES: USDA, *Foreign Agriculture Circular*, FG 12–75, October 7, 1975. Personal communication with FAS, USDA.

TABLE I-4. WORLD TOTAL WHEAT AND RICE SUPPLY AND CONSUMPTION,
MARKETING YEARS 1960-1961 THROUGH 1975-1976[a]
(IN MILLIONS OF METRIC TONS)

Year	Total Wheat[b] and Rice[c]		Ending Wheat Stocks[d]	Wheat Stocks as Percentage of Total Wheat and Rice Consumption
	Production	Consumption		
1960-1961	467.4	464.3	76.9	16.6
1961-1962	464.6	476.4	65.1	13.7
1962-1963	491.2	485.8	70.5	14.5
1963-1964	488.6	497.1	62.0	12.5
1964-1965	539.9	529.8	72.1	13.6
1965-1966	522.6	541.4	53.3	9.8
1966-1967	566.6	541.8	78.1	14.4
1967-1968	578.6	574.8	81.9	14.2
1968-1969	612.5	587.3	107.1	18.2
1969-1970	604.6	617.9	93.8	15.2
1970-1971	619.0	640.5	72.3	11.3
1971-1972	656.7	655.6	73.4	11.2
1972-1973	638.1	660.0	51.5	7.8
1973-1974	692.9	687.7	56.7	8.2
1974-1975[e]	678.2	680.5	54.4	8.0
1975-1976[f]	700.0	702.0	52.4	7.5

[a] Data are based on an aggregate of differing local marketing years.

[b] For countries for which stock data are not available, or for which no adjustments have been made for year-to-year changes, consumption estimates assume a constant stock level.

[c] Rice consumption is assumed to be approximately equal to rice production, and few countries maintain appreciable stocks.

[d] Stocks data are only for selected countries and exclude such important countries as the USSR, the People's Republic of China and part of Eastern Europe for which stocks data are not available; the aggregate stocks level have, however, been adjusted for estimated year-to-year changes in USSR grain stocks.

[e] Preliminary.

[f] Projections.

SOURCES: USDA, *Foreign Agriculture Circular*, FG 12-75, October 7, 1975. Personal communication with FAS, USDA.

(Table I-4). Few countries maintain appreciable stocks of rice, and therefore the burdens of shortfalls in total food grain production must be met largely from reserves of wheat.

From a world perspective, the supply situation in 1971–1972 was considerably less bountiful than the U.S. position appeared when considered in isolation. Rising world consumption and lower world stock levels had combined to reduce considerably the margin of insurance provided by reserve stocks. While not yet obvious to most observers, the United States was now in a position where the world

TABLE I-5. WORLD COARSE GRAINS SUPPLY AND CONSUMPTION, MARKETING
YEARS 1960–1961 THROUGH 1975–1976[a] (IN MILLIONS OF METRIC TONS)

Year	Production	Consumption[b]	Ending Stocks[c]	Stocks as Percentage of Consumption
1960–1961	416.0	406.4	99.8	24.6
1961–1962	397.1	412.0	84.9	20.6
1962–1963	417.2	419.4	82.7	19.7
1963–1964	425.8	422.5	86.0	20.4
1964–1965	427.9	434.7	79.2	18.2
1965–1966	443.4	460.3	62.3	13.5
1966–1967	474.6	470.4	66.5	14.1
1967–1968	495.7	484.7	77.5	16.0
1968–1969	501.1	497.6	81.0	16.3
1969–1970	522.6	529.2	74.4	14.1
1970–1971	518.9	535.1	58.2	10.9
1971–1972	573.8	557.7	74.3	13.3
1972–1973	559.4	577.1	56.6	9.8
1973–1974	608.2	611.5	53.3	8.7
1974–1975[d]	570.6	578.2	45.7	7.9
1975–1976[e]	592.4	590.4	47.7	8.1

[a] Data are based on an aggregate of differing local marketing years.

[b] For countries for which stock data are not available, or for which no adjustments have been made for year-to-year changes, consumption estimates assume a constant stock level.

[c] Stocks data are only for selected countries and exclude such important countries as the USSR, the People's Republic of China and part of Eastern Europe for which stocks data are not available; the aggregate stocks level have, however, been adjusted for estimated year-to-year changes in USSR grain stocks.

[d] Preliminary.

[e] Projection.

SOURCE: USDA, *Foreign Agriculture Circular,* FG 12–75, October 7, 1975.

view of supply and demand was relevant to domestic prices and availabilities. Decision makers in both the private and the public sectors would become acutely aware of this fact as events unfolded.

USSR production of total grains in 1972–1973 was only 156 million tons, 13 million tons less than in 1971–1972 which was, in turn, less than 1970–1971 production (Table I-6). Nearly all of the decline took place in wheat. Such variation was not unusual but well in line with past experience. It was also not unusual for the Soviets to make large purchases in world markets when their production fell below trend levels (see 1963–1964, 1965–1966, and 1971–1972 in Tables I-6 and I-7). However, belt-tightening in the form of reduced use of feed through liquidation of livestock was also typically a part of their adjustment process in short crop years.

TABLE I-6.   USSR PRODUCTION AND CONSUMPTION OF GRAINS, 1961–1962 THROUGH 1975–1976 (IN MILLIONS OF METRIC TONS)

Year	Wheat		Coarse Grains[a]		Total Grains	
	Production	Consumption[b]	Production	Consumption[b]	Production	Consumption[b]
1961–1962	66.5	62.4	56.1	53.0	122.6	115.4
1962–1963	70.8	63.3	57.7	54.2	128.5	117.5
1963–1964	49.7	55.8	46.8	47.9	96.5	103.7
1964–1965	74.4	61.4	61.6	52.0	136.0	113.4
1965–1966	59.7	74.6	50.8	53.5	110.5	128.1
1966–1967	100.5	77.2	58.6	57.0	159.1	134.2
1967–1968	77.4	79.6	58.4	57.8	135.8	137.4
1968–1969	93.4	84.8	63.5	62.9	156.9	147.7
1969–1970	79.9	86.6	63.6	68.7	148.5	155.3
1970–1971	99.7	97.0	74.8	74.0	174.5	171.0
1971–1972	98.8	98.4	70.6	72.0	169.4	170.4
1972–1973	86.0	99.6	70.4	75.4	156.4	175.0
1973–1974	109.8	100.2	96.5	99.3	206.3	199.5
1974–1975[c]	83.8	89.2	96.8	100.8	180.6	190.0
1975–1976[d]	85.0	95.5	77.0	91.5	162.0	187.0

[a] Corn, barley, oats, sorghum, and rye.
[b] Includes estimated waste due to excess moisture and foreign material.
[c] Preliminary.
[d] Projection.
SOURCES: USDA, *Foreign Agriculture Circular*, FG 21–74, August 23, 1974, and FG 12–75, October 7, 1975.

The crucial first step in the Russian grain deal was a credit arrangement.[13] In late May 1972, Nixon and Brezhnev discussed credit terms at the Summit Meeting, and the credit agreement was triumphantly announced at the White House on July 8.[14] The USSR agreed to purchase $750 million of wheat, corn, sorghum, oats, barley, and rye during a three-year period beginning August 1, 1972; at least $200 million would be purchased in the first year.[15] The Soviets were granted total credits of $750 million with a $500 million ceiling at any one time in a manner similar to other purchasers of agricultural products.[16]

Beginning in early July and continuing through early August, the Soviets made huge purchases of about 21 million tons of wheat and feed grains for their 1972-1973 needs (see Table I-7). The bulk of these were purchased from U.S. private export companies. About three-fourths of the purchases, 15 million tons, were of wheat. The 13-million ton drop in production of grains in 1972-1973 was fully offset by increased import purchases of 13 million tons. The USDA estimate of USSR grains consumption showed a rise of 2.7% from 1971-1972 to 1972-1973 rather than a decrease which would reflect belt-tightening (Table I-6).

The USDA had guaranteed to continue subsidies on wheat exports throughout the period of the Russian purchases. These subsidies

TABLE I-7.   USSR TRADE IN WHEAT AND FEED GRAINS, CROP YEARS
1963-1964 THROUGH 1975-1976 (IN MILLIONS OF METRIC TONS)

Crop Year	Wheat and Products[a]		Feed Grains[b]		Total Grains	
	Exports	Imports	Exports	Imports	Exports	Imports
1963-1964	2.7	9.7	1.3	0.1	4.0	9.8
1964-1065	2.2	2.2	1.4	c	3.6	2.2
1965-1966	2.6	8.5	2.2	c	4.8	8.5
1966-1967	4.4	3.1	0.5	0.2	4.9	3.3
1967-1968	5.3	1.5	0.7	0.4	6.0	1.9
1968-1969	5.8	0.2	0.9	0.5	6.7	0.7
1969-1970	6.4	1.1	0.9	0.1	7.3	1.2
1970-1971	7.2	0.5	0.9	0.3	8.1	0.8
1971-1972	5.8	3.4	0.7	4.3	6.5	7.7
1972-1973	1.3	14.9	0.4	5.9	1.7	20.8
1973-1974	5.0	4.4	0.9	6.1	5.9	10.5
1974-1975[d]	4.0	2.4	0.5	2.5	4.5	4.9
1975-1976[e]	1.5	12.0	0.5	13.0	2.0	25.0

[a] Grain equivalent.
[b] Corn, sorghum, barley, and oats.
[c] Less than 50,000 tons.
[d] Preliminary.
[e] Projection.
SOURCE: USDA, *Foreign Agriculture Circular*, FG 12-75, October 7, 1975.

continued in effect and increased as prices rose. The export subsidy was designed to maintain the U.S. competitive position in world trade while domestic producers were receiving higher prices. Exporters received a payment for the difference between the domestic price and a fixed world price of about $1.63 to $1.65 per bushel or $60 per ton. The USDA objective, as expressed by the official in charge, Carroll Brunthaver, was "to move as much wheat . . . as possible" by keeping the export price at $60 per ton.[17]

In view of the decline in world food grain production, it was not surprising that the farm price of wheat in the United States rose quickly from $1.32 per bushel in July to $1.51 in August to $1.73 in September. The subsidy likewise increased from its initial low level of 2 cents per bushel to a peak of 47 cents per bushel as the United States sought to maintain a constant export price.[18] American taxpayers had clearly subsidized Soviet wheat consumers and were being asked to do the same for other foreign purchasers. On August 25, Caspar Weinberger, Director of the Office of Management and Budget, ordered the subsidy revoked in a process extending over the following four weeks, despite earlier assurances of Brunthaver to exporters that the subsidy would remain in effect.[19] A total of about $300 million was expended in the third quarter of 1972.[20] The farm price of wheat reached $2.38 per bushel by December; many wheat growers had sold in June and July for $1.38 per bushel or less.

It is important to note that the Soviet purchases were not the sole source of the increased demand for U.S. wheat. U.S. exports of wheat and flour increased by 15.0 million tons from 1971–1972 to 1972–1973. Of this total, Soviet sales accounted for 9.5 million tons, about 63%. The remainder of the increase was shared among the rest of the world, with the exception of Africa.

The USDA announced a very restrictive 1973 wheat program on July 17, despite the announcement of the Soviet agreement just a few days earlier.[21] The goals were "a reduction of stocks, improving farm incomes, and providing farmers flexibility." The set-aside acreage was set at the maximum allowed by law. All doubts as to the ineptness of such a restrictive policy should have been erased by the end of July, or possibly as late as August. A change in the program at this juncture would have led to increased planting of winter wheat in the fall of 1972 and greater production in 1973. The Cost of Living Council, including Secretary of the Treasury George Shultz who had become chairman in June 1972, argued for such a change. However, Secretary Butz opposed relaxing the program, and the White House supported him—partly for political reasons associated with the November elections. The change would eventually come in early 1973, but it would occur too late to affect winter wheat production.

To summarize this crucial sequence of events related to food grain prices, the root cause of price increases was unfavorable weather and thus lower world production. However, U.S. policies accentuated the cost to U.S. consumers, partly in favor of foreign consumers. A careful monitoring of world stocks relative to consumption might have shown the need for a turn to less restrictive production policies in late 1971 or early 1972. By the end of August 1972 there was little or no excuse for not taking such action. This error, as will become clear later, contributed to a new surge of prices in 1973-1974. The subsidy was clearly continued too long. Phasing out the subsidy at an earlier date might have reduced foreign purchases; it certainly would have led to lower costs for U.S. taxpayers and greater foreign exchange earnings.

PHASE III: JANUARY 11,1973—JUNE 12, 1973

The general economic picture changed markedly during Phase III, with food and agriculture playing a crucial role. Real GNP and real per capita disposable income registered significant gains from the fourth quarter of 1972 to the first quarter of 1973, but rose very little in the following quarter. Real compensation per man-hour began dropping in the second quarter of 1973 and continued to fall throughout the remainder of the Economic Stabilization Program (ESP) despite significant gains in nominal terms. Output per man-hour, i.e., labor productivity, followed the same pattern of decline beginning in the second quarter of 1973. Unit labor costs thus increased rapidly, adding pressure for price increases and leading to a softer labor market. The unemployment rate, however, continued to decline through Phase III. Finally, the dollar was devalued a second time in February and subsequently allowed to fall further in a system of floating exchange rates. This devaluation, in contrast to the first, occurred in the context of an economy operating near capacity and of low reserve stocks of grains and oilseeds. The value of the dollar relative to the currencies of major agricultural customers fell approximately 9% from January to mid-1973. This brought the total devaluation from the mid-1971 value of the dollar to 17%. (See Appendix Table V-12.) Prices of imports tended to rise and foreign demand for U.S. products rose, resulting in increased upward pressure on the domestic price level.

The total CPI increased at an annual rate of 9.1% from January to June in 1973, a rate well in excess of Administration goals and expectations. As was true in Phase II, the index for all items less food grew much less, 5.4% per year, over this period. Food prices rose at an annual rate of 22.2% in the January–June interval, destroying the credibility of the Stabilization Program with each leap.

Those people planning and administering Phase III were not caught completely unaware by the surge in food prices, although its magnitude was a surprise. As 1972 was ending and the discouraging news was unfolding in the early months of 1973, the frustration of many people with USDA analyses and policies reached new levels. The story of the pressure they generated is an appropriate starting point for the discussion of the Phase III period.

Pressures on USDA Policies

As noted earlier, USDA announced a restrictive wheat program soon after the Russian wheat deal—and resisted efforts to change it. In December 1972 USDA announced the 1973 feed grain program. While not so limiting as the very restrictive 1972 program, the program was designed to yield a set-aside of 25 million acres. This set-aside would be about one-third less than in 1972 (37 million acres) but still greater than the 18 million acres in 1971. Although not so obvious an error as in the case of wheat, the feed grain program clearly reflected a greater willingness to risk high feed grain and soybean prices rather than low prices and higher government costs.

The "marketing guide" program of the USDA probably provided as much ammunition (or more) to USDA detractors in late 1972 and early 1973 as any other action. The USDA marketing guides made specific recommendations to farmers on how much to produce during future time periods. The guides were issued for poultry, fruit, and vegetable producers. Throughout 1972 the USDA egg marketing guide recommended a reduction in egg production in order to gain "improvement" (a rise) in egg prices. In late 1972 and early 1973 egg prices rose sharply, moving from 55 cents per dozen at retail in November to 74 cents in January. Consumers were furious and their complaints deluged the Price Commission, which, in turn, blamed USDA. To make matters worse, in January the USDA recommended a cutback in broiler production—at the very time when poultry and meat prices were skyrocketing.

The influence exerted by the marketing guides is questionable. Many market observers and participants felt that they had little impact. Some even argued that the guides had a perverse impact. They argued that many producers assumed that others in the industry would follow the recommendation; these producers reasoned that the best action would be to expand when others contracted and vice versa.

However, there can be no doubt that dissatisfaction with USDA policies had grown to very high levels in the Cost of Living Council and Price Commission by early 1973. This feeling was shared by others, notably Secretary of the Treasury Shultz. The result was the creation of a special Food Committee of the CLC, chaired by Secretary Shultz and including Secretary Butz. The intent of the Food Committee was to stimulate a greater emphasis on consumer interests, i.e., increased supplies and lower food prices, in food and agricultural policy. The primary target for change was the USDA, but inputs were to be made to other agencies such as the Office of Management and Budget (OMB) and the Council on International Economic Policy (CIEP).

The CLC Food Committee had no authority other than that delegated to it by the President. The full membership of the Committee was:

> George P. Shultz, Chairman, Secretary of the Treasury
> Herbert Stein, Chairman of the Council of Economic Advisers
> John T. Dunlop, Director of the Cost of Living Council
> Earl L. Butz, Secretary of Agriculture
> Roy L. Ash, Director of the Office of Management and Budget

Shultz was clearly the head of the Committee by virtue of his title as chairman and his superior access to the President. The formation of food and agricultural policy was effectively lifted from the USDA to an interagency level. The White House would have more information transmitted from agencies sympathetic with less inflationary prices: Secretary Shultz, rather than Secretary Butz, would be the person most likely to provide the information to the President.

An important element in this critical institutional change was the creation of an independent staff for the CLC Food Committee, directed by Kenneth J. Fedor. The staff was sufficiently large so that a mix of expertise, with regard to commodities and institutions, was available. It was capable of generating independent proposals and forecasts, as well as reacting to USDA work. Access to information and people in other agencies was greatly aided by the legitimacy conferred by the CLC Food Committee. Although the Food Committee staff fulfilled a real need in the Executive Office, it had serious drawbacks. The staff was young and inexperienced for the most part. It did get some forced cooperation from USDA because of the nature of the short-term crisis, but it could not have provided a long-term solution to the basic problem of a lack of an institutionalized *food* policy mechanism within the federal government. The USDA bureaucracy tended to overwhelm it, especially in the final stages of Phase IV.

The final component of the new policy machinery was the creation of a Food Industry Advisory Committee, chaired by Donald S. Perkins, Chairman of the Board and Chief Executive Officer of Jewel Companies, Inc.[22] The Advisory Committee was an important source of ideas and independent evaluation. Its recommendations were often influential, as in the case of ending the Wheat Certificate Program (to be discussed later), and such recommendations were always given careful attention, even if rejected. Its members opened communication links throughout the food sector which were especially important to the inexperienced Food Committee staff. The Advisory Committee added significantly to the credibility and effectiveness of the CLC Food Committee.

Not surprisingly, the pace of action increased markedly in late 1972 and early 1973 as food prices rose and USDA's influence diminished somewhat. Some of the actions will be discussed in more detail later, but a brief listing is instructive. In late December the Administration suspended quotas on meat imports throughout 1973 and also increased quotas on imported nonfat dry milk. A 50% increase in cheese import quotas for four months was instituted. Dairy price support levels continued to be set at the minimum level required by law. The wheat and feed grain program acreage restrictions were relaxed. Disposal of Commodity Credit Corporation stocks of grain was accelerated. All direct subsidies on the exportation of farm products were ended. Marketing guides were eliminated. All decisions to implement marketing orders or regulations were cleared through CLC.

Despite these actions, food prices continued to rise sharply in early 1973. The feeling persisted among CLC and White House personnel that the USDA lacked dedication in the battle to hold down food prices. USDA officials argued that they were moving as quickly as was prudent, but others perceived foot-dragging. The issue came to a head on March 12 in the Cabinet Room of the White House.

The leaders of the USDA were told in frank language that their efforts had been unsatisfactory. *The Wall Street Journal* captured well the flavor of the meeting.[23] "The Agriculture Department's top bureaucrats were marched to the White House woodshed yesterday to be told they will have to try harder to get food prices down. The farm aides . . . were told to apply the same zeal to reducing eating costs that they have shown for years in trying to push farm income up." Quoting the article further, Ehrlichman stated to newsmen, " 'We are having to turn the Department of Agriculture around to work in the other direction' after many years when it 'had as its task keeping food prices up for the benefit of the farmer.' "

USDA officials resented the implication that they were not responsive. They felt that decisions were forced upon them by people with much less knowledge of the food and agricultural sector. Such decisions, in their view, were often destructive—rather than helpful—to the public interest. However, their ability and willingness to fight successfully on important issues was obviously eroding rapidly. The conflicts are best illustrated by the disposal of government-held stocks of grain.

In mid- and late-1972 the government owned large quantities of wheat and feed grains as a result of price support programs. As the demand for grain rose and prices reacted upwards, there was agreement among all government agencies that government stocks should be sold in order to moderate the price rise and reduce government storage costs. Agency representatives disagreed, however, on the rate at which the sales should be made. In January, CLC personnel, with support from the Department of the Treasury, argued that the sales should be made as quickly as possible in order to exert maximum, immediate downward pressure on prices. USDA representatives, with some support from the Office of Management and Budget, countered that the transportation system was already overloaded, and additional supplies in private hands would have little or no price effect at terminal markets. The price spread between terminal markets, especially port facilities, and country (farmer-country elevator) markets, had more than doubled as the result of transportation problems. Forcing sales immediately, USDA continued, would lead to a transfer of grain ownership at country locations with no increase in physical movement; private grain merchants would gain at the expense of the government and farmers. USDA lost the argument, but their arguments were certainly valid to a large extent. To the author's knowledge, no study of the question has been made, but it would not be surprising if the forced sales in early 1973 cost taxpayers millions of dollars relative to what a more orderly procedure would have yielded. It should be noted that CLC was very much aware of the logistics problems and took part in substantial efforts to relieve congestion and reduce abnormal price differentials.

At the March 12 meeting the White House announced it wanted a *weekly* report to the President on actions taken to increase food supplies and reduce food prices. The Food Committee staff and leadership within CLC had major responsibility for preparing the report, which was reviewed by the CLC Food Committee prior to transmittal to the White House. The need to identify options and exhibit quick progress was intensified by this measure, and it proved to be an effective tool of policy.

Feed Grain-Livestock Sector, Including Protein Meals

Meat, poultry, and fish prices rose an astounding 16.4% from December 1972 to March 1973—an annual rate of increase of 83.5% (Figure I-3). Over these three months the farm value of beef rose 24% and the farm value of pork rose 23%; the farm-retail price spreads increased slightly from low December values, but these were not a major cause of the price problem (Figures I-4 and I-5). Meat prices were the primary factor behind the rise of the CPI in early 1973, and they were even more important in the public's perception of the inflation rate.

The underlying factors were the same as have been discussed in earlier periods—rising incomes and declining supplies (Figure I-3). Compared with a year earlier, the first quarter of 1973 real per capita disposable income was up 7.8% and per capita supplies of meat and poultry were down 3.3%. A drop in total pork supplies of 7% was primarily responsible for the overall decline in meat production from a year earlier; beef registered a very small gain while poultry registered a similarly small decline. The liquidation of hogs in late 1971

FIGURE I-5. PORK: RETAIL PRICE, FARM VALUE, AND FARM-RETAIL SPREAD:
JANUARY 1970–DECEMBER 1974

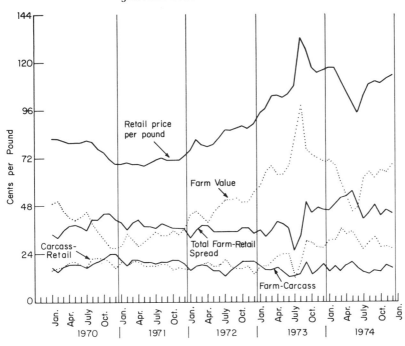

SOURCE: USDA, *Marketing and Transportation Situation* and *Agricultural Outlook.*

and all of 1972 was showing up with a vengeance. Exports of pork in the first quarter increased from 11 million pounds in 1972 to 52 million pounds in 1973, primarily as a result of Japanese purchases stimulated in part by the devaluation; while exports equaled only about 1.6% of domestic production, these purchases added upward pressure on meat prices. A wet, cold winter, which increased death losses and reduced rates of gain, was also a contributing factor.

In response to these increases in meat prices, the President, on March 29, imposed ceilings on the wholesale and retail prices of red meats (beef, veal, pork, and lamb). This was primarily a political decision, rather than an action in response to economic arguments. The Food Advisory Committee and nearly all Administration economists advised against it. Congress was debating the renewal of the ESP, and considerable pressure existed for price rollbacks. Some of the President's political advisers were arguing for a freeze on all food prices; there was a strong feeling that the Executive Branch ought to "do something." However, there did exist some elements of an economic rationale. At the time the ceiling prices were imposed, some federal officials felt that meat prices had peaked, or nearly peaked. The ceiling prices, it was hoped, would have little impact on market prices but would reassure the public that meat prices would rise no further. The hopes were based primarily on two factors: (1) indications of future meat supplies and (2) favorable feed-livestock price ratios.

Meat supplies were expected to improve substantially from low first quarter levels. The USDA's semiannual survey of hog inventories, *Hogs and Pigs*, taken in December, revealed an increase of 1% in market hogs under 60 pounds, which should be marketed beginning in late March. Even more encouraging was the outlook for a 7% increase in the December–May pig crop (births), based on the same survey. A March survey of hogs in 14 Corn Belt states reinforced this conclusion. This optimistic balloon was punctured when a revision appearing in June showed that both figures were too high by four percentage points. If the numbers originally published in December had better reflected final figures, the many statements holding out hope for lower prices later in the year would undoubtedly have been tempered greatly. The January results of a quarterly survey, *Cattle on Feed*, showed a 4% increase in total cattle on feed. The number of steers on feed in the 500–899 pound classes was up 11% over 1972 levels; most of these would normally be marketed in the second quarter of 1973.

The second promising factor in late March was the favorable state of feed-livestock price ratios. Grain prices were sufficiently low, relative to meat ceiling prices, so that producers of red meats still had an incentive to expand production (Figures I-1 and I-6). It was not anticipated that the ceiling prices on meat would disrupt supplies in either the short or the long run. However, feed grain and protein meal prices rose rapidly in the weeks and months following the imposition of ceiling prices. Producers of animal products found themselves in an increasingly tight squeeze between feed costs and ceiling prices as Phase III continued. The origins of the rise in feed costs will now be explored—picking up from where we left off in Phase II.

As noted earlier, 1972 was a year of restricted feed grain production in the wake of low prices in 1971. A very good growing season was followed by a wet, cold, snowy harvest season which reduced the quantity and quality of feeds. USDA estimated that in early January 1973 about 12% of corn, 10% of sorghum, and 15% of soybean acreage remain unharvested.[24] Reduced production, weather delays, and reduced feeding of high-priced wheat and soybean meal combined with growing export demand led to higher prices in the fall of 1972. Corn prices reached the 1971 blight year level by December, but this was not particularly worrisome to policy makers. The price of soybean meal at $135 a ton in October–December 1972—nearly double the fourth quarter levels of 1971—was a cause for greater concern.

Soybean meal prices were responding to a slowdown in the rate of increase in world protein meal supplies at a time of growing demand.

FIGURE I-6. ESTIMATED NET RETURNS TO CATTLE FEEDERS,
JANUARY 1970–MAY 1974

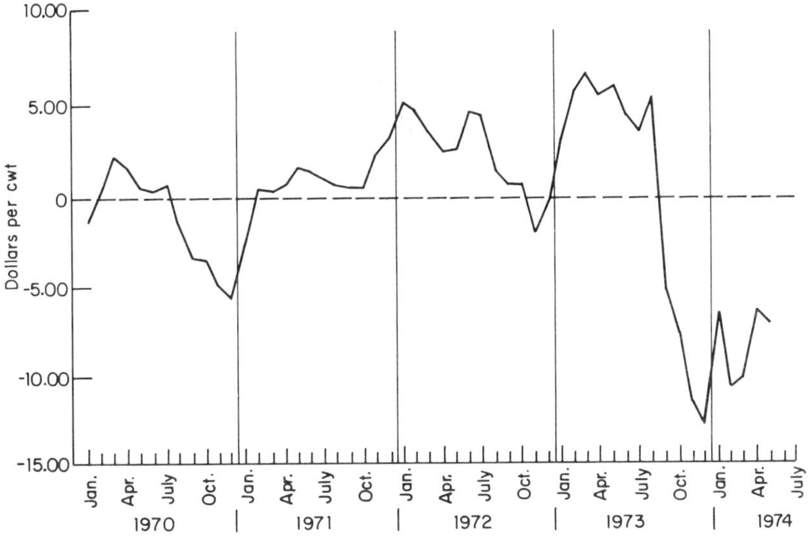

SOURCE: Cost of Living Council.

Protein meal feeds were necessary for growing the livestock products demanded in increasing amounts as per capita incomes increased throughout most of the world. World production of protein meals, shown in Table I-8, grew by an average of 2.1 million tons per year from 1960 to 1970. The growth from 1970 to 1973 averaged only 1.2 million tons per year. Fish meal production declined in each year after peaking in 1970; the disappearance of the anchovies off the Peruvian coast was a major cause. U.S. acreage restrictions in 1971 and 1972 were also an important factor. As a result, ending stocks of U.S. soybeans had declined in every year after August 1969 (Appendix Table I-9). This alone should have led to a concern before a crisis was reached in 1973.

On December 11, 1972, USDA announced the 1973 feed grain program. As mentioned earlier, the goal of a set-aside acreage of 25 million acres was less restrictive than the 1972 program—but certainly not a particularly expansive program. Rising prices and the January 1 planting intentions report led to an announcement on January 31 designed to stimulate additional production. After prices continued to rise and the March 1 planting intentions report was announced, the 1973 feed grain program was further modified on March 26 to gain greater production. These two adjustments reduced the set-aside acreage to 9 million acres from the original 25 million acres. A reduction to zero set-aside would have led to a large increase in program costs (estimated to be $400 million) with little anticipated

TABLE I-8.   WORLD PRODUCTION OF MAJOR OILSEEDS AND MEALS
(44% SOYBEAN MEAL EQUIVALENT BASIS), 1960–1975
(IN MILLIONS OF METRIC TONS)

	Location			Commodity				
Year	U.S.	Foreign	Total	Soybean	Fish	Cotton	Peanut	Other[a]
1960	13.56	17.95	31.51	14.80	2.90	4.98	3.45	5.38
1961	14.13	18.85	32.98	14.74	3.58	4.98	3.82	5.86
1962	16.58	19.94	36.52	17.29	4.09	5.03	3.97	6.14
1963	16.48	20.07	36.55	17.11	4.15	5.28	4.02	5.99
1964	17.07	21.01	38.08	17.42	5.17	5.53	4.13	5.83
1965	17.08	22.76	39.84	17.54	5.09	5.76	4.53	6.92
1966	20.08	23.33	43.41	20.59	5.87	5.89	4.39	6.67
1967	20.92	24.92	45.84	22.46	6.62	5.21	4.44	7.11
1968	21.67	25.71	47.38	23.44	7.18	5.08	4.57	7.11
1969	24.89	24.96	49.85	26.30	6.70	5.80	4.17	6.88
1970	25.7	26.8	52.5	27.0	7.7	5.6	4.4	7.8
1971	25.5	28.1	53.6	27.7	7.4	5.5	4.5	8.5
1972	26.4	28.1	54.5	29.8	5.6	6.1	4.8	8.2
1973	28.8	27.3	56.1	32.8	5.1	6.5	3.9	7.8
1974	34.3	31.4	65.7	40.7	5.8	6.6	4.1	8.5
1975[b]	27.8	33.6	61.4	35.6	6.8	6.7	4.2	8.1

[a] Includes sunflower, linseed, rapeseed, copra, and palm kernel meals.
[b] Forecast.
SOURCES: USDA, Foreign Agriculture Circular, FFO 7-74, June 1974, and FOP 2-75, April 1975.

change in production; it also would have created inequities among producers, deriving from their earlier acreage diversion commitments. Thus, changing circumstances and the new decision structure in the Executive Branch led to a major change in feed grain policy from December to March.

But corn prices and soybean meal prices continued to increase in response to export demand. The Decatur soybean meal price in May 1973 was $315 per ton, three times that of a year earlier and four times the 1970–1971 average. The May corn price received by farmers, $1.61 per bushel, was 40% above the year earlier level; the Chicago price was up 57% to $2.01 as the farm-to-terminal-market spread widened. By late May and early June, when Phase III gave way to Freeze II, livestock and poultry producers were in a tight cost-price squeeze (Figures I-1, I-6, and I-7). Producers responded by withholding marketings and cutting back production; these actions will be discussed in more detail in a following section on Freeze II.

Wheat

There was only one major development in wheat in the first half of 1973. On January 11 USDA announced a change in the wheat pro-

FIGURE I-7. ESTIMATED NET RETURNS FOR BROILER PRODUCTION,
JANUARY 1970–MAY 1974

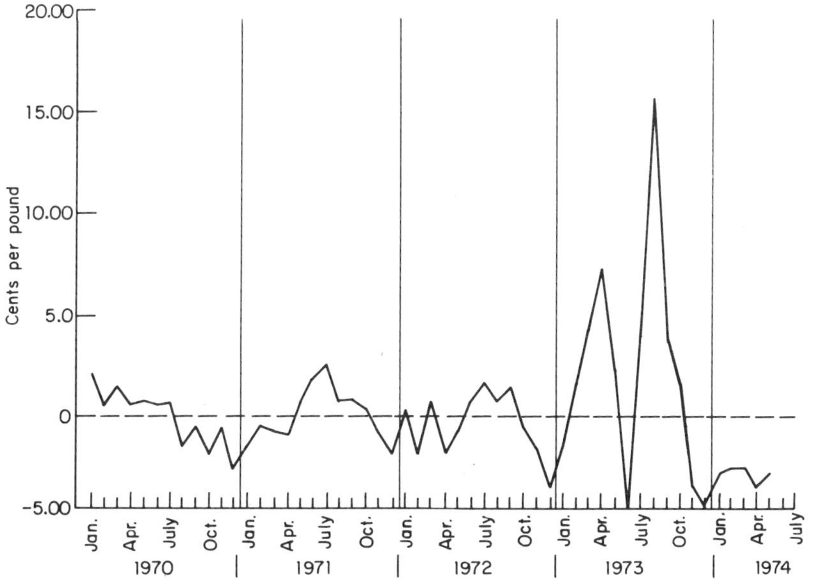

SOURCE: Cost of Living Council.

gram to encourage greater production. The announcement came too late to affect winter wheat plantings, which accounted for about two-thirds of total production in 1971–1972. However, spring wheat producers were able to adjust and increase plantings 25% above 1972 levels, in stark contrast to the 2% increase for winter wheat.

Wheat prices declined slightly after reaching peaks in December and January. Although the Russian grain sale was a continuing topic of controversy, center stage in food and agricultural policy debates was now taken over by the meat and soybean problems outlined above.

Dairy Products

In late 1972 and early 1973 dairy products became an increasingly important focal point for policy action, a state of affairs which would continue through the end of the stabilization program in mid-1974. The basic ingredients were: (1) rising demand and prices for dairy products as a result of higher incomes and the substitution of dairy products for meats with their higher relative prices, (2) a cost-price squeeze on dairy farmers as increases in feed costs outran the rise in milk prices, (3) large supplies of nonfat dry milk and cheese available from foreign markets, (4) government-mandated price support levels, and (5) government-mandated import quotas. The struggle between producer and consumer interests was intense throughout Phases III and IV. Prior to late 1972 dairy product prices were a very minor cause of inflation; the index of consumer dairy product prices rose only 1% from October 1971 to October 1972 (Appendix Table I-10).

Milk production declined in the fourth quarter of 1972 after two years of steady growth. The immediate cause was a slackening in the rate of increase in milk production per cow so that the 1972 fourth quarter level was only 0.8% above a year earlier. Meanwhile the total number of cows continued to fall at an annual rate of 1% to 1.5%, which was consistent with previous trends. The more basic factor underlying the drop in milk production was the squeeze on producers' margins. The rise in milk prices was outpaced by the gain in feed prices (Figure I-8).

Milk prices rose as a result of income gains and substitution from meat products as well as because of declining supplies. The demand for fluid milk and cheese was particularly strong relative to the demand for butter. In late 1972 and early 1973 the market prices of cheese and nonfat dry milk moved well above federal support levels while butter prices remained at, or near, minimum guaranteed levels. The support level was set at 75% of parity, the minimum required by law.

The production and pricing of dairy products are somewhat complex, and a brief review may be helpful. Milk sold in the relatively inelastic fluid market receives a higher price than milk sold for man-

FIGURE I-8.   ESTIMATED NET RETURNS FOR MILK PRODUCTION, JANUARY 1970–MAY 1974

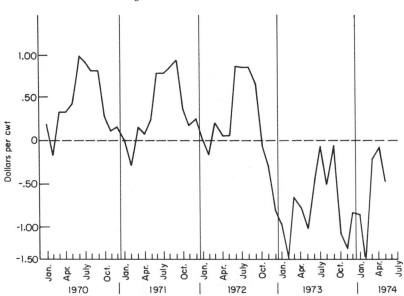

SOURCE: Cost of Living Council.

ufacturing into products, principally cheese, butter, and nonfat dry milk. This classic form of price discrimination is typically implemented by large cooperatives and supported by federal policy, in the form of "marketing orders" or "marketing agreements" defined over geographical areas.[25] Within each order or agreement, producers receive a "blend price" equal to the average of the fluid and manufacturing prices weighted by the proportions going to each use. Producers near large metropolitan areas, where most of the milk is consumed in the fluid form, such as those near New York, prefer a large differential between the price of fluid and the price of manufacturing milk. Those in more remote areas, where much of the milk is processed into products, such as Minnesota and Wisconsin, prefer little or no price discrimination between fluid and processing milk. Minimum differentials in each order are specified by the federal government, but the dairy cooperatives often charge a premium on fluid milk, i.e., increase the differential. The base price to which the differential is added is usually the average price paid for manufacturing milk in Minnesota and Wisconsin. Finally, prices for manufactured dairy products are supported by the USDA through offers to purchase butter, nonfat dry milk, and cheddar cheese at specified prices. Imports are restricted primarily in order to insure that federal purchases are not inflated by available foreign supplies; the restrictions continue, however, when domestic market prices rise above support levels.

Dairy prices are thus the product of a circular feedback system. The fluid milk market usually is supplied with all the milk it will absorb at prevailing prices, in any given period. The remaining supply of milk enters the manufacturing market where competitive forces or USDA price supports determine prices. If the manufacuring milk price rises, the fluid milk price rises by a similar amount after a two-month lag—and vice versa in cases of falling manufacturing milk prices. Price changes in the fluid milk market affect the quantity sold and, in turn, the quantity remaining for manufacturing purposes.

In late 1972 prices of cheese and nonfat dry milk (NFDM) rose significantly. Increasing demand for fluid milk in combination with declining production left a smaller residual for the manufacturing market. Among manufactured products, the demand for cheese was growing faster than that for butter. This led to higher prices for cheese and a greater use of milk by cheese plants relative to butter plants. Since NFDM is a joint product of butter, NFDM production declined and the price rose 14% from September to December. End of November NFDM stocks were down 55% (61.5 million pounds) from year earlier levels.

The rise in the NFDM price concerned CLC because of both its immediate effect on consumer prices and its lagged effect on fluid milk prices. On December 30 the annual NFDM import quota of 1.8 million pounds was raised temporarily by 25 million pounds. The temporary quota was filled by January 15; Canada supplied the bulk, 19.6 million pounds or 78%.[26] The imports of NFDM appeared to stabilize prices of manufactured dairy products in January–February 1973 (Appendix Table I-11).

The next major action was the announcement on March 8 of price support levels for 1973–1974, effective March 15. Two aspects of the program were particularly significant. First, the support level continued at 75% of parity, the minimum provided by law; because of rising costs, the 1973–1974 minimum was 7% above the 1972–1973 support price. The second important feature was a strong "tilt" toward cheese in fixing the relative prices used to implement the support level, as shown in Table I-9. The purpose was to discourage butter production, which tended to exceed demand, and encourage cheese production in order to satisfy the rapidly growing demand for cheese. Simultaneously with the price support announcement, President Nixon directed the Tariff Commission to study the need for a temporary increase in cheese import quotas, which would also aid in satisfying consumer demand.

The announcements provoked anger among producer groups. Dairy producers felt a higher support level was warranted by higher costs. Only by such action, they argued, could domestic milk producers be encouraged to increase production; February milk production was nearly 5% below the 1972 level (Appendix Table I-13). A further increase in imports, they continued, would lead to lower prices, a worsened plight for domestic producers, and greater reliance on undependable, subsidized foreign producers. Those producers selling to butter plants were of course greatly upset over the decreased support price for butter. They argued that the building of cheese plants was already proceeding at a maximum rate, so that the tilt would have no positive effect, while unjustly discriminating against many producers.

CLC estimates confirmed that dairy producers were caught in a cost-price squeeze, but consumers were also being squeezed. The costs of dairy producers rose about $1.60 per cwt. of milk produced from February 1972 to February 1973, according to CLC estimates. Milk prices rose $0.47 per cwt. over the same period, resulting in a decline of about $1.13 per cwt. in producers' net returns (Figure I-8). Nevertheless, CLC continued to reflect the interests of consumers in repeated attempts to blunt the rise in dairy prices.

The new price supports led to a decline in butter prices, but most other dairy product prices resumed their upward trend in April (Appendix Table I-11). Wholesale butter prices fell 6.1 cents per pound, 9.0%, from February to April; retail prices declined only 2.0 cents per pound, 2.3% (Appendix Table I-10). From February to April wholesale cheese and NFDM prices rose 3.1% and 10.8% respectively.

Two additional dairy import actions were taken during Phase III

TABLE I-9. DAIRY SUPPORT PRICES, 1972–1973 THROUGH 1974–1975

Date	Butter		Cheddar Cheese		Nonfat Dry Milk		Whole Milk Equivalent[a]	
	Price (cents/pound)	Percent Change	Price (cents/pound)	Percent Change	Price (cents/pound)	Percent Change	Price (dollar/hundredweight)	Percent Change
1972–1973	68.75	—	54.75	—	31.7	—	4.93	—
1973–1974								
April 1	62.0	−10	62.0	+13	37.5	+18	5.29	+7
August 14	62.0	0	65.0	+5	41.4	+10	5.61	+6
1974–1975								
April 1	62.0	0	70.75	+9	56.6	+37	6.57	+17

[a] No actual purchases are made of whole milk.

SOURCES: USDA, *Dairy Situation*, DS-344, March 1973, p. 4; DS-347, September 1973, p. 7; DS-349, March 1974, p. 4.

with strong support from CLC. On April 25 the President signed a proclamation increasing cheese import quotas by about 64 million pounds for the period ending July 31. The additional import quota, filled by April 27, equaled about 9% of quarterly disappearance. Cheese prices continued to rise in May and June. On May 10 President Nixon signed a proclamation authorizing additional imports of 60 million pounds of NFDM for the period ending June 30. This quota was also quickly filled, by May 25. The quota equaled nearly 25% of May–June 1972 NFDM commercial disappearance, but prices continued to advance in May and June to new highs.

In early June, just prior to Freeze II, retail dairy product prices were 4.9% above their level of six months earlier—an annual rate of increase of 10%. While they undoubtedly had a dampening effect, the increased imports had clearly not stopped the rise in dairy prices. Dairy farmers remained in a cost-price squeeze; milk production continued at a level significantly below 1972 output.

Although not directly related to U.S. prices, it is interesting to note that in mid-1973 the Russians purchased 441 million pounds of surplus butter from the European Community (EC) at about 19 cents per pound.[27] The cost of the sale to the EC was estimated to be $240 million.[28] The resemblance to the Russian wheat deal with the United States is striking. This purchase demonstrated anew that a buyer, especially a state trader, can often find excellent bargains in international markets when some countries choose to support prices at high levels which leads to surplus production.

Freeze II: June 13, 1973—July 18, 1973

By early June the pressure for changes in the Phase III controls toward even more stringent controls had grown intense. Congressional pressure for changes was clear in the debate leading up to the one-year extension of the Economic Stabilization Act signed into law on April 30, the day on which previous authority would have expired. In early April the House Banking Committee reported out a bill requiring a rollback of prices and interest rates to pre-Phase III levels, i.e., to January 10, 1973. This and other similar efforts were successfully resisted by the Administration in April. The debate continued, however, and on June 5 the Senate Democratic Caucus gave its unanimous support to the introduction of legislation imposing a 90-day freeze on all prices, wages, interest rates, dividends, and rents. Administration officials and others were apprehensive that the widespread support for mandatory controls was itself a source of inflationary pressure. It was feared that prices, wages, rents, and other similar items were being raised by people hoping to avoid being caught in a squeeze by new, stiffer controls.

The agricultural provisions of the ESP were a source of much irritation to many nonagricultural groups. The nonfarm portion of the food industry and the nonfood sectors felt the burdens of controls, but agricultural and food prices continued to soar. Many farmers—especially large grain producers—were obviously enjoying greatly expanded profits. Net income of farmers (including valuation of inventory change) in 1973 reached $33.1 billion, 82% above 1972 net income of $18.2 billion and more than double the 1971 total of $14.2 billion.[29] The disposable personal income per farm person was 28% below that of nonfarm people in 1971 and 19% below in 1972 but 7% *above* that of the nonfarm population in 1973.[30] Sizable increases in agricultural prices and incomes undermined the credibility of the entire controls program and threatened to destroy it. In such an event wages would have almost certainly taken a large and permanent boost.

The second Freeze on prices, not to exceed 60 days, was announced by President Nixon on June 13. Wages were not frozen but remained under the Phase III control system. Rents and raw, unprocessed agricultural product prices at the farm level continued to be exempt from controls, but no pass-through was allowed in the freeze period. The ceiling prices on red meats remained unchanged. The purposes of the Freeze were: (1) "to administer shock therapy" in order to dispel widespread inflationary psychology, (2) to stop the destructive speculative pricing activity noted above, and (3) to provide time for planning a Phase IV program which would be more stringent than Phase III.[31]

It quickly became apparent that Freeze II was a disastrous policy for the food and agricultural sector. Although the Freeze on the industrial and service sectors continued through August 12, the food and agricultural sector shifted to Phase IV on July 19 because of numerous distortions caused by the Freeze. The problems of the Freeze II period will be examined under two subheadings: (1) general impacts and (2) feed-livestock sector.

General Impacts

The timing of Freeze II with respect to price movements was much worse than in the case of Freeze I. As pointed out earlier, most food prices had attained, or even passed, their seasonal peaks at the time Freeze I was imposed on August 15. The Freeze II base period was June 1–8, more than two months earlier than Freeze I. The aggregate index of food prices normally rises seasonally from June to July. For some commodities, such as apples, oranges, and potatoes, the seasonal rise from May–June levels is very strong (Table I-1). Not surprisingly, numerous price freeze problems for fruits and vegetables arose. Fresh tomatoes and potatoes were a particularly severe problem because of low prices during the base period. The movement of products left normal market channels and entered undocumented, disorganized market paths. Compliance with freeze regulations became difficult, if not impossible, to ascertain.

In addition to normal seasonal movements, agricultural prices were in the midst of a strong upward trend in June 1973—as opposed to the decline coming after August 1971 (Figure I-2). The farm value of the market basket of food rose 5.4% from May to June and 3.0% from June to July; the farm-retail spread fell 1.4% and 1.1% in each period, respectively. Many processors and retailers experienced a severe squeeze between uncontrolled raw material prices and frozen product prices. CLC monitoring efforts disclosed that about 180 food and feed firms curtailed activity or closed during the Freeze with a maximum of 80 firms closed at any given time. The maximum loss of jobs was estimated at 8,000.[32]

The grain milling industry provides a good example of the problems caused by the Freeze. Ceiling prices were based on prices for shipments during the week of June 1–8, but most of these shipments were filling contracts written at least 30 days previously. The shipment prices thus reflected much lower raw material costs than millers had experienced since signing the above contracts. The freeze regulations prevented them from passing on the higher costs. The losses to firms were considerable in many cases. Numerous other examples could be cited.

Feed Grain-Livestock Sector

Reduced marketings, higher feed costs, and cutbacks in production plans were confronting policy makers during Freeze II. Although the Freeze was an important factor leading to distortions, other events also played a significant role. The major policy initiative, in addition to the Freeze, was a dramatic attempt to lower feed costs by placing an embargo on exports of soybeans and related products.

Beef prices were up to ceiling levels by mid-June, and hog prices moved up to ceilings later in the month (Figures I-9 and I-10). The dip in prices after the ceilings were imposed in late March was a result of declining demand as consumers purchased less meat. A well-publicized meat boycott in early April was instrumental in raising people's awareness of how much prices had increased and in legitimizing the omission of meat from meals. Producers responded by reducing marketings of cattle and hogs; broilers were nearly impossible to withhold for a significant period because of the short feeding period. Beef production was down 9.3% in the second quarter of 1973 compared with a year earlier, pork production was down 6.1%, and total meat and poultry production was down 6.7%. The withholding practiced by producers reflected an attitude that the underlying trend of prices was upward. By delaying marketings, producers expected to receive higher prices and larger profits when ceilings were removed. In the short run the attitude proved to be a self-fulfilling prophecy,

FIGURE I-9. SLAUGHTER STEER PRICES, 1972–1974

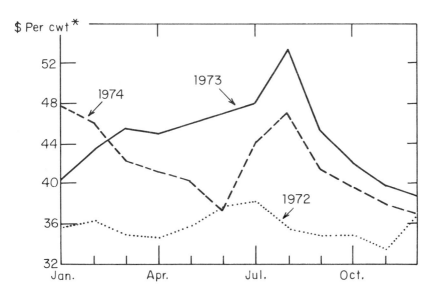

SOURCE: USDA, *Livestock and Meat Situation,* LMS-201, February 1975, p. 2.

* Choice grade, sold out of first hands at Omaha.

FIGURE I-10. HOG PRICES, 1972–1974

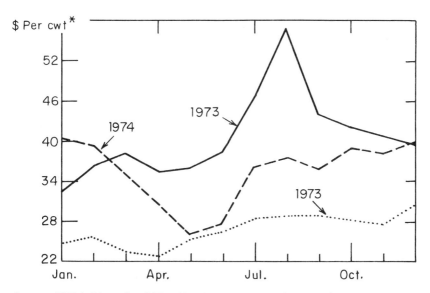

SOURCE: USDA, *Livestock and Meat Situation,* LMS-201, February 1975, p. 2.

* Barrows and gilts at seven markets.

i.e., withholding created price strength which, in turn, caused more withholding, and so on.

As prices pressed against ceiling levels in late June and early July, the tendency of producers to delay marketings grew stronger. Shortages of meat, both actual and potential, were receiving a great deal of attention. Producers expected Phase IV to include a removal of meat ceiling prices and to result in higher prices. Their actions increased the upward pressure on ceiling prices. Processors and retailers were increasingly squeezed between exempt raw material prices and frozen final product prices.[33]

Livestock and poultry producers were also in a cost-price squeeze. Feed costs continued to climb as they had done throughout Phase III. The price of corn (Chicago) went from $2.01 per bushel in May to $2.42 in June and $2.52 in July; these were increases of 57%, 94%, and 95%, respectively, over a year earlier. Similarly, the price of soybean meal (Decatur) advanced from $315 per ton in May to $412 in June; the June price represented an astounding increase of 333% from the June 1972 price of $95 per ton.

The profitability of livestock and poultry production had deteriorated greatly from March to June (Figures I-1, I-6, and I-7). The price of corn had risen 52% and the soybean meal price had risen 106% over this period. Farm prices of beef and pork had risen slightly, but consumer resistance and the back pressure of retail price ceilings had limited advances. Broiler prices were not frozen until mid-June, but they were only slightly higher in June than in March. Placements of cattle on feed in the second quarter of 1973 were 10% below year earlier levels. Reports of pregnant sows being slaughtered and of cutbacks in broiler production became widespread. A TV news item on the drowning of baby chicks was particularly important in shaping public opinion, although the incident—by itself—probably had little impact on policy makers. A more influential statistic was the drop in the number of eggs set in incubators to a level 8% below 1972, after trailing 1972 levels by only 2% in early June. Data which became available after the Freeze showed June sow slaughter in 1973 actually down 25% from 1972, rather than up (no data are available on pregnant sow slaughter).

On June 27 the Secretary of Commerce announced an embargo on the export of soybeans, cottonseed, and related products.[34] This followed by exactly two weeks the announcement of a requirement that exporters report export commitments of grains and oilseeds on a weekly basis by country of destination, reports which USDA had resisted since March. Upon examination of the initial reports, government officials judged that remaining supplies would not satisfy domestic and export commitments, even at the prevailing high prices. The embargo was replaced by a licensing system on July 2; allocations as a percentage of unshipped contracts were soybeans, 50%; soybean meal, 40%; cottonseed and related products, 100%. On August 1 all allocations were increased to 100%, and on September 21 all export controls were terminated.

The immediate impact of the export controls was dramatic. Cash soybean prices at Chicago fell from a range of $11.30 to $11.45 per bushel on June 20–25 (the price had reached $12.27 on June 5) to $6.15 to $6.25 per bushel on July 6–9. While significant, the final price impact of the export controls—as measured by broader averages rather than the extremes—was considerably smaller. Chicago cash soybean prices in Chicago fell to $8.69 per bushel in July from $10.87 in June. Similarly, soybean meal prices dropped to $311 per ton in July, down 25% from $412 in June. Foreign customers were irate. The sudden breaking of contracts for supplies of an important feed, and in some cases foodstuff, was in their opinion a serious breach of faith. U.S. officials emphasized that the action was an emergency measure taken in light of the domestic price freeze and the oversold condition of soybeans, but foreign customers were obviously not mollified.

Despite the anger in other countries, the most important consequence of this foray into export controls was a change in domestic attitudes rather than in policies of other nations. Export restrictions were now an acknowledged alternative in discussions of how to control domestic inflation. Such restrictions were no longer regarded as illegitimate or unrealistic; they would reappear, albeit less formally, in succeeding years. The export monitoring system continues to be a tool in public decisions regarding exports as well as a means for improving price information in private markets. Opinions differ as to whether admitting export controls into the realm of possible actions leads to better national policy, but few—if any—would deny that the option exists.

Phase IV: July 19, 1973—April 30, 1974

As the result of many problems, the food sector moved from the Freeze to Phase IV on July 19—several weeks earlier than the August 13 date applicable to the industrial and service sector. The most important features of the program dealt with the ceiling prices on meat and the cost pass-through provisions. As originally announced, the ceiling prices on beef were continued through September 11, but all other meat ceiling prices were immediately terminated. In computing pass-throughs prior to September 12, retail and manufacturing food firms were permitted to raise prices only enough to reflect raw agricultural cost increases since June 8 on a dollar-for-dollar pass-through basis. Beginning September 12 all costs could be passed through on a basis very similar to the regulations for the industrial and service sector. The two periods divided by September 12 were designated "Stage A" and "Stage B," respectively.

On September 7, a Friday, the September 12 date for the beginning of Stage B was changed to September 10, primarily for two reasons. First, there was concern that producers would withhold livestock in large numbers on September 10-11, creating short-term shortages, in expectation of higher prices beginning on September 12. Second, the change would ease administrative and enforcement burdens because many food firms start their accounting periods at the beginning of each week. The new change-over time was midnight Sunday rather than midnight Tuesday.

General economic conditions deteriorated in Phase IV. Real GNP grew at an annual rate of only 2% from the second to the fourth quarter of 1973; it then declined at an annual rate of 4.5% from the fourth quarter of 1973 to the second quarter of 1974. Although total employment continued to rise, the unemployment rate shifted upward from 4.6%-4.8% in the second half of 1973 to 5.0%-5.2% in the first four months of 1974. Inflation continued to worsen despite the economic slowdown. Consumer prices rose at an annual rate of 11.4% in the nine months of Phase IV (July 1973 to April 1974) compared with an annual rate of 6.5% in the preceding nine months (October 1972 to July 1973). Output suffered and inflation was more severe as a result of the Arab embargo on oil exports to the United States, followed by oil exports to the United States at a threefold to fourfold increase in price.

The rise in food prices continued to outpace that of nonfood prices. Consumer food prices rose at an annual rate of 17.1% in the nine months of Phase IV, approximately equaling the 17.4% annual rate observed in the preceding nine months. Even though the annual rate of inflation of nonfood prices nearly tripled in the corresponding periods, from 3.5% to 9.5%, it remained considerably below that of food.

Throughout late 1972 and early 1973, the USDA had consistently underestimated the rise in food prices in 1973. The USDA estimate of the increase from 1972 to 1973 changed from about 3% in November 1972 to 6% in February and to 9% in May. In mid-1973 many others felt a larger estimate was warranted; later events substantiated this for the actual year-to-year increase was about 15%. The forecasting errors of USDA were, of course, very upsetting since policy makers based many of their statements and actions on the USDA estimates. In the fall of 1973 John T. Dunlop, Director of CLC, requested that the Executive Branch obtain an independent appraisal of deficiencies associated with food price forecasting in 1973. Karl A. Fox of Iowa State University agreed to undertake the assignment. In his report Fox concluded that no one had forecast well the increase in agricultural and food prices because of a lack of adequate data and an absence of an adequate analytic framework encompassing the world economy.[35] Fox concluded: "The overriding need is this: The economic intelligence function must be given increased salience in the organizational structure of the U.S. Department of Agriculture and in the attention and concern of the Secretary of Agriculture." His recommendations included the following: that an assistant secretary for this area be established, that Economic Research Service (ERS) personnel grades be upgraded, that ERS be insulated from political issues, and that the ERS budget be increased.

Feed Grain-Livestock Sector

Meat prices continued to occupy center stage through Stage A as the continued ceiling on wholesale and retail beef prices led to major market and price distortions. Stage B, however, was characterized by lower meat prices as beef supplies bulged as a result of marketings of a backlog of cattle and an apparent shift in consumer beef buying habits. Feed prices, especially corn prices, remained high but did not reach the crisis stage seen in soybean meal.

The decision to maintain ceilings on beef prices but not on other meat prices led to a host of problems. The rationale for maintaining beef ceiling prices until September 10 had several elements.[36] First, one of the goals of Phase IV was to spread the bulge of post-freeze price increases over several months. Policy makers sought to delay the expected rise in beef prices into September—and into October so far as CPI figures were concerned.[37] Second, beef was the logical choice for the continuation of ceiling prices because the long-term effects on production were not likely to be negative. Feeder cattle prices were very high relative to costs of production so that ranchers were continuing to expand their herds. Available data indicated that hog and poultry producers, on the other hand, were cutting back production. Third, market prices would be available to guide decisions at the time of peak movement of feeder cattle from ranches to feedlots in September-November. Fourth, policy makers recognized that some cattle feeders would withhold cattle from the market in expectation of higher prices after September 10. However, such a strategy involved feeding cattle to weights where feed-to-meat conversion is very inefficient, and the withholdings would create a glut on the market in September if the strategy became widespread. Withholding was a self-defeating process, they continued, and cattle feeders should recognize it as such—and thus not withhold in excessive amounts.

Opponents of the beef price ceilings argued as follows. First, the price bulge was spread over time very little, if at all, since pork and poultry prices in Stage A were much higher than would have been the case if beef was not being withheld because of ceiling prices. Some contended that the aggregate index of meat and poultry prices would fall if beef ceilings were removed. Second, high prices were preferable to shortages and enforced rationing by nonprice means at lower prices. Third, the beef industry was suffering from severe distortions which were creating inefficiencies and unnecessary hardships. Cattle were being custom slaughtered and beef was increasingly moved in black markets. Many packers, processors, and retailers—especially meat specialty shops—were forced to curtail operations or close. Fourth, withholding was a potentially successful strategy. The profit could be "locked in" by hedging in the October future at a price above prevailing levels. But even unhedged cattle could be withheld successfully, the argument continued, because the resulting backlog would not be sufficiently large relative to demand to depress prices. Finally, a further delay in removal of beef ceiling prices would lead to continued low placements of feeder cattle into feedlots and thus jeopardize future production.

Both sides of the argument had some merit. The aggregate index of meat and poultry prices peaked in August at a figure 17% above July and 8% above the following October (Figure I-3). The immediate post-freeze price bulge was massive and evidently not spread into later months. Shortages and distortions were commonplace. Perhaps the greatest surprise was the willingness of food chains to absorb very large losses by bidding up farm prices of cattle in the face of a retail price freeze. Many firms did shut down. Placements of cattle on feed were low. However, CLC officials were certainly correct in their opinion that withholding was a self-defeating process. Despite this, most cattle feeders withheld cattle from the market; many feeders passed up prices of over $50 per cwt. in August only to be confronted by prices in the high $30's and low $40's in late September through the remainder of 1973 (Figure I-9). Cattle prices rose somewhat in 1974, but a large backlog of fed cattle continued to be a depressing influence on prices. Losses to feeders of $100 or more per animal were common throughout late 1973 and early 1974 (Figure I-6).

Retail prices of beef and pork did not drop by the same proportion as cattle and hog prices when the latter declined precipitously in September, October, and November. Producers, with some encouragement from USDA officials, laid blame for part of their economic problems on excessive margins charged by middlemen. If the margins were smaller, producers argued: (1) retail prices would be somewhat lower and farm prices somewhat higher, (2) meat consumption would increase and the glut at the producer level would disappear more rapidly, and (3) middlemen could still realize a profit comparable with that of preceding years. USDA data did show a large increase in farm-retail spreads in September-November, relative to the preceding months (Figures I-4 and I-5). However, much of the increase reflected a recovery from abnormally low spreads; i.e., middlemen were unable to pass on all increases in meat costs when cattle and hog prices were rising. In addition, costs other than meat—especially transportation costs—were increasing rapidly. Finally, retailers and others in the meat sector continued to dispute the accuracy of USDA data.

In retrospect the opposing arguments concerning meat price

spreads largely reflect differing interpretations of what the spread data represented rather than measurement errors.[38] The farm-retail price spread for a food item is the difference at one point in time between the average retail store price and the average value of a corresponding amount of raw food material as sold and priced at or near the farm. The item is typically defined in precise terms in order to insure that the spread is an index of price change not compounded by changes in quantity or quality. For example, the price spread for beef is computed from choice cattle which are estimated to be yield grade three and from choice retail cuts. The prices of all other beef items have no direct impact on the spread calculation despite their importance to producers, packers, retailers, and consumers. Thus, the very important conclusion is that price spreads are *not* equivalent to gross margins (or, obviously, net margins). The gross margin is the difference between sales of goods and the cost of goods sold, where the latter includes an adjustment for inventory valuation. The mix of goods often varies significantly over time (e.g., the increasing importance of "grass fed" as opposed to "corn fed" beef in 1974 and 1975) with a consequent impact on margins, but as noted above, the spreads do not reflect such changes. Producers, industry spokesmen, and consumers who regarded the spread data as measures of margins were clearly misinterpreting the USDA data.

Several other underlying concepts must be noted if spreads are to be properly interpreted. The conversion factors used to transform farm, wholesale, and retail prices to an equivalent base apply only to the specific items incorporated into spreads. Again, changes in product mix are *not* incorporated since the USDA intent is to compute a price index with fixed quantity and quality weights. Another important matter is that price spreads generally reflect price differentials at a point in time, while normal business practices contain lags as a result of physical product flows, information flows, and decision frameworks. As a consequence, USDA price spreads tend to narrow when prices are trending upwards and widen as prices are declining—even if businesses maintain a constant margin on each physical item. Finally, USDA adjusts retail prices of beef and pork—but no other items—to take into account the increased volume of sales when items are "specialed." Industry spokesmen argue that such adjustments have been too small.

Summarizing the events surrounding meat prices, the continuation of beef ceiling prices by CLC during Stage A (July 19 through September 9) would almost certainly have to be judged an error in view of the results. However, the judgment of cattle feeders was also very poor and the decision by food chains to resort to custom slaughtering compounded the problem.

While discussing beef, it is once again instructive to digress for a moment and note how the Russians have enjoyed subsidies as a result of support policies in the Western world. In mid-1974 the Russians purchased about 50,000 tons of surplus beef from the European Community at a price of about $830 per ton. World market prices were about $984 per ton, and the cost to the EC was about $30 million.[39]

Shifting to feeds for a moment, in a follow-up to the announcement of Phase IV food regulations, Secretary Butz announced on July 19 that there would be no set-aside acreage for feed grains, wheat, or cotton in 1974. Unconstrained production of feed grains and soybeans began in the spring of 1974 for harvest in the following fall.

The 1973 corn crop got off to a bad start because of a wet spring. This was especially troublesome since it followed a cold, wet fall which had prevented extensive preparation of fields after the 1972 harvest. Forced planting delays led to an increase of soybean acreage at the expense of corn and cotton. Although corn yields were down from the record 1972 level, total corn production in 1973 increased slightly because of greater harvested acreage (Appendix Table I-1). Strong export demand raised prices to the $3 per bushel range (Chicago) in early 1974. While substantially above the $2.52 price recorded in July 1973, the price was not sufficiently high in the eyes of the Administration to impose export controls—the only meaningful policy measure which could reduce prices at this juncture.

Soybean meal prices trended downward through October 1973, under the combined influence of export controls (through September 20) and the new crop. The downward trend was interrupted briefly in November and December as crushers seemed unable to catch up with demand, but meal prices resumed their decline in 1974.

The major attention in grains shifted from feed grains and oilseeds back to wheat in 1973–1974.

Wheat and Related Products

Prices of wheat, flour, and related products rose at a rapid rate in 1973–1974 as strong export demand for wheat continued in the presence of reduced total supplies (beginning stocks plus production). Policy makers were pushed to the brink of imposing export controls but rejected this alternative. Other measures, with fewer undesirable consequences but with less impact on domestic prices, were adopted.

Beginning stocks of wheat on July 1, 1973, were 439 million bushels, down 424 million bushels or about 50% from a year earlier. Production was up only 166 million bushels, largely as a consequence of waiting until after winter wheat was seeded to announce a release of set-aside acres. Total wheat supply in 1973–1974 was thus down 258 million bushels, 11% less than in 1972–1973.

The first policy decision of the new crop year, and coming almost simultaneously with the Phase IV announcement, was the July 19 declaration of no set-aside acreage for wheat, feed grains, or cotton in the coming year. The government's position was one of total commitment to expanding grain and oilseed supplies, although some officials in USDA and OMB were concerned that a bumper crop would drastically lower commodity prices and raise government costs.

Wheat prices increased dramatically in late July and August as strong export demand entered the U.S. market. The average price received by farmers moved from $2.47 in July to $4.45 in August and $4.62 in September. Prices were more than double those of a year earlier, which were considered high as a result of the Russian wheat sale.

Strong export demand was reflected in two series of data readily available to all observers. First, actual export shipments (reported weekly) were proceeding at a record rate. Exports of wheat, flour, and related products totaled nearly 400 million bushels in July–September. USDA projected exports of 950 million bushels for 1973–1974 in May, but it became obvious that this estimate was too low.[40] In August the estimate was revised upwards to 1,100 million bushels.[41] Even this seemed too small to many observers who noted that the USDA estimate implied that the export rate would drop about 40% in the remainder of the crop year.[42] Second, the new reporting system for outstanding export sales showed a rapid increase in sales for 1973–1974, despite the fact that record shipments were being made and thus converting outstanding sales to actual sales. Outstanding sales grew from 750 million bushels as of June 29 to 1,003 as of July 20 and to 1,136 as of August 17.[43] In late July and early August it was a simple matter to add actual and outstanding export sales figures to yield a result which was impossibly high; i.e., the implied ending domestic stock level of 0–100 million bushels was below minimum working stock requirements of about 180 million bushels. In the absence of other rationing devices, prices clearly needed to rise in order to ration available supplies among domestic and foreign users.

Prices remained strong despite a record increase in world grain and rice production in 1973–1974 (Table I-2). Production increased over 100 million metric tons, 9%, from 1972–1973. However, stocks remained at low levels as consumption equaled production. Foreign buyers, mindful of low world stocks and the soybean export embargo, were probably anxious to obtain commitments for available supplies early in the crop year. The distribution of exports by country changed significantly from 1972–1973 to 1973–1974. Shipments to the USSR fell by nearly 250 million bushels, and Japan's purchases dropped about 11 million bushels. Exports to the People's Republic of China rose by nearly 100 million bushels and those to India were up over 40 million bushels; increased exports to other Asian countries, Africa, and South America were also important.

Flour, bread, and other wheat product prices increased rapidly as wheat prices rose. Consumers were upset, especially in view of the earlier subsidized sale of wheat to Russia. Consumer and producer interests, with strong support from CLC and the CLC Food Industry Advisory Committee, combined to eliminate the Wheat Certificate Program, that is, the "bread tax," in August. The Certificate Program required millers to purchase a 75-cent certificate from the federal government for each bushel of wheat milled into flour for domestic consumption. The proceeds, about $400 million annually, helped to offset the costs of wheat price support activities. Certificate requirements were suspended retroactively to July 1 as part of the Agriculture and Consumer Protection Act of 1973, enacted on August 10. The suspension of the Certificate Program added to the federal deficit by reducing taxes, which was inflationary. However, the suspension probably slightly reduced the rise in wheat product prices which occurred; this had the greatest impact on low- and middle-income groups, who consume more flour and bread than high income groups. Wheat prices probably rose slightly more than they would have with a continuation of the program.

After a slight downturn in September–November, wheat prices resumed their upward climb in December–February. The sum of actual exports plus outstanding sales continued to maintain a level of over 1.3 billion bushels, instead of declining to a conceivable range of 1.1 to 1.2, i.e., a level consistent with minimum working stock requirements. Fears grew that the United States had oversold its wheat supply and that a price explosion similar to the 1973 soybean experience was in the offing. January wheat prices exceeded $5 per bushel at the farm level and were in the neighborhood of $6 at many major markets.

On January 8 the Chairman of the American Bakers Association asserted at a press conference that a coming wheat shortage might lead to bread prices of a dollar per loaf. He strongly urged that government action be taken. In response Secretary Butz labeled this "an irresponsible scare tactic . . . to catch the headlines and perpetrate a hoax on consumers." The controversy continued in the public eye with a hearing before the Senate Committee on Agriculture on February 4. Secretary Butz correctly pointed out that a dollar per loaf bread price would occur only if bakers increased their margins to very high, most would say unreasonable, levels.

While few, if any, government officials expected bread prices to reach a dollar per loaf, they were very much concerned with the possibility of further price increases. The CLC Food Committee met in early January to review the situation and discuss policy alternatives. Limitations on imports were suspended on January 25 for a period extending through June 30, 1974. USDA officials urged foreign buyers and U.S. exporters to defer shipments until new crop wheat could be substituted for old crop; the major positive response came from the Soviet Union. USDA officials also urged other potential sellers, notably the European Community, to export additional wheat.

Prices continued to rise despite these measures. The Food Committee reconvened in early February and again in late February to discuss the progress on actions taken and the need for further initiatives. Pressure continued to be exerted on USDA to utilize all its potential influence on foreign buyers and U.S. exporters. Export controls were rejected.

Pressure was exerted on the Department of State to limit concessionary sales under PL 480 to the minimum consistent with high priority policy objectives. Requests for food aid were scrutinized carefully with regard to the needs in the recipient countries, the ability of recipients to handle shipments, and the contribution to U.S. foreign policy objectives. Representatives of CLC and the Department of State often disagreed strongly on what action should be taken. Concessional sales of wheat and flour fell to only 64 million bushels in 1973–1974; shipments had totaled about 500 million bushels per year in the mid-1960's and about 250 million bushels per year in the late 1960's and early 1970's. The cutback in foreign food aid was clearly an important factor limiting price increases, but the inherent questions of equity between U.S. and needy overseas consumers were difficult ones.

Wheat prices fell sharply after peaking at $5.52 per bushel (farm) in February. Export shipments failed to meet expectations as the result of vessel delays, a labor strike, a postponement of some shipments, and a People's Republic of China refusal to accept delivery because of contamination by dwarf-smut.[44] Farm prices reached the $3.50 to $3.60 per bushel range in May–June. The decision not to impose export controls in the middle of the crop year, supported by USDA and the Department of State and viewed less certainly by CLC, proved the correct course of action.

Dairy Products

Issues related to dairy prices and products were an important component of policy in Phase IV. However, the basic elements of the situation, as presented in Figure I-8 and Appendix Tables I-10–I-13, were the same as outlined earlier. Milk prices received by producers rose but so did feed and other costs. Dairy producers were caught in a cost-price squeeze; domestic production of milk declined in each month of Phase IV relative to a year earlier.

Government price supports continued to be set at minimum levels. Two adjustments were required by law. First, the Agriculture and Consumer Protection Act of 1973 enacted on August 10 required that manufacturing milk prices be supported between 80% and 90% of parity through March 31, 1975; after this date, the previous range of 75% to 90% would be restored.[45] The new support prices are shown in Table I-9. Wholesale prices were well above support levels so that the change had no effect on market prices. Second, on March 8 the USDA announced that the new support levels for the 1974–1975 marketing year beginning April 1 would continue at the minimum required by law (Table I-9). A large increase in the NFDM price relative to the cheese price, while not changing the butter price, restored equality of returns to milk entering butter-NFDM and cheese plants. Dairy producers were pleased with the end of the "tilt" but unhappy with the minimum support level. CLC officials were happy with the minimum support level, and they were now willing to let the market provide the incentive for switching from butter-NFDM to cheese production. Wholesale prices exceeded the support levels in March but dropped to support levels in June (Appendix Table I-11). The decision to maintain minimum price supports reduced government costs and lowered dairy product prices, but reduced returns to dairy farmers.

The other major policy actions dealt with imports. CLC consistently pushed for greater imports while USDA resisted. Producer groups, of course, argued against imports, but they also contended that—at a minimum—countervailing duties should be levied to offset foreign subsidies. Nearly all government officials desired to avoid further complicating the U.S. trade stance by levying such duties.

Authorized imports of NFDM were increased by 80 million pounds on July 18, 1973, 100 million pounds on August 28, 1973, and 150 million pounds on March 5, 1974 (only 114 million pounds were delivered under the last authorization because New Zealand did not fill its quota).[46] NFDM prices rose 45% from July 1973 to April 1974, but fell to support levels in June.

Authorized imports of cheddar cheese were increased by 100 million pounds on January 2, 1974; actual imports under this authority were 98.8 million pounds.[47] Cheese prices had risen 31% from July 1973 to January 1974; they rose 1.4% from January to a peak in March, but then fell back 22% to support levels by June.

Finally, authorized imports of butter and butter oil were increased by 84 million pounds (butter equivalent) on November 1, 1973; 83 million pounds entered.[48] Butter prices had risen 25% from July 1973 to October 1973 but declined 24% to support levels by May 1974.

Imports of dairy products were clearly useful in reducing the rate of increase in dairy product prices or even bringing about price decreases. The timing, however, could have been much improved; the imports should have entered earlier in most cases. The typical pattern for such actions was a CLC proposal followed by weeks of discussion and delay while other government agencies were consulted. USDA was a major cause of delays but certainly not the sole source; the clearance process was lengthy and even the simple problem of putting the item on the President's agenda for signing consumed time. The downward pressure on prices undoubtedly reduced the returns to dairy producers, who were in a poor profit position throughout Phase IV.

Fruit and Vegetable Marketing Orders

Federal marketing orders[49] regulate the marketing of about half of all fruits, vegetables, and nuts produced in the United States. The scope of regulation varies with each commodity and ranges from the prohibition of packing operations on Sunday (Texas lettuce) to mandatory weekly limits on the amount sent to fresh markets (California navel oranges, lemons, and Valencia oranges). Most orders are used to regulate the quality of produce going to fresh markets.

Most federal marketing orders were established during periods when farmers exercised little market power and farm prices fluctuated widely both between seasons and within seasons. They originally were designed to maintain orderly marketing conditions that would regulate the flow of products so that farmers could avoid periodic gluts on the markets and disastrously low prices which could bankrupt substantial groups of farmers within one season.

In most instances, federal marketing orders have a direct effect on the price of the commodity they regulate. The effects are slight when the orders establish liberal grade and size limitations to eliminate poor quality products, usually unacceptable to consumers. However, the effects can be significant when the marketing order restricts the amount of product reaching the market place.

The specific regulations of each marketing order are recommended by a committee composed of producers and handlers of the commodities involved. The Secretary of Agriculture then has the responsibility of accepting or rejecting the committee's recommendation.

Concern over the adequacy of food supplies and the level of food prices led the Cost of Living Council, early in 1973, to seek a full review of all marketing orders in conjunction with USDA. After this CLC reviewed almost all major marketing orders decisions to insure that supplies of food were not being unnecessarily restricted from market channels. The controversy surrounding the Navel Orange Marketing Order in the first half of 1974 is a good illustration of the issues involved.

The order, established in 1953, controls the fresh marketing of navel oranges in Central and Southern California and in Arizona. Through the mechanism of weekly prorates to producers, the order places a limit on the number of navel oranges which can be shipped to fresh markets each week. Oranges that do not go to fresh markets are sold for processing, generally at a price below the cost of production because navel oranges have very little value as a source of juice. In 1972–1973, 35% of the navel orange crop was diverted into processing outlets; 60% was shipped to the fresh domestic market, and about 1% went to export.

By diverting oranges to processing, the industry is able to maintain prices of fresh oranges above the price that would result if all oranges went into fresh uses. This is a typical case of price discrimination between markets with different demand elasticities, analogous to the milk case cited earlier. Some of the oranges ordinarily would go to processing because they do not meet grading standards for fresh market.

The size of the 1973–1974 crop was projected to be 14% larger than that of the previous year. The Cost of Living Council became concerned when, despite the expected increase in production, total permissible weekly shipments (prorates) were below 1972–1973 levels and prices remained well above a year earlier. In the face of these statistics, the CLC concluded that the marketing order committee was acting to enhance the price of fresh shipments by restricting the amount reaching the market.

The CLC Food Committee requested the Secretary of Agriculture to raise the weekly prorates above the shipping schedule proposed by the marketing order committee in order to insure that all quality fruit was available to consumers. USDA and industry officials resisted, but the USDA finally ruled higher prorates should become effective at the end of January. This revised schedule of weekly shipments limitations did not foreshadow the demise of the marketing order, as some growers indicated. Handlers' and growers' associations retained the right to pick, pack, and ship as few cars as they wished and did not have to ship an amount equal to the prorate.

Fresh market shipments increased in February and March, and the wholesale price declined after a short lag in which the distribution system accumulated sufficient stocks to force prices down (Appendix Table I-14). The wholesale price dropped from $3.86 per carton in the first week of February to $3.31 in mid-March, a fall of 14%. The price of Valencia oranges also declined, despite a smaller crop than in the previous year. In January and February 1974 the retail price of fresh oranges (as measured by the CPI) was 8% above a year earlier. In early April 1974 the price had fallen 2.3% below the January–February prices and was only 0.6% above the 1973 level. Orange growers were angry; they claimed that (1) a price of over $4.00 per carton was need to provide incentives for increased production, and (2) the increased supply was too much for retail outlets to handle in an orderly manner. USDA estimated that costs of production at the f.o.b. position were about $3.40 per carton, and CLC estimated about $3.20 (break-even prices do not generally provide much incentive for increased production, of course). At the invitation of CLC, representatives of growers, retailers, USDA, Department of Justice (to insure that antitrust laws were not violated), and CLC met on March 28, 1974, to discuss the navel orange situation. CLC urged retailers to feature navel oranges so that consumers would be aware of the large supply and reasonable prices; growers were urged to continue to ship all fruit of adequate quality to the fresh market.

The uproar from growers continued. They successfully marshaled influential Congressional support for their position. In early April CLC lost the support of the White House. The lower prorates recommended by producers were approved by USDA. Shipments declined. Prices rose.

The illustration of how marketing orders can affect prices, especially in the short run, is clear. Realistic solutions must deal with the political variable.

Agricultural Legislation

The Agriculture and Consumer Protection Act of 1973 was signed into law on August 10, 1973—in the early portion of Phase IV. Although it had very little immediate impact on agricultural and food prices, a brief review of its enactment is useful since it is the major piece of farm program legislation. The potential impacts of its provisions are important and must be considered in a discussion of major policy issues in the food and agricultural sector.[50]

The Executive Branch sought an act that would facilitate a transition toward freer markets for agricultural products on a permanent basis, but administrative flexibility was desired so that particularly severe impacts of the transition on farm prices and income could be counteracted. There was a strong desire to eliminate income supplement payments unrelated to production adjustments, such as existed for cotton and wheat producers. The authority to pay producers for reducing production was to be retained; the feed grain payments were of this nature. Allotments to producers for individual crops were to be phased out in favor of a single allotment for each farm covering all crops; this allotment would provide the means to restrict production and raise agricultural prices if the federal government desired to do so. The Executive Branch favored the single allotment because it would give greater freedom of choice to farmers and would allow geographical shifting of cropping patterns to areas of most efficient production. Finally, the Administration desired a domestic program compatible with the objective of expanded exports of agricultural products without extensive federal subsidies.

With regard to strategy the Administration chose not to send a formal bill to Congress but to rely on informal consultation with the House and Senate Agriculture Committees. The Administration feared that a formal bill would be an obvious Administration target to be attacked as "anti-farm" and would reduce the chances of achieving a bipartisan result. The House Committee and Secretary Butz strongly favored this approach. OMB preferred that a formal bill be presented in order to provide an identifiable administrative position; this would facilitate building support for the position, especially among nonfarm groups who were increasingly dominant in Congress.

In partial acceptance of OMB's arguments, the Administration made a public announcement of the position that it would support in the consultation with Congress. Although CLC was involved in legislative discussions, USDA and OMB were clearly the leaders at this stage within the Executive Branch.

While the legislation was evolving in Congress, the Administration's position and strategy were of little influence. The leader in OMB on agricultural matters, William Morrill, transferred to an assistant secretary position in HEW, leaving a vacuum in the Executive Branch with regard to coordination on agricultural legislation. CLC, OMB, and the Council of Economic Advisers attempted to influence events but with little apparent effect. Secretary Butz was the clear representative of the Administration, and he felt little or no pressure to confer with other Executive agencies.

Congress quickly rejected the Administration program and substituted its own. Deficiency payments, a form of income subsidy not directly related to production restraints, were adopted; farmers were to be guaranteed a fixed return per unit of production, with the federal government providing the difference (if any) between market prices and the guarantee levels. Allotments were to be established for individual crops. The critical issues in final passage of the bill were, first, limitations of payments per farmer and, second, food stamps for strikers. After a complex series of failing coalitions and floor votes, a coalition of liberal-labor and rural-Southern Democrats hung together sufficiently long enough to pass a bill. The payments limitation was set at $20,000 per farmer, but this provision was riddled with loopholes. Food stamps for strikers were kept intact; in addition, a separate minimum wage bill strongly supported by labor was passed with critical support from rural interests. These provisions remained in the bill submitted to the President, who signed it on August 10, 1973.

Agricultural interests must win the backing of other groups to gain sufficient support for their own positions. Despite a persistent decline in their numbers, they have been fairly successful in their attempts to build the needed coalitions. A combination of strong commodity groups in the private sector, Congressional committees dominated by agricultural interests, and the USDA form a complementary set of relationships which nonagricultural interests find difficult to confront successfully.

CONCLUSION

A few summary comments on the causes of the price explosion and the government's response are offered here. The principal causes of the rapid inflation of food prices in 1972–1974 were as follows.

(1) Adverse weather reduced world supplies of grains and rice.
(2) Rising incomes due to expansionary policies and rising population, to a

lesser extent, led to large increases in demand; incomes rose coincidentally throughout much of the world.

(3) U.S. policies restricting production and marketings continued too long; this was especially important with regard to grains, oilseeds, and rice but also applied to many minor commodities such as peanuts and oranges.

(4) Two devaluations of the dollar plus an upward float by other major currencies, made U.S. grains less expensive for foreign buyers.

(5) Beef and pork production cycles are factors with long histories but no less important for their familiarity.

The government policies designed to deal directly with food prices varied in their impacts and acceptability:

(1) Direct price and wage controls as structured in the stabilization program had very little impact relative to the total rise in food prices because:
  (a) Raw agricultural commodity prices were exempted.
  (b) Price spreads of processors and retailers tended to be under downward pressure when raw material costs were increasing.
  (c) Greatest impact on food resulted from rigid price ceilings whose net benefits were very much in question in view of the distortions created.

(2) The most significant measures were those designed to increase domestic production and marketings which, somewhat ironically, were primarily cases of re-examining internal government policies; CLC played an important role in this re-examination but—at least conceptually—this role did not derive from CLC's power to regulate prices and wages.

(3) Export controls were a potentially effective tool for reducing prices of grains, oilseeds, and their products—but considerations of international commercial relations and politics sharply constrained their use as a short-run policy instrument while the reluctance to reduce exports, farm prices, and domestic production incentives served to prohibit the use of export controls as a long-term policy alternative to combat fluctuating food prices.

(4) Imports offered an effective means of reducing prices of some commodities, especially those such as dairy products where foreign producers had a comparative advantage (e.g., Australia and New Zealand) or in which other governments accumulated stocks through price support programs (e.g., European Community); domestic producers objected strenuously to admitting such supplies.

CHAPTER II

The Agribusiness Market Structure and Controls

RAY A. GOLDBERG

RAY A. GOLDBERG

Ray A. Goldberg is the George M. Moffett Professor of Agriculture and Business at the Harvard Business School. His research and teaching are concerned with analyzing the organization, structure, and arrangements that coordinate the functions and policies of the U.S. and world food system. His books include A Concept of Agribusiness, Agribusiness Coordination, *and* Agribusiness Management for Developing Countries.

Professor Goldberg has served as chairman of the Governor's Food Commission for the Commonwealth of Massachusetts, subgroup chairman for the World Food and Nutrition Study, National Academy of Science, and as a consultant to the Price Commission, National Commission on Productivity, the U.S. Department of Agriculture, Commodity Futures Trading Commission, as well as to various foundations, business firms, and farmer cooperatives.

CHAPTER II

The Agribusiness Market Structure and Controls

THE PURPOSE of this chapter[1] is to describe briefly some of the effects of price controls on the U.S. agribusiness* market structure. To make such a descriptive analysis one must keep in mind the historical perspective of controls on the U.S. food system. At the same time, it is difficult to isolate the impact of controls from other factors influencing agribusiness, including

technological changes;

cycles for different commodity systems;

new grading systems (e.g., Beef);

new bookkeeping systems (e.g., LIFO and FIFO);

high input and energy costs;

investor incentives;

devaluation of the dollar;

decline of the Peruvian fish catch;

development of various marketing orders; and

the price support program, consumer subsidies, and import and export policies of domestic and international customers and competitors.

---

* "Agribusiness" as used in this chapter is taken from the book, *A Concept of Agribusiness* by J. H. Davis and R. A. Goldberg (Harvard University Graduate School of Business Administration, Division of Research, 1957) and includes all the farm inputs, farm production, food and fiber processing, and distribution entities utilized in the production and ultimate distribution of food and fiber products to U.S. consumers and to U.S. export markets.

FOCUS

This chapter examines selected commodity systems and points up, through the aid of historical hindsight, some of the uncertainties felt by farmers, farm suppliers, processors, and distributors and the actions they took based on their past and future perceptions of the Cost of Living Council's pricing policies. Some of these policies inadvertently led to distortions of certain kinds of price signals, which in turn led to strategic errors by managers reacting to the distorted price signals. In addition, the biological nature of parts of agribusiness required different time horizons from short-term market and price control mechanisms. The different perceptions in agribusiness and the biological nature of the products involved resulted in decisions that affected the market structures of major agribusiness commodities.

HIGHLIGHTS OF FOOD PRICE POLICIES EXPERIENCE, 1971–1976

In order to place this chapter in perspective, the reader should keep the following points in mind:

(1) Price policies in foods had to deal with a system already heavily controlled.

(2) Existing controls were very complex, but wheat and feed grain price supports were the primary leverage.

(3) Up to the 1971–1972 period, grain prices were stabilized reasonably well as long as there was money enough to provide incentives for farmers to keep acreage idle and as long as the United States could afford the cost of storing huge reserves for the whole world. This system was partly economic, partly political, with conflicts between the two.

(4) The animal economy was basically allowed to function with free markets, with only the cost and availability of feeds as the prime stabilizer. Internationally, the livestock-meat economy was relatively insulated. (Dairy products were an exception in that they had detailed domestic controls and important international impacts.) The livestock economy had more fluctuations than the cereals, but cycles were not intolerably violent up to the early 1970's. Supplies were adequate, and consumption was rising.

(5) By the early 1970's considerations of cost, of humanitarian politics, and the conviction that grain stocks were overhanging markets and penalizing farmers, had led to a program to cut down reserves. Increased quantities were exported, much of them on a concessionary price or credit basis.

(6) Later events proved that this liquidation went too far. The economy was unable to sustain the added drains of 1972–1975, triggered by the huge pre-emptive Soviet purchases but reinforced by widespread droughts and crop failures in many areas.

(7) U.S. imposition of price ceilings at this time proved a disaster. The cattle cycle, poised for a downturn into a liquidation phase, was dammed up by distorted price and cost relationships and holding back of supplies, only to break loose later. The grain economy was only belatedly released from acreage restrictions. The systems of controls already in place produced other abortions or diversions of resources which might have stimulated expanded production.

(8) There is a progressively increasing world involvement in matters relating to the food and agricultural economies. They will continue to be heavily controlled in one way or another. The Common Agricultural Policy (CAP) of the European Economic Community is an example. The inevitable involvement of developing countries as they become more commercialized and rise above bare subsistence levels is another consideration. The spate of various national commodity marketing boards and of proposals for international trade agreements moves food and agriculture more and more into the political sphere. An early end of these trends is not in prospect.

(9) Lower living costs cannot be legislated by imposing fiat ceilings. Rather, a whole complex system of controls and guidelines already in place demands a recognition of incentives and controls already in operation or available.

(10) This broad-brush criticism relates to the *methods* of attaining price-stabilization objectives. It takes advantage of a focus based on a single purpose and of a perspective based on hindsight. In this sense it is not entirely fair.

Historical Perspective

In the past 50 years, with the exception of World War II, most elements of a U.S. food price control policy were originated at the farm level and resulted in ramifications throughout the food system.[2] Dating back to the 1932 depression the U.S. price support legislation was developed to provide a minimum price level for basic food and fiber producers as a means of maintaining commercial agricultural productivity for the country and at least a minimum income for the producer. Price supports were raised during World War II as an incentive to spur much needed agricultural production.

> In addition to price support incentives for the production of crops needed for lend-lease and for military use, the Department gradually relaxed penalties for exceeding acreage allotments, provided the excess acreage was planted to war crops. In some areas during 1943 *deductions* were made in adjustment payments for failure to plant at least 90% of special war crop goals. Marketing quotas were retained throughout the war period on burley and flue cured tobacco to encourage production of crops needed for the war. Marketing quotas were retained on wheat until February 1943.[3]

Besides price incentives, a variety of price control programs were developed during World War II.

From May 1942 to May 1943, retail prices were frozen by the General Maximum Price Regulation, but many *farm* product prices were excluded by statutory restrictions and only brought under controls later in the year. Consequently while the consumer price index for all commodities rose 7.8%, food prices rose 17.6%. During the "hold-the-line" period (May 1943 to June 1946), the consumer price index for all commodities increased 6.6% and food prices less than 2%. In these years, dollars-and-cents ceilings were applicable on most food items, some prices were "rolled back," and processor subsidies were used on some items. When controls were lifted rapidly beginning in July 1946, prices rose at the sharpest rate ever recorded. Hence the period from June 1946 to March 1947 saw the overall index rise 17.3% and that for food 30.2%.[4]

In addition to specific farm commodity incentives and price controls the government established processing margins for each commodity and by type of technology. For example, in the soybean processing industry, hydraulic press processing plants, expeller press plants, and solvent extraction plants each had different "cents-per-bushel crushing margins" by size of plant and technology used.[5] Also, soybean price supports were higher than the equivalent ceiling prices of meal and oil (the two major products of the soybean). At this time the government paid the extra cost of the processor's soybeans so that the processor would be certain of an adequate crushing margin.

During the Korean War, commodity ceiling prices were again set for soybeans, meal, and oil (February 12, 1951). The soybean, meal, and oil prices were all set high enough at ceiling in relation to each other to provide an "adequate" crushing margin. But in the early months of 1952 soybean meal remained at the ceiling price, oil prices dropped to less than 50% of the ceiling, and soybean prices remained high. The result in the industry was "custom" crushing for mixed feed manufacturers, barter arrangements with producers, and "adulterating" the meal by mixing less valuable ingredients with it to change the classification of the product.[6] These specific examples are noted here to indicate the similarity of the adjustment problems of different commodities in preceding time periods to those that developed in the 1972–1975 period. These experiences led to the reluctance of public policy makers to put specific price controls on at the farm level in the 1973–1974 period. In both of these wartime periods farm prices rose more rapidly than the off-farm components and hence the "farmers' share of the consumer's dollar" on most items increased.[7]

Price supports were raised during World War II as an incentive to spur much needed agricultural production. At the same time ceiling prices were instituted for basic grains such as wheat in order to share the burden of the cost of food and rationing at the consumer level. Other programs were derived partly by design and partly by accident from these price support programs and included a government grain storage program to build storage for grain obtained under the price support program.* Similarly, a PL 480 program was developed partly to aid the less fortunate population in developing countries but also to reduce the U.S. surplus; some $25 billion of shipments took place. In addition, domestically surplus disposal, school lunch, and food stamp programs were developed partly to aid low income groups in the United States and partly to dispose of surpluses of both "basic" and other agricultural commodities. These domestic price supports were normally above "world prices" which, in turn, led to export "subsidies" to enable U.S. grain to be sold in the world market. These price supports and export subsidies became a stable "world grain price support pattern."

Under the Kennedy, Johnson, and Nixon Administrations, attempts were made to lower high price supports so that more of the commodities produced would get into the private domestic and international markets. Even though the United States was and is the major cereal, feed grain, and oil seed exporter, it had a conservative export policy and provided an umbrella under which competitors sold their exports first by undercutting the U.S. price and the United States became a residual, but major, export supplier. The domestic surpluses of wheat, corn, soybeans, and other commodities kept these prices relatively stable in both the domestic and international markets. Also the price support program provided for the selling of government stocks only if the market price reached 110% of the price support level, which meant a very narrow band of price movement before government stocks became available. In essence, the price support program and the resultant surplus stocks for 25 years preceding 1972 were the *principal devices* used to influence price levels of the entire food system. Price fluctuations were determined more by changes in price support levels than by market conditions with the exception of wartime. The stocks provided a shock absorber to most major supply and demand changes. For example, from 1950 to 1971 St. Louis No. 2 Red Winter wheat varied from a low of $1.35 a bushel to a high of $2.11 a bushel. Similarly from 1959 to 1971 corn prices varied from a low of $1.00 a bushel to a high of $1.33 a bushel in 1970 when corn blight affected some 20% of the crop.

With this kind of background it is understandable that most general economists and agricultural economists felt that the excess capacity at the U.S. farm level and the idle farm capacity of 60 million acres were important counterbalances in fighting inflationary pressures in the nation. One exception that concerned the Nixon Administration was the decision of how to react to the corn blight problem and the resultant increase of corn prices to $1.33 a bushel which in time put pressure on livestock and poultry producers and ultimately consum-

---

* Some six billion bushels of storage capacity was built in the United States on and off the farm with low interest loans and guaranteed occupancies to pay for the construction of the facilities.

ers. The decision was to release more corn acreage and still have corn farmers eligible for the price support program. The result of this decision was an increase in both corn acreage and corn yields and a price decline to $1.08 per bushel.

At this time, President Nixon changed Secretaries of Agriculture and Dr. Earl L. Butz became the new Secretary, succeeding Dr. Clifford Hardin. As this was an election year, Secretary Butz assured the farmers that the Administration would help them and went out into the open market and *purchased* 800 million bushels of corn. These purchases did not affect the market very much but they did affect the attitude of the Administration with respect to decisions that would be made subsequently. When the Soviets were desirous of purchasing both wheat and corn in the United States, after 25 years of surpluses and excess capacity and the recent purchase of 800 million bushels of corn, such a sale to the USSR was welcomed by both political parties and by all economists. The surpluses of the past had acted as a buffer to major international changes and in a way temporarily isolated the U.S. food system from these changes. The result was that U.S. domestic food policy, which was primarily promulgated at the producer level, could be largely insulated from commodity programs in other nations. Export subsidies permitted U.S. grain to enter the "World Market" while import quotas and tariffs protected the U.S. price support program.

Therefore it is not surprising that in practically every major governmental decision the greatest concern was to avoid adding to surpluses and to excess capacity. When there was any doubt, the decision was made not to add additional acreage to government price support production programs or to permit additional imports of specific commodities. Timing therefore became critical and the possibility of shortages seemed then to be remote. In reality this 25-year surplus history continues to affect the attitude of many public decision makers and represents the fears of many agricultural producers. In some crops, for example, wheat, their fears had already proved justified in 1977. But during the price pressure period of 1972–1975, such fears fueled a set of industry-wide and individual commodity decisions that added greatly to the food price crisis.

Setting

There was an upheaval in the U.S. food economy during the 1971–1975 period consisting of a serious decline of feed and food grain reserves, an energy crisis, devaluation of U.S. currency, unprecedented food price inflation, a spate of international cartels and state trading, and a national and world-wide economic boom and recession. Superimposed upon these major changes in the U.S. and world food systems was the impact of a variety of old government programs that were developed primarily to deal with surplus grain supplies and new government programs set up to deal with what many considered "temporary" and others "long-run" food, energy, and environmental problems.

Agribusiness Background

After the early 1950's the major concern of U.S. government food policy was what to do with excess productive capacity at the farm level and how to handle excessive grain production induced by price supports that were traditionally above world price levels. Although the United States supplied 40% to 50% of all the grain exported in the world, during most of this time it had to pay an offsetting subsidy to its exporters in order to enable them to be competitive in world markets. Domestic surpluses and price supports provided price stability for many commodities in the U.S. market, provided abundant and stable priced feed for the poultry and livestock industries, and provided a price umbrella for international commodity competitors as well as some semblance of global commodity stability.

In essence, these pre-1972–1973 surpluses, now called reserves, made U.S. agribusiness a safe place to invest money. This industry which encompasses 60% of the world's population engaged in farm supply, farming, food and fiber processing, and retail and institutional distribution also utilizes most of the world's capital. In fact, in the United States over 50% of all the assets of all corporations and agriculture combined are utilized by agribusiness operations. The twin safety valves of price supports (around which prices varied only slightly) and surpluses (that were used as alternative markets for the farmer and inventories for the processor and retailer) provided a cushion of price and inventory stability for all the participants in U.S. agribusiness from farm supplier to ultimate consumer. Of course, there was a major cost factor of carrying these inventories and payments at the taxpayer's expense.

For the input suppliers, price supports became a means of insuring the mortgage value of farm land, the purchasing power needed for commercial inputs such as fertilizer, machinery, seed, pesticides, and animal health products, and a stable price for feed as an input for poultry and livestock producers. Price supports also assured the Farm Credit Administration and private commercial investors of a "hedge" for their fixed land investment and their short-term commodity investments.

For the farmer, price supports provided an assured futures market. The opportunity to utilize inputs on limited acreage to increase yields for an assured market led to a highly capital-intensive development of the U.S. farm sector. As yields improved, the resultant increased production was capitalized into land values. The storage program and nonrecourse loans led to on-farm storage and uniform marketing.

For those processors with little storage capacity in excess of minimum requirements, the government program provided readily available inventories stored at the government's expense.

For the retailer, surpluses provided stable costs which permitted him to charge prices high enough to earn a reasonable net return on his assets; surpluses also provided the price underpinning of several private label items manufactured by the retailer from bread to milk and was an underpinning of stable consumer prices.

Price responsiveness during this period was based not only on changing supply and demand conditions; it also took into consideration the continued existence of Commodity Credit Corporation stocks. For example, domestically a 1% change in the supply of corn usually resulted in a 2% change of price in the opposite direction. But in 1973, when the reserve stocks were sold, a 3% decline in world grain production resulted in a 250% increase in U.S. farm prices.* These grain price increases led to higher prices on other crops that had to compete with grain for land, such as some fruits, vegetables, and sugar beets. Collectively, these commodity price increases and rapid increases in consumers' income over the 1972–1974 period led to a 33% increase in retail food prices, with 50% of the increase the result of farm value changes (see Table II-1). These commodity price changes, together with increased energy costs, were one of the principal spurs to both U.S. and world-wide inflation.

The Changing Nature of U.S. Agribusiness

In Table II-2 the changing nature of U.S. agribusiness is summarized. Farm input purchases increased from $38 billion to $72 billion a year from 1967 to 1974. This increase in input costs has made the producer more dependent on a higher break-even sales revenue and thus more vulnerable to changes in both input and commodity prices. It also means that the input suppliers from credit, feed, and animal health products to farm machinery have also become more dependent upon the farmer's commodity values.

Net farm income increased from $12 billion to $27 billion during the same period, reaching a high of $32 billion in 1973. In that year, for the first time in reported statistics, on-farm income per capita in the United States was higher than off-farm income. The decline of farm income from $32 billion in 1973 to $27 billion in 1974 was the result of the cost-price squeeze faced by the poultry and livestock producer who was caught between high feed grain prices and resistance by consumers in a world-wide recessionary economy. From the fourth quarter in 1973 through the fourth quarter of 1974 the livestock industry had a $1.7 billion negative margin and a $15 billion inventory loss compared with the third quarter of 1972 to the third

---

* Naturally there were many other factors occurring at the same time that caused this price increase such as the fear factor triggered by Soviet's pre-emptive buying coup and a world-wide economic boom with consumers' income moving up rapidly.

TABLE II-1.   ALL FOOD—THE MARKET BASKET,[a] 1969-1976

Year	Year-to-Year Increase	Retail Cost	Farm Value	Off-Farm Value	Farm's Value Increase (in percent)
1969		$1,179	$481	$ 698	
1970	$ 49	1,228	478	750	−6
1971	22	1,250	480	770	+10
1972	61	1,311	524	787	+72
1973	226	1,537	701	836	+78
1974	213	1,750	747	1,006	+22
1975	126	1,876	784	1,084	+29
1976	19	1,895	749	1,146	−184

[a] The Market Basket includes estimated quantities of farm food products purchased annually per household in 1960-1961 by urban wage earner and clerical worker families and workers living alone.

SOURCE: USDA, *Marketing and Transportation Situation,* various issues.

TABLE II-2.   THE CHANGING NATURE OF U.S. AGRIBUSINESS
(IN BILLIONS OF DOLLARS)

	1967	1972	1973	1974
All farm inputs	$38	$ 52	$ 65	$ 72
Net farm income	12	18	32	27
Amount in subsidies	7	7	8	6
All farm marketings	43	63	89	93
U.S. imports	4	6	9	10
U.S. exports	7	8	21	21
Net U.S. food processor purchases	40	61	77	82
Assembly, processing, and distribution value added	54	62	67	83
Total consumer food expenditures	94	123	144	165

SOURCE: USDA, *Agricultural Outlook,* various issues.

quarter of 1973 positive margin of $1.9 billion or a margin swing of $3.6 billion.[8]

For the cash crop producers, 1973 and 1974 were bonanza years. Many of them utilized their additional income to acquire more farm land, thus capitalizing high commodity prices back into higher land values. Farm land values went up 25% between 1973 and 1974. This higher land cost structure and higher input cost structure such as fertilizer, feed and farm machinery at the farm level meant an increase in the total cost base of the American farmer.

Food processor purchases from the farming segment increased from $40 billion to $83 billion from 1967 to 1974. With the selling off

of surpluses, world markets came up to domestic U.S. markets, subsidies for exports were cut out or back, and food processors have had
to compete with overseas users of U.S. commodities. The procurement officers of most firms have become more important in total
corporate decision making. The use of the futures markets has become essential for all key corporate and cooperative managers,
whether they are chief executives, product managers, or procurement
officers. Suddenly, brand differentiated product managers have
realized that they are really speculating by not using the futures
market because they are perpetually committed to shelf space at the
retail level and market share of the institutional markets. All kinds of
food firms, from chewing gum to soft drink and fruit and vegetable
canners, have once again realized that they are part of an agribusiness
commodity system and need to know how to use the futures markets
not only to hedge but as part of their total long-range planning,
corporate, marketing, and procurement strategy. A price variation of
over $1 a bushel in one year compared with 50 cents a bushel over 15
years has caused a major rethinking in most agribusiness industries.
Previously, profitability of firms was dependent upon manufacturing
or production efficiency of fractions of a cent, given relatively stable
commodity prices. Now procurement and marketing decisions and
the hedging of risk receive much higher priority as they determine
the profitability of a firm to a much greater degree than do effective
and efficient operating procedures.

Value added by assembly, processing, and distribution increased
from $54 billion in 1967 to $83 billion in 1974. The added new
product costs placed pressure on supermarkets during the price
stabilization period when net income averaged 0.5% of sales and
return on investment averaged about 8%. Statistics for 1976 indicate a
widening of their net profit margins back to the traditional 0.7% of
sales and a corresponding increase in net return on investment. However, labor, which had had its net income held down in relation to the
cost of living (1973), was desirous of catching up on wage increases, a
situation which added to the cost structure at the retail level. Labor
costs in all food marketing averaged a 10% increase in the year ending
in the third quarter of 1974, but food retailing and restaurant labor
costs were 22% higher in the same period, and labor costs accounted
for more than 50% of total retail and institutional costs. Similarly,
energy costs for food retailing and institutional outlets went up 52%,
packaging 30%, and transportation 10%.[9] These cost increases show
no sign of leveling off, and thus will contribute to keeping prices at
retail at current or high price levels irrespective of lower farm commodity prices.

In addition to the price, cost, and income changes in U.S. agribusiness, the market structure has changed domestically. Farm cooperatives continue to be one of the most important coordinating entities in
agribusiness, with farmers themselves supplying over 20% of the $75
billion of farm inputs from chemicals and fertilizers to manufactured

feed. Similarly, farm cooperatives handle or process some 30% of the $95 billion of farm marketings ranging from small percentages of some crops to 90% of such items as cranberry products. Even though the number of farmers in the United States remained relatively stable from 1971 to 1973 at about 2.9 million, the growth of farms with $100,000 of gross farm income or more increased from 58,000 farms out of 2,909,000 in 1971 to 109,000 farms out of 2,844,000 in 1973. The net income of these farms went up over fivefold during the same time period, from $2 billion to $11.2 billion. These same types of farmers represented over 45% of gross farm income in 1973.

Consolidation in Agribusiness

Although, in general, there is consolidation in all areas of agribusiness, in some industries such is not the case. For example, in the cattle industry the small breeder still accounts for a large percentage of the U.S. beef supply with about 1.7 million farmers carrying less than 200 cows and 50,000 enterprises carrying more than 200 cows. Two-thirds of the farms in the United States have some cattle. However, the feedlot, in spite of financial reverses, still is becoming and will become more important in the food system. In 1975, 73 feedlots (or one-twentieth of one percent of the feedlots) with a capacity of 32,000 head or more supplied 20% of the grain-fed cattle in the United States. Thirty-one of the 73 were located in Texas.

The consolidation in agribusiness represents certain efficiencies of large-scale enterprises partly in production but even more important in the changing logistics of the industry. For example, in 1973 some 100,000 farms out of 2.9 million or 3% represented 45% of gross sales volume while some 20 supermarket chains out of 30,000 mass retailers and over 200,000 other outlets represented 50% of the retail food sales volume. Similarly, some eight fast food restaurant chains accounted for 52% of U.S. fast food sales. Some six exporters handled over 50% of U.S. grain exports. For most entities in U.S. agribusiness, therefore, a few large firms are of major importance to those who sell to them and to those who buy their products. However, excess capacity at the farm level is also matched by excess capacity in most major commodity processing facilities and at the supermarket level (as witnessed by the closing of A&P stores, for instance). Therefore, consolidation has apparently not affected competition and the increasing presence of farm cooperatives in all parts of agribusiness has also added to the competition in the industry. The greater potential capacity at the farm level in some commodities and the greater consolidation at the retail and institutional level have also encouraged a policy of providing minimum price assurance to the producer, for it is he who in the past had to bear most of the brunt of adjustment when prices fell. For the most part that adjustment was down, not up. Therefore, an attitude developed that the producer would not be one to be concerned about in an inflationary economy.

Given the above setting and brief historical perspective, this chapter will examine one commodity industry structure in detail (beef-feed grain) to provide a brief summary of the impact of the Cost of Living Council on the market structure of this and other commodity systems and their participants.

BEEF INDUSTRY

The beef industry represents an important segment of U.S. and world agribusiness (cattle and calf marketings represented over $20 billion in farm sales in 1975, and over 50% of the cost of producing meat was represented by feed costs). By reviewing in detail this commodity system, one can obtain a more specific view of the structural changes that were partially caused by the Economic Stabilization Program (ESP) from 1971 to 1974. It is difficult to isolate the effects of the ESP program from the political and economic decisions that were made with respect to price support activities, acreage restrictions, import controls, and export sales, as well as other factors occurring in the industry such as the stage of the cattle cycle, rapid rise in consumer incomes followed by a recession, the development of boxed beef, new grades, the packer and stockyard rules and regulations against vertical integration from commercial feedlot to meat processing, excess capacity at retail store levels and resultant price wars, investor interest in cattle feeding, impact of use and control of futures markets, stop-loss guarantees, new retail cuts, beef specials, direct consumer sales by farmers and cooperatives, consumer boycotts, producer antitrust suits against chains, and truckers' strikes. One attempt to place a value on several causes of the meat price inflation of 1973 was the study by Albert J. Eckstein and Dale M. Heien, prepared for the National Commission on Supplies and Shortages,[10] characterized on the basis of a statistical computer model. In their summary and conclusion they claim that "all" meat prices rose 23% in 1973 as a result of:

domestic income growth	38%
feed cost inflation	52
other factors and errors	10
	100%

Feed cost increases were the major factor with feed costs rising 78% because of the following:[11]

high meat and livestock prices	42%
domestic acreage policy	28
devaluation of the dollar	4
Russian grain deal	12
world demand growth	9
world supply short-falls	5
	100%

Integrating the feed cost increases in the overall analysis, Eckstein and Heien summarized as follows:[12]

domestic price and income growth	38%
domestic acreage policy	15
devaluation of the dollar	4
Russian grain deal	9
world demand factors	7
world supply factors	5
price freeze II	4
other factors and errors	18
	100%

Eckstein and Heien *estimated* the "cost" of these increases as follows: policy values not increasing the use of diverted acreage rapidly enough, selling grain to the Russians at too low a price, etc., at $5.8 billion to the consumer; "feedback on overall inflation" at $3.2 billion to the consumer; and "equity losses to feedlots in 1973–74" at $1.7 billion to feedlot owners and cattle owners in the feedlots—a total of $10.7 billion.

As mentioned previously, these so-called "costs" are *extremely* inexact because of a mixture of normal "beef cycle" activity taking place in the United States and also because these estimates include all meat and not just beef. At the same time, world-wide supply and demand factors affected by unusual climate conditions on the supply side and an unusual "economic boom" followed by "recession" on the demand side were beyond the "control" of even the best intentioned governmental policy makers. The public policy decisions on the beef system in other countries also intensified the swings in the U.S. beef cycle. U.S. imports increased in 1973, while world demand for meat was increasing. In 1974 some international meat contracts for high-priced meat were broken by several countries, putting supplies back into the world market at a time when market gluts were already occurring.

The livestock and beef industry provides one of the best illustrations of the effect of price controls and other government policies on the market structure of a food industry. Throughout the Economic Stabilization Program, from 1971 to 1974, beef received particular attention and was the subject of special regulation, for example, the meat price ceilings during the spring and summer of 1973. Livestock and its closely related sector, feed grains, experienced some of the worst price inflation among all the commodities. Policy makers in the United States, and indeed world-wide, are particularly sensitive to the effect of rising beef prices on their constituents because of its high visibility as an item in the consumer's market basket and diet.

It is of primary importance to realize that the wage and price controls were merely a superimposing of more government regulation over a system which was already strongly influenced by government policies evolved through the years. Figure II-1 contains a

FIGURE II-1. GOVERNMENT POLICIES AFFECTING THE BEEF SYSTEM

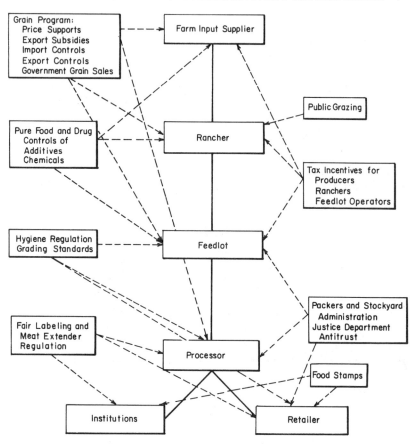

NOTE: Policies of the Occupational Safety and Health Administration (OSHA); and the Environmental Protection Agency (EPA) together with irrigation, water control, transportation, energy, and pollution affect the entire system.

graphic representation of the commodity market system at the junctures where policies regarding livestock and beef have an impact on this system. It can be seen that the beef industry, like the grain system, has been increasingly surrounded and affected by government policies. These policies, including price controls, hygiene regulations and grading standards, import quotas, tax incentives for feedlots and ranchers, subsidies, antitrust provisions, price supports on feed inputs, and food stamps, are coming to influence the market structure of the beef industry just as similar policies in the past have been a major force in shaping the structure and organization of the dairy and grain sectors.

The beef system will be analyzed by market segments, giving first a brief outline of the components of and participants in the industry and a history of the market forces and trends prevailing in the industry prior to 1971 when the ESP was inaugurated. The second part will examine chronologically the various phases of the controls period as to their effects on the different segments of the industry. Third, some of the continuing impacts of the ESP on the livestock and beef sector will be examined, as much as they are apparent in the period since controls were lifted. Finally, some conclusions will be drawn as to the lessons that might be learned from the price control period.

The purpose of this chapter is to make an evaluation of how government policies influence the conduct of the participants in the industry, the kind of evaluation which perhaps was not done as carefully as it might have been prior to the institution of controls in 1971.

Composition and Recent Historical Trends of the Beef System Prior to the ESP

Producers. Figure II-2 is a schematic diagram of the beef system setting forth the number of participants in each segment and the size in dollars of the key inputs and outputs of each segment. Starting at the top of the chart with the inputs to the producers, composed of cattle ranchers and feedlot operators, feed is the most important external input (other than land) to the producer segments. Feed grains, comprising 22% of the costs of the feedlots in 1970, are seen to be particularly important to this group which in recent years has produced most of the beef for the market in this country. The importance of feed grain prices on the livestock sector is further magnified when it is realized that high grain prices tend to lower the price of feeder cattle going into the feedlots.

Through its policy of price supports, the United States had built up an enormous surplus of feed grains after World War II, which provided cheap and stable inputs to the livestock sector. Stocks were reduced sharply from the early 1960's to 1970's without a large impact on grain prices. This may suggest that the pressure of a limited amount of government stocks and a fixed resale policy tends to stabilize the market between the price support minimum and the resale maximums. The price supports on grain and the excess capacity situation thus acted as the underpinning of the beef system for many years. The producers were less concerned with feed costs as an input and could concentrate more extensively on the marketing of and demand for their products. There were production cycles caused by the long lead time of breeding cattle, periodic building up and liquidating of herds corresponding to approximately ten-year cycles after the 1930's with prices usually rising during the build-up phase.*

Beef cows are normally bred at 15 to 18 months. The gestation period is 283 days. Cows should produce a living calf every 12

---

* The price swings were accentuated as producers held cattle on the range longer during the price rises and liquidated their herds en masse during the price declines.

FIGURE II-2.   THE BEEF SYSTEM, 1973

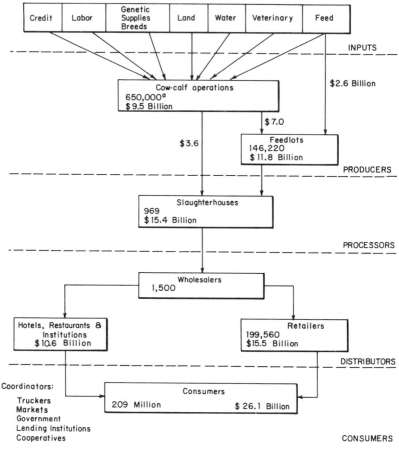

^a Includes only ranches with marketings over $2,500 annually.

SOURCE: *Livestock and Meat Statistics,* June 1974.

months. The calf is then weaned after eight to ten months and becomes a "stocker" at 300 to 400 pounds, and grazes on a ranch until it becomes a "feeder" of 550 to 750 pounds over a period of seven to nine months. Then it normally goes into a feedlot for four or five months until it reaches 1,050 pounds and is then sold for slaughter. A flow diagram of this time sequence is shown in Figure II-3.

Seven beef cycles have occurred since 1896. The cycles are characterized by two phases: (1) a build-up phase in cattle numbers that range from six to eight years with cattle being held back to build up breeding stock; and (2) the liquidation phase reduction in cattle numbers varying from eight to ten years in early cycles and from two to three years in more recent cycles. The total beef cycle has varied from eight to sixteen years in duration. At the time that controls were

FIGURE II-3.   RELATIONSHIPS PREVAILING IN THE BEEF SYSTEM
PRIOR TO THE ESP

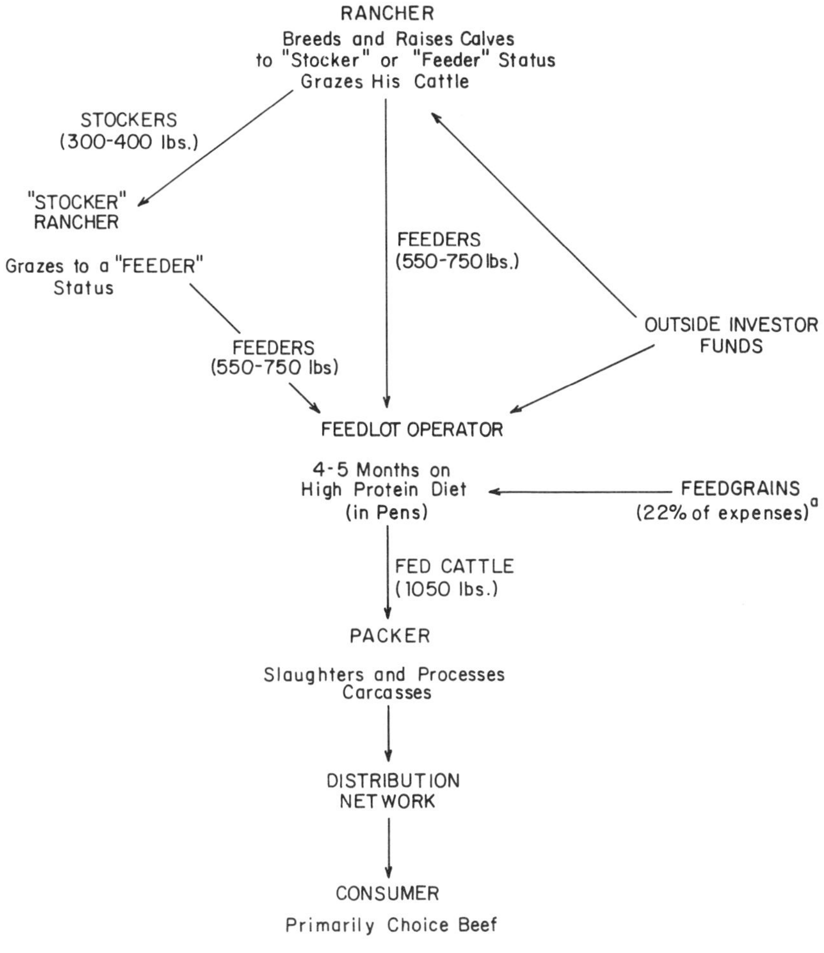

RANCHER
Breeds and Raises Calves
to "Stocker" or "Feeder" Status
Grazes His Cattle

STOCKERS
(300-400 lbs.)

"STOCKER"
RANCHER

Grazes to a "FEEDER"
Status

FEEDERS
(550-750 lbs.)

FEEDERS
(550-750 lbs)

OUTSIDE INVESTOR
FUNDS

FEEDLOT OPERATOR

4-5 Months on
High Protein Diet   FEEDGRAINS
(in Pens)   (22% of expenses)[a]

FED CATTLE
(1050 lbs.)

PACKER

Slaughters and Processes
Carcasses

DISTRIBUTION
NETWORK

CONSUMER
Primarily Choice Beef

[a] Does not include the cost of the feeder cattle.

instituted the cattle cycle was historically coming up to its peak. The emphasis by the producer during this time was on trying to smooth out supply and up-grade the quality of his product. He could cope with the rather predictable but difficult cycles and felt he knew pretty much what his downside risk was because the price of his feed grain input was so relatively stable. What occurred was that high prices had overstocked feedlots in early 1973. Then ceilings led to further holding back until it was found that the ceilings were not a guarantee of high prices which led to liquidation and feeder losses in 1974; that is, retail ceilings caused cattle to back up and then to glut the market as overdue liquidation took place.

There were approximately 650,000 livestock ranchers in 1969 (with annual marketings over $2,500). Greater than 80% of these cow-calf operations were individually or family owned. The average size of a herd was under 50 animals, indicating the continuing supplementary character of the cattle enterprises on many cattle-raising farms. Of the 146,220 feedlots operating in 1973, the large majority were also individually owned. While 2% of the feedlots accounted for 55% of grain-fed cattle marketings in 1970 and almost two-thirds of the marketings in 1973 in the 23 major states, this 2% still included over 2,000 feedlots. In 1976 there were 138,000 feedlots in the United States (down 10% since 1972). Over 98% of these were run by farmer feeders (defined as feeders with a capacity below 1,000 animals). These farmer feeders marketed 35% of the grain-fed beef in 1976. Commercial feedlots (feedlots with capacities over 1,000 animals) dominated the market, producing 65% of the grain-fed beef from only 2% of the feedlots. The largest 400 feedlots marketed nearly 48% of the grain-fed beef.

A "surplus government feed price support policy" coupled with the logistic economics of developing concentrations of feeding capacities in close proximity to surplus grain growing areas led to the logical development of a grain-fattened beef cattle industry. This "grain-fattened" cattle development also resulted in more choice grade meat being consumed. The USDA grading standards encouraged this shift as did consumer desires for tender, tasty meat.

Income tax legislation helped to encourage the investment transfer necessary to provide the capital for the expansion of the beef grazing and feeding segments of the industry. Allowable cash-basis accounting and favorable capital gains treatment for breeding animals appealed to investors that had high ordinary earnings from business activities. In addition to these incentives, depreciation allowances and investment credits encouraged these high income investors from outside the industry to enter it to take advantage of tax shelter possibilities. The larger feedlots which were thereby encouraged went to year-round feeding and produced a more uniform quality of beef on a consistent and regular basis. This outside participation became an important factor when investors pulled their funds out of feedlots during the controls period, placing additional strains on the livestock market structure. At the the the same time many of the livestock feedlots used guarantees for their investors which added to the vulnerability of the feedlot corporations.

Processors. The meat packer segment, composed of approximately 1,150 firms in 1970, was pleased to have an assured, high-quality supply. In an industry where profits average only about 1% of sales, consistent throughput and volume are the key considerations. The late 1960's saw the decline of the dominance of packing by the "Big Four" (Swift, Armour, Wilson, and Morrel) and a new era of corporate and cooperative groups entering the industry.* In the United States modern, smaller slaughter plants were built closer to the surplus grain and new feedlot production areas in the Midwest and eventually the Oklahoma-Texas Panhandle area, reducing the distance live cattle moved to market. Improved highways for the shipment of live cattle and modern mechanized and controlled atmosphere systems of refrigerated transport for beef facilitated this process. As the whole beef industry became more dependent on the transportation system, particularly the truckers, its vulnerability to transportation and labor disruptions was increased.

Retailers. For the retailer, beef played a crucial role. Beef is the focal point of the average American diet and thus a key traffic builder and top advertising lead. Beef is also a significant percentage of store volume, usually 8% to 12%, and gross margins are normally in the 18% to 22% range with net margins below the average of other commodities to build store traffic. Prices are extremely competitive because they are watched so closely by consumers. The retailer, like the packer, benefited from an assured supply of uniform-quality meat. Robert Braunschweig, Vice President of The Kroger Company, testifying before a Congressional Committee in November 1974, made this statement:

> Beef, because of consumer preference, is one of the most essential ingredients. For this reason, our own company's emphasis on continuous merchandising and promotion of beef received top priority. Without a successful beef or meat program—i.e., without a consumer response to our beef promotions—we cannot be successful retailers. To assume otherwise—i.e., that we do not continually attempt to optimize our beef and meat tonnage—is to ignore the facts of life in food retailing.

Consumers spent $7 out of every $10 of their retail food store purchases at the supermarket, while the remaining $3 went to smaller stores, some 167,000 of them, as compared with around 32,000 supermarkets. The supermarkets included corporate chains, voluntary chains, cooperatives, and independents. There had been a tendency for major food chains to set up their own regional carcass breaking and processing centers, thus making them more interdependent with other segments of the beef system.

Consumers. The end of the beef chain is the consumer. Consumption per capita of beef grew at approximately 5% from 1960 to 1970. The expenditures per person and as a percentage of income spent for

---

* The meat packing sector had been experiencing a shakedown and the number of participating firms were declining rapidly. The 1973 total of 969 was down from 2,833 firms in 1963. Concentration, however, was lessening as the top four and eight firms had accounted for, respectively, 39% and 51% of sales in 1954 and in 1970 accounted for only 23% and 37%, respectively.

red meat has not declined over the past 20 years. Personal consumption expenditures for all food showed a decline of disposable income spent for food from 20.0% in 1960 to 17.1% in 1975, with a slight year-to-year increase in 1974 and 1975. This is in sharp contrast to beef consumption. The consumer has demanded and received an ever-increasing supply of beef, primarily choice, grain-fed meat. The number of head slaughtered annually increased slightly in the 1972–1975 period, but the shift from grass-fed to grain-fed cattle has increased the average weight per steer slaughtered and the quality of the meat available. The restructuring of the beef system over the past 20 years has enabled it to satisfy consumer demand which has often been embodied in the form of government policies.

The Economic Stabilization Period

With the commodity system clearly in mind, this section will analyze how the beef industry was affected by and responded to the wage and price controls in effect from 1971 to 1974.

Freeze I and Phase II: August 15, 1971—January 10, 1973. This period can be disposed of relatively quickly. Food prices were a major concern to policy makers until the very end of 1972, but the pressure of government stocks and tough price competition at the retail level kept prices relatively stable. Indeed the first freeze caught the food cycle at a time when prices were declining seasonally as the harvest came in. During the first half of 1972, Price Commission Chairman C. Jackson Grayson and Secretary of Agriculture Earl Butz debated the potential problem of food prices. Mr. Grayson had an immediate concern. Secretary Butz wanted to do nothing that would dampen producer incentives. Beef prices, however, rose 8% from August 1971 to December 1972. This was a sharper rise than had been experienced in previous years, and much higher than the Consumer Price Index change of 3.29% in 1972. Throughout much of 1972, slaughter steer prices remained relatively stable while feeder steer prices advanced.

Ranchers' and feedlot operators' margins were excellent during this period. Feed margins were favorable and consumption was setting a new record in 1972. Rancher profits for the most part were good as feeder-steer prices were advancing. Feedlot profits were at all-time highs throughout most of the year as the lots were at full capacity in response to high consumer demand. The beef cycle was still continuing on its expansion phase based on favorable feed ratios caused by perceived surplus grain supplies. Raw agricultural prices were not frozen and pass-through provisions were in effect except for the brief preliminary freeze. During the first freeze period, the abundance of cattle and the availability of relatively cheap feed resulted in little upward pressure on raw meat prices that might place the strains on the system that were present in 1973. There was probably a certain amount of cost absorption during Phase II in the meat-packing and retailer segments. Profits declined somewhat for packers in the second and third quarters of 1972 and rather drastically for retail food chains, but this latter occurrence was at least partly the result of other competitive pressures such as excess capacity at the retail level.

Phase II was chiefly noteworthy for the policy that was set and was to continue throughout the ESP of not controlling raw agricultural prices. One assumption behind this policy was that of excess capacity at the farm level so that farm price increases would be temporary. Other assumptions included the following: (a) a belief that prices could not effectively be controlled; (b) that if they could, it might act as a disincentive to the producer; and (c) political pressures would not make it possible. But during this period the Russian grain purchases took place, feed grain stocks declined, while land set-asides mandated by the USDA remained relatively high. Feed grain prices moved up strongly which depressed profits that feedlot operators could figure on in the fourth quarter of 1972 to less than one-third of the profit level of preceding quarters. For a time, feeders held back cattle expecting prices to rise, but this strategy cut two ways as it produced a plethora of over-fat cattle later. Meanwhile, the beef cow herd was expanding rapidly as optimistic ranchers held heifers back from slaughter. The short-term effect was to slow the growth of supply at the consumer level at a time when real personal income was growing both in the United States and overseas.

The result of all this was a strong surge in retail beef prices from December 1972 to March 1973 of 18% or (as the press tended to report it) an annual rate of more than 90%.

Phase III and Freeze II: January 11, 1973—July 18, 1973. When Phase III was announced in January 1973 there was strong pressure to control food prices, particularly beef prices, which were becoming the cutting edge of inflation. This set the stage for the meat ceilings imposed at the end of March. The beef price cycle was coming up to its peak, and producers were angered at having the government cut off this peak, as they perceived it, while leaving them the valleys. Their response was to keep their cattle on the range longer and to hold them in the feedlots in anticipation of the de-control of meat prices. Since it had been announced when the freeze would end, it was their intention to hold back supplies and wait for the increase in prices that were expected when controls were over. Profits for feedlot operators were at all-time highs during the first half of 1973 (a net margin of $580 million in the second quarter of 1973), because the price of beef had been frozen at the wholesale and retail levels at the highest price beef had ever attained. By picking this high price as the ceiling, it became a floor in the eyes of the producers. Beef slaughter declined sharply in the second quarter of 1973; beef production for the whole year was down 6% from the previous year. By 1974 the situation was reversed and the second quarter of 1974 indicated a negative margin of $457 million for grain-fed cattle. The public policy assumption was that backward pressure from the retailer and processor would result in lower cattle prices. In the long run this would have had a dampening effect such as in the case of consumer boycotts, which are notoriously short-lived, but in a short-run situation the life cycle of a cow and the alternative of grain-fed and grass-fed conversions would have more immediate effects on cattle prices.

The pressures on the packer and retailer segments were much more acute during Freeze II from June 13 to July 18, 1973. Packers' prices were frozen while their raw material costs were not. Slaughter steer prices were still rising, and over 75% of packer expenses are the cattle they slaughter. As cattle coming off feed declined, many were forced to shut down plants or go out of business entirely. By August 24, 64 plants were closed and slow-downs at 94 plants were reported.[13] Because consistent throughput is the key to making money in this business on extremely slim margins, disrupting the packers' supply through freezing their prices but not their input costs was a sure way to send them into the loss column.

Actually, however, meat packer profits declined only from 1% as a percentage of sales in the first quarter of 1973 to 0.9% of sales in the second quarter because retailers were forced to take over a portion of packer losses through custom killing. Many packers were thus able to utilize much of their capacity and make their customary margins while picking up some extra profits through the selling of offal and other by-products of the slaughtering process which the retailers could not use. In order to fill their meat counters, retailers bought live cattle and paid packers to slaughter them, taking a considerable loss. For example, one very large food chain lost $4 million in its meat department in two months of custom slaughtering. Retailers were forced by the packers to take the whole carcass, and thus they had to market unaccustomed and undesirable cuts. Similarly, wholesale distributors began to notify their accounts that the ceiling price would not permit them to replenish their stocks at "current custom costs" (see Appendix II-1). Further depressing retailer and wholesaler profits was their lack of any quality control. They had to take what was in the pen. During the freeze period after June 13, 1973 the quoting of actual wholesale beef price transactions was difficult to ascertain; prices became totally negotiated. Exports continued to expand with the second devaluation of the dollar and much higher prices were obtainable in other countries compared with those in the domestic market; but imports of other meats more than offset the exports.

Consumption of beef declined about 6% as farmers reduced marketings and retailers reduced specialing or promoting beef, especially in March 1973 when red meat ceilings were imposed. One retailer estimated that in normal times as much as 70% of beef tonnage moves at specialed prices. In addition, at this time, consumer resistance to high prices was increasing. There was a fairly wide-spread meat boycott in the spring. It is difficult to divide the responsibility for the drop in beef consumption between consumer resistance and the lack of promotion on the part of retailers. Another complication which entered in at this time was the practice by retailers of switching to higher margin meat cuts in order to minimize losses.

Retailers were experiencing cost problems in other areas. Their wage costs were rising as wage approvals were given by the Cost of Living Council and they were unable to pass these along. Profits on all products hovered around 0.5% of sales for the first three quarters of 1973, which was similar to the last three quarters of 1972.

Futures Market Impact of Freeze II. The initial price freeze, which did not apply to futures or to raw agricultural commodities, distorted many of the price spreads and rendered useless one of the most sensitive and subtle price signals sent by futures markets. Businessmen who were using price spreads between products and by-products and between time periods in the decision models suddenly found no reliable prices available to guide them in making such decisions as plant operating capacities and inventory levels.

In the case of individual commodities, each person in the delivery process of a futures contract could have a different price ceiling. Nobody knew what the highest price was that could be paid for a product; and, when delivery time came, price ceilings for different participants varied significantly. An individual person could be getting delivery from two different producers or from two different mills owned by the same producer at substantially different prices. In addition, in the case of some products such as lumber and plywood, the product could be shipped across the line to Canada and then immediately brought back into the United States exempted from the price ceiling and available for delivery at a very high price.

Perhaps the aspect of the price freeze which disrupted the futures market more than anything else came after June 13, 1973, when a freeze was established (see Appendix II-2). After some confusion it was decided that the freeze would also apply to futures contracts. This was evidently done because someone thought that, unless ceilings were placed on the futures also, the shorts whose futures contracts were made at prices above their individual cash ceiling prices would be prohibited from making delivery on their futures contracts and forced to cover by making offsetting transactions in the futures markets. This would act as a restriction on the right to delivery and, of course, could disrupt hedging operations. If the futures prices were allowed to exceed cash prices at the time of delivery, it would be to the short's economic advantage to purchase a cash commodity and make delivery. This could create an artificial demand for the commodity in the cash market, and would raise cash prices to the ceiling for those commodities in which such prices would otherwise have remained at a somewhat lower level.

Since people knew that the 60-day price freeze would only last for no more than two months and that the freeze was on futures as well as cash, they completely altered their buying and selling decisions. The result was that prices for deferred months went very high, while those in the near-by months were restricted. Those who had spreads in the market took substantial losses.

Then to make matters worse the freeze on the actual physical commodity and the futures in the food industry was removed earlier than the originally announced date. The cash prices shot up. Cash product was withdrawn from the market and futures price could not respond because of daily price limits, and the exchanges were faced with extending delivery periods for July and shortening them for August, raising daily price limits and increasing margins in order to reach a point where the futures price could reflect cash values and market participants would be treated equitably.

The most dramatic case in point occurred in pork bellies.* The situation that the applicants complained about relates to an emergency measure taken by the Chicago Mercantile Exchange to terminate trading in the August 1973 frozen pork belly futures on July 25, which would normally have expired on August 24. The Exchange further ruled on August 7, 1973, which was the last delivery day set by the Exchange, that failure to make delivery on contracts still open after the close of trading on July 25 was to be considered unintentional, and the Exchange established a settlement price for closing out the remaining open contracts.

The Chicago Mercantile Exchange faced this emergency situation following price control actions directed by the Cost of Living Council during June and July 1973. On June 13 the Council placed a price ceiling on processed agricultural products, which included frozen pork bellies. This directive was subsequently extended to include trading in the July and August 1973 pork belly futures. On July 18 the Cost of Living Council removed all price controls of cash and futures contracts in frozen pork bellies. The market developments that resulted from these actions caused cash pork belly prices to rise considerably above futures prices during July, resulting in a market disruption and a potentially serious problem in liquidating the July and August pork belly futures contracts. As a result of this market disruption, the Commodity Exchange Authority on July 23, 1973, sent the following telegram to the Chicago Mercantile Exchange:

> In view of the disparity between pork belly cash and futures prices and in view of the deliverable supply situation, CEA requests your Board of Governors to take prompt action to liquidate the 1973 July and August pork belly contracts in a fair and equitable manner. We are especially concerned that no action taken or permitted by the Exchange increases the cash price of pork bellies.

---

* On May 20, 1977, an adminstrative law judge of the CFTC ruled that the Chicago Mercantile Exchange had acted properly. As of this writing (June 1977) the ruling may be appealed.

The Chicago Mercantile Exchange took action with respect to the July and August 1973 pork bellies futures in extending trading in the July pork bellies and foreshortening the period of trading in the August pork bellies, and in increasing the allowable daily price fluctuation limits.

Futures markets are not only used by U.S. food participants but also by private and public managers throughout the world so that price control decisions in the United States affect countless cash and futures contractual relationships on a global basis.

Phase IV: July 19, 1973—April 30, 1974. This final period saw the effects of the previous controls, particularly the meat ceiling, catch up with the beef system. In fact this period began earlier for foods than for other products, indicating the impracticality of freezing commodity prices. The retailers and packers experienced some relief because they were able to pass through at least part of their increased costs, and profits rebounded sharply in the final quarter of 1973. The producer segments, on the other hand, went into a serious decline from which they had not yet recovered in May 1977. There was a predictable rush of cattle to market when the ceiling was lifted in September 1973. Both feeder steer prices and slaughter steer prices began to slide from their August peak. Margins turned negative for feedlot operators as feed costs continued high. They experienced a cumulative realized loss of $1.3 billion in the three quarters of Phase IV.

Ranchers, who had been increasing their herds over the past several years, were left with high inventories at a time when feedlots were not putting animals on feed because they were losing enormous amounts of money on every animal they fed. The pulling out of investor funds from feedlots and ranching during this period exacerbated the situation. Outside investors who had been encouraged by deferred tax incentives to invest in cattle raising and feeding had lost their equity, and had more tax and real losses than they had ever counted on.

Typical of the loss at the rancher level was the Thurber Livestock Company (see Table II-3). By 1976 Thurber's net worth had declined from a high of $162,000 in 1973 to $12,000 in 1976 on a land at cost basis (1971 value). The ability of this rancher to exist during this dramatic adverse period is based primarily on the dramatic increase in his land value based on the change in alternative crop values and the location of the property. Other ranchers less fortunate have left the industry.

Throughout the Economic Stabilization Program, regulation of other areas of the beef industry besides prices continued and escalated. Environmental and health awareness was growing which led to bans on the feeding of hormones such as di-ethyl stilbestrol (DES) to cattle to encourage faster weight gain. Dieldrin, a herbicide which was used on pasture and corn, was similarly banned because of its possible harmful effect on the end product, meat. Stricter hygiene regulations

TABLE II-3. THURBER LIVESTOCK COMPANY (IN THOUSANDS OF DOLLARS)

	1971	1972	1973	1974	1975	1976
Sales	$320	$380	$340	$580	$440	$700
Net income	(2)	6	17	(102)	(27)	(21)
Net worth	139	145	162	60	33	12
Return on net worth:						
Land at 1962 estimated price level		4%	12%	(63%)	(45%)	(64%)
Net worth:						
Land at assessed value	240	277	356	317	383	773
Land appreciation		31	62	63	93	411
Return on net worth:						
Land at market value		3%	6%	(29%)	(9%)	(5%)

SOURCE: Company files.

in slaughter houses were instituted, causing some plants to become uneconomic. The Occupational Safety and Health Administration was promulgating more stringent safety rules which necessitated capital investment for safer equipment and facilities. All these factors increased the cost pressures on the industry at a time when prices were being held down by controls without regard to expenses being incurred as a result of other government regulations.

The Post-Controls Period. Despite the fact that wage and price controls were lifted on April 30, 1974, the disruptions caused by this period on the livestock and beef sector continued. It should not be assumed that all the problems in this industry were caused by the government or its use of a variety of programs. Rather it was the use of government programs that did not take into consideration potential hazards, for example, the effects of drought in the United States and Europe, which could again end up with a surplus of cattle and a shortage of feed. Since cattle are not storable but feed is, the logical need for adequate grain reserves is obvious.

Beginning with producer segments, cattle inventories were finally declining in 1976—down 9% after going up 3% in 1974 and 4% in 1975. Feeder steer prices declined throughout 1974, but turned up sharply in 1975. Prices in 1976 were 25 cents below their abnormal peak in August 1973, however. The economics of grass-feed production are such that the cow-calf rancher has the ability to keep his animals on grass longer during times of depressed prices without incurring crippling losses. But even he had liquidated some cattle herds because poor range conditions in 1974 and 1975, coupled with poor returns for the calves he produced together with tight money and restricted credit policies by bankers, left him with little flexibility or incentive. The feedlot operator, on the other hand, must push an animal through his lot once he has taken it on feed, although the time in the lot can vary from two to four months depending on type of finish.

The plight of the feedlots is, therefore, more serious in the short run. Placements of cattle on feed began to decline in the first quarter of 1974 until by the fourth quarter they were 24% below the figures for the previous year. Cattle and calves on feed as of January 1, 1975, were down 29% from the preceding January. Feedlots sustained heavy losses throughout 1974. They were unable to use the futures markets to hedge their feeding margins because the relative margins in the futures market were below a breakeven. Outside investors, of course, stayed away from the industry. After the extremely short feed grains crop of 1974, the price of feed inputs skyrocketed, adding an increasing cost factor to an unused feedlot capacity cost problem. A further complication was that the amount of overcapacity was not uniform throughout the major geographical feeding areas. In the Texas-Oklahoma Panhandle area, which had been experiencing the most rapid growth in recent years, total grain-fed cattle production declined from a high of 4.9 million head in 1973 to only 2.5 million head in 1974. Several feedlots went out of business during this period, some being taken over by large grain merchandising firms of other corporate entities, thereby reducing slightly the percentage of individually owned business in the feedlot sector.

The situation had repercussions for the packer also. Companies were affected by the fall-off of cattle on feed. This decline threatened to disrupt their lines of supply in certain areas of the country. In an industry dependent on high volume for profits, this became a serious concern. One large meat packer, Iowa Beef Processors, completed a $30 million plant in the Texas Panhandle area in 1974. It was forced to truck cattle uneconomic distances in order to fill the capacity of the new plant. The second largest meat packer in the Panhandle, American Beef Producers, went into bankruptcy in 1975.

There was a marked shift in 1975 to more grass-fed cattle in the slaughter mix. The percentage of grain-fed cattle in the commercial slaughter was 77% in 1973. It was 55% in 1975 but increased in 1976. Ranchers were holding cattle on the range longer and doing more selling directly to packers. Since most meat packers' meat merchandising systems are based on fully fed-out choice steers, the change in their product mix became a problem. The packer was faced with a new set of meat merchandising economics. Lighter, leaner carcasses yield different-sized cuts from traditional choice carcasses. Such a change affects processing costs and merchandising margins. Some packers and feeders have been experimenting and feeding cattle for their own account to assure choice supply.

When grain-fed cattle were important, retailers had to struggle with how to merchandise these new cuts and how to respond to competitive pressures. Donald Perkins, Chairman of Jewel Companies, in a presentation before a USDA-sponsored Conference on Food Productivity in November 1974, stated that Jewel had lost over $5 million before charges for interest and taxes on sales of $95 million of fresh meat in the first half of 1974. He offered to open up the company's books for federal inspection and released figures which showed a significant decline in beef gross margin in 1973 and 1974.

Consumption of beef rebounded to reach a new high in 1974 and continued upward in 1975. Consumers at that time ate much more nonchoice beef as a result of the change in the cattle slaughter mix. As the supply of choice beef declined in 1974 and 1975, the spread between choice beef and good beef widened, which was probably an indication of retailers' reluctance to disrupt their consumer franchise for the tendered beef. It is unknown whether there was consumer resistance to the new kind of beef appearing in the meat counter. But by mid-1975 the situation reversed and consumers went back to purchasing "choice" meat.

Farm-retail spreads widened throughout most of 1974 and 1975. This phenomenon was mostly the result of skyrocketing marketing and distribution expenses throughout the system, particularly labor, fuel, transport, and packaging. With the change in the product-mix of retail beef cuts, the government must reassess its calculations of margins in the industry. Indeed, the USDA only publishes price and spread data for choice grade beef, so it is not known what the average price of beef is that consumers are actually paying or what the average retail margin is. In 1976 beef prices at retail declined. With a decline in beef numbers, the 1977 outlook was for higher beef prices.

Many of the traditional relationships prevailing in the beef system prior to 1971 were disrupted during the Economic Stabilization Program. Several of these disruptions were well-meaning attempts to protect the consumer without adversely affecting the industry. Nevertheless, the disruptions cited above did occur.

It can be seen that high feed grain prices and the poor economic condition of the feedlots resulted in ranchers holding cattle on grass for longer periods and placing cattle in lots for "short feeding" up to a low-choice weight. This practice eased the margin squeeze on the feedlot operator somewhat because he had to feed with less high-priced grain. Ranchers were also selling more cattle directly to packers. Some packers and meat processors invested in production facilities for textured vegetable protein (TVP) and ground beef blending. When carcass beef prices went into their long slide in 1974, these investments became white elephants because TVP could not compete with the low carcass beef prices.

Conclusions

In essence, the beef commodity system, as well as most other U.S. commodity systems, has been greatly influenced in the development of its structure by the government programs that affect costs and market opportunities. All commodities have a common land base with varying degrees of alternative cropping patterns and alternative uses of the crop—e.g., direct human consumption or feeding to provide animal protein. This means that controls cannot be developed for one commodity group without affecting the structure and organization of other commodity systems.

Particular problems arose in the livestock industry when the prices for grains (which were not placed under the freeze because they were raw products) rose to very high levels, while live animal prices were restrained by the price ceiling on meat products. Producers could not afford to continue feeding high-priced grain to animals that were selling at artificially low prices; hence, they began liquidating their herds. This had the effect of temporarily driving prices down and altering the normal production and marketing cycles. All of the old relationships between feed and end products were altered considerably. The livestock economy was just beginning to recover several years after the fact.

If a 25-year-old "control" policy is already in existence through the use of domestic price supports, grain storage programs, acreage set-aside programs, and export subsidies, to superimpose "new controls" and "new procedures" without making maximum use of existing tools seemed to give different signals to different parts of the food system. In addition, Occupational Safety and Health Administration and environmental programs that are obviously important but also add to cost structures were being implemented at the same time that the national policy on inflation was to hold down costs. For the most part, the government through its *existing* programs was in a better position to influence U.S. food prices than any new "control" system. Given the build-up of stocks in 1971–1972, given 25 years of "surplus" history, and given the "market orientation" of the Administration, the decision to keep acreage set aside, the decision to encourage export sales, the decision to sell off government supplies slowly in the domestic market, these were all consistent with *past* history. Unfortunately, no one knew how much surpluses had been relied on to buffer the economy against drought, against unusual export sales, as a hedge for grain sales and purchases, and as an underpinning for the livestock and poultry industry. Once the decision was made on the disposition of U.S. surpluses, and all-out production finally encouraged, it became difficult to separate out the Cost of Living Council's exact effect on the industry because of unusual crop and economic conditions both in the United States and abroad. Also, agreements with other nations on their agricultural pricing policies and export policies, such as providing feed grains to Europe in exchange for their making available export wheat crops, all affected the grain-livestock relationships in this country.

From a structural point of view the volatility of grain and oil seed prices coupled with the rigidities of price control activities led to the following changes (keeping in mind that price control activities were only *one* factor in the change):

(1) Custom processing gave additional advantage to those innovative firms that had gone into "boxed beef" and other forms of "fabrication" prior to beef controls. The advantage to these firms was that retailers' resistance to boxed beef and their dependence on a few firms was broken down when the alternative was no meat.

(2) Second guessing on price levels and holding back of supplies to anticipate the end of price controls with a common build-up of temporary "shortages," followed by massive dumping on the market coupled with "dry grazing conditions," added to the problem. This increased price volatility. In reality, this was a highly exaggerated cattle cycle "peak out." Profits and losses went as high as plus and minus $200 per head.

(3) Bankruptcy of some feedlots and processing firms and the acquisition of these enterprises at a below book value basis added to the competitive structure of the industry. New higher cost feedlots were forced out while older, smaller feedlots could buy new facilities at cheap prices.

(4) Retailers were also adversely affected, some changing the mix and grade of beef as feedlot production of "choice" cattle declined.

(5) The futures market controls at ceiling prices led to serious price distortions both domestically and internationally and made a "risk transference" device unavailable.

(6) Price was only one of many variables in determining product movement. Once price was interfered with, the nonpricing factors became more important, such as contractual integration and change in product mix in both type and composition. In essence, a processing "contract" took the place of price as a "market exchange."

(7) The factors affecting the domestic meat system also affected the international meat system. President Nixon removed import controls in 1972 and 1973, and meat imports increased. Although meat prices were not controlled, the profit margins for those handling the imports were. The surpluses and shortages at the domestic level were mirrored internationally. The build-up in the United States was matched by the build-up in the European Community. They collapsed together, but in the EC the livestock producers were given more aid as the bottom fell out.

(8) The distortions of the meat system and the changes in product flow, product specification, and production orientation were similar to the distortions that occurred in other commodity systems during the World War II and Korean experiences.

On the other hand, some positive results occurred such as:

(1) The development of better hedging utilization of the futures market (provided that price controls do not distort futures price quotations).

(2) The acceptance by most in agribusiness that buffer reserves of some sort are a necessity provided that the pricing corridor for the use of the reserves is wide enough to let "normal" market forces work.

(3) The development of better coordination in the industry—e.g., long-term contract.
(4) The development of better data to be used by both private and public decision makers.

OTHER EXAMPLES

Poultry System

Although there is a much shorter grow-out period for poultry, many of the same factors that affect the beef system affect the poultry system. Poultry is even more dependent on feed prices (some 60% of the cost of broiler production). Just as there were relatively stable corn prices from 1962 to 1972, so were there relatively stable broiler prices. Although there were regional and seasonal price variations from 1961 to 1972, the U.S. annual average liveweight farm broiler price varied only from a low of 13.3 cents a pound in 1967 to a high of 15.2 cents a pound in 1969. The "breakeven price" on broilers was so close to the sales price that minor changes in the average price could be the difference between major profit and loss operations. These thin margins meant that efficiency of fractions of one cent per pound were critical competitive tools, as were marketing savings or product differentiation. In fact, from 1967 to 1972 the *cost* of broiler production at farm level fluctuated from 13.5 cents a pound to 14.3 cents a pound.

The 1972–1973 surplus disposal-feed grain explosion led to tremendous price volatility and profit variations in the poultry industry which went from a range of plus 1.1 cents per pound of dressed poultry to a loss of 1.2 cents a pound during 1972; in 1973 variations went from plus 6.3 cents a pound to minus 4.3 cents a pound; in 1974 minus 0.7 cent a pound to minus 3.9 cents a pound, and in 1975 a plus 0.3 cent a pound to a plus 11.9 cents a pound. (None of these were actual results, just concurrent spreads.)

A number of firms in the poultry industry had decided to leave the industry just prior to or during the feed grain price volatility because of the poultry cycle alone; this, coupled with feed grain price volatility, had encouraged firms such as Ralston Purina, Pillsbury, and Quaker Oats to leave the unbranded poultry industry. These exits from the industry were offsets to the value added occurring in the industry such as "chill-pack" that required larger and fewer plants so that the concentration of the industry remained fairly stable. Two forces were at work, the "break up" of national firms into regional firms and the basic technological forces encouraging large-scale plants.

The impact of price controls on meat affected poultry first as an alternative to beef and finally as a price competitor with a per pound price of some beef being actually *lower* than broiler prices. These distortions cannot be attributed solely to the actions of the Cost of Living Council, but to the Council's inability to convince other parts of the governmental agribusiness system to work in tandem with the Council by encouraging more feed grain acreage and by insisting on controls on both feed grains and the processed products using feed grains. It is apparent that "partial controls" or controls that attempt to pressure downward, end up with the utilization of crops going to the highest legal or "illegal" bidder. In the case of a "lid on the top," the commodity bailed over at the sides and went to export or other markets without lids. Eventually the feeder—be he poultry or livestock producer—must reduce his operation or get out of production. This has the opposite long-run effect of helping the consumer.

The broiler grow-out cycle is much shorter than that of cattle. A breeder pullet takes six months to grow and has a laying period of twelve months. A broiler chick takes 26 days to hatch and has a growing period of six to eight weeks; processing takes only one day. Poultry supply and price cycles in recent years have spanned approximately 30 months, in contrast to the 10-year cattle cycle. The industry has been plagued with volatile earnings as a result of the periodic build-up of flocks. The wide swings in profits from year to year are evident even with the underpinning of cheap surplus feed grain supplies which was present at this time. The fact that the broiler cycle is short and that decision-making is concentrated in relatively few firms allows producers to react, and over-react, with extreme rapidity to changing market conditions.

During the critical transition period from Phase III to Phase IV in the late summer of 1973, producers who were experiencing a margin squeeze responded by sharply reducing their flocks. Off-farm consumption declined in 1973 to 37.7 pounds per capita from 38.8 pounds in 1972, reversing a steadily upward trend since 1961. The reduction in production was not so great as it was for beef. Prices peaked in August after the ceiling was lifted on all agricultural products except beef, hitting a high of 60 cents per pound at wholesale. By November, prices were back down to 34.8 cents per pound. Overall commercial broiler production was down 2% in 1973 from the 1972 marketing year.

As feed grain prices climbed in 1973 and 1974, feed price ratios for broiler and egg producers turned increasingly unfavorable. Despite a jump in feed costs of 82% in 1973, the net returns were still positive because of the very high prices which prevailed during much of the year. In 1974 prices were below costs, however. This situation turned around in 1975 and 1976 to result in the best profits in the industry in years.

Price controls during the period 1971 through 1974 added to the problems of earnings volatility which beset the poultry industry. The distortions occurring in the beef system further impacted on broiler production and prices because of the high degree of substitutability between these two products. From a market structure point of view it hastened the exit of large, multinational firms and helped to create new marketing and procurement strategies of an industry responding to severe economic pressures.

Hog System

The hog system encompasses many of the same animal cycle characteristics as do the beef and poultry systems. It was thus under similar kinds of pressures from 1971 through 1974. The hog cycle was disturbed by the imposition of price controls, and producers responded by reducing their sow farrowings and liquidating their herds. Because the hog life cycle is shorter than beef but longer than poultry, requiring only six months to grow out, plus a gestation period of four months, herd rebuilding requires 10 months, and a rapid adjustment in the system was possible. Total commercial slaughter went down 11% in 1972 from 1971, and down another 10% in 1973. Commercial hog production, like broiler production, is dependent on prepared feed so that the producer felt the strong impact of rising feed grain prices when surplus grain stocks disappeared. In addition, since many hogs are owned by corn farmers who have the alternative of feeding their crop to their hogs or marketing the raw crop, a producer was able to make an individual decision as to whether to liquidate his hog inventory. He could react rapidly to changing market conditions and feed-price ratios. During much of this period, high corn prices encouraged him to get out of hog production temporarily.

Even after the end of price controls in the spring of 1974, farmers continued to trim their hog inventories. On December 1, 1974, there were just over 55 million hogs on farms, the fewest since 1965. Market hog inventories were cut by 10% from a year earlier and breeding stocks were reduced 15%. Sow farrowings were projected to be at the lowest rate since 1924. Corn price ratios and feeding margins which rose for a while during 1972 and 1973, as a result of the reduced availability of pork along with the withholding of supplies during the meat freeze, plummeted to low levels in 1974 because feed grains were scarce and expensive.

Retail hog prices remained very high. In the second quarter of 1975 prices were 76% above the comparable quarter in 1971; per capita consumption in 1974 was 10% below the level of 1971. The feed-price ratio provided little incentive for the producer to expand his herd, although this was changing in 1975 when hog producers had received favorable returns, and production increases were again occurring in 1976 with continuing favorable returns.

From a structural point of view the unusual distortion of the price control program occurred at a time when the industry was becoming more commercially oriented to large-scale, year-round hog feeding operations. The Cost of Living Council probably caused more short-term pressure on these large-scale units that did not have the flexibility to get into or out of hog production—but at the same time forced them into long-term marketing arrangements that in the long run may add to the stability of the industry. In many ways the Cost of Living Council in each commodity system caused a closer coordination of procurement and marketing to take place.

Wheat and Flour Milling

This sector has been closely regulated by the government for many years through such programs as grain price supports, CCC credit operations and storage, land set-aside programs, and export subsidies. During the Economic Stabilization Program, when price controls were added onto this already complex system of controls, the industry received some severe shocks.

As in the feed grain and livestock systems, huge grain surpluses have overhung the market for many years thereby providing cheap and stable inputs to the milling and baking industry. The U.S. wheat price was always maintained above the world price through price supports, and export subsidies were used to enable the United States to be competitive in world markets. In 1972, however, when much of the domestic stocks were sold off and prices subsequently climbed, the miller's situation changed. The world economy was booming, resulting in increased demand for U.S. food grains. Export subsidies remained in effect through August 2, 1972, and the miller was put in the position of having to compete with foreign customers for raw wheat. He was under severe pressure as exports soared. Since the government was still giving a subsidy to grain exporters to meet the world price, domestic customers had to bid the price up continually in order to be competitive in the market.

A limited one-month price freeze in 1973 added to difficulties with wheat prices uncontrolled. Other problems concerned the definition of "mill-feed" which is 25% of the total volume of flour milling and is considered a "co-product." With no pass-through provisions on mill-feed, for a limited time it was difficult for the miller to maintain his margin as mill-feed competed with feed grains which had no controls. Some flour millers indicated that each mill in the industry had different controls based on the current history of the mill's operations which affected some locations adversely and vice versa.

At the same time baking firms were also complaining about squeezes. Typical is the quote from the *American Bakeries Company Annual Report for 1975* indicating that the loss before income taxes in 1973 was attributable to three factors, one being "price controls in a year of rapidly increasing uncontrolled raw material costs" and that in 1972 operations were adversely affected by "the impact of existing price control regulations." Margin statistics indicate that the industry *in general* did not have its *average* margin squeezed, although individual firms and individual mills did, with some of them closing as a result.

Fats and Oils

The oilseeds situation paralleled in many respects that of the grains. Export demand, which had been rising steadily throughout the 1960's boomed in the early 1970's as world-wide income and demand grew together. The income elasticity of both protein and fat is high, so that there was a strong demand for soybeans, in particular, for their protein content to be used directly in the human diet, for their use as an animal feed, and for their oil content. The domestic market found that it had to compete with the rest of the world for oilseeds. The devaluation of the dollar further spurred exports.

U.S. soybean stocks, which had been building up somewhat at the end of the preceding decade, were reduced to extremely low levels by 1973. Prices doubled for soybeans and tripled for soybean meal and soybean oil simultaneously, an unprecedented occurrence. This tight supply situation culminated in the export embargo during the fall of 1973.

Price controls once again added to the extremely difficult situation facing the fats and oils processors, wholesalers, and retailers. The margins of these industry participants were suffering because they had difficulty catching up with their exploding raw material costs. The price ceiling period created a scenario where retailers were actually having problems filling their shelves with margarine. The product was simply not available.

At the processor level, companies used this unusual supply dislocation period to try and gain market share. Those firms which through a combination of foresight and good luck happened to build high inventories of oil in anticipation of market needs were able to buy market share through the sharing of these unusual inventory prices with their customers by lowering prices. Thus the effects of the price controls fell unequally on different industry members depending on what their stock position happened to be when controls were imposed. Also, because of the competitive nature of the industry, those with inventory profits provided the margin leadership in the industry. Because timing is so critical to agribusiness operations, imposing price controls at one moment in time could not help but create a long-term advantage to those firms which by accident were in the best margin position at that time. Similarly, with price rationing of existing soybean, meal, and oil inventories, the government had little choice but to impose an embargo if it wanted those few remaining supplies to stay in the United States until the new crop and new "crush" became available. The firms with cheaper inventories could weather the storm.

Wholesale and retail prices for fats and oil products experienced very high inflation from 1972 through 1974. Vegetable oil products such as margarine were subject to a far higher degree of inflation than was margarine's substitute, butter.

Dairy Industry

The dairy industry has been closely regulated for decades by support prices for manufactured milk based on feed prices and organized by Federal Milk Marketing orders. Thus it would seem that the dairy sector might not be as severely affected as the other commodity systems by the unusual situation prevailing from 1971 through 1974. The participants in the dairy system discovered, however, that in a time of rapidly rising feed input prices there was a serious time lag in keeping wholesale manufactured milk prices in line with feed prices because they had to rely on the USDA for their price base. In other words, some commodities, such as milk and peanuts, that rely solely on the government for a price level, depend on the government to make adjustments. If the government over-adjusts, it disrupts a program such as that of the Cost of Living Council; if it under-adjusts or reacts slowly, the industry—in this case the producer—is adversely affected. The milk-feed price ratio, the general indicator of dairy farmer well-being, declined seriously in 1973 and even further in 1974. It began to stabilize in 1975 and improve to a profit level in 1976. This is another case of one government program needing to be changed to fit into the needs of another government program.

Farmers reacted predictably to this unfavorable situation by reducing grain and concentrate feeding rates and failing to add protein supplements to their dairy rations. As a result, milk output per cow dropped 1% in 1973, the first annual decline since 1944. Production remained at the same low level in 1974, reversing the trend of the past decade when dairy farmers were achieving a 3% annual average gain in output per cow, for the most part by increasing grain and concentrate feeding by approximately 5.5% per year. The culling rate also picked up sharply in 1973 because of high feed costs and increased slaughter cow prices. After three successive years of increase, milk production in 1973 dropped about 3.5% to the smallest annual output since 1952.

Output of manufactured dairy products in 1973 also declined some 5%, with butter and nonfat dry milk showing the largest declines. The processor was caught in the familiar cost-price squeeze, along with the dairy farmer, which was worsened by the one-month ceiling on wholesale and retail prices. To offset this decline in domestic production, import quotas were increased in 1973, allowing additional imports of butter, butter oil, nonfat dry milk, and cheese. Dairy product imports in 1973 reached about 3.9 billion pounds milk equivalent, up from 1.7 billion pounds in 1972 or more than double. Additional imports were authorized for 1974 also, although they fell somewhat from the previous year.*

These sharp cutbacks in production, which an increase in imports did not entirely offset, created serious periodic shortages of dairy products at the retail level. The consumer was hit with high prices, causing him to reduce his consumption in 1974. The amount of time manufacturing laborers had to work in order to earn money to purchase dairy products increased sharply in 1974, placing the burden for inflation of staple good products on those who could least afford it.

The Fruit and Vegetable Markets

The fruit and vegetable commodity system, particularly the processed portion of the system, did not experience severe price inflation until the last few months of the controls period. This was primarily the result of the inventory "overhangs" that existed in the citrus and fruit and vegetable industries generally. These industries absorbed many increases of costs, such as fertilizer and cans, because of the inventory overhangs. Supplies declined and prices rose in the latter half of 1973 mainly in reaction to what was happening in other commodity groups, particularly the feed and food grains and the oilseeds. These other commodities compete with many fruits and vegetables for land. As land values rose with the high income generated by grains and oilseeds, acreage was bid away from fruits and vegetables to keep up with their opportunity costs of switching to corn, for example. The structure of the industry into marketing orders and bargaining units caused the farmers' demands for higher prices to be well-organized.

During 1972 and 1973, consumption of all fresh and processed vegetables moved up strongly because vegetables were cheap by comparison with many other foods which were experiencing price inflation and tight supplies. Prices of processed vegetables were being held down by price ceiling restrictions, while fresh produce prices were moving up more rapidly. Canners and processors were reducing their stocks of vegetables in response to the low returns resulting from price controls. In addition, canned fruits and vegetables were subject to increased export interests intensified by USDA export subsidies for such items as canned peaches. With the subsidy of $1 a case for exports of peaches which prevailed at this time, it was more profitable for the canners to sell some inventory abroad than to sell in the United States under ceiling prices.

---

* The timing of import permission is also important such as in the "Cheese War" with the EC, when imports finally arrived at the time when a U.S. surplus situation was occurring in 1974–1975.

The increased cost structure at the farm level has aggravated the farmer's position. In essence, because of the time lag at the producer level the fruit and vegetable system has acted like a re-run movie portraying all of the actions affecting the food system in 1972–1975, starting one year later.

Conclusions

1. Price stabilization in the food system is as dependent upon government actions with respect to commodity programs and commodity market structures as it is on direct food price control programs and their implementation. The excess capacity at the farm level was partially regulated by acreage control programs and the disposition of government stocks as well as the level of agricultural price supports. These were really the "price control" mechanisms that affected raw and processed agricultural products from World War II to 1972. These control structures already in being probably should have been used, reorienting and reinforcing them instead of adding the confusion of another layer of controls.

Raw agricultural prices were the one part of the economy it was thought could be ignored in an anti-inflation program. Once the decisions were made not to use available acreage and to push for agricultural exports during a world-wide economic boom, control of the raw farm sector of the food economy was lost but no one wanted to admit it. The result was that all the burden of adjustment was placed on the manufacturing, wholesaling, and retailing segments of the food system. This was done by administrators who were well-intentioned but who were not familiar with the special market structure arrangements of each commodity system that had been built upon the unique agronomic crop and livestock characteristics of these industries and the unique inventory position each commodity system held at that particular moment of time.

The institutions that had been created to help these commodity systems work effectively under surplus conditions, such as futures markets, farm cooperatives, and contractual coordination agreements, became distorted only during the brief period of a freeze or export controls, and wide swings occurred when government surpluses no longer existed. Futures markets became unfair for a seller or a buyer when a freeze or a soybean embargo took place. Cooperatives, through their transfer pricing arrangements with their producer members, in some cases had more access to raw agricultural materials than their proprietary corporate counterparts. Finally, those that had unique long-term contractual arrangements, by using either the cash or the futures market, in some instances anticipated the huge raw agricultural price rise. With their resulting profits or savings, these firms had the opportunity to gain market share by holding prices below replacement costs for their competition or to enhance their profits and at the same time establish margin relationships that were untenable for the remaining competitors in the industry.

2. In essence, food price controls are not workable if they cover only a part of the economic system. Imposing them on the manufacturing, wholesaling, and retailing segments without making the primary producers or exporters subject to controls ultimately produces severe distortions which lead to artificial shortages and accelerated price increases. When reliance is placed on limited application of controls, the end result is just the opposite of the original objective. Instead of controlling inflation, such steps lead into unforeseen directions such as those described in the meat system. Even when food price controls are developed for the total system, distortions occur as was noted in the review of World War II programs.

3. Some industries or individual firms within those industries were caught with unusually low profit margins at the time of the imposition of controls. The disruptions of cattle, hog, and poultry production are cases in point and these were increased by the Cost of Living Council's activities. Government administrative decisions, because of the unique character of each firm and each industry, cannot be applied in a uniform manner. The result is a change in competitive costs of firms within the industry arising from government actions rather than from market forces and the firms' response to those market forces.

4. Shortages in one sector of agribusiness, because of its interrelated and interdependent structure, automatically affect the other sectors. The fruit and vegetable producers, for example, who could raise alternative crops demanded price increases in their production contracts with processors. If they did not receive the price increases, they threatened to divert their acreage to cereal or feed grain crops, provided such diversion was agronomically feasible. Thus on the West Coast the price of peas increased from $100 a ton to $200 a ton to compete with West Coast wheat prices. This added another group of commodities to the food price push and illustrates the fact that "farm land" is a farmer's "factory" and the price of one commodity is automatically reflected in alternative crops that compete for use of the land. Similarly, controls on beef products in the spring and summer of 1973 led to artificially high increases in poultry price levels and subsequently extremely low price levels when beef controls were removed, causing a flood of beef to hit the market. This interdependency also works to the consumer's advantage because of the variety of nutrition foods he has available. He is able to substitute one food for another, thus lessening the need for controls over any one segment of the food system.

5. One of the most difficult aspects of the food price control program *was the uncertainty and confusion of many of the rules and regulations.* These uncertainties led to individual interpretations within and be-

tween firms to the point where many decisions became based on "get what you can." Some products were rerouted through uneconomic logistic patterns in order to be eligible for higher margins. Other processors introduced cheaper sources of raw materials such as imported flour from Canada, where the Canadian government had set a cheaper price for domestic wheat and hence flour and a higher price for exported wheat. The inequities usually were their worst at the start of each program because firms had little time to prepare for the new competitive situation dictated by controls. For example, in wheat flour milling, margins for some firms were as low as 30 cents. The more the millers sold, the more they lost. Eventually corrections took place but only after severe company losses and market structure distortions had occurred.

6. Figure II-4 indicates farm-retail price spread and farm value from July 1972 to September 1974. From this chart it is apparent that farm value was going up while farm-retail spreads were remaining stable or slightly declining through the middle of 1973. This put severe pressure on processors and retailers as previously noted. Profit margins in 1976 returned to normal in the industry, and farm-retail spreads widened as a result of lower raw agricultural prices and higher labor, packaging, and transporation costs. Labor costs, although increasing in an uneven way during the price control period, did not increase as rapidly as other costs until the 1973–1975 period when labor caught up with increases of over 20% at retail and institutional levels during 1974. Energy costs were up 52%, packaging 30%, and transportation 10%. In 1975, with additional Russian grain purchases and indications of a long-term, five-year contract with that country, agricultural grain prices reversed their decline and once again accelerated. Hence, even with bumper crops, the pressure of increased and rigid processing and marketing costs, together with potential long-range export contracts, may lead to continued price pressure in the food area. By 1976 bumper crops again reduced raw agricultural prices, but inflexible cost structures—primarily labor and energy costs—kept prices at retail at the same or slightly higher rates.

7. What then can we say should be our first priority in bringing back some semblance of price stability to the U.S. food system? The answer appears to be obvious—namely, *some sort of a reserve system* at the raw agricultural commodity level that protects the producer during times of gluts and the rest of the food system as well as the consumer in times of shortages. Certainly most participants in the agribusiness system want the market place to provide allocations between the extremes of severe shortages and gluts, and the existence of a reserve system seems to be the simplest way in which to provide for economic stability in this important segment of the U.S. economy. If drastic action should be called for in the future, *controls need to be placed on all parts of the food system without reducing the incentives needed to provide more output at the farm level.* Such controls should not be imposed without

FIGURE II-4.   FARM-RETAIL PRICE SPREAD AND FARM VALUE
JULY 1972—SEPTEMBER 1974

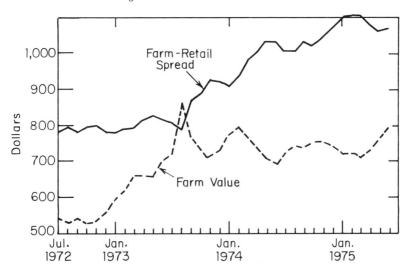

relating them to the agricultural commodity programs, export and import programs, environmental and Pure Food and Drug Programs, and antitrust activities that affect these control programs and, in turn, are influenced by them. The reduction in growth stimulants in feed mixtures and the ban on certain corn herbicides have economic costs that must be reviewed in relation to other human benefits. A commodity system approach on a commodity-by-commodity vertical market structure basis will be useful in determining what food control programs, if any, are needed. In all analyses the consumer perspective must be represented as well as the interests of participants in each segment of the food system from input supplier through ultimate distributor.

The history of food price controls leads to the inescapable conclusion that they are only workable if applied to the *total* economic system—the private sector and the other public laws that affect that sector. Even then, as previous histories suggest, they may not be effective.

8. The impact of the Cost of Living Council's price program on the market structure of the food system is difficult to isolate from all the other factors affecting the food system such as drought, new production areas (e.g., Brazil), farm labor unrest, and changes in the support levels for tightly controlled products (e.g., dairy products). Traditionally all controls created distortions. In World War II, soybean manufacturers did not sell soybean meal because it was controlled; they mixed oats with it, called it "mixed feed," and sold the lower

protein product at a higher price than soybean meal. In the 1972–1974 period each commodity system had its location and product distortions; one of the best defenses against such distortions may be a "reserve system" that acts as a buffer between extreme shortages and gluts. The market system can handle normal volatility; what is needed is a safety valve of commodity inventories to alleviate abnormal situations. Most participants in the food system agree to a reserve. The argument is concerned with the size of the reserve, its cost, its ownership, and the wisdom to administer it in a political environment. All of these are issues that go beyond the description of different effects of the Cost of Living Council's program.

9. Finally, without reserve stocks the political pressures to use other commodity and acreage legislation as a current expedient response is the greatest potential distortion to the U.S. food system. At the same time U.S. programs are greatly influenced by the food programs of other nations and therefore must be related to the international commodity agreements currently being developed on a regional and global basis. Table II-4 indicates that the food component of the Consumer Price Index in selected countries went up in spite of a whole variety of control programs. Reserve food stocks have been the safety valve of both the U.S. and world food systems in the past. We may argue about their control, their cost, and their interference with "normal" market activities, but there is general agreement that such reserves lessen the distortions of alternative "control" programs.

TABLE II-4.   THE FOOD COMPONENT OF THE CONSUMER PRICE INDEX
IN SELECTED COUNTRIES, 1972–1976 WHERE 1970 = 100

Country	1972	1973	1974	1975	1976
Argentina	231	359	413	1187	—
Australia	108	124	143	154	—
Canada	109	125	145	164	168
Israel	123	149	215	314	353
Japan	110	124	157	180	190
Netherlands	111	120	129	140	147
United Kingdom	121	139	164	206	234
United States	108	123	141	153	157

SOURCE: International Labor Office, *Bulletin of Labor Statistics,* October 1976, p. 9.

CHAPTER III

The Design and Implementation of Food Price Regulations

KENNETH J. FEDOR AND REGINALD J. BROWN

Kenneth J. Fedor

Kenneth J. Fedor is Vice President of Economics and Planning, The Quaker Oats Company. He held various positions at the Cost of Living Council including special assistant to the director, executive director of the Food Committee, and administrator of the Office of Food.

Dr. Fedor taught economics at the U.S. Military Academy, West Point, while in the military. He spent over two years as an economist in the U.S. Embassy and AID Mission in Brazil.

Reginald J. Brown

Reginald J. Brown is principal analyst for natural resources in the Congressional Budget Office. He served as deputy administrator, Office of Food at the Cost of Living Council.

Mr. Brown has worked as director, Washington Administrative Operations for Mitre Corporation, as assistant vice president for management for the Urban Institute, and as associate director, Economic Analysis for the Defense Manpower Commission. He was an assistant professor of economics and of government at the U.S. Military Academy, West Point.

CHAPTER III

The Design and Implementation of Food Price Regulations

Two QUESTIONS are of particular importance in the design of price regulations for the food industry. The first is to what extent should the regulations limit price increases by forcing firms to absorb rising costs? One design extreme incorporates fixed price ceilings at either the manufacturing or the retail level, preventing any pass-through of higher costs. This system was employed on three different occasions in the food industry during the Economic Stabilization Program. At the other end of the design spectrum, regulations can permit unlimited pass-through of costs. This set of regulations was never applied to the food industry but was in operation for most of the rest of the economy during Phase III subject to profit margin limitations. The second important question is to what extent should all segments of an industry by controlled? In the food industry this question involves the issue whether prices of raw agricultural products should be controlled directly.

The resolution of these two design questions will determine the essential elements of the structure and scope of a regulatory system imposed on the food industry. Once they are resolved, issues such as choice of base periods and definition of allowable costs must be addressed prior to the implementation of any set of regulations. The resolution of these implementation issues, perceived by the press and the public to be only technical changes in the regulations, has major implications for firms subject to the regulations; they define the degree of restrictiveness or permissiveness of the regulatory scheme, and consequently, influence the impact that the regulations have on pricing behavior in the food industry.

Primary Issues

Fixed Price Ceilings

The issue of whether to impose fixed price ceilings, or "price freezes" as they are called in the popular press, is likely to be debated often throughout the course of any stabilization program. The most direct method of dealing with rising prices appears to be simply to order them to stop. The simplistic appeal of this bold policy action is guaranteed to gain consumer support initially since it is a dramatic response to the "do something" nature of the public debate of the inflation problem.

A price freeze also provides a rationale for pursuing other policies which could not be justified in the absence of a freeze. During the 1971 Freeze, for example, an excessively stimulative fiscal policy was instituted. Similarly, the export embargo on soybeans was imposed during the 1973 Freeze.

Virtually all economists and businessmen agree that the very blunt tool of freezing prices should be considered only under the most extraordinary circumstances such as the emergency conditions surrounding the outbreak of war. Since governments throughout the world continue to resort to price freezes under circumstances which could hardly be described as "emergency conditions," any analysis of food price regulations should begin by reviewing the arguments which continue to be weighed in government policy decisions regarding the imposition of price freezes. It will also be helpful to proceed by presenting the well-known set of economic arguments against price freezes on the food industry since most of the arguments against direct food price controls are really arguments relating to the shortages and distortions caused by fixed price ceilings rather than the more flexible types of price regulations.

Economic Arguments Against Food Price Freezes. Ceiling prices must be set below the level of prices determined by the market if they are to be effective. Whenever government-dictated prices are set below market clearing levels, they inevitably result in shortages since someone's demand will be unsatisfied at the prevailing price. Whenever the market place is thereby rendered ineffective as a mechanism for rationing available supplies in the short run, some other method for deciding the merits of various claimants on available supplies must be imposed. All nonmarket methods of rationing, whether they are government-imposed or consist of special deals and arrangements among businessmen or between producers and consumers, are inefficient and create unacceptable burdens.

Before discussing the rationing implications of effective price ceilings, the meaning of the term "shortage" should be clarified. If the market accurately registers the relative valuations of both consumers and producers when it is operating effectively, then a shortage may be assumed to exist whenever the quantity demanded exceeds the quantity supplied at a given price level. Under such conditions of excess demand, there will be pressure on prices to rise, which could be interpreted as evidence that a shortage exists. This interpretation of shortages rests on the role of price as an allocator of supplies available in the short run. This type of "shortage" would disappear if prices were allowed to rise to reduce excess demand. If prices are not allowed to rise to their equilibrium levels, the statement that a "shortage" exists is somewhat tautological.

The popularly held view of shortages is that a shortage exists whenever a smaller supply is available at one point in time compared with an earlier period. Alternatively, a sudden surge in demand may create the impression of a shortage if supplies cannot be increased immediately to meet the higher level of demand. When prices cannot rise because of government-imposed ceilings, however, one needs to look at factors other than rising prices as indicative of shortage situations, e.g., incidence of queues and empty meat counters.

The relevance of this discussion of shortages is that whatever is used as evidence that a shortage exists, the problem of insufficient supplies to meet the existing demands is not solved in the short run by rising prices if excess capacity is not immediately available. Higher prices or longer lines at the meat counter are simply alternative ways of rationing the supplies available in the short run. Although the choice of rationing method can have important long-run implications, let us initially limit the discussion of arguments against price freezes to short-run considerations, as is often the case in public policy debates.

The fact that effective price ceilings require government-mandated rationing schemes has been acceptable in the past in the United States (World War II) and continues to be acceptable to nonmarket economies in the Soviet Union and Eastern Europe. A key point to be considered, however, is that government-imposed rationing systems on an economy as complex as the United States requires the utilization of an extremely large number of government employees to administer the program. Since it is never feasible to set up such a large agency during the short period of time for which prices are frozen in nonemergency times, available supplies have been rationed in some other way.

Queues, special customer arrangements, and black market influences may perform the function. Although inefficient from an economic point of view, some of these alternatives may prove politically acceptable for a time. The experience of the Economic Stabilization Program (ESP) with beef ceilings invoked on March 29, 1973, and lifted over three months later on September 9, 1973, provides an illustration of political acceptability of economic inefficiency. In addition to long lines at meat counters, the effects of this period of beef ceilings were monitored in daily price and slaughter reports, and in weekly reports of Beef Packing Closures. As an illustration, the weekly closure report on August 24, 1973, almost three months into the ceilings, indicated the following:

(a) 68 packing plants had closed down;
(b) 94 packing plants were experiencing slowdowns;
(c) the average daily slaughter rate for cattle for the week was 103,000, compared with 122,000 for the same week in 1972.

Many are quick to point to these statistics as conclusive evidence of the distorting effects and folly of using ceilings as price control devices. Although no one denied that slaughter rates declined and plant closures occurred, the fact that ceilings were not lifted implies that these costs were acceptable to the government. In spite of the reduced supply of meat, clearly related to the price freeze, no form of government rationing was attempted, nor was the need for such recognized officially at any time. As a consequence, another form of rationing emerged. Many food retailers decided to insure the flow of some beef to the supermarket via "custom slaughtering" in order to avoid empty meat counters, long queues, and potential loss of customers to competitors who were able to offer meat for sale. Reacting to the fact that beef prices and availability are significant factors determining where customers shop, retailers partially reduced the extent of the beef shortage by continuing to supply meat even though they absorbed the losses implicit in the ceiling prices.

In summary, the experiment with ceiling prices on beef in 1973 provides another vivid illustration of the short-run economic costs of imposing freezes. The policy decisions made also clearly imply that the Administration was willing to tolerate the short-run costs of the nonprice/nongovernment form of rationing that inevitably evolved.

The second argument often made against price freezes is that prices should always be allowed to rise to provide incentives to producers to increase output, thereby permitting demands to be satisfied and prices stabilized in the long run. Increasing output is said to be the only real solution to the inflationary problem in the long run.

Even those policy makers who are interested in the longer-run implications of their decisions may find this argument against price freezes inapplicable under certain circumstances. The freeze on beef prices in March 1973 can again be used to illustrate one form of the "special circumstance" argument.

Beef ceilings were imposed at the retail and processor levels in March. Transactions involving the sale from rancher to feedlot and feedlot to processor were not controlled even though rising livestock prices were clearly the cause of rising meat prices at retail during the previous four months.[1] The internal government forecast when beef price ceilings were imposed, however, was that cattle prices were very near their highs in March and, although they might rise seasonally throughout the spring and summer, the pressure on the ceilings would be tolerable until the fall when prices would decline and ceilings could be removed. The hoped-for effect of the ceilings, then, was to avoid the temporary seasonal peak in meat prices, thereby avoiding the permanent inflationary effect this might have through the impact on long-term wage settlements.

There were two assumptions implicit in this reasoning which seemed quite plausible at the time. First, it was felt that imposing price ceilings at the packer and retailer levels would force pressure back down the production chain to a point where live cattle prices would actually stop rising because neither packers nor retailers would be willing to incur the reduction in margins caused by the freeze on the prices that they charged for beef while the costs they incurred to purchase beef continued to rise. Second, the level to which live cattle prices had risen in March 1973 was fairly high by historical standards and seemed to provide more than ample incentives for the cattle producers to increase output and thereby provide a long-term solution to the problem of rising beef prices.

Models and forecasts based on a simulation of market behavior in the absence of government regulations were not, in this instance in any case, very accurate in terms of predicting what actually did happen after the imposition of the Freeze on beef prices in late March. Live cattle prices actually peaked in August following the announced decision by the government to delay lifting ceilings on beef until September even though the Freeze was lifted for the rest of the food industry in July. The government's action induced farmers to withhold cattle in August in anticipation of the lifting of the ceilings, causing cattle prices to spurt another 20% above what were already historical highs in July. Some cattle were withheld as a "strike" to force elimination of the ceilings. The flood of cattle that came to market in September combined with the experience of consumers who had learned to reduce their consumption of beef the preceding month resulted rather in lower prices and depressed profits in the cattle industry, thereby reducing the supply of beef for at least the next 18 months.

The final argument which we will review against imposing ceiling prices is particularly relevant in the food industry in the United States since large portions of agricultural production, particularly grains, are exported. To the extent that prices are frozen on domestic transactions below world market prices, a larger portion of the available supply is likely to flow into export channels, thereby further exacerbating the problem of domestic inflation. Beef and pork exports were monitored weekly by the Cost of Living Council during the Freeze of 1973. Although exports clearly increased substantially during that period,[2] no action was taken to limit meat exports because the total amount of meat exports never exceeded 10% of the available supply. A more significant increase in meat exports would have lured the government into the next logical step; namely, export restrictions. As it turned out, only soybeans, a primary input into the production of livestock, were embargoed in the summer of 1973, partially justified by the fact that meat prices were frozen.

In the final analysis, arguments denouncing the effectiveness of price ceilings hinge on the proposition that government-imposed prices cannot do as well as competitively determined prices in efficiently rationing available supplies in the short run, allocating scarce resources to increase production in the long run, and can easily be circumvented by exporting goods which are normally traded in world markets. Even though agricultural commodity markets evidence the characteristics of an efficient/competitive market, there seems to be a growing reluctance to accept the proposition that an efficient market mechanism *equitably* distributes available supplies. Future decisions about the advisability of imposing price freezes, especially in the highly visible food area, will be made in the public policy arena on the basis of the trade-offs between political conceptions of equity and the costs in terms of lost efficiency in the functioning of agricultural markets.

These trade-offs will, of course, never be addressed directly. The enormous political pressure that emerges to "do something" to deal with the perception of inequities caused by substantial food price increases may lure government policy makers into any action program which is both politically and administratively convenient. What could be more tempting than a temporary program to freeze prices without government rationing under the "special circumstances" that will appear to exist the next time?

Raw Agricultural Product Prices

Rising agricultural product prices were the principal cause of food price problems throughout the 1971–1974 period. Although the issue of whether to control agricultural prices was debated throughout the program period, the decision to exempt agricultural prices made in August 1971 by the President at Camp David immediately preceding the imposition of wage and price controls proved to be irrevocable. There were two basic reasons for deciding against controlling prices at the farm level. First, most agricultural commodity markets, although imperfect in many ways, are often thought to be the closest approximation of free markets in operation in the United States today. Indeed, many agricultural products are sold in auction markets which do exhibit the characteristics of the model of a perfectly competitive market. The underlying conditions of demand and particularly supply are, of course, oftentimes significantly influenced by government agricultural programs. Second, the specter of a cumbersome administrative apparatus and physical forms of rationing were never acceptable to an Administration which never anticipated that the controls would last more than a year.

Since a program to regulate farm level prices directly was administratively and politically inconvenient, there was little reason for the Administration to interfere directly with agricultural markets in 1971 since farm prices were not rising rapidly. The critical importance of the raw product sector later in the Program period was, however, widely recognized by the controllers. A January 8, 1973, Cost of Living Council memorandum on Food Price Regulations, for example, addressed the merits of substantial changes in Phase II food price regulations when the raw product sector was exempt. In support of the option for "no change in food price regulations," it was argued that:

> No dramatic change in food prices would occur as a result of changes in the regulations . . . . rising food prices basically reflected the strong increase in farm prices in 1972. Farm-retail spreads rose only 0.6% over last year. Consequently, the prospects for short-term stabilization of food prices by squeezing this segment of the food industry are remote.[3]

The underlying assumption of that memorandum was that control of the raw product sector was out of the question. The administrators of the price and wage stabilization program, recognized all along that without controls on the primary sector, they were dealing with the relatively insignificant causes of food price inflation during the particular period under review. Indeed, the experience of 1973 was even more pointed than that of 1972. Council data at the end of the year showed that two-thirds of the food price inflation of 1973 was directly attributable to rising raw agricultural prices. John T. Dunlop's February 1974 testimony before the Senate Committee on Banking, Housing, and Urban Affairs stated the following:

> Consumer food prices accelerated from annual rates of 3.0% in 1971 and 4.3% in 1972 to an unprecedented rate of 14.5% in 1973. The overwhelming cause of the sharp rise was a 26% increase in agricultural prices at the farm level in 1973 . . . the share of the retail food dollar going to the farmer jumped from 40% to 45% in 1973, and the income of farm proprietors rose 32.7% compared to 11.9% for total national income in 1973. . . .[4]

Revised data published in the July 1976 issue of *Farm Income Situation*, USDA Economic Research Service, shows that the rise in farmers' income in 1973 was a more significant factor causing food price inflation than had been thought at the time. Farm operators' total net income (realized net income adjusted for inventory changes) in 1973 was $33.3 billion, compared with 1972 income of $18.7 billion, an increase of 78%. Going beyond the period covered by controls, total net farm income fell to $26.5 billion in 1974 while retail food prices escalated another 14.4%, a pace quite similar to the 14.5% rate of 1973. Although farm prices did increase somewhat (7%) in 1974, the potential impact of a system of price regulations limited to influencing cost increases beyond the farm level would have been much different in 1974, the year the controls were lifted.

To control farm prices directly with the type of regulations administered by the Economic Stabilization Program was politically and administratively unacceptable and unfeasible. Yet many government programs had an important impact on demand, supplies and prices in various agricultural markets. The choice is never simply a question of whether the government should control (in the general sense) agricultural markets, but in reality it is a question of the type and intent of government intervention. The Administration's ability to change agricultural programs to reduce their inflationary impact in a year like 1973 is limited because the administration of many programs is written in detail in legislation. Legislatively determined programs which artificially raise the general demand for food are particularly restrictive, such as food stamps, school lunch programs, and PL 480.

There are many instances where government policies constrain prices or supplies in specific product markets. The following examples offer some illustrations of programs whose administration Congress has left more to the discretion of the Executive branch. Dairy prices are, for example, by and large regulated by either state or federal governments throughout most of the nation. The primary effect of governmental price regulation of milk is to set minimum, not maximum, prices. It can be argued that nearly 20 of the 50-odd USDA agricultural marketing orders can be used to raise price levels in the short run for a number of vegetables, fruits, and nuts.[5] These marketing orders effectively sanction the operation of grower cooperatives in price setting. The operation of navel orange growers, lemon growers, and almond growers are prime examples of how noncompetitive these markets can be. The main objective of these marketing orders is to prevent prices from falling below specified levels, thereby reducing the risk to growers.

In summary, the myriad set of government agricultural programs could, if administered in a manner which gives higher priority to restraining agricultural price increases rather than raising minimum prices, offer an alternative or complementary method of controlling food prices juxtaposed on direct price controls at the retail/wholesale level.

In concluding this section on design issues of price regulations, it bears repeating that although it is accepted that market-determined price changes in competitive markets provide the efficient allocation of scarce goods among alternative demands, in times of rampant inflation both the efficiency and the equity of the market mechanism will be questioned. The imposition of meat price ceilings can be used to illustrate how "special circumstances" provide the economic rationale for freezing prices and indirectly controlling raw agricultural prices. The only acceptable and administratively available method of stopping the rise in cattle prices in the short run was to impose ceilings at the processor/distributor level and squeeze their margins to the point where meat packers would refuse to pay higher prices for live cattle. For whatever reasons, the stability of cattle and hog prices in April, May, and June 1973 tended to support the effectiveness of this approach to controlling raw agricultural prices.

The limitations of this approach, however, became obvious as weeks turned into months and it became obvious that the legislated ceilings on beef were unable to withstand the pressure of rising feed costs, expanding meat exports, and the explosion of all other food prices when Freeze II was lifted in July 1973. The incidence of meat packing plant closings and marked reductions in gross meat margins experienced by those retail chains which engaged in custom slaughtering, cited earlier, provide ample evidence that price ceilings at the processor/distributor level are an ineffective measure of controlling raw agricultural prices when a strong market and speculative forces are creating upward price pressure. This section would be incomplete if it ended without identifying other significant dangers of controlling raw agricultural prices by any method.

It will always be tempting, particularly because of the sensitivity of wage rates to sharp run-ups in food prices, to try to delay food price increases by tampering with the relatively competitive but still imperfect market mechanism which exists in the agricultural sector. There are four principal problems in implementing any program designed to regulate price behavior at the raw agricultural level. First, there is a long lag between price changes, production decisions, and eventual output responses in agriculture. The second is that food price increases are seldom, if ever, acceptable. An economic rationale for further delays in permitting food prices to rise can always be found. Whether the delays are temporary or permanent, the variety of government programs which influence agricultural production decisions must be used as the primary method of bringing about the required changes in output. The government really does not need to resort to food price freezes or other means of direct price controls to utilize this method.

Even if this is accepted by any Administration, a third problem in implementing the policy is to convince the USDA to increase production in order to lower agricultural prices—a proposition which is hardly popular among many USDA constituents. The recognition of this aspect of the problem of regulating food prices during the Economic Stabilization Program was clearly reflected in the wording of the Executive Order[6] establishing the Food Committee of the CLC in Phase III:

> There is hereby established the Cost of Living Council Committee on Food which shall be composed of the Chairman of the Council, who shall be its Chairman, the Vice Chairman of the Council, the Director of the Council, the Secretary of Agriculture, the Director of

the Office of Management and Budget, and such others as the President may, from time to time, designate. *The Committee shall review Government activities significantly affecting food costs and prices and make recommendations to the Chairman of the Council concerning these matters.*

Even though this administrative apparatus was established and used extensively, only limited and short-lived progress was made in changing USDA programs.

The fourth problem is that there is a huge escape valve for agricultural products, the domestic prices of which are not allowed to move in accordance with world prices—the export market. This subject is dealt with in detail in Chapter V.

The temptation to impose export controls is mentioned in this discussion of controlling raw agricultural prices merely to put its rationale in the proper perspective and to illustrate the scope of the problems inherent in successfully implementing a program to control food price behavior via the route of influencing the allocation of agricultural resources. The abrupt decision to embargo soybean exports in the summer of 1973 was the final step in the logic of trying to moderate food price increases caused primarily by uncontrolled and rising raw agricultural prices.

This list of problems which arise when implementing a program designed to control raw agricultural prices is not exhaustive but simply represents the main problems which emerged during the 1971–1974 Economic Stabilization Program. They do, however, illustrate the complexity of the task facing any Administration which contemplates controlling farm prices. Our conclusion is that the thrust of an anti-inflation program in the food/agriculture area, at least in the economic and political setting of 1973–1974, should be limited to changing government programs and policies which themselves contribute to food price pressure.

FOOD PRICE REGULATIONS

Having decided that ceilings and controls of the raw product sector were unacceptable, many implementation issues of significance to firms which had to operate under the system of cost pass-through rules remained to be resolved. The premise upon which the regulations promulgated at the beginning of Phase II for the economy as a whole were based on allowing firms to raise prices to the extent that they had experienced permanent cost increases. The theory was that inflation was caused by administered prices, set independently from costs, by a few firms in concentrated industries. The regulations adopted were consistent with the administered price theory of inflation in that the regulations were intended only to control margins of prices over costs rather than to control prices directly. These rules were applied also to food manufacturers, wholesalers, and retailers even though the theory did not apply in the food industry because raw material inputs constitute a large percentage of total costs. For most forms of food processing, raw agricultural product costs for commodities like cattle, cash grain crops, and sugar represent approximately 40% of total costs. In some sectors such as meat packings, raw material costs represent about 80% of the total. In normal circumstances, nonagricultural cost elements such as labor, packaging, transportation, and overhead account for approximately 60% of the costs of processing and distributing food. Consequently, under a normal set of circumstances, unlike those prevailing in 1973, a scheme of price controls based on regulating the speed and extent to which costs could be passed through could potentially have only a limited impact on food prices when raw agricultural prices are not controlled.

Our discussion of the regulatory issues raised during the Economic Stabilization Program period will proceed by describing first the general evolution of the food price regulations from August 15, 1971, through April 30, 1974.* An analysis of specific regulatory issues which were raised and debated in Phases II, III, and IV will follow in the next section. The discussion throughout these two sections focuses primarily on events in 1973 and 1974 because this was the period when food inflation was greater and the food sector was singled out for special treatment.

Special Considerations for the Food Sector

The decision to impose controls on August 15, 1971, did not envision separate treatment for the food sector beyond the exemption on raw agricultural products. In fact, the behavior of food prices just prior to the first freeze had been quite stable, and food prices actually fell during this freeze. In this context, it was not surprising that a strong program designed to fight rising food prices was not an item of major concern to government policy makers.

The absence of special concern for food prices continued through the formulation of a control scheme for Phase II. It was not until the accumulation of experience in Phase II, combined with the intensification of world-wide food price pressures, that distinctly different problems associated with food began to point to the development of a separate program for food prices and wages. When Phase II regulatory experience was coupled with substantial increases in agricultural commodity prices toward the end of 1972, the regulation of food prices emerged in Phase III as a scheme distinct from the treatment accorded to the rest of the economy with the notable exception of the health care and construction industries which were also singled out for special treatment. The distinctive treatment of the

---

* A chronology of specific regulations can be found in Appendix III-1.

food industry continued through the design and implementation of Phase IV to the final decontrol of food prices on April 30, 1974.

Freeze I: August 15—November 13, 1971

The rise of food prices during the summer and fall of 1971 was clearly not an item of concern to the Administration. Indeed, the Freeze operations memorandum submitted by Arnold Weber, a public member of the Pay Board, and used at Camp David, provided for the exemption of the entire food sector "because of the seasonal variation of food prices and their relative stability."[7] This recommendation was modified to exclude raw agricultural products, but not to a comprehensive exclusion of the entire industry. The rather special food price problems that were to loom large in subsequent phases were virtually ignored during this freeze period. Although the food sector was not totally exempt, prices of raw agricultural products were not subject to the Freeze.

The same set of Freeze regulations that were applied to the economy as a whole were also applied to the manufacturing and distribution components of the food industry. The 90-day freeze imposed a set of ceiling prices calculated on the basis of prices in effect during the 30-day period from July 16 to August 14, 1971. For the most part, firms subject to the Freeze were limited to prices that they had in effect just prior to the Freeze, including temporary special deals and allowances. Specifically, the ceiling price allowed was equal to the highest prices charged for at least 10% of the sales by class of purchases from July 16 to August 14.

Phase II: November 14, 1971—January 10, 1973

The character of the price regulations designed during the planning for Phase II was bound to reflect the diverse and not wholly compatible influences on those with the responsibility for designing a domestic price restraint program following a set of policy actions announced on August 15, 1971, implemented initially to deal primarily with long-term international monetary problems. The salient factors were:

(1) Economic distortions caused by strict price ceilings meant that the Freeze had to be relaxed;
(2) Political pressures arising from the popularity of the Freeze dictated a continuation of some form of controls; and
(3) A perceived need for "equity" precluded any system other than a comprehensive program.

Herbert Stein, the leader of the task force planning Phase II, identified its objective to be "to move from freeze to free markets with reasonable price stability."[8] In this context, a cost pass-through scheme of controlling prices by regulating allowable margins, contrasted with actual price levels, was adopted by the Price Commission. In addition, proposals recommending changes in government programs that it was thought would be effective in increasing available supplies (e.g., reduction of import restrictions, increased livestock grazing on diverted acreage, amendments to the Sugar Act, review of USDA marketing orders, restructuring of farm price supports, and the elimination of subsidies for beef exports) were submitted, but were relegated to the back burner.[9] Beyond these recommended strucutral modifications, however, no systematic or special treatment for the food sector was suggested or sought in the planning for Phase II.

The Phase II control scheme for food firms was identical to that employed for the rest of the economy. The Phase II program allowed prices to be adjusted in relation to movements in costs provided that aggregate firm-wide historical profit margin limits were not exceeded. Firms could adjust prices above freeze levels provided they submitted evidence substantiating that they experienced cost increases adequate to justify the new price. Manufacturing firms with sales of $100 million had to prenotify these price increases 30 days in advance. Retailers and wholesalers were allowed to maintain their customary percentage markups over costs of goods purchased. They were not required to prenotify price increases because of the large number of items sold and the frequency of changes in the costs of goods purchased from a variety of suppliers.

Volatile Pricing Authority

During the implementation of Phase II, fluctuating raw material prices became a stumbling block to the smooth administration of a prenotified price control scheme. Some firms, primarily meat packers, found the 30-day prenotification requirement particularly onerous, because raw material costs were subject to drastic and unpredictable changes requiring instantaneous price adjustments if they were to avoid cost absorption. The Price Commission decided early in Phase II to exempt such firms from the prenotification requirement provided they requested exemptions and could substantiate that they were victims of this volatility. This exemption was called "Volatile Price Authority." The volatility of food raw material prices was later to become a major consideration in tailoring a special set of rules for food manufacturers.

Phase III: January 11—June 12, 1973

While the food, health, and construction sectors continued under mandatory controls in Phase III, the remainder of the economy was allowed to self-administer a more flexible set of regulations. The cost pass-through system that comprised Phase II was continued in the food sector into Phase III with minor modifications, principally in the regulations for wholesalers and retailers.

The basic design of the regulatory aspects of food price stabilization in Phase III did not result from an effort to tailor a system designed to restrain large increases in raw product prices. The difference in the approach to food price stabilization between Phases II and III was not regulatory in nature but was reflected in a series of actions taken to expand supplies of agricultural products in order to address the principal cause of the increase in food prices at the time. These actions are described elsewhere. It will be sufficient to note here that the time lag between actions designed to increase agricultural supplies and their eventual impact on the market were sufficiently long to preclude any impact on the explosion of agricultural commodity prices in the spring of 1973.

Despite the effort to implement agricultural program changes in response to the explosion in food prices, it is essential to note here that the dimension of the ensuing problem of rising farm prices was seriously underestimated by the USDA, the Council of Economic Advisers, the Cost of Living Council, and private forecasters. The consensus forecast at the end of 1972 envisioned some mild farm price pressure (3% to 4%) through the summer, pressure which would subside when the new crop was harvested in the fall. It is obvious now that the Phase III regulatory scheme, based on the cost pass-through concept, was not able to prevent the rapid rise in food prices caused by higher farm level prices. The only effective actions which could have been taken to limit food price increases in the first half of 1973 would have had to have been implemented in 1972; e.g., reduced acreage controls to expand production (spring, 1972) and export restraints at the beginning of the crop year (fall, 1972). Having failed to take these politically unpopular steps in an election year, the alternatives available in 1973 were rigid price ceilings and export embargoes, which not only failed to stop food price increases for more than a few months but also created costly distortions, artificial shortages, and foreign relations problems.

Meat Ceilings

The retreat from the general policy of gradual decontrol of the economy through self-administration, which initiated the introduction of Phase III in January, began in the food industry with the imposition of meat ceilings on March 19, 1973. Meat ceilings were initiated during the period when the extension beyond April 30, 1973, of the Economic Stabilization Act was being reviewed by the Congress amid political pressure to "do something" about the quickening pace of food inflation following the switch from Phase II to Phase III. Many measures to freeze prices or roll them back were seriously discussed in the Congress. Since red meat prices were leading the surge in inflation and activist consumer groups were calling for a boycott of meat, meat prices seemed like an ideal target for some dramatic regulatory action by the Administration—a policy step short of the widening call for a more general freeze and tightening up of the regulations. Since red meat prices had already reached levels which provided more than sufficient incentive for meat producers to expand output, it was felt that placing ceilings at the levels achieved in March would not create any serious production distortions.

The establishment of ceiling prices for meat alone provided an opportunity to account more easily for the peculiarities of that industry in drafting the rules. The selection of an appropriate base period, the definition of meat products, and the requirements for freeze price posting could be addressed without the need to consider the peculiarities of other industries which would be the case if price ceilings were applied to the economy as a whole. The March base period was selected on the basis of the dynamics of the meat industry alone. This base period would not, for example, have been appropriate to the circumstances faced in the canned fruits and vegetables industry.

The raw agricultural product, fed cattle, was still exempt. The rationale for continuing that exemption rested on the large number of feed lots and perceptions regarding the competitive nature of primary cattle production. The theory was that ceilings at the retail/processor level would contribute to restraint on livestock prices.

Freeze II: June 13—July 18, 1973

The move from meat ceilings to Freeze II was rapid—meat ceilings on March 29, 1973, a general freeze on June 13, 1973. Public dissatisfaction with economic developments intensified in May 1973, exacerbated by a weak dollar and fears of shortages. Recognizing the impracticability of effectively dealing with these problems through changes in fiscal policy and the political unacceptability of a freeze limited to meat prices, the President instructed the Cost of Living Council staff to draft a plan to tighten Phase III. Nothing short of another freeze across the entire economy was acceptable to the President as being sufficiently dramatic or capable of having the required psychological and political impact. The regulatory provisions for the food industry in Freeze II were virtually identical to those promulgated during the 1971 Freeze. The second freeze, however, was implemented during the period immediately preceding rather than after the harvest which meant that the exempted raw agricultural prices were not only rising but reflected world-wide pressures on agricultural products that were not experienced in 1971. The tremendous pressure on ceiling prices caused by rising farm prices in 1973 was in sharp contrast with the 1971 Freeze period.

Phase IV: July 19, 1973—April 30, 1974

Although the second freeze was maintained on nonfood prices until August, the food industry was afforded a cost pass-through provision on July 18, 1973, in recognition of the fact that rapidly rising raw commodity prices were not controlled. The separate treatment for the food industry was granted to provide a transition stage between the Freeze and Phase IV. A transitional period was required to enable the controlled segments of the food industry to survive the tremendous cost pressures caused by rising raw agricultural commodities until a workable set of Phase IV rules could be devised. The Freeze of 1973 was beset by many problems caused by rapid increases in the prices of basic agricultural commodities; some of the more noteworthy examples were broilers, fresh vegetables, hogs, feed-grains, and soybeans, all basic ingredients in the process of producing finished consumable foods.

The key new regulatory feature of Stage A of Phase IV was a certification system which required firms at each point in the production and distribution process to certify, using appropriate invoices, that they had experienced the raw agricultural product cost increases needed to justify higher prices. While this certification process was viewed by many firms as administratively cumbersome, it was the only system known to the controllers and was designed as an interim feature far preferable to continued cost absorption implied by remaining under fixed ceiling prices.

Stage B of Phase IV marked the final evolution of a set of rules designed to regulate the food industry in a manner distinct from the rest of the economy. Those regulations provided for the continuing exemption of raw agricultural products. Although they were designed as a cost pass-through system, they were intended to be tighter than the control scheme employed during Phase II.

Phase IV rules were "tighter" in the sense that manufacturers were not allowed to maintain percentage margins over rising raw agricultural costs. The Stage B rules prohibited firms from widening the absolute dollar/cent difference between revenues and costs on a per unit basis. In order to maintain this cost/price relationship, of course, firms which were at their allowable revenue level were forced to lower prices when costs declined. As an offset, food manufacturers were not required to apply for and receive prior approval for price adjustments whenever their raw agricultural costs changed. Finally, Phase IV rules for food retailers/wholesalers were "looser" in the sense that they were allowed broader options for choice of base periods and category as opposed to item control. This latter point will be discussed in more detail below.

Three major conclusions can be drawn from this description of the evolution of a set of price regulations specifically designed for the food industry:

(1) In the beginning, food was not considered to be a troublesome sector, even though some of the industry's unique characteristics were recognized.

(2) The decision to exempt raw agricultural products made during the early phases of the Economic Stabilization Program remained operative throughout the program period, affecting the design of subsequent phases.

(3) The development of cost pass-through rules associated with Phase IV was the outgrowth of large food price increases in the spring of 1973, coupled with the accumulation of industry experience associated with prior phases.

ISSUES OF COST PASS-THROUGH REGULATORY SYSTEMS

Cost pass-through issues constituted the fabric of the regulatory scheme actually used in the periods of the Economic Stabilization Program when fixed price schemes were not in effect. Although the discussions of these issues within the Council and its staff, in advisory committees, and public hearings and written comments were highly technical and, consequently, of limited interest to the public and the press, the resolution of these issues had a significant impact on specific companies and the prices they charged. These issues were resolved quite differently as the program went through three phases. The changing degree of program "tightness" or "looseness" was largely determined by the outcome of the debate on these seemingly "technical issues."

A cost pass-through system of controls is based on the presumption that individual firms have the market power required to influence the relationship between the costs they incur and the prices they charge, i.e., their margins. The price regulations were designed to accomplish the limited objective of preventing firms from taking advantage of this market power by expanding margins to levels higher than some "competitive norm." The basic problem in implementing this concept is to determine a practical definition of "competitive norm." Throughout the program period, the regulations made the simplifying assumption that the margins earned during some past period (base period) were a useful proxy for the "competitive norm." The stated policy was to allow firms to raise prices to maintain their base period margins over costs throughout the Economic Stabilization Program except when prices were frozen.

The implementation of this general policy differed through the nonfreeze phases depending on the latitude given firms in choosing base periods for costs and prices, the definition of margins and allowable costs for price justification purposes, and the lag between the time when costs were incurred and the time when firms were permitted to raise their prices. Since the regulations applied quite differently to food manufacturers and food distributors (wholesalers and retailers), each of these implementation issues were resolved separately. The discussion will proceed by examining each segment of the food industry separately.

Manufacturing Regulations

Base Periods, Price, and Cost. The problem of determining appropriate formulas for measuring the movements of costs and prices was approached by requiring firms to calculate and report a price level based on the prices in effect during a "base period." This price was called the base price, and adjustments in allowable prices were measured from that level. Similarly, a period of time was also designated as the base-cost period. Firms would calculate cost changes from the level of costs established during the base-cost period.

The base price of a product or service was that price charged by a seller to a particular class of purchaser within the time frame specified. In Phases II and III, base periods for prices and costs were established in such a way as generally to account for the legal price and cost changes that had occurred since the beginning of the period. A chronology is outlined below:

	BASE PERIODS	
	Price	*Cost*
Phase I	Prices in effect (not necessarily charged) on at least 10% of sales made in the 30 days prior to August 15, 1971.	Not applicable since price adjustments were not allowed.
Phase II	Same as Phase I	Costs at the time the last price change was instituted prior to August 15, 1971.
Phase III	Authorized as of January 20, 1973.	Cost at the time the last price change was instituted before January 11, 1973.
Meat Ceiling	30 days prior to March 28, 1973.	Not applicable.
Second Freeze	June 1—June 8, 1973.	Not applicable.

Base price and cost periods took on a different significance during Phase IV. The regulatory scheme went through a major alteration which in effect made previously approved or instituted prices no longer relevant as the base level from which costs and price changes were to be measured.

In each of the prior phases the base periods were set to account for previous price levels; e.g., prices that were either approved or in effect during the base period. Price increases, then, were justified on the basis that costs had risen above levels on the *day* of the last price increase. The simplifying assumption was that all costs would have been captured in some normal sense at the time the last price increase was instituted. Since it was highly unlikely that prices and costs change on the same day, the Phase IV rules tried to approximate more closely the timing of relative cost/price movements in actual markets by widening the periods for measuring both base costs and prices. In addition, it became apparent to the controllers that regulations in Phases II and III would not be effective in dealing with cost decreases. The previous regulatory mechanisms would come into play only when the firm had requested a price increase (provided it did not exceed its profit margin limitation). During the planning for Phase IV, however, there was a strong expectation that agricultural costs were likely to decline from the levels achieved in the sharp increases in agricultural commodity prices in the spring and summer of 1973. In this context, a formula for dealing with these expected cost decreases was particularly relevant. The Phase IV scheme required monthly measurements of average cost changes from the base cost period as justification for the average prices charged during the compliance period. In this sense, firms were forced to follow costs down, when and if those costs declined. The history of agricultural commodity price declines in the fall of 1973 verified the expectations of the controllers.

It is also apparent that the determination of base price and cost periods can be juxtaposed to each other in such a way as to be more or less stringent. When prices are measured from one period and costs from another, it is conceivable that the firm can be placed in the intolerable situation where its prices will always be below its costs. This criticism was levied against the Phase IV rules. During the opening days of Phase IV, the relevant base price period was four consecutive fiscal quarters during the eight fiscal quarters ending prior to May 11, 1973. The base cost period was the fiscal quarter immediately following the base period. An example is outlined in Figure III-1.

Given the base price period selected in Figure III-1, the firm would prefer to measure cost increases from the level depicted by line 1 rather than from that at line 2. The regulations would permit a firm to use the cost increase from the line 2 level to the line 3 level as a basis for increasing prices from the base price level. The difference between lines 2 and 1 was denied to the firm. If costs actually did rise between the base periods for measuring revenues and cost, the firm would be denied some cost justification.

The reason for separating base cost and price periods was to prevent the double counting of costs caused by the necessity of allowing firms to measure labor cost increases on the basis of the difference between the labor rate in effect on the first day of the base cost period and the rate in effect on the last day of the current cost period. This rule for measuring labor costs meant that if the base period and the

FIGURE III-1.   BASE PERIOD IMPLICATIONS

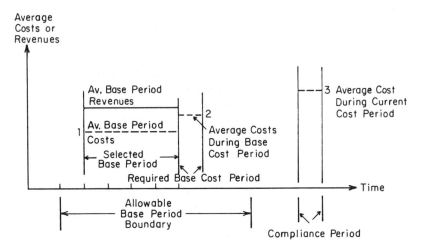

base cost period were to overlap, the firm would be able to count some of its labor cost increases twice.* Given the need to make quick decisions combined with the propensity to decide doubtful or ambiguous choices in favor of price restraint in Phase IV, it was decided initially to maintain the separation of the base period for establishing price levels from the base period for establishing cost levels before the implications were reviewed fully.

Because the cost justification procedures allowed revenues to be increased only by the amount of the increase in costs since the base cost period, whatever cost changes that occurred between the base price period and base cost period (the difference between lines 1 and 2 in Figure III-1) was lost for cost justification purposes. This result could have affected a particular firm in one of three ways:

(1) Those that had increased prices to account for any of those cost gaps would have lost those price increases, even though they would have been able to retain whatever revenues they had received prior to the current period.

(2) Those that had not increased prices would have received no credit for their efforts (intentional or unintentional) to keep prices from rising in spite of rising costs.

(3) In a few cases, firms experiencing declining costs between the two base periods and rising costs since the base cost period would have received a windfall because they could measure their cost increases from a lower base. Further, if they had failed to decrease prices in line with cost movements during the base period, they would also have been able to retain those "unjustified" prices.

---

* See Appendix III-2.

Although the double counting of labor costs was the main reason for separating the two base periods initially, the Council subsequently recognized that the proposed approach would force an unsustainable amount of cost absorption on many firms. When time finally permitted, the extensive analysis of commodity cost movements revealed that the majority of commodities could not be placed in any of the five possible base period base cost periods which would yield steady or declining raw material costs. There were, however, at least five commodities where at least one combination of base periods did yield declining raw material costs: cattle, corn, flour, milk, and soybean oil. In all other areas, the significant rise in commodity costs between each of the allowable base periods made it quite clear that many food manufacturers would have had to absorb costs to the extent that they would be forced to incur losses in order to abide by the regulations.

The Council decided in this instance to change the base cost period for food raw material to be coincident with the base period. This decision was able adequately to solve the problem of meat packers and processors of edible oils, but fruit and vegetable canning firms continued to have problems complying with the regulations even after this major modification. Two factors caused these problems: a large portion of canners' costs were not food raw material costs (as much as 60% to 70%). In some cases (e.g., meat packers), the nonfood proportion of the total was under 20%. Canners were confronted with seasonal packing periods during which they experienced the bulk of their costs for a particular product line. When this fact was coupled with the requirement to use only one base period base cost period for the entire firm, some canners were unable to find a base period in which they were not placed in a loss situation. Many found themselves in loss positions for some product lines. Because the circumstances of the canners were not a general phenomenon, the Council elected to treat those problems on an exceptions basis. Requests for exception were received from two major canners on those grounds. These requests were never granted because subsequent detailed analysis showed that the firms were not forced to absorb costs as claimed.

The length of time allowed for each period is another important aspect of base period definition. Food raw materials experience considerable seasonal fluctuations in price. Presumably, during a period of sufficient length, average raw material cost levels could be established which would absorb the disparities due to seasonal fluctuation. Because all firms do not follow the same practice for purchasing raw material, whatever the designated period of time (from which a base period of specified length is to be selected), it should be long enough to enable diverse firms to find a base period which they feel would provide a reasonable approximation to their raw material cost level.

In selecting a base period, firms had to consider the impact of several factors operating at the same time; the effect of ranging lengths of time between the base period and current period, the degree of price increase that had occurred in the interim, and changes in product mix and relative cost/price relationships between the compliance period and any base period. Since the time available to write regulations never was sufficient for the controllers to develop the detailed knowledge of industry structures, it was impossible to tailor regulations to fit the unique circumstances of each industry segment, much less those of individual firms. In the absence of such detailed knowledge, this discussion of choice and definition of base periods illustrates the degree to which the regulations can be written tightly or loosely depending on the directions in which the controllers seek to move at any given time.

Allowable Costs. The regulations need not permit all cost increases to be used as a justification for higher prices. Some cost increases within a firm or industry can be attributed to practices that may be inherently inflationary or may tend to exacerbate inflationary pressures resulting primarily from other casual factors. During a period in which a program is trying to moderate the rate of inflation, having given up its most effective and direct tool (control of raw agricultural prices), the question of allowable cost becomes extremely important. This question tended to be viewed by industry as one of providing sufficient documentation that a cost increase had been incurred. While controllers recognized that necessary documentation was part of the problem, it was not the entire problem. One illustrative issue relating to the allowability of cost increases arising from sales commissions will be reviewed here to provide another concrete example of the changing interpretation of regulations to reflect the degree of program tightness designed in different phases.

Bread delivery men and milk delivery men typically have labor contracts which include a percentage of the gross sales as compensation. The resolution of the issue of whether such compensation increases should be treated as allowable costs changed from Phase II to Phase IV. The Phase IV practice was more stringent, in that only those increases in commission expenses that were attributable to negotiated and Council approved increases in commission rates were permitted. In earlier phases, increases in commission expenses attributable to either volume or price increases were treated as wage increases and therefore could be used as allowable costs.

When this change in the interpretation of the regulation was instituted during Phase IV, a number of baking firms complained that partial allowance of commission expenses caused cost absorption they could ill afford. The Council's Phase IV interpretation was predicated upon two principles:

(1) Commission cost changes should be treated in the same way as labor cost changes, and allowed only to the extent that a rate change had actually occurred.
(2) The concept of limiting rising raw material costs to dollar-for-dollar pass-through would have been violated. In a situation of rising wheat

prices, higher bread prices could, in turn, be used to generate additional costs (commissions). The result would certainly be inconsistent with the stringent regulatory program desired in Phase IV.

The Council decided to continue its practice of allowing only that portion of commission expenses that was consistent with labor rate increases. This decision recognized the fact that bakers had to absorb some costs because their labor contracts with commission payments were inflationary. The Phase IV interpretation also illustrates that the definition of allowable costs can protect consumers from bearing the full brunt of price increases resulting from inflationary industry practices.

Formulas for Cost Pass-Through. Price regulations can allow firms to raise prices to reflect cost increases on either a dollar and cents or a percentage markup basis. The choice depends on the structure of the industry and the degree of program restrictiveness desired. The differences between these two formulas can be illustrated by the following example. Assume that there is an industry where roughly 80% of the product price is represented by allowable cost elements. The normal markup over costs is 25%, or 20 cents on every 80 cents of costs per unit. The same distinction can be made when margins are used for control purposes where margins are defined as the ratio of the difference between price and costs per unit divided by price. If costs increase by 40 cents, from 80 cents to $1.20 per unit, percentage markup maintenance would mean that the final product price would be allowed to increase to $1.50 per unit (a 25% markup over costs of $1.20 is 30 cents). A dollar and cents pass-through system would allow the product price to increase to $1.40 per unit, reflecting the simple addition of 40 cents cost increase to the base period price of $1.00 per unit. When costs are rising, the dollar and cents pass-through system is a more stringent control measure than that which allows percentage markup maintenance.

The differential impact of these two approaches on profit margins is apparent. Assuming that the firm can sell its product at the higher price allowed by percentage markup maintenance, that system will allow firms to earn greater absolute profits as costs rise. In this example, if the initial 20 cents markup over initial costs of 80 cents is considered to be profit, permitting prices to rise to $1.50 means that profitability, which is normally measured in percentage terms, remains constant ($.20/$1.00 = $.30/$1.50 = 20%). Under the dollar and cents pass-through system, the same 40-cent increase in costs leaves absolute profits unchanged at 20 cents while profitability declines ($.20/$1.00 = 20%; $.20 = $1.40 = 14%). On the other hand, when costs are declining the dollar and cents pass-through system preserves absolute profit levels and raises allowable profitability while the margin system forces allowable profits to decrease while again maintaining profitability. Under a scenario in which costs are moving unpredictably in both directions, a firm would have greater incentives to limit cost increases if it were operating under the dollar and cents system of controls. To the extent that costs are forecast to increase because of forces outside the control of individual firms (e.g., rising prices in world commodity markets), profitability can be squeezed by adopting a dollar and cents system of regulation.

Prenotification and Volatility. The principle of prenotification was applied throughout the program. It was generally well suited to application in nonfood manufacturing. Firms above a certain size were required to provide cost justification at least 30 days in advance of raising prices, giving the controllers an opportunity to audit, question, and accept/reject the supporting data. This feature was not very popular with any manufacturers, but food manufacturers were particularly disturbed. The delays associated with prenotification forced at least temporary if not permanent cost absorption, and it provided controllers with a very tempting device to force cost absorption by the simple administrative practice of requesting additional data, thereby further delaying price increases whenever public or political pressure so dictated. The administrative delays which caused significant cost absorption were viewed as particularly onerous and inequitable by manufacturers, particularly because of the arbitrary nature in which they could be applied. Administrative delay can be quite costly because if it is used to excess it results in a loss of support for the program by firms in general—a support which is recognized to be necessary for effective compliance with program regulations.

Food manufacturers argued that the volatile nature of raw agricultural prices made prenotification particularly onerous because they had to operate in volatile markets for the products they purchased and sold. Since raw commodity prices fluctuate daily, food manufacturers argued that they needed to make quick adjustments in their product prices. Their ability to respond quickly, in the view of the prenotification requirement, was stifled. The problem was particularly acute for meat packers. The initial solution to this problem was to allow firms to apply for "Volatile Pricing Authority" in advance. This authority enabled firms which qualified to provide cost justification of price increases, based on food raw material prices, after the fact. The Volatile Pricing Authority, however, only allowed firms to pass-through volatile costs on a dollar and cents basis.

Although the volatile pricing rule obviated the necessity for prenotification of those price changes that could be justified by changes in the cost of materials, it was not a panacea. There were numerous problems with administering it. There was no uniform set of standards for determining when volatile pricing authority was appropriate. The initiative for requesting and the burden for demonstrating the need for volatile price authority rested with the firm. Each firm was required to provide data on the price fluctuations that affected their own ability to comply with the regulations. The decisions to grant such authority were, consequently, made on a case-by-case basis. As of January 1973, there were 180 volatile pricing agreements covering 25 commodities. In addition to the absence of any clear criteria for determining who qualified for the volatile pricing authority, only the meat packing industry had a reasonably clear formula for determining price changes once such authority was granted. No special forms were devised to measure compliance with the provisions of volatile pricing authority in Phases II or III.

In Phase IV the problem was reduced markedly by the adoption of a gross margin formula similar in some respects to that devised to deal with volatility in meat prices in Phase III. Firms were allowed to adjust prices based on food raw material price increases automatically, without prior approval. Other costs, however, had to be prenotified. Whether or not firms prenotified other costs, the Phase IV regulations required firms to submit quarterly reports showing that their revenues and costs in the reporting period did not exceed the same relationship in the base period. Since this relationship had to be measured on an absolute dollar and cents basis for each category of products, there was a method for forcing compliance with the dollar and cents cost pass-through rule.

As we have indicated, the attractive feature of prenotification as a control device was that it provided an opportunity to review and veto, since it was the controllers who made the decisions on the allowability of costs and timing of price increases. It was also a feature that provided for at least a 30 to 60 day delay in the pass-through of costs. For a program whose life was never conceived of in more enduring terms than months, a 30 to 60 day delay can be significant. If the time period for prenotification had been increased, the cost absorption impact could have been more severe.

Special Regulations for Retailers and Wholesalers

The high volume and large number of items handled by retailers and wholesalers prevented the application of the dollar and cents cost pass-through approach to regulation because it would require the allocation of overhead expenses to individual items or groups of items. Such an allocation would, under most circumstances, be administratively difficult and highly arbitrary. Consequently, Phase II regulations for retailers and wholesalers adopted the percentage markup principle. This principle for retailers and wholesalers remained in effect through the duration of the Economic Stabilization Program.

The rules were designed to allow these firms to mark up costs of merchandise purchased at their historical rate which was supposed to be sufficient to cover other expenses such as rent and utilities which were also rising. The historical rate was called the customary initial percentage markup and was applied to the purchase price of material inputs plus freight charges and fixed at base period levels.

Firms controlled by the percentage markup method could obtain greater profits per unit whenever costs of merchandise rose faster than other costs or gross profits could be increased by increasing the volume of sales and holding margins constant. It was presumed that additional gross margins earned through increasing either merchandise costs or volume would be sufficient to cover increases in either overhead or labor. These firms were also subject to profit margin limitations.

As experience was accumulated with this system of control, a number of problems developed in the implementation of the program:

> Although it varied over the program period, about one-half of the 30 largest food retailers were never forced to price in order to remain within their customary markups because they qualified for loss/low profit treatment. The basic requirement for qualifying for such exemption was a low return on equity. The limited number of food retailers forced to abide by the regulations introduced the possibility of havoc in some individual geographical markets. The Internal Revenue Service (the enforcement arm of the Cost of Living Council) attempted to get firms to agree to item-by-item control, which in many cases reduced pricing flexibility of retailers and forced increased prices on those products which were under inflationary pressure.

> Many firms claimed that the lack of choice of base periods to determine customary markups did not permit sufficient additional revenues to cover rising nonmerchandise expenses.

Each of these problems is discussed below.

Base Periods for Determining Customary Initial Percentage Markups. Some of these retail/wholesale problems were largely addressed in program modifications. Food retailers were given a longer time frame from which to select base periods in Phase IV (either of the last two fiscal years ending before February 5, 1973). This greater flexibility in base period selection was designed to help them find base margins which were more in line with historical norms. During 1972 the food industry had gone through a period of price discounting, spurred mainly by the effort of the A&P program to recapture a greater share of the market. Table III-1 illustrates the extent to which profit margins were actually depressed during this period. The historical profit performance of the food retail industry depicted in this table illustrates the dangers inherent in refusing to tailor the administrative rules of the stabilization program to the dissimilar characteristics and historical performance of various segments of a broadly aggregated industry.

So far as overhead costs outstripping merchandise input costs under the customary initial percentage markup system, 1973 proved to be a year of such high merchandise cost increases that the Phase II overhead problem was diminished. In 1974 overhead costs rose more rapidly than merchandise costs. If the program had been continued, it might have been necessary to change the regulatory approach again. The fact that the theoretical efficacy of a particular control

TABLE III-1.   PROFIT RATES AFTER FEDERAL INCOME TAXES OF FOOD
RETAILERS ANNUAL 1964–1974, QUARTERLY 1973–1974 (IN PERCENTAGES)

| | Return on Stockholder's Equity | | Return on Sales | |
Year	(15 leading firms)	(excluding A&P)	(15 leading firms)	(excluding A&P)
1964	11.5		1.3	
1965	11.3		1.3	
1966	11.4		1.3	
1967	10.3		1.1	
1968	10.3		1.1	
1969	10.4		1.1	
1970	10.6	11.7	1.0	
1971	9.6	11.7	.9	1.1
1972	5.1	8.4	.5	.8
1973	8.2	9.6	.7	.8
1974	4.8	11.1	.4	.9

SOURCE: Compiled from *Moody's Industrial Manual.* Two series are shown for the years 1970–1974 because of the low profit levels of A&P in that time period.

device is likely to be found wanting when it is applied to an industry under different circumstances, none of which accurately fits the average parameters on which the theory was based, serves to underscore the need for administrative flexibility in adapting theory to the practical world and individual industry conditions.

Category Versus Item Control. In consonance with the increased flexibility in base period selection, the level of product aggregation at which controls were applied gave retailers more pricing flexibility as the program progressed through its several phases. Phase II regulations provided incentives for firms to choose to be regulated on an item-by-item basis to make compliance enforcement easier and more publicly visible. The item-by-item control of Phase II was relaxed in Phase III to allow for a broader aggregation of items, which in turn was replaced by a single store-wide category scheme in Phase IV. This question had long been a complicated one. The item-by-item approach contrasted with schemes with fewer categories, each of which included a large number of individual items (e.g., produce) representing varying degrees of tightness. The consuming public's interface with controls in the retail store created a strong temptation to devise a system of visible item-by-item controls. However, the possibility of item-by-item control was complicated by the nearly 8,000 items that appear in the typical retail store. The Phase II rules provided for exceptions to item control, and in Phase III those provisions were formalized. Items were accounted for in Phase III by broadly common categories: meat, produce, dairy, and groceries. Controls paralleled these general product groupings. During Phase IV, however, the dismal profit performance in the retail sector in 1972 and early 1973 coupled with requests for pricing flexibility (the ability to shift costs among categories) to deal with extraordinary rises in meat prices, led to the adoption of a single store-wide category for all merchandise in the retail food store.

Even if one were to discount the poor profit performance of retailers in 1972, the trade-off between item-by-item and category control must be made carefully. The administrative problems of tracking costs and prices on 8,000 retail items are considerable; yet that type of control would inevitably come closer to regulating the price movements of particular items in accordance with price fluctuations in the raw material components of those items. Category control more closely parallels the normal marketing behavior of retailers and tends to dampen the retail price impact of rapid fluctuations caused by individual raw material. It is much easier to administer but may quickly take on the appearance of no controls at all in public perceptions.

The issue of item-by-item versus category control is illustrative of the general problem faced by the designers of a control scheme. Mainly, the choice lies between tailoring a control scheme which parallels normal industry practices and one which the public perceives as being "tough" even though it may have a perverse effect on either the actual or the perceived rates of inflation. Typical retailer pricing behavior tends to moderate the relatively abrupt swings in prices of individual raw agricultural products. Raw egg prices are, for example, quite volatile. When raw egg prices go up by ten cents a dozen, the typical retailer marks up egg prices by something less than ten cents. Egg cost increases are then offset partially by raising prices of other items, resulting in little if any cost absorption by the retailer. Food retailers argue that consumers find this practice much more acceptable than one in which retail egg prices would rise and fall in proportion to the change in egg prices at the farm level. It should be noted, however, that this retail pricing pattern is quite short term in nature. If egg prices at the farm level continue to rise over time, retail prices will eventually reflect this trend.

Regulations based on category pricing allowed retailers to follow traditional pricing practices which consumers presumably find acceptable under normal circumstances. Item-by-item control, on the other hand, is much more visible and is much more conducive to compliance checking. In addition, item-by-item control may be "tougher" in that retailers may not be able to increase prices of individual items (eggs) because market demand and competition may not permit them to increase prices by an amount equal to the cost increase in the short run. Consequently, if retailers are not allowed to use the rise in cost of one item to justify increasing the price of another, they may have to absorb these cost increases, thereby lowering the rate of inflation. This must be weighted against the consumer's perception of the rate of inflation which is very sensitive to the rate of price changes on individual items frequently purchased (eggs).

It must be repeated, however, that retail profits represent a very small percentage of the food price pressure experienced during the stabilization period during which retail profit margins were low by historical standards and represented less than 1% of the total cost of consumer food expenditures.

Cost Decreases. In addition to the question of program toughness in Phase IV, there was a continuing concern during the entire program about how and to what degree firms were to be required to reduce prices in light of cost decreases. Although the concept of cost-justified price increases included the notion that prices should be reduced when costs decreased, the development of a stringent set of rules to require these decreases did not take place until the adoption of the Phase IV gross margin formula based on the concept of dollar and cents pass-through. Prior to Phase IV there was a tendency for pre-viously approved and implemented price increases to become minimum prices. This result was not so disturbing until the large raw material price increases in the spring of 1973 required the controllers to consider explicitly ways to induce cost absorption.

One form of cost decrease that was adopted early in the program (during Phase II) and remained throughout was the requirement that firms offset labor cost increases by labor productivity increases. The regulation concerning labor productivity adopted in Phase II stipu-lated that productivity gains had to be taken into account in the calculation of all cost increases during any fiscal year, and that the full offset for productivity must be satisfied before any cost increase could be used to justify higher prices. As Phase II moved through Phase III, and a second freeze to Phase IV, more than one fiscal year elapsed for a number of firms between the base cost period and current period. Multiple fiscal years raised the question of whether cost increases had to be reduced by more than one productivity offset. This question also stirred quite a bit of controversy because multiple productivity offsets could have had the impact of forcing price decreases. There were four realistic alternatives that had to be evaluated:

(1) One productivity offset for each whole or fractional fiscal year since the end of base cost period.
(2) One offset for each whole or fractional year between the beginning of base cost period and the end of current cost period.
(3) One offset for each whole or fractional calendar year since the begin-ning of the base cost period.
(4) Fractional offsets in proportion to the number of fiscal quarters since the beginning of the base cost period (number of quarters/4).

The Council staff's analysis of the impact of these alternatives on permissible revenues established that none of them deducted sig-nificantly more than 100% of the revenue gain attributable to productivity increases. However, the second alternative proved most stringent, taking 100% more frequently, while the fourth alternative proved more lenient, usually taking less than 75% of the gain. The Council adopted the third alternative as a moderate posture that was also consistent with previously established interpretations.

The underlying rationale for either of the alternative offset treatments rested on the view that labor productivity gains were in effect cost decreases that had been experienced during the preceding year. Firms were forced to use average industry productivity increases (average annual gains based on a 12-year period prior to the onset of controls). This offset proved to be an irritant to many firms because they denied that they had in fact experienced such increases in productivity. The Council's view was that some firms experienced gains in excess of the industry average, while others gained less than the industry average.

The offset rule was viewed by the Council as an incentive to higher productivity levels. Businessmen objected to the rulings on productivity, regardless of the rationalizations espoused for exacting offsets, because the primary incentive for raising productivity is potential increases in profits. They wanted to maintain the option of using productivity increases to reduce prices, raise wages, or increase profits. In a regulatory framework looking for ways to lower the rate of price increase, productivity offsets provided another available tool for lowering the rate of price increase whenever the controllers wanted to use it.

This section on the technical aspects of implementation issues should be concluded by highlighting the degree of latitude provided the framers of any price regulation system to design and implement that system in a variety of degrees of restrictiveness.

Any regulatory scheme designed to allow prices to move upward to reflect cost increases continually raises issues concerning the degree to which cost absorption should be required. The officially stated policy followed by the Council was to permit prices to rise to reflect all fully justified cost increases, provided that historical profit margins were not exceeded. There were, however, several alternative policies which were considered and sporadically employed during the course of the program. During Phase II and Phase III, a degree of cost absorption was forced through prenotification requirements and other delay tactics, requirements somewhat arbitrarily and implicitly imposed. This form of cost absorption was not the result of planned attempts to achieve some specified level of price restraint but was the consequence of regulatory decisions taken on other grounds. Essentially, three alternatives to force cost absorption were considered at different times during the program:

(1) Formulas for partial pass-through of costs:
    (a) limitations on allowable costs; e.g., exclusion of some parts of bread deliverymen's compensation and exclusion;

   (b) dollar for dollar instead of percentage margin maintenance when
       costs were rising; and
   (c) fractional pass-through; i.e., only some portion of cost increases
       would be allowed.
(2) Limiting price increase on the basis of other rationale:
   (a) prospects for declining costs associated with transitional events;
       e.g., seasonal increase in agricultural commodity costs; and
   (b) lengthening the 30-day prenotification period to allow for more
       thorough analysis.
(3) Negotiated absorption.

With the exception of the adoption of the dollar and cents cost
pass-through alternative in exchange for the lifting of prenotification
requirements in Phase IV, none of the other alternatives was formally
adopted in the food industry. Some of these others, such as fractional
cost pass-through in the automotive industry, were adopted in specific
cases. Of course, virtually every firm that had to abide by the prenotification requirements would claim that the controllers arbitrarily
lengthened the prenotification period by requesting that additional
data be supplied by firms seeking price increase approvals. Indeed,
the basic reason that staff recommendations to employ one or more of
the alternatives to limit cost pass-through outlined above were rejected by Council members was in order to reduce the degree of
discretion already possessed by over-zealous controllers at the staff
level.

Summary and Conclusions

   The evolution of a regulatory system for price control in the food
industry as described here, with the benefit of a historical perspective,
might leave the reader with the misapprehension that it was a system
rationally designed and improved over the two and a half years of the
Economic Stabilization Program. Nothing could be further from the
truth since the evolution could more accurately be described as somewhat arbitrary and subject to rapid changes. The countervailing political pressures caused by consumers and their representatives complaining about the spurts in food prices in the face of the existence of
controls and by food and agriculture industry representatives dis-
tressed about the inability to pass-through rising costs caused frequent changes in the regulations and program policies.
   The behavior of food prices as measured by the Consumer Price
Index rose over 14% per year during the two full years in which
controls were in effect. The history of the period is further depicted
by the data shown in Table III-2 which summarizes the changes in
costs eminating at the farm, wholesale/manufacture, and retail levels
during the various phases and freezes of the Economic Stabilization
Program as well as the periods immediately preceding and following

TABLE III-2.   MOVEMENT IN MARKET BASKET STATISTICS BEFORE AND DURING
ECONOMIC STABILIZATION PROGRAM (SEASONALLY ADJUSTED
ANNUAL RATES IN PERCENTAGES)

Period	Retail Cost	Farm-Retail Spread	Farm Value
8 months prior to Phase I			
(January 1 to August 1971)	3.9	4.3	8.9
Phase I			
(August to November 1971)	3.2	−6.4	14.0
Phase II			
(November 1971 to January 1973)	8.4	1.5	17.4
Phase III			
(January to June 1973)	20.6	12.2	37.2
Phase IV[a]			
(June 1973 to April 1974)	18.1	26.9	7.4
During controls			
(August 1971 to April 1974)	14.4	10.8	19.7
6 months after termination of			
controls (April to October 1974)	5.0	3.7	8.6

[a] Including a general price freeze from June 8 to July 9.

NOTE: The market basket contains the average quantities of domestic, farm-originated food products purchased annually per household in 1960 and 1961 by wage earners and clerical worker families and workers living alone. Its retail cost is calculated from retail prices published by the Bureau of Labor Statistics. The farm value is the gross return to farmers for the farm products equivalent to foods in the market basket. The farm-retail spread (difference between the retail cost and farm value) is an estimate of the total gross margin received by marketing firms for assembling, processing, transporting, and distributing the products in the market basket.

SOURCE: Marvin H. Koster, *Controls and Inflation; The Economic Stabilization Program in Retrospect,* Washington: American Enterprise Institute for Public Policy Research, p. 78.

it. Three salient observations can be made on the basis of the data shown in this table:

(1) Food prices rose faster during the August 1971 to April 1974 period than either before or after the Economic Stabilization Program. This was also true for each phase of the program with the exception of the first freeze in 1971 when farm prices actually fell slightly (0.8%) although they rose on the seasonally adjusted basis shown in the table.

(2) Food price inflation was led by the rise in costs at the farm level which out-paced cost increases at other levels of the food processing/marketing chain.

(3) The regulations did not prevent costs emanating at the production/distribution level from being passed through to the consumer. This should not be surprising since the regulations were designed to control the relationship between costs and prices. The only times when prices themselves were controlled were the brief periods when price ceilings were imposed, forcing firms to absorb temporarily any increase in costs. These ceiling prices or freeze periods never lasted more than a few months.

(4) The principal cause of cost pressures on food prices changed dramatically over the course of the program, especially during Phase IV when the rate of increase in the farm-retail spread was higher than the rise at farm and retail levels.

Although Table III-2 shows what happened to food costs during the Economic Stabilization Program, it would be misleading to draw conclusions from these data alone about the effectiveness of the regulatory scheme employed in Phases II, III, and IV. It should be kept in mind "that the farm-retail spread is a measure of differences in prices only at two levels of the marketing system while profit is a measure of the differences between revenue and outlays by firms providing selected marketing services."[10] The explicit policy of the program throughout Phases II through IV was to allow firms to pass-through all costs, whether they originated in the exempt agricultural sector or in the non-exempt sectors of the economy providing items such as packaging material, freight and utility services, and labor inputs to food processors and distributors. An estimate of the change in the two major components of the nonagricultural costs of processing and distributing food is shown in Table III-3.

The rates of increase in costs of nonagricultural inputs began to escalate dramatically with the termination of Freeze II on the general

TABLE III-3.   MOVEMENTS IN COMPONENTS OF THE FARM-RETAIL SPREAD: 1970–1974 (CHANGES IN PERCENTAGES AT ANNUAL RATES)

Year and Quarter	Intermediate Goods and Services[a]	Hourly Earnings of Employees[b]
1970	6.2	6.7
1971	6.2	6.9
1972	5.0	6.5
1973	6.5	6.1
1974	18.7	9.0
1973		
I	6.4	8.2
II	12.9	5.7
III	6.1	3.3
IV	12.3	9.0
1974		
I	24.9	11.1
II	20.3	10.8
III	31.6	9.4
IV	10.0	10.3

[a] Excluded wages.
[b] Weighted composite of production employees in food manufacturing and nonsupervisory employees in wholesale and retail trade, calculated from data of the Department of Labor.
SOURCE: USDA, *Marketing and Transportation Situation*, MTS-195, various issues in 1974 and 1975.

economy during the third quarter of 1973. The regulations permitted these costs to be passed through to the consumer, with food manufacturers being allowed to maintain percentage margins under virtually the same rules in Phase IV that had existed in Phases II and III.

It will be recalled that the Phase IV regulations for food manufacturers were designed to be more restrictive by limiting the pass-through of agricultural costs to a dollar and cents basis. Consequently, one important reason why these "tougher" rules did not have the impact intended was that the underlying causes of the pressure on food prices shifted from the rising farm prices to other sectors of the economy.

The data shown in Table III-4 illustrate that food manufacturers were able to maintain their historical rates of profitability throughout the entire period of controls. They were also able to increase their profit margins in Phase IV, even during the third quarter of 1973 including the second freeze and the highly restrictive Stage A of Phase IV. This expansion in margins during Phase IV was possible under the regulations which permitted percentage margin maintenance because the rapid rise in nonagricultural costs could be used to justify much higher prices. The slight improvement in return on sales in the October 1973 to March 1974 period could easily be explained by changes in product mix. The more significant increases in both measures of profitability in the last half of 1974 cannot be attributed to a post-control program explosion in prices following pent-up cost pressures because the margin maintenance shown in Table III-4 clearly implies that food manufacturers were not forced to absorb costs during the Economic Stabilization Program.

Aggregate profit margin data for 15 leading food retailers presented in Table III-1 above show a clear decline in the rate of profitability during the stabilization period. Whether these margins were reduced by the controls themselves cannot be demonstrated conclusively because of the impact of the A&P discount price program during the early parts of the period. The data for rates of return to the leading retailers, excluding A&P, show a less significant decline during 1972 and 1973. Subsequent analysis conducted by the Federal Trade Commission indicates that competitive pressure of the A&P discount price program reduced the profitability of stores competing directly with A&P.[11] It is, of course, entirely conceivable that margins of individual retailers (as well as manufacturers) could well have been larger in the absence of controls.

Although one cannot end conclusively the debate about the extent to which controls were employed in an effective manner, the weight of evidence presented above provides further support for earlier statements that the food price inflation which characterized the 1972–1974 period was caused principally by rapidly rising agricultural prices. Direct controls on prices were neither designed nor able to prevent these costs from being eventually passed-through to the consumer.

TABLE III-4. PROFIT RATES AFTER FEDERAL INCOME TAXES OF FOOD
AND OTHER MANUFACTURERS, ANNUAL 1964–1974,
QUARTERLY 1973–1974 (IN PERCENTAGES)

Year	Percentage Return on Stockholders Equity		Percentage Return on Sales	
	All Food Manufacturing	All Manufacturing	All Food Manufacturing	All Manufacturing
1964	10.1	11.7	2.7	5.2
1965	10.7	13.1	2.7	5.6
1966	11.3	13.6	2.7	5.6
1967	10.9	11.8	2.6	5.0
1968	10.8	12.2	2.6	5.1
1969	10.9	11.5	2.6	4.8
1970	10.8	9.3	2.5	4.0
1971	11.0	9.7	2.6	4.1
1972	11.2	10.6	2.6	4.7
1973	12.8	12.6	2.6	4.7
1974	13.9	14.9	2.9	5.5
1973				
Jan–Mar	10.8	11.6	2.4	4.5
Apr–June	12.3	14.0	2.6	5.1
July–Sept	13.3	12.3	2.7	4.6
Oct–Dec	14.7(15.0)	13.4(14.3)	2.8(3.0)	4.7(5.6)
1974				
Jan–Mar	12.4	14.3	2.7	5.6
Apr–June	12.8	16.7	2.7	6.0
July–Sept	15.4	15.4	3.2	5.7
Oct–Dec	14.7	13.2	3.0	4.8

SOURCE: Compiled from "Quarterly Financial Report for Manufacturing Corporations" published by the Federal Trade Commission. Data for 1974 are imperfectly comparable with prior data because of significant changes in accounting methods. Statistics were collected by both the old and new methods for the fourth quarter of 1973. Ratios for the new method are shown in parentheses.

CHAPTER IV

Wage Stabilization in the Food Industry

William M. Vaughn, III

WILLIAM M. VAUGHN, III

William M. Vaughn, III is currently the director of personnel, corporate services, The Stop and Shop Companies, Inc. He served as executive director of the food division, Office of Wage Stabilization, Cost of Living Council, from April 1973 until June 1974. He was also deputy administrator of the Office of Wage Stabilization from March 1974 to June 1974.

During the period of Phase I and Phase II of controls, and prior to joining the Cost of Living Council, Mr. Vaughn worked for the Stop and Shop Companies, Inc., in applying the regulations for this retail firm.

Mr. Vaughn has a Ph.D. in Economics from Massachusetts Institute of Technology and has taught economics and labor relations at the Graduate School of Business, University of Chicago, 1968–1971.

CHAPTER IV

Wage Stabilization in the Food Industry

THIS CHAPTER deals with the wage stabilization aspect of price and wage regulation in the period August 15, 1971, to April 30, 1974.[1] Particular attention is concentrated on the experience of the Tripartite Food Industry Wage and Salary Committee (to be referred to as the Committee), which functioned from February 26, 1973, until April 30, 1974. While much of the experience discussed is applicable to the entire food industry, this chapter concentrates on the retail food industry sector. The reasons are twofold: this is where the author had most experience, and this is where most of the more complex problems and issues arose.

This chapter has two major objectives. First, it seeks to provide more evidence on some of the issues of wage stabilization that have been raised before, during, and after every attempt at wage stabilization in the United States. These issues include:

(1) Can wage stabilization be effective by controlling just the large units?
(2) Can a single number or standard constitute effective wage stabilization?
(3) Is dispute settlement an integral part of wage stabilization?
(4) Does price control necessitate wage control?
(5) Should a stabilization program be administered by a tripartite body or an all-public body?

These issues, which have been extensively discussed elsewhere,[2] are set forth here as an integral part of the story of the Committee's efforts at wage stabilization. Second, this chapter attempts to suggest through the Committee experience some of the practical problems that any stabilization program must confront.

The term "wage stabilization" will be used extensively in this chapter. Unfortunately, depending on the context, the term may have different meanings. As used here, the term will always include salary and fringe benefits, such as vacation, holiday, pension, and sick leave. The term may also include work rules and dispute settlement activities if these are judged to be part of the stabilization activity. In short, the term "wage stabilization" can only be given meaning in this chapter by the context in which it is used.[3]

This chapter is divided into four sections. The first section describes the economic background and industry characteristics which serve as a backdrop for the Tripartite Food Industry Wage and Salary Committee. The second section briefly traces the control periods prior to the Committee's formation. The third section portrays the Committee in action. The final section attempts to evaluate the food wage stabilization experience, list some of the lessons that were learned, and discuss some unresolved questions flowing out of that experience.

THE ECONOMIC AND INDUSTRIAL RELATIONS BACKGROUND

All during Phase II food was perhaps the biggest problem for the price stabilization program. Food prices rose rapidly, responding to crop conditions, foreign demand arising from widespread prosperity in the Western World, and the sale of grain to the Soviet Union.

This situation held clear implications for wage stabilization. As a major component in the average wage earner's budget, rapidly rising food prices stimulate wage demands throughout the economy. Wage earners, including those in the food industry itself, were particularly cognizant of and sensitive to rapidly rising food prices. Public and governmental attention focused on the food industry. Political and consumer pressures in late 1972 were demanding action on food prices. Since wages are a significant component of food prices, particularly at retail, and it would be difficult to regulate prices without restraints on compensation, the political and public concern over food price increases was reflected in the need for a wage stabilization program in the food sector.

The markets for retail food and associated labor constitute a difficult setting in which to control wages. The retail food product market is very competitive. The products sold are essential and in the main basically nonpostponable in sale and purchase. Food stores, even though they may offer neighborhood convenience, are highly substitutable in consumers' minds. These basic factors, in their cumulative impact, put pressures on collective bargaining in the retail food industry.

The industry is characterized by low profit margins per dollar of sales. Furthermore, labor is the largest "controllable" expense item in the food industry. In 1974, for retail firms, total payroll and fringe benefits constituted 67% of all expenses other than the cost of goods sold.[4] In food wholesaling, the figures were comparable (56%).[5] (Cost of goods sold is of course the dominant expense for retailers and wholesalers in the food industry. In 1974 cost of goods sold for wholesalers was 93% of all expenses).[6] Also, in 1971 nonsupervisory workers accounted for almost 90% of the employees in the retail food industry.[7] Hence, labor costs, especially wage levels, have a significant impact on the food industry's profitability and price level.

Other features of the industry influence the wage-setting process. Food retailers in any given market generally include a mix of local firms and "national firms" such as A&P, Safeway, and Kroger. Local firms have most of their operations in a few localities while national firms spread their risks over many areas. Also, the presence of national firms in any one market means that wage and benefit settlements elsewhere may influence directly the particular local labor market.

Many food retailers also own and operate nonfood retail establishments. In 1967, multi-industry companies in the food industry, while less than 1% of the total companies, accounted for over 50% of employment.[8] This meant that when Phase III left food employees under mandatory controls with pre-approval necessary for pay increases, a food retailer's nonfood employees were not subject to the same detailed pre-approval requirements and procedures. To the extent that the firm had a consistent and coordinated wage policy for both its food and nonfood employees, with similarity in the timing of any adjustments, issues of relative equity for food employees were made the more severe. Also, it is generally true that intense competition in the food industry in both the product and labor markets operates against permissible cooperation with competitors. There had been no industry effort to collect information on wage rates, compensation practices, or other data that might have proved helpful to the wage stabilization effort. There were no industry-wide procedures to coordinate company or union collective bargaining policies nationally. Furthermore, retail food unions sometimes compete for the same members during organizing campaigns. These factors not only complicated the wage stabilization process but also the attempt to form and operate a food industry committee composed of labor and management representatives.

Retail food employees are relatively high paid among retail trade sectors. In January 1973 average hourly earnings for nonsupervisory workers on private nonagricultural payrolls was $3.77; in retail trade it was $2.78; and in grocery, meat, and vegetable stores it was $3.20. In June 1975, the figures were $4.50 (private); $3.33 (retail trade); and $4.01 (grocery, meat, etc.). The norms for comparison outside the retail food sector are thus controversial, one side referring to industry generally and the other to retail trade.[9]

The level of average hourly earnings in retail food stores is affected by the prevalence of part-timers in the sector. Geographical variations as well as substantial differences in wages by the size of grocery companies contribute to the over-all average level. It is also true, however, that virtually every high-paid occupation (carpenter, truck driver, plumber, electrician, mechanic, etc.) can be found in small numbers in the food industry, often employed directly by the retail company. These workers, especially where organized, often receive the prevailing area wages. Hence, while the average wage level in the retail food sector may be relatively low (as compared with the level in other industries), the existence of high wage workers working side by side with lower wage workers complicates wage setting.

The unions in the retail food industry are several. The Teamsters, Retail Clerks, and Meat Cutters are, by far, the most important and prevalent, but almost any union can be found either in the retail food industry or possibly exerting an influence on workers in the retail food industry. Union jurisdictions are often not well defined, and it is common to find retail establishments organized entirely by either the Retail Clerks or Meat Cutters, and, in at least some cases, the Teamsters. Other firms can have Retail Clerks in the front end of the stores and Meat Cutters in the back of the stores, creating the need for jurisdictional boundaries inside the store and the possibility of different contract expiration dates and leapfrogging.

Furthermore, the degree of unionization in the retail food industry is varied. Good statistics are not available, but the Cost of Living Council estimated that the production employees in the retail food industry in 1974 were approximately 70% organized. In 1964 the Super Market Institute, based on a survey, reported that 58% of the companies in the industry were organized. However, only 20% of the companies in the Southeast and 36% in New England were organized while 100% and 69% were organized in the Pacific and West North Central regions respectively. Also, part-timers had the lowest degree of organization while warehousemen and truckmen had the highest.[10]

Bargaining is decentralized with small units being the norm. Bargaining in local product markets is often not coordinated with other unions or other employers. Also, as stated above, local firms—"independents"—are often picked by the unions to be pattern setters in negotiations since they have more at stake and possibly, therefore, would be less willing to resist or more willing to settle.[11] (The fact that there were many firms and many unions and hence, many, many more "appropriate employee units" added also to the administrative burdens connected with governmental wage stabilization.) Finally, local settlements can spread rapidly across labor markets or craft lines, constantly putting pressure on the wage level and creating ample opportunities to distort traditional wage relationships.

The prevalence of part-timers in the industry with their short duration of employment has put added pressure for increased wages on the bargaining table. In 1974, 46% of employees in the supermarket industry were part-time employees.[12] They are a factor in contract ratification (and union elections). Fringe benefit payments for these part-timers are expensive given their normal short duration of employment. Furthermore, the presence in the industry of well-compensated union employees, such as Teamster drivers under the Master Freight Agreement, has brought additional pressure to the bargaining table for "improved conditions" for all food industry employees, including part-timers.

Job security has become a significant issue in the industry. The prevalence and growth of part-time employees have been viewed as a threat to full-time jobs. Also, the threat of automation in the form of centralized meat cutting ("break down" of meat in a central location rather than in store back rooms) and automated front ends (computerized cash registers with scanning devices doing the "checking out," thus eliminating, partially at least, the need for clerks to price the items individually) have made job security and the ability to automate important issues in negotiations.[13]

All these factors, cumulatively, compounded the problems involved in trying to achieve a measure of wage stabilization in the retail food industry, particularly in a period of rapidly rising food prices. These very factors, however, convinced concerned individuals of the need to improve the structure and performance of collective bargaining in the industry.

THE LEGACY OF PRIOR PHASES OF STABILIZATION

The Tripartite Food Industry Wage and Salary Committee's efforts to stabilize wages in the food industry were also influenced by the legacy of wage stabilization administration and policies in the period from August 1971 to January 1973.[14,15]

Phase I and Freeze I: August 15, 1971—November 13, 1971

Freeze I is well-known. It was the program—comprehensive in coverage and covering virtually all wage earners—that, *for a short period of time,* was the easiest to administer, for all questions concerning increases could be answered by "no," since nearly all prices and wages had to remain at or below levels that existed on August 15, 1971—the date the Freeze was imposed. The Freeze, by its very nature and specific design, had to be a short-run program. While prices and wages in most markets were frozen, some, notably commodity and stock markets, were not. Interest rates as well as import prices also were not frozen. Furthermore, any freeze on a specific date was bound to catch transactions in various stages of completion. It is inevitable, therefore, in a dynamic economy that a freeze is bound to create distortions and inequities that grow with the passage of time. The Freeze also introduced the Internal Revenue Service as "stabilization agents" that developed strong opposition from the labor movement, and it made the public familiar with the Federal Register as a source of complex regulations.

The Freeze provided examples of the arbitrariness and inequity of wage changes being allowed or not allowed by reference to a single freeze date. It also produced the first examples of "game playing" with the regulations. Conflicting IRS interpretations were encountered at local levels and "experienced game players" began to learn the rules and where to go to get more favorable answers to their questions. Because of its seeming success, controls were regarded increasingly as the answer to the nation's inflation problems.

Phase II: November 14, 1971—January 10, 1973

The Freeze was followed by a more flexible program. Phase II, as enunciated by the policy makers, had at least four other features. First, Phase II was to be short in duration. It was viewed as an emergency expedient and only a small bureaucracy was to be created to administer it. Second, no structural reforms in the labor market or in the structure of collective bargaining were considered. Third, controls were intended to discourage inflationary expectations. As a result, they came to have a strong public relations orientation. Delay was probably used as an instrument of policy, and on the wage side prime attention was concentrated on big employee units. Fourth, the goal was to keep the labor movement involved in the program. As a result, President Nixon signed the "Meany" memorandum which guaranteed the independence of the Pay Board in policy areas.[16] Hence, while Phase II had a Pay Board and a Price Commission with the Cost of Living Council functioning as an overseeing body, the Pay Board's independence was promised as a condition of labor's involvement.[17] These features of Phase II had implications for the Committee's efforts following the end of Phase II.

Besides these policy features, Congress imposed certain mandates upon the policy makers during Phase II. Special consideration had to be given to small businesses, to certain fringe benefits called "qualified benefits" which were essentially pension and health and welfare benefits, and to certain "low wage " employees.

Furthermore, the focus of Phase II was not on wage stabilization so much as on controlling labor costs. This followed from the primary emphasis in Phase II to control or to moderate the increase in prices. The Pay Board allowed without further approval increases in wages and salaries of 5.5% (plus 0.7% for qualified benefits) based upon a measure of hourly earnings and benefits in every unit, irrespective of whether wages and benefits had lagged or moved ahead in the dynamics of the wage-setting process. The differences in objectives— controlling labor costs versus wage stabilization—can in the short run lead to different programs which in the long run may not lead to compatible results.[18] This point is important and requires further elaboration because this difference constituted one of the major differences in the wage side between the Pay Board and the Committee's efforts.

Wage stabilization, in the viewpoint of Dunlop (and this author), consists of the *definition* and *restoration* (or establishment) of appropriate wage and benefit relationships over some period. The fundamental task of wage stabilization, then, "is the achievement of a wage and salary structure, a complex of differentials or relativities, which is generally acceptable and respected, and which does not contain within itself the distortions for continued self-generation of inflation." (Automatic adjustments due to price increases [escalator clauses] complicate the process but must be considered.)[19]

Several important consequences follow from this view of wage stabilization. The definition of appropriate relationships means detailed analysis of wage relationships, historical studies, and reliable data. The acceptability criterion implies the persuasion and acquiescence of the affected parties; it also requires their formal or informal cooperation and involvement. Finally, it holds that a single number or guideline to be applied to all cases is not an acceptable standard of wage stabilization for the following reasons: such a number will become a floor to bargaining even where not economically justified (a Phase II phenomenon); it is hard to reduce the value of fringes (particularly pensions) to a single number given differences in seniority and occupational mix (more below); work rule changes do not lend themselves to precise monetary evaluation but they are vital in evaluating the economic consequences of different collective agreements; no single number is appropriate for all circumstances;[20] and focus on a single standard, no matter how loose the exception criteria, will inevitably force the stabilization agencies and affected parties to focus on the number (and deviations therefrom) and not on wage rates and historical relationships and thus create further distortions, the seeds of continuing wage inflations.

Wage stabilization, on the other hand, necessarily also leads to stabilization of labor costs. (It may, however, take longer.) The shift away from a single standard after January 1973 to the stabilization of the wage and salary and benefit structure was made more difficult by the inequities and distorted relationships created by the Freeze and the subsequent adherence to a single standard as general policy in the food industry. The intervention of the Pay Board in individual cases in Phase II, without comprehensive wage and salary data, tended to create even more anomalous results which could not persist.

The food industry had been treated like all other industries in Phase II and hence no special attention was given to it and little or no staff expertise was developed in this sector. Phase II rules proved to be cumbersome. A substantial number of undecided cases remained (many of them the hard ones); some erroneous decisions, IRS involvement, complicated wage decisions, and the delays created claims for retroactive payments for as long as 14 months. Also, organized labor in the spring of 1972, with the exception of the Teamsters, walked off the Pay Board as a consequence of continuing policy disputes and national politics. Besides these problems, Phase II developed no infrastructure in the Pay Board to attack the problems in the future. Computer programs were lacking, forms were not suitable to wage stabilization, no wage data base had been developed, and immediately prior to Phase III the administrative capacity of the agency was limited; the mail delivery system, for instance, still was not functioning.[21]

General Wage and Salary Standard. The comprehensive coverage of Phase II, the short time envisaged for the program, and the determination to keep the bureaucracy small all contributed to the necessity for a general regulation approach to wage stabilization in contrast to a case-by-case handling of applications. Since a freeze could not continue indefinitely, the general regulations provided for implementation of some level of wage increase without further approval of the government.[22] The result was the adoption of the "general wage and salary standard" of 5.5% plus 0.7% for qualified benefits. The general standard was said to be the combined effect of the average long-term increase in productivity (3.0%) and the desired rate of increase in the cost of living by the end of 1972 (2.5%).[23]

The public began to identify a single number as being consistent with stabilization, and any larger wage or salary increase, no matter how justifiable, as violative of stabilization. The success of the wage program in the public mind came to be judged solely by the degree of adherence to the single standard. Moreover, as mentioned above, there was some tendency for the single standard to set a floor for bargained settlements and management wage decisions. Also, the number "5.5%" became very hard to change even after the underlying economic rationale for the number had changed dramatically in 1973. From a stabilization point of view, a single number expressed as a percentage can be destabilizing if the underlying wage structure is already distorted or if wage differentials among closely related units at different wage levels are linked on a cents-per-hour basis.

Regulation Approach. Phase II clearly opted for a general regulation approach to stabilization rather than a case-by-case approach. Rules promulgated under Phase II often did not reflect the collective bargaining or wage-setting process. They proved difficult to change, notwithstanding the difficulties they created. Two examples of these problems can be cited: The first was the so-called "tandem" regulation which permitted increases in one unit, beyond the general wage standard, provided a consistent relationship in timing and amount could be shown with a legal increase in another unit. This device was found necessary to mitigate some of the impractical results of a freeze and the single general standard. The administrative rules permitted a tandem between two employee or bargaining units provided there was a "six-year" consistent wage or bargaining history. This rule did not reflect the realities of bargaining where often one party leads one year and follows the next year. The rule also led to "game playing." At least one union had a master chart of all settlements across the country so that it could pick out tandem relationships that fitted the definition but possibly had no relationship to economic factors or industrial relations realities.[24] The second example was the importance of the choice of the "appropriate employee unit."[25] One unit had to be chosen for measuring changes in compensation whereas in reality there were often several units—one for wages and another for fringes. The regulation approach often did not permit enough flexibility and at other times was too lenient. But it had the advantage of general rules and a small bureaucracy.

Pay Board Forms (PB-3, PB-3A). The official forms adopted by the Pay Board during Phase II were called PB-3 and PB-3A.[26] They were not available until June and November 1972, respectively, thus adding to the delay. These forms were designed to translate wage increases into percentage terms to compare with the general wage and salary standard. They reflected the concern of the program with labor costs rather than wage and benefit rates. No provision was made for reporting occupational wage rates.[27] These forms also introduced the concept of "rollup" which was strange to most bargainers and which introduced a new and often troublesome feature in most wage negotiations.[28]

These forms, in the author's opinion and experience, did not help the stabilization process. The forms did not identify wage rate or fringe changes explicitly. All changes were included in a single number. The allowable percentage increases for two collective bargaining units covered by an identical contract could differ based on such factors as a different seniority structure or occupational structure (more meat cutters—fewer part-timers), thus adding to wage rate disparities and collective bargaining problems. The forms and regulations only considered the impact that changes would make on the *current* workforce in the next year. Changes with no short-run impact but substantial long-run cost implications, such as in vacation eligibility and pension, were allowed if their effects were not current.

The Pay Board generally only considered economic factors which could be costed onto the forms. Such factors as work rule or seniority system changes, which may have substantial effects on labor costs, were not considered explicitly by the forms even where they formed a basis for trade-offs for ordinary compensation terms. This fact merely reflected the Pay Board's view and focus on compensation factors. In short, while the forms may have been consistent with short-run objectives to limit labor costs, they were hardly consistent with a program trying to stabilize wage rates and industrial relations. The Pay Board was, of course, free to take such factors into account in the handling of individual cases; indeed the Congress mandated that it consider changes in productivity.

Treatment of Prestabilization Increases (Deferred Increases). The labor movement felt strongly that contracts negotiated prior to stabilization which provided for further increases to go into effect at future dates should be allowed to do so. Failure to do so, they held, struck at the heart of the sanctity of contracts. Labor also maintained that these prefreeze or prestabilization contracts with deferred increases were often secured in a trade-off or as a quid pro quo for changes in working conditions and work rules. To take away the wage increase and to leave the working condition change favorable to the employer was patently unfair. For this reason, and others, the Pay Board essentially adopted a policy of allowing such deferred increases to go into effect unless they were challenged by the Board or parties at interest. This policy, coupled with the large number of multi-year contracts in the food industry, assured a very large number of challenged deferred increases that were to leave a legacy of potential retroactivity and bitterness.[29] Continuing problems resulted because it was harder to cut back a deferred wage increase which had been in effect for some time and because, given the small Pay Board staff, it was almost impossible to identify such increases before they took effect. Hence this policy, while perhaps necessary to assure "equity," caused continuing serious stabilization problems for the Pay Board as well as later for the Committee.

Delay in Processing Cases. Delay in case processing is almost inevitable with a new program administered by a small bureaucracy. Furthermore, delay may have been used as an instrument of policy during this period. The final Pay Board forms were not issued until June (PB-3) and November (PB-3A) 1972, almost six months after the start of the program.[30]

Such delay, however, was very critical in a 14-month program. It assured leftover cases for the succeeding stabilization phase and such cases were often the most difficult. Also the delay was exacerbated by the multi-level, multi-time appeal process and the limited delegation to the IRS.[31] This delay and interpretation of initial IRS decisions caused problems for the Committee later when more facts became known.

Limited Attention to Support Facilities and Staff. Limited attention was paid to building proper staff support facilities and programs as a consequence of the desire for a small stabilization staff and the belief that the program would be short-lived. When the Committee came into existence, the mail was still not being delivered properly, and a computer program to track cases was not working properly. It was not until late in the program—around February 1974—that the food wage staff felt "comfortable" with the data. The computer experience underscores the need for advance planning and effective logistical support in any stabilization program.

Low Wage Employees. Congress mandated that special attention be given to "low wage employees." The stabilization agencies during Phase II did not adequately address this problem. The low wage levels proposed were too low to be acceptable. As a result, the court in July 1972 disapproved the level—$1.90 per hour—set by the Cost of

Living Council. As a result of the court's action the Council raised the level to $2.75 effective July 1972. This was followed in April 1973 by Congressional enactment of a specific low wage exemption of $3.50 an hour.[32]

This situation merits emphasis because it illustrates that if a stabilization agency does not responsively address a problem, the Congress or the courts may well impose a solution that may be more disruptive to the program.

The low wage exemption issue was very important to the retail food industry. The industry employs many low wage part-timers. Their exemption from wage stabilization and the calculation rules subsequently issued by the Pay Board to determine allowable percentage increases for the employee unit as a whole caused problems for the higher wage members of the unit. A specified dollar exemption level is bound to have an uneven impact because of regional variations in wage levels. Furthermore, the Pay Board's reaction to the court decision was a "rule" that was literally logically impossible and prohibitively costly to implement.[33]

The factors listed above derived from Phase II, created a legacy and an agenda of issues which materially influenced the work of the Committee in meeting its stabilization objectives. Phase II ended on January 10, 1973.

The Introduction of Phase III: January 11, 1973

Phase III was designed to prepare the economy for decontrol, give the economy room to grow, try to bring organized labor back into this program, and focus on specific problem sectors, including food. Short-term and long-term solutions for these problem sectors were to be explored and encouraged.

Under Phase III the economy was divided into three segments: mandatorily controlled, "voluntarily" controlled, and decontrolled. Food wage and price adjustments continued under mandatory controls.[34] The Pay Board and the Price Commission were eliminated and administration of the stabilization program was consolidated under a single director, John T. Dunlop. Also the general wage and salary standard was continued in principle but greater flexibility was envisaged in its application. "No single standard or wage settlement can be equally applicable at one time to all parties in an economy so large, decentralized and dynamic." (Statement of the Labor Management Advisory Committee, February 26, 1973.)

The design of Phase III caused some problems for the Committee. Immediately the unions raised the question of why food wages were retained under mandatory controls while other wages (except for construction and health) were left to self-administration. Possible answers were that food wage control was needed if food prices, which were rapidly rising, were to be controlled and food retailing wage adjustments were often singled out in Phase II as being destabilizing. Moreover, there was some recognition of a need for reforms in the bargaining structure of the organized portion of the food industry. Yet it was quite clear that the decision to control food industry wages during Phase III was basically concomitant to the decision to control food prices.

Another problem for the Committee, created by Phase III, was that a sectoral approach to stabilization required a specific definition of the food industry to remain under mandatory controls.[35] This definition raised equity arguments because any definition would be somewhat arbitrary. It is important to realize, however, that the Committee did not write the definition—it was given to the Committee by the Cost of Living Council. The Committee was free to propose subsequent changes in the scope of the industry.

The definition caused the Committee problems, since the distinction between food and nonfood is not so clear-cut in the labor market as in the product market. A truck driver employed by a contract hauler delivering food was not subject to mandatory controls whereas a truck driver working directly for a food retailer was so controlled. Similar definitional problems involved, for example, can makers and farm workers, some of whom were direct employees of a food retailer or processor, whereas others were employees of commercial can manufacturers that supplied cans to numerous food processors. These definitional problems were also exacerbated by the diversity of retailers. Their nonfood operations, often in the same shopping centers, were not under mandatory controls.[36]

A further problem of Phase III was that of staff morale. Phase III came as a complete surprise to the staff that had to adjust to the sectoral and case-by-case approach as opposed to the general regulatory approach. Finally, many of the staff viewed the director of the Cost of Living Council with some suspicion, because of his prior feuds with the Pay Board over the Construction Industry Stabilization Committee's policies.

The preceding discussion describes the setting of the assignment of the Food Committee which held its first meeting on February 26, 1973.

THE TRIPARTITE FOOD INDUSTRY WAGE AND SALARY COMMITTEE

Background to Formation of the Committee

By the end of Phase II it had become clear that the method of deciding cases by formula could not continue. Different decisions had been made by the Pay Board in the food industry among crafts in a single locality that had historically related wages and benefits. Expertise familiar with the food industry and its industrial relations was definitely needed. Experience with handling cases in isolation led to the strong belief that cases should be decided in patterns, whenever possible, so as to reflect more accurately the wage-setting process and not to distort it. Some Phase II case decisions added to the distortions in the wage structure rather than alleviating or correcting them.[37] This suggested that many Phase II case decisions on appeal would have to be re-examined by more knowledgeable individuals during Phase III.

Phase III included objectives broader than wage stabilization alone. Structural reform, where necessary, was to be encouraged. If the collective bargaining system in the food industry needed strengthening, this could only be done on a lasting basis by directly involving the participants in the process. Also, if dispute settlement was to be an integral part of the wage stabilization program, this, too, suggested involving the participants.

Another factor was that tripartite committees had seemed to be successful elsewhere. The director of the Cost of Living Council had long experience with such committees, starting with the War Labor Board during World War II and continuing with the Wage Stabilization Board during the Korean emergency. The Construction Industry Stabilization Committee (CISC), which he chaired, had been in operation for about two years and its success came to be widely recognized. Furthermore, a Food Advisory Committee, particularly concerned with policies relating to prices and products, had recently been established under the Council.*

Also a tripartite approach would mean that labor and management members from the food industry (along with public members) would have to meet together to discuss and it was hoped to resolve common problems. These relationships could endure (and remain useful) long after the current stabilization program terminated. The labor and management members would know each other's problems better and the process might generate public members who could prove useful to the industry as arbitrators, fact finders, mediators, and consultants.

Besides labor, management, and public representatives, a member of the Federal Mediation and Conciliation Service (FMCS) was an integral part of the Committee. The experience of CISC, the necessity of getting information to and from the field, and the concern and the hope that dispute resolution would be consistent with stabilization objectives were all reasons for the FMCS inclusion. Also past experience suggested that their participation would strengthen that agency's interest in the success of the stabilization effort—rather than be indifferent or hostile[38]—and make them more an integral part of the

---

* Mr. Dunlop once explained part of the reason for his belief in tripartitism was that 10,000 union business agents and their management counterparts would negate any piece of paper or rule that a stabilization agency might issue unless they were persuaded to help design and enforce the program. The collective bargaining process as well as the experience of Phase II attested to the wisdom of this statement.

bargaining process under wage and price controls. The Committee's actual experience demonstrated the usefulness of FMCS participation.

It is important to observe that members of the food industry—both labor and management—while in some instances reluctant, were willing to serve on the Committee. Reasons as to why these members were "willing" are important. The Executive Branch and Congress (April 30, 1973) extended controls, in a *peacetime* economy, even after almost 18 months of controls. From the management perspective, labor settlements were still large, at a time when profit margins were narrowing and constraints on wages were felt essential; consumer and political pressure made some form of price controls for food almost inevitable and therefore some form of wage control was needed; many "mechanical" initial decisions by the Pay Board were in need of review and management preferred to be involved; and some management leaders realized that something had to be done about the structure of collective bargaining in the industry and were willing to participate in a program that might be of some long-term assistance. Labor shared some of these views and also felt that some inequities had occurred during Phase II while they were "on the outside looking in," and their participation might alleviate these problems in the future as well as help correct past "incorrect" decisions; "leapfrogging" of large settlements into new areas (part-timers, South, rural areas) was probably limiting the unions' membership gains; the international unions in the controls period were losing a degree of control over local unions and local settlements, and finally, and because of the above factors, the top Labor Management Advisory Committee, which included leaders of the AFL-CIO, recommended involvement by food industry labor leaders. These factors also help to explain the wide degree of compliance with controls and the decisions of the Committee and the agency.

Committee Function and Composition

The scope of the Committee's functions and operations was basically defined in a charter written by the Cost of Living Council, issued before the Committee was named. Consultations between the Committee and the Director subsequently settled several issues as to whether the Committee had jurisdiction over certain questions (executive compensation—no, nonunion cases—yes) and the standards to be used to process various cases (e.g., Phase II cases were to be processed under Phase II rules).

> The charter prescribed five basic functions for the Committee: review all remaining food industry wage and salary cases filed before January 11, 1973, and advise on the disposition of these cases under Phase II regulations; review all new food industry wage and salary cases filed after January 11, 1973, and advise on the disposition of these cases under

existing regulations; advise the Cost of Living Council and the Labor Management Advisory Committee relative to any wage stabilization policies which are necessary to meet the special problems of the food industry (and its various branches) within the general framework of wage stabilization policies; cooperate with labor and management organizations in the food industry which operate under collective bargaining agreements and with appropriate government agencies in order to facilitate the settlement of disputes in 1973 within stabilization policies and to encourage longer-run dispute settlement machinery and procedures; and work with labor and management organizations in the food industry under collective bargaining agreements to improve the structure and performance of collective bargaining in the industry.

Some broad observations on the charter are in order. The charter made clear that the committee would both recommend policy and handle cases. The charter reflected the feeling that cases make for better policy and that policy lasts only if evolved from cases. Furthermore, through case processing, the parties are better able to understand the problems of the industry. And finally, decisions and policy are better explained and defended if the principals are involved in making that policy.

The charter also made it clear that the Committee was technically to advise rather than to make final decisions. The director of the Cost of Living Council had the authority to make final decisions. This proved to be a good safety valve for the Committee and led to consultations with labor, management, and public members and the Director on several occasions (very hard cases such as the Dallas Teamsters, Louisville Meat Cutters, and others.)[39] On the other hand, the Committee would not survive if it was frequently overruled. In fact, its recommendations invariably prevailed. The fact that the Committee advised and did not make final decisions obviated the need for Congressional confirmation of Committee members.

The charter dictated that the Committee's jurisdiction extended only to wages and salaries, not prices. Two of the labor members as well as representatives of management in the retail and manufacturing of food, however, also sat on the general CLC Food Advisory Committee, thus providing some contact on price and production policy matters. Also, as mentioned above, all stabilization agencies—price and wage—were directly part of the Cost of Living Council, instead of functioning as separate agencies. Hence, while pay and price were still separate, they were coordinated at the top through the CLC.[40]

Since there were three major or dominant unions in the food industry (especially in the retail sector) and since it might be difficult to recruit public members, this further suggested that the Committee not be too large. The decision was made to limit the Committee to 12, comprised of four public, four labor, and four management members. In addition, an at-large union member and an at-large management member (both nonvoting) were to be designated to insure broader representation and to provide a link between the Food Wage Committee's activities and the Labor Management Advisory Committee—a top level, tripartite committee that advised the Council on overall stabilization policies. In addition, a representative of the Federal Mediation and Conciliation Service attended meetings but without vote.

On the labor side three unions had to be represented by virtue of their pervasive representation: the Teamsters, the Meat Cutters, and the Retail Clerks. The fourth union chosen was the Bakery and Confectionery Workers. (This proved to be a good choice because the bakery industry submitted many cases that presented problems.) The interests of the other unions in the food industry were always considered. One other union (the Retail, Wholesale and Department Store Union) was represented as an alternate. The labor at-large delegate as well as committee members contacted other affected unions for their positions on issues or on cases involving these other unions.

The selection of management representatives involved the issue of whether they be labor relations officers or company presidents. Those selected represented a mix of both: the principal labor relations executives from The Great Atlantic and Pacific Tea Company, Swift and Company, and Safeway Stores, and the chairman of the board of the Kroger Company. The Safeway representative subsequently resigned and was replaced by the president of Colonial Food Stores. Representatives from Acme Stores, Oscar Mayer, and the Southern California Food Employers' Council also served as employer alternates on the Committee.

Representatives of the public proved to be hard to recruit. The food industry had not developed many neutrals, familiar with the industry's industrial relations and compensation problems, who were acceptable to both sides. The labor and managment members of the Committee were asked to recommend public members. Eventually five public members were appointed. (This provided for one alternate.)[41]

The labor and management members received no compensation or expenses for their work on the Committee. The public members received a government per diem plus travel expenses. The Committee met regularly several days each week in full session or subcommittee; it was a hard working committee. It was perhaps regrettable that on the union side, unlike the Construction Committee, only one general president represented its union, although two other union representatives were vice presidents.

Committee Organization

A quorum rule was adopted which provided that at least two members from each side had to be present for business to be conducted.

Each meeting had an agendum available in advance. This enabled committee members to prepare for the meeting and to solicit views of affected parties prior to the session. Until November 1973 the meetings were closed to the public. Minutes were recorded, approved by the Committee, and available to the public.

When hearings were held, the Committee tried to move away from a formal legalistic approach. Parties directly involved rather than their lawyers were encouraged to present their cases.

Individual votes of members were never recorded. Unanimous or majority recommendations were always forwarded to the director of the Cost of Living Council since the Committee was advisory only. However, when one or several of the affected parties felt strongly about a decision, written minority and majority reports could be forwarded to the director of the Cost of Living Council[42] for final decision. At least once (Dallas Meat Cutters) three position papers were forwarded to the director. No split votes were cast by labor or public members; only once did management split (Philadelphia Meat Cutters).

While an attempt was made to have alternates that represented other interests of the food industry serve on the Committee, in practice the alternates often turned out to be individuals on the organizational staff of the Committee members. This occasionally led to a delay in decision making since these alternates were reluctant to make hard decisions without consulting their principals.

The Committee was very careful not to delegate its responsibility to others. In contrast to Pay Board practice, staff delegations, until the final days of the Committee, were very few. Such delegations were carefully defined and subject to review by the Committee. One of the Committee's first decisions was to seek to eliminate the Internal Revenue Service from its role in Phase II in handling cases. All files were to be returned to the Committee for processing.

The Committee had a separate support staff, which comprised an integral part of the Cost of Living Council's Office of Wage Stabilization. Members of this staff reported to the director of the Food Division. The executive secretary of the Committee, the author of this chapter, was appointed by the director of the Cost of Living Council and also served as the director of the Food Division. (This organizational structure proved initially cumbersome but by July 1973, when the Office of Wage Stabilization was reorganized under a new Administrator, it began to function effectively.)[43] The Committee did use the full support services of the Cost of Living Council, especially the Office of the General Counsel. Eventually full-time staff working exclusively on food cases exceeded 50 individuals plus the occasional and part-time support of numerous other Council members, not to mention Committee members and their associates. (The total staff of the Pay Board, at the end of Phase II, did not exceed 250 individuals.)

The director of the Cost of Living Council was always available for consultation with the whole Committee or interested group members. These consultations were both formal during working hours and informal after working hours. The director also tried to keep the Committee informed on all aspects of the Cost of Living Council through this direct contact and through the executive director of the Committee. This enabled the Committee to have a broad picture of the Council's function as well as providing firsthand information for Committee members on the functioning of the Council.

Until decontrol was actively being discussed, the Committee had no direct relationship with the "price side" of the Council. The director of the Cost of Living Council was of the view that conditioning wage increases on price policy in individual cases, as had been done in 1946–1947, was destructive of stabilization. He regarded it as important to maintain a distance between individual price decision apparatus and the individual wage decision apparatus. Wage policy and price standards usually were, of course, related at the level of general policy. Moreover, if a wage committee was to get involved in specific price decisions, the confidentiality issue on price and cost data would surely be raised. On the other hand, failure to coordinate individual price and wage decisions more directly left some important information gaps which adversely affected decision making on both the wage and price side.

In practice the director of the Cost of Living Council seldom, if ever, overturned the Committee's "advice." Never was a recommendation by the public members on a particular wage case overturned. However, this degree of acceptability was not so consistent in the area of policy recommendations. The Committee's policy recommendations had to be weighed against their effect on the whole stabilization program, including prices. Fortunately no policy clash ever occurred between the Committee and the director of the Cost of Living Council, although certain issues such as changing the "general wage and salary standard" or recommending decontrol could have caused such a confrontation.

In practice any information that was submitted to the Cost of Living Council that was pertinent to a food wage or salary case was available to the Committee members. The issue of confidentiality of such information was always a potential problem but seldom caused operational difficulties. Confidentiality was discussed almost exclusively in relation to nonunion or salary cases.[44]

Two developments might have dramatically affected the Committee's operations. The first was the "hearing requirement" which Congress imposed on April 30, 1973. This provided that before an order was issued which had the effect of reducing wages or salaries in effect, or proposed to be put into effect, the affected parties must be offered a hearing. (Before the hearing requirement was imposed, the Committee had used hearings but had scheduled them in significant cases.) Through a device called an "Interim Decision and Order" the Committee was able to minimize the procedural and administrative problems that might have occurred under this requirement by allowing the parties to decide whether a hearing was necessary after an "Interim Decision and Order" was issued.[45] Relatively few chose to do so in these circumstances.

The second development occurred on November 9, 1973, when Judge Green issued a decision that required Committee meetings to be open to the public under the requirements of the Advisory Committee Act. This requirement in practice did not cause a problem (probably because of the dullness of the subject matter to the public)[46] but could have limited the frankness of the debates and the ability of partisan committee members to compromise if the public had attended consistently and in large numbers. Informal sessions were always possible, or meetings of some public members with one side or the other in private could be used to move toward the resolution of a difficult issue.

The main point that should be emphasized is that both factors—the hearing requirement and the open Committee meeting requirement—could have been used by the parties or factions among the parties, if they wanted, to throttle the effectiveness of the Committee operation. At the minimum, full use of these factors would have involved considerably more staff time. At the maximum, both requirements could have posed insurmountable difficulties to the effective functioning of stabilization efforts. That neither occurred is a credit to the Committee.

The Committee and Case Processing

The Committee's charter mandated that it was to process both Phase II cases that were undecided or on appeal and cases filed subsequent to January 11, 1973. The Committee started operating in February 1973 with a backlog of 254 cases. By November 1973 the backlog had reached a peak at some 3,600 cases. By mid-June 1974 the Committee had processed over 12,000 cases (a volume comparable to the number processed by the Pay Board in all industries during Phase II)[47] and had only 31 cases remaining.[48] The Committee and the Cost of Living Council expired on June 30, 1974, although controls authority had lapsed on April 30, 1974.

The Committee never processed or considered a case with an established collective bargaining relationship until an agreement had been reached and an agreement or memorandum of understanding had been signed by the affected parties. The Committee would not become a party to the collective bargaining process although it was available to aid in the process of dispute resolution. Also the Committee would never modify a decision to accommodate a delicate bargaining situation or to alleviate economic conditions of one of the parties after an agreement had been reached.[49]

The goal of the Committee was to arrive at a recommendation in short order by consensus whenever possible. Delays by the Pay Board had caused serious problems for labor and management.[50] Indeed, one of the main reasons labor and management representatives agreed to serve on the Committee was to rectify the perceived mistakes of Phase II. The procedure developed to meet this goal was to narrow the case universe to those major or "lead cases" (see Regulations below), get those cases ready for recommendation, make a recommendation, and transmit the decision to the affected parties. Other follower cases could be handled in this framework by staff with Committee approval. All this required the development of expertise that would aid the decision-making process.

The Committee made special efforts to make clear by regulations and by workshops the types of information that the Committee would need to aid it in the decision-making process. Furthermore, the Committee instructed and insisted that the staff scrutinize submissions for completeness.

Simultaneously, the staff that served the Food Division was organized in such a manner as to develop specialized knowledge which would facilitate the Committee's decision making. Retailing and wholesaling cases were divided into three geographical divisions, each with a supervisor and staff members. Processing and manufacturing constituted another division, and still another dealt with nonunion and merit plan cases. This administrative structure was designed to develop staff specialization so that cases would no longer be processed in isolation of closely related cases. Considerable effort was made to utilize the computer to serve as an effective tool to aid the Committee's work. A standard format was developed for all data input. Eventually, this allowed grouping of related cases to facilitate the decision-making process.

The Committee fluctuated from time to time between a strict, careful case-by-case decision-making process resulting in a backlog threatening to destroy the creditability of the program and a policy of deciding groups of related cases of seemingly minor significance. It was always painfully clear that a large backlog would undermine confidence in the program.

Over a period of time the Committee recommended and the Council issued regulations to cut down the universe of cases under its jurisdiction. It started by eliminating restaurants and eating places from mandatory food controls on June 27, 1973. It subsequently exempted mobile catering firms, restored the small business exemption to firms employing 60 or fewer employees in the food industry, decontrolled fruit and vegetable processors, and in February 1974 abandoned the requirement whereby firms making wage adjustments within the general wage and salary standard had to report these adjustments to the Cost of Living Council. This series of exemptions were premised on the belief that they would not be destabilizing.

These decisions, issued as Regulations, markedly reduced the Committee's case load.

The Committee also made some "group recommendations" on the basis of a careful grouping of cases by the staff, assisted by the computer. Such actions took the form of approving groups of cases that met certain criteria. Among the criteria were that the percentage wage adjustment fall below a specified level, that the dollar amount of the adjustment fall below a specified level, or that the pay adjustment in question was one involving a pre-Phase II case and that the adjustment was already in effect. These group recommendations were not adopted until the summer of 1973 when the backlog became critical. The criteria for approving the group cases were debated carefully and at length by the Committee.

The Committee readily decided that the number of employees in a unit was not a good basis for any action. Small units had both large increases and historical relationships with larger units. The staff also made sure that the cases actually fitted the criteria. Finally, any individual case, even though it met the criteria, could be challenged by any member of the Committee if he felt that it still could have a destabilizing effect.[51]

Ordinarily, the staff did not make recommendations to the Committee. The tripartite Committee was zealous to preserve its leadership and to keep the staff neutral. The Committee, with great reluctance and care, did delegate to the staff the right to recommend approval of certain limited types of cases, e.g., where parties requested hearings and did not appear or appealed a decision without submitting new information. Such cases were listed by the staff and recommendations were presented to the Committee. Again, any Committee member could challenge the list or a particular case and request that the case be given further consideration. In a similar matter, the staff was allowed to process cases that were strictly follower cases to key decisions. The Committee, however, always reviewed the staff's work.

The Committee also used a task force of lower rank labor and management members drawn from the food industry to aid in case processing. (It also used with much more limited success a subcommittee of the full Committee.)[52] This task force, coordinated by a nonvoting staff member of the food division, would initially consider all cases that did not meet the criteria mentioned above. If the task force could reach a unanimous recommendation, all such cases were listed and presented to the Committee for consideration and action. Members of the full Committee worked closely with task force members and provided them with guidance as to what factors they considered important and which cases were of special interest to the Committee.[53]

Cases not disposed of by the expedited methods mentioned above were handled directly by the Committee. New issues came before it, as did the more emotional and tough cases which tended to involve a combination of retroactivity and an organization represented on the Committee. These cases usually were formally decided by the public members' recommendation. A few cases were appealed to the Director of the Cost of Living Council for a final decision.

Mandatory hearings, required after April 30, 1973, in cases involving a reduction of wages and salaries in effect or proposed to be put into effect, were conducted by the staff (over 250 such hearings) and the report was given to the Committee before final recommendations were made. The Committee also, at its request, conducted voluntary hearings (about 25) when the Committee felt it was necessary to get the facts. Such hearings were held by the full Committee, a subcommittee of the full Committee, or a public member of the Committee, always with staff present. These hearings to "get the facts" proved quite useful. They also permitted informal conversations with local representatives directly involved in the negotiations under consideration.

The nature of the Committee's recommendations varied. The Committee, by a Decision and Order, often recommended solutions by allowing x percent, disallowing y percent, allowing x cents per hour, disallowing y cents per hour, allowing certain occupational rates, altering the timing of wage increases, disallowing retroactivity but allowing contract rates or vice versa, or by utilizing a combination of these actions. Facts were always insisted upon including the appropriate relative wage rates—industry, occupational, and geographical. In certain difficult cases, the Committee encouraged the parties to work with Committee members to arrive at a suitable resolution of the case which was compatible with stabilization objectives. The focus of stabilization concern was always the level and relative position of the parties at the end of the control period in order to leave a relatively stabilized wage and benefit structure.[54] Innovation and imagination constituted important tools for the Committee's efforts. Never was the process reduced to a single number or formula for lead cases.

The Federal Mediation Service as well as Committee members constantly kept in touch with what was happening in the field. In so doing, the Committee was able to process cases based on current information. It also minimized the possibility that a recommendation would be made on a "follower" case before the lead case had reached the Committee.

The Committee considered many cases but had very few decisions result in law suits, despite the fact that it modified hundreds of agreements.[55] Tripartitism no doubt contributed to this low incidence of legal appeals. Decisions were clearly better understood and explained than had they been made by a purely administrative staff.

The Committee and Dispute Settlement

The Pay Board had never regarded dispute resolution as a part of its assignment or as an integral part of wage stabilization unlike earlier periods of stabilization in this country. Dispute settlement was, however, assigned to the Committee by its charter.

The fact that a representative of the Federal Mediation and Conciliation Service attended all Committee meetings helped the dispute settlement function as well as serving as an information channel. Working with its field staff, the FMCS representative was able to funnel information about the Committee's activities and policies to local labor and management. Also, it was hoped, stabilization goals would be recognized in dispute settling attempts. The FMCS field staff as well as labor and management members of the Committee kept the Committee posted about key negotiations. Furthermore, on occasions when local parties in dispute were invited to Washington for FMCS mediation efforts, they also met and conferred with the Committee. (Philadelphia Retail Clerks, California Retail Clerks.)

The Committee's role in dispute settlements was varied. It held hearings with the parties when it was deemed advisable (some even after work stoppages had commenced) and offered informal advice and guidance (but never a guarantee of approval of any settlement reached). Committee members were available, upon request, to counsel with parties to a dispute and to advise them of Committee policies. Furthermore, on at least one occasion, by agreement of the parties a public member of the Committee became a formal fact finder in a dispute, making specific recommendations (California Retail Clerks).[56] The Committee also advised the Director of the Cost of Living Council when a major labor dispute in the food industry was brewing and members of the Committee often sought his advice and possible assistance. Also, the Committee made it clear that it would assist the Mediation and Conciliation Service if deemed appropriate.

A major problem faced by the Committee was to avoid becoming too deeply involved in the bargaining process. The Committee steadfastly avoided approval of any settlement before it was negotiated and a contract signed.

Because of the relatively short period of its existence, the Committee's role in dispute settlement does not provide a decisive basis for judgment as to the merits of combining stabilization and dispute settlement. Labor disputes clearly worried the Committee. What can be said is that the Committee did what it could to facilitate dispute settlement. This experience, however brief, adds support to the argument that some form of dispute settlement or involvement may contribute to effective wage stabilization.

With these sections as background, we turn to a discussion of the Committee in operation.

The Committee in Operation: Continuing Problems and Issues

One recurring problem concerned the extent to which the Committee should conform to or break away from Phase II regulations and forms. This issue was epitomized in the constant discussion about the general wage and salary standard. The debate had two aspects: (1) Should the general wage and salary standard of 5.5% plus 0.7% for qualified benefits be changed? (2) Should "self-implementation" of wage and salary adjustments be permitted up to a specified level or "standard" rather than requiring advance approval of all wage and benefit adjustments? As stated above, the Director of the Cost of Living Council strongly believed that a single standard did not constitute a workable wage stabilization program. Nonetheless, in view of the practical necessity of having to process a large number of cases, failure to allow some self-implementation, up to the level of some figure, might have caused the entire system to become unadministrable or subject to widespread noncooperation, particularly after the universal character of self-administration in Phase II. Furthermore, as prices continued to rise after January 1973, the old standard of 5.5% became less palatable. The 5.5% figure never was changed, but the issue fostered frequent and prolonged debates within the Committee. Over time, in practice, the Committee paid less attention to this standard.

A further problem, related to the issue of breaking with the past, concerned adequate information for decision making and communications with the parties. The limitations of the PB-3 forms, noted above, became more evident as the Committee concerned itself increasingly with wage rates and benefit levels and relationships. Cases processed during Phase II provided almost no useful wage and benefit data for the Committee. Still the forms were not abandoned in a program in which the parties had gradually become accustomed to the unusual form and its cost-oriented concepts. Instead the Committee sought other means of getting needed data, including relying on the organizations represented on the Committee. In addition, the Committee requested and enforced the requirement to provide supplementary information with the PB-3 forms, such as collective bargaining agreements and wage and salary plans. When data were lacking, pertinent information needed by the Committee (such as area and occupational wage rates) were either requested by the Committee's staff, or obtained through the direct efforts of Committee members. The "service requirement," under which all parties to a wage case were to notify the other parties concerning any submission to the Council, was strictly enforced. (Much to the author's surprise this requirement caused many problems. Parties often, and sometimes deliberately, would not keep other parties informed.) Finally the staff conducted a series of regional wage workshops in the fall of 1973 which explained the Committee's purpose and procedures. (This also had the merit of introducing the staff and involving the staff in the food industry.) Following these workshops a detailed series of questions and answers, based on actual questions raised at the workshops, were published in the Federal Register better to inform the industry.

The Committee also developed special forms for use in large clear-cut pattern-setting wage situations. These forms, tailor-made to the specific situation, were designed to expedite the processing of major cases and the myriad of related cases that follow such major settlements. These forms were used for the 1973 Master Freight and Meat Packing settlements. These special forms, however, seemed to have been adopted with some acrimony on the management side. There was concern that these simplified procedures could influence the collective bargaining process; i.e., that an expedited form could lead parties which had not been part of the pattern-setting negotiation in the past or had not regularly followed to conform to the pattern in the interest of a larger settlement or expedited treatment.

In a related effort, the Committee tried to develop a data base for the future. A questionnaire for parties in the food industry was developed and cleared by the Office of Management and Budget, but was adopted too late for use before controls were eliminated in April 1974. The continued use of the PB-3 form, however, precluded establishment of an effective wage data base as well as developing quantitative estimates of the effect of the Committee's action on wage rates.[57] No usable wage data came out of the 1971–1974 food wage control experience, unlike the wage and benefit data bank developed under construction controls in the period 1971–1974. The absence of such data, in the author's viewpoint, is one of the most disappointing features of this controls experience. Moreover, others have used Phase II data, and others may want to do so in the future, to describe the effectiveness of Phase II and the Pay Board, and it is essential to be aware of the limitations of the available data.[58,59]

Another set of problems that took much of the Committee's time revolved around the definition of the food industry, the precise employees to be included under mandatory controls, and the jurisdiction of the Committee. The resolution agreed upon combined equity and pragmatic considerations and required coordination with the price controllers. Two major definitional issues were: (1) how to classify employees outside the "food industry" whose wages and benefits directly affected food wages (contract truckers, for example); and (2) employees not normally classified as in the food industry (captive can workers for a food processing firm). The former problem was resolved by coordinating the Committee's efforts with the "self-administered" sector; the Committee never expanded the original definition to include additional workers who were not initially included. The latter problem was resolved by excluding can workers from mandatory coverage. Other examples that raised definitional questions included "captive farm workers," workers who made ice cubes, grain millers, and workers harvesting kelp.

The Committee constantly wrestled with improving case processing techniques and procedures. That it was never able to develop an exact formula probably reflects the intricacies and complexities involved in the wage-setting process even in one sector. The Committee constantly sought past regularities and patterns. In general, in handling food processing and manufacturing cases, the Committee looked for national patterns. In bakery cases, however, the Committee discovered that, with some notable exceptions, regional patterns predominated. As a rule, processing and manufacturing cases were less complex to handle than food retail cases.

In food retailing complications were almost endless: "areas" were not always readily defined; union jurisdictions overlapped; nonunion firms were important in some areas; the proportion of part-timers varied within and between areas; craft differentials varied and showed fluctuations over time; and so on. Inter-area relationships, sometimes present, presented additional problems. These complications were not surprising given the structures of the food industry and food labor market mentioned above. Yet compensation relationships within an area were considered most important in retailing, and stabilized area wage rates for key crafts and occupations were often set and other retail food enterprises in the area were allowed to come up to the level of the stabilized rates.

Because nonunion firms were important in some areas, a constant source of debate was the weight to be given to the degree of nonunion competition and nonunion wage rates in deciding cases of unionized firms in the area. The nonunion rates were often well below the union rates but in some situations represented most of the food retail labor market.

Another problem was how much to allow the wage leaders in an area, if anything.[60] This problem most often occurred with a unionized unit in a strong nonunion area. Again both problems were never resolved at the level of principle. They were handled on a case-by-case basis.

With respect to nonwage compensation, the Committee tended to adopt Pay Board rules on fringe benefits such as pension and health and welfare plans. This practice may have spurred a more-than-normal negotiation of these fringes in the food industry. However, quantitative evidence is lacking. When it came to productivity and work rule changes, the Committee recognized only discrete work rule changes. Arguments for approval of wage increases based on general productivity improvements often lacked supporting evidence. Unions presenting such petitions on productivity generally claimed that management was unwilling to supply the adequate data. Where discrete work rule changes were negotiated, with relatively clear-cut and demonstrable actual or potential cost savings, the Committee tended to ratify the trade-off arrived at through collective bargaining.

Deferred increases, those negotiated prior to the stabilization program, always presented a problem. Deferred increases often raised the prospects of establishing higher levels which in turn could be used to claim inequities to leverage still higher adjustments elsewhere. Also, the large backlog of inherited cases made it virtually impossible to identify such deferred increases before they took effect. Once increases had been placed into effect it was most difficult to reduce or eliminate the increase. The deferred increase issue was a key factor in one of the most emotional cases brought before the Committee—the St. Louis Retail Clerks case. The case involved three pre-Phase II agreements that had been cut by the Pay Board during Phase II. The question the Committee had to decide was what could legally be put into effect during the next year of the agreement: the contract rate actually negotiated in the prestabilization agreement for the second year, or the contract increment for the second year on top of the lower first-year rate established by the Pay Board. To allow the contract rate, and thus permit the rate to "spring" back to the original negotiated rate, would undo the prior Pay Board decision. To allow only the contract increment meant limiting a pre-Phase II contract without an explicit decision by the Committee. The case evoked strong expressions of feeling, reflecting, in large measure, labor's view of the sanctity of contracts negotiated in good faith as well as equity considerations.

The treatment of deferred increases being limited remained a controversial issue. Indeed when the stabilization program ended in April 1974 there were still agreements with higher specified rates than the stabilization program had permitted to go into effect, and the unions sought to have these higher rates enacted immediately. The only way to reslove this issue well would have been for the parties actually to change the agreement following a stabilization agency decision.

Related to the treatment of deferred increases was the issue of whether the Committee could challenge such an increase going into effect. Legally such a challenge could be instituted, but the Committee used this procedure sparingly. Ordinarily employer groups affected by a proposed increase exercised the right to raise a challenge. The Committee, unlike the Pay Board, did not allow parties to an agreement to challenge their own deferred increases.[61] Few acts could be more disruptive to industrial relations than for an employer to agree to an increase in collective bargaining and then request the stablization agency to reduce the increase.

The treatment of low wage employees also produced much debate in the Committee. As noted above, the courts and Congress mandated that the stabilization agency could not limit wage increases as long as the wage increases left employees' wage rates below $2.75 or, after April 30, 1973, below $3.50 per hour. These mandates affected the food industry because in many instances the wages of many part-timers and even some of the full-time employees fell below the low wage level. To meet the problem of processing cases which included low wage employees, the Committee required the submission of two PB-3 forms, one for the employees whose rates were $3.50 or above, and one for the entire unit; the Committee then considered each on its own merits. Resolution of the low wage issue and specific cases took up much debate but did not create a major problem for the Committee.[62]

The Committee, and the Pay Board, never had a strong organized compliance program, but compliance with its decisions did not seem to present a major problem. The Committee could, and did, effectively use the influence of labor and management members to gain compliance. If necessary, the Committee could call upon the Internal Revenue Service to conduct a directed investigation as well as recommend other Cost of Living Council sanctions such as injunction or fines. This power was never exercised and reliance was primarily on voluntary compliance and labor-management cooperation, which seemed to be adequate.

The issue of retroactivity was probably the Committee's single most troublesome problem. It arose in virtually every controversial case (the Louisville, Kentucky, meat cutter cases invloving Kroger and A&P were the outstanding examples). It caused a few hours' walk-out by labor members of the Committee.[63]

Labor held that because a case was old and hence might involve significant back payments, this should not affect the decision as to the level of wages and benefits. Management was concerned over the size of large retroactive payments and wished to reduce the extent of back payments by making increases effective at a later date than originally specified in the collective agreement. Delays in case processing and appeals from earlier rulings exacerbated the issue. Also, Internal Revenue Service tax rules on accruals against pending wage cases did not help the situation.[64] The Committee handled retroactivity claims, at best, on a case-by-case basis with combinations of compromises, trade-offs, and equity considerations: higher amount approved with limited retroactivity, lower amount approved with full retroactivity, renegotiation with all decisions based somewhat on what caused the delay and hence the retroactivity.

Another problem confronting the Committee was management's participation in cases involving their own companies. The cry of bad faith was often raised by labor representatives on the Committee, where a labor relations vice president on the Committee was voting for or advocating that a contract affecting his company be reduced in economic terms and the same individual had either directly negotiated or had authorized the wage settlement being decided. Since the Committee could not approve more than the parties had negotiated or requested for approval, the same problem did not occur because of labor's participation in their own cases. Labor fought to preserve what the parties had agreed to in their contract, and this was consistent with their contract and committee behavior.

These, then, represent some of the major ingredients which conditioned the Committee's determinations. It is probably true, given all the problems mentioned above and the large number of cases, that the Committee (especially considering its short duration) concentrated its efforts more on not creating new wage and benefit distortions rather than eliminating older ones.

Before ending this section, it is appropriate to highlight four of the harder types of cases the Committee encountered during its operation:

(1) *Bakery consecutive workweek.* This group of cases presented the most difficult manufacturing situations the Committee encountered. Bakeries, because of consumer shopping patterns and the limited shelf life of products, prefer to produce their products by working a split workweek (close down on Tuesday and work on Sunday). Bakery workers would prefer to have two consecutive days off (instead of Tuesday and Saturday). Several bakery contracts effective in 1973 contained provisions that provided for a premium for any worker who did not work a consecutive workweek. The issue was whether the Committee and Council should approve the provision. The debate, instead of focusing on the economics of the issue and the fact that the contracts were arrived at through collective bargaining, tended to focus on the technical question of whether the payment was chargeable under the Regulations. The "chargeable" side argued that it represented a cost to the employer since work on Sunday would represent more pay for the same hours of work. The nonchargeable side argued that if the consecutive week was worked, no additional wage payment would be forthcoming and hence the consecutive workweek was nonchargeable. The premium therefore was a trade-off for a nonchargeable adjustment. This group of cases was complicated by the Regulations and the focus on the costing of work rules. In the end the Committee and Council approved the premium, holding that it would not *per se* be destabilizing.

(2) *Allowable increase to wage leaders.* Another class of cases that caused problems was the adjustments to allow the wage leaders increases in a given area. Because of the general wage standard which was self-administered, it was difficult to hold any unit below 5.5%.[65] Since these units were already "ahead," the general standard put them further ahead in dollar terms. An analogous situation presented itself when one or two union units came up in a predominately nonunion area. The Committee never satisfactorily resolved this at the principle level but rather tried for compromises on a case-by-case method.

(3) *Overlapping labor markets.* Cases covering large geographical areas (many labor markets) caused difficulties because of the problem of which labor market to consider in deciding the case. In at least one case, the Committee recommended different amounts for different areas rather than the uniform amount negotiated.

(4) *Craft or occupational differentials.* A problem similar to (3) above arose when one craft—say meat cutter—in a bargaining unit got ahead of similar crafts in an area but the other crafts in the unit—clerks, wrappers—were even with or behind comparable workers. The Committee had to decide on the amount to allow each craft. The problem was especially difficult when the unit negotiated uniform increases for all crafts. Again, in at least one case, the Committee—

albeit not unanimously and with great acrimony—held the leader craft to less money than the other crafts in the unit.

Other examples could be given. These, however, amply attest to the difficulties of wage stabilization and the Committee's assignment. We turn now to a discussion of the Committee and Regulations.

The Committee and Regulations

The Committee was directed to advise the Cost of Living Council and the Labor Management Advisory Committee relative to any wage stabilization policies necessary to meet the special problems of the food industry. The Regulations adopted by the Food Committee, approved by the Director of the Cost of Living Council, and published in the Federal Register, suggest how the Committee fulfilled this mandate. The Regulations were not the only method of giving advice but they were the most general. Several informal meetings and many discussions over these Regulations were held with the Director of the Cost of Living Council by the Committee, groups of members, and staff.

On March 29, 1973, on instructions of the President, the Cost of Living Council published Regulations establishing price ceilings on meat. Meat prices had been rising rapidly. In conjunction with these price regulations, the Council also published Regulations that affected wage adjustments in the food industry. However, before publishing these latter Regulations, the Director of the Council sought the advice of the Food Wage Committee and obtained its agreement. These food wage Regulations abolished all size categories in the food industry and treated all units the same for purposes of reporting and approval (prior to the changes and under the Pay Board the wage world was divided into units of less than 1,000 employees, units of 1,000 to 4,999 employees, and units of 5,000 or more employees. Each size category had rules governing reporting and self-implementation with the rules being stricter the larger the unit);[66] the small business exemption for food industry wage adjustments was revoked; the Regulations required prenotification and approval of all such wage adjustments, subject, however, to the provision that wage adjustments in contracts negotiated prior to March 29, 1973, which were prenotified to the Council but which were not acted upon by the Council within 60 days, could go into effect, subject to later Council review and possible rollback; an explicit "service requirement" by a filing party on the other party involved was included; and contracts or evidence of pay practices were required to accompany any submission to the Cost of Living Council. These Regulations gave the Committee total control over all pay adjustments, regardless of the size of the employing unit, or size of adjustment. In the short run, this constituted a de facto freeze on all wage adjustments in the food industry.

These Regulations reflected the Committee's feeling that decisions to be equitable had to be timely (the 60-day clock). The Regulations also recognized that there was to be no automatic entitlement to the general wage standard of 5.5%. They reflect the view that in the case of wage leaders, particularly those far out in front, any percentage adjustment might potentially be destabilizing in that wage leaders would move further ahead, making it harder for followers to catch up. Finally, it was hoped that these Regulations would be a first step in allowing the Committee to begin building a data base for the future.[67]

Almost overnight, the Committee and its staff realized that the Regulations were too constraining. No wage adjustments could be granted without prior approval but the Committee was not yet well enough organized to provide speedy relief. There was an honest fear that if the Regulations remained in effect the program would be overcome by its backlog and be unadministrable. The Committee actually received many submissions on many types of forms and even letters stating that they intended to give various employees so much of an increase.[68] On April 20, 1973, acting on the Committee's advice, the Council published "interim rules" which: (a) essentially reinstituted Phase II regulations, but retained the requirement that *all* pay adjustments were to be reported to the Council; and (b) continued the abolishment of size categories. These Regulations also published for the first time in the Federal Register an address for submission to the Council (this address did help the mail problems). Finally, the date for full implementation of the March 29, 1973, rules was deferred until November 1, 1973. It was still hoped that the "ideal" system could be implemented by November.

This hope was never realized. On October 26, 1973, the latter date was extended to February 1, 1974, and on January 28, 1974, the "interim rules" were made permanent. Hence, practical limitations prevented the Committee from ever implementing a program that may have been most desirable for a complete stabilization program. It is possible that these Regulations could have been implemented on the date originally set, had the Committee started its operations without a backlog, but even this is doubtful given the staff size limitations.

The Committee's experience with the "interim rules" demonstrated the practical limitations of a stabilization program that begins with little data, operates with limited staff, and starts with a backlog. That experience, inextricably linked to the pre-existing stabilization policies which conditioned the Committee's operations and decisions, transformed the charter mandate to develop a wage stabilization program consistent with the needs of the food industry to a program somewhat short of what might have been an ideal stabilization program.

The Committee and Decontrol

The issue of full or partial decontrol (of the food industry) was raised by both labor and management Committee members at various times. Other industries were being decontrolled starting in the fall of

1973, and the unions were particularly anxious to see controls on food ·
eliminated and free collective bargaining fully restored. The Committee soon learned that it is often harder to get out of controls than into
controls. This suggests that before embarking on a control program, a
program or plan as to how to get out of controls should be considered.
Coordination with price decontrol had been started through the Food
Advisory Committee (on which two labor Food Wage Committee
members sat) before Congress made it clear that authority for the
stabilization program would not be extended after April 30, 1974.
The Director of the Cost of Living Council set the parameters for
these discussions. First, to the fullest extent possible, prices and wages
were to be decontrolled together. Second, food did not have to be
decontrolled all at once; sectors of the food industry would be considered for decontrol based on their own merits. Finally, the Director of
the Cost of Living Council in testimony before Congress, although
recommending extending the life of the Cost of Living Council, did
not request continuation of mandatory controls for food after April
30, 1974.

The criteria used by the Cost of Living Council to decontrol industries were the projected effects upon supply and capacity, the extent
of price and wage increases, and the commitments that affected
parties were prepared to make to stabilization objectives in the event
of decontrol. On the wage side, factors such as the ratio of labor to
total cost, bargaining relationships in the industry, and the timing and
structure of bargaining were considered important. Labor factors,
because of the strong interrelationships among unions, were often a
drawback to decontrol of a sector because of the effect on other
sectors still under control.

Decontrol of food wages presented special problems because the
food industry had been under mandatory controls since November
14, 1971. These problems involved decisions on:

(1) "Paper rate problem"—it must be decided if and when parties which
    have had wage rates reduced by the Cost of Living Council can reinsti-
    tute the reduced portion of the wage rate.
(2) "Cases-in-house"—it must be decided how to handle cases-in-house
    either initially or on appeal once the pay adjustments affecting these
    workers have been decontrolled.
(3) "The effect of issued Decisions & Orders"—it must be decided whether
    Decisions & Orders that have been issued by the Cost of Living Council
    pertaining to a period prior to the day of decontrolling the product or
    sector in the food industry still are in effect.
(4) "Retroactivity"—depending on how the other problems are handled,
    retroactivity could be a problem for cases-in-house where no decision
    has been rendered if the pay adjustments are suddenly decontrolled.
(5) "Negotiations presently in progress"—it must be decided whether the
    Council will take jurisdiction over proposed pay adjustments scheduled
    to be effective prior to the date of decontrol but which were not

submitted to the Council because the contract was being negotiated or the appropriate forms were being filled out when decontrol was announced.

The Committee finally decided to retain jurisdiction only over all payments paid for work performed prior to decontrol. Realistically, Congress was about to dictate this solution anyhow. If Congressional action had not been imminent, these issues would have been debated much more intensely.

The sequence of decontrol of the food industry was as follows. Inadvertently, vending machines were decontrolled on February 1, 1974. The error was due to the use of SIC codes to determine what type of firms were decontrolled and the failure of the Cost of Living Council to coordinate this action with the Food Wage Committee because of the policy to keep proposed decontrol decisions secret. This premature decontrol, however, caused no problems.

On March 18, 1974, prices of canned fruits and vegetables were decontrolled, primarily out of concern that failure to do so might have reduced plantings in the 1974 season. The general principle of linking price and wage decontrol actions was followed here as elsewhere, despite the great interdependence of wages in this sector of the food industry with other sectors in food. Many members on the Committee would have preferred universal wage decontrol of the food industry. The labor members especially felt that piecemeal decontrol would only cause internal problems in the industry and within the various unions. In this case, however, the Director of the Cost of Living Council felt that the benefits to the public from early decontrol of the prices and wages of fruits and vegetables clearly outweighed any objections. In return for decontrol, ten major fruit and vegetable firms, accounting for 30% of the industry's total production, agreed with the Council to increase production by amounts ranging up to 25% of individual product lines as compared with 1973 production and to keep price increases at levels authorized on March 1, 1974, on all product lines until the new crop became available.

On April 15, 1974, food retailing and wholesaling were decontrolled. A major reason for this early decontrol (although the end of the program was already near) was that labor and management in the retail food industry had agreed to form a Joint Labor-Management Committee with public member Wayne Horvitz as Chairman. This committee was to explore and consider labor-management relations problems in the retail food industry and to devote its efforts to improving the industry's collective bargaining structure and performance. The JLM committee, which contained many members of the Food Wage Committee, could well be the most important legacy that the food wage control program left for the industry. It was during the decontrol process, then, that the Committee accomplished part of its final charter mandate to work with labor and management organizations in the food industry under collective bargaining agreements to improve the structure and performance of collective bargaining in the industry.

Finally, on April 30, 1974, the Congress let the statutory authority for the control program expire and thus the rest of the food industry (basically processing and manufacturing) was decontrolled.

Some Rough Statistical Evidence

The discussion above describes how the Committee responded to the mandates of its charter. Despite the data limitations mentioned before, it is appropriate to examine briefly some data—where applicable—relating to the Committee's performance to see if they add anything to the story of the Committee's activities.

The fact that the Committee processed over 12,000 cases, prescribed regulations to meet the special problems of the food industry, and worked to improve the structure and performance of collective bargaining in the food industry (aided in the formation of the Joint Labor-Management Committee) has already been discussed. This section, then, will focus on the Committee's possible[69] quantitative effects on dispute settlement and wage stabilization.

Dispute Settlement. The concerns of the Committee about dispute settlement and its consequent efforts toward dispute settlement have been mentioned above. Unfortunately few data are available to measure these results.

Table IV-1 contains some statistics published by the Bureau of Labor Statistics relating to work stoppages[70] by various industries during the period 1971–1974. These statistics, while admittedly rough and very responsive to the underlying economic conditions, the degree of unionization by industry, and the bargaining schedule for each year, do suggest that the Committee may have promoted or encouraged labor peace in the food industry during its tenure (basically 1973). In manufacturing, food and kindred products, despite rapidly rising prices in 1973 the number of work stoppages was lower in 1973 than in 1971, 1972, or 1974. Furthermore, this was especially pronounced in the bakery industry—an industry that occupied a great deal of the Committee's attention.

In food retailing the picture is less dramatic but still suggestive of positive accomplishment. Again, labor disputes during 1973 were lower (48) than either the last partial precontrol year (1971) or the first partial postcontrol year (1974).[71] Only in 1972 were labor disputes in food retailing lower—30—and this may indicate the initial uncertainty prevailing during this period under the Pay Board. Most likely, however, it indicates that wage controls—whether dispute settlement is made an integral part of the program or not—have an initial dampening effect on labor disputes.

Finally, the figures indicate that the segments of the food industry

TABLE IV-1. WORK STOPPAGES BY INDUSTRY, 1971-1974

Industry	1971	1972	1973	1974
All Industries	5,138	5,010	5,353	6,074
Manufacturing	2,391	2,056	2,282	2,823
Food and kindred products	215	190	186	265
Food and kindred products, bakery products	35	32	18	43
Nonmanufacturing	2,762	2,954	3,072	3,253
Wholesale and retail trade	502	389	499	549
Wholesale trade	271	198	274	317
Retail trade	232	191[a]	225	232
General merchandise stores	28	26[a]	38	28
Food stores	53	30[a]	48	89

[a] Because of a printing error the data for retailing in 1972 are incorrect. The author has corrected the error and the data published here would appear to be correct.

SOURCE: Bureau of Labor Statistics, *Analysis of Work Stoppages* 1971-1974, Table A-14.

contained in the table had the greatest percentage increase in work stoppages in 1974 when controls were ended, as compared with 1973. Bakery manufacturing increased by 138%, food retailing by 85%, food and kindred products (which includes bakery) by 42%, compared with an all-industries increase of 13%, manufacturing by 23%, nonmanufacturing by 6%, retailing by 3%, and a decline of 26% in general merchandise retailing. These data suggest the possible effectiveness of the Committee's activity in dispute settlement and its role in preventing relationships from deteriorating further after a period of controls administered without labor and management direct participation.

To summarize, the data are rough but they are consistent with the proposition that the Committee, during its tenure, as part of its wage stabilization efforts, enhanced industrial peace in the food industry. The data also strongly indicated that a wage control program—even Pay Board style—of short duration may have a definite dampening effect on work stoppages.

Wage Stabilization. To measure the Committee's real impact is very difficult, if not impossible, for at least two basic reasons. First, there is a real scarcity of accurate, consistent data available to measure the Committee's efforts toward wage stabilization. Second, even if such data were available, it is true that what *did* happen is being measured, given the Committee's existence, not what *would have* happened if the Committee (and controls) had not been in existence.

Table IV-2, based on a computer printout requested by the author from the Cost of Living Council gives a qualitative picture of the Committee's actions (and the state of the wage data) as of May 24, 1974.[72] This table indicates: (1) by far most of the cases processed by

TABLE IV-2.   FOOD WAGE COMMITTEE ACTIVITY, BY DISPOSITION,
FROM JANUARY 11, 1973—MAY 24, 1974
(11,804 CLOSED CASES—2,618,846 EMPLOYEES)

Items	Total Cases	Not Audited	Approved in Full		Partly Approved and Partly Denied	Denied in Full	Items Not Requested
			Within Standard	Over Standard			
Wages and included benefits	11,804	5,885	4,317	1,247	322	27	6
Qualified benefits (pension, health, and welfare)	11,804	5,892	3,087	415	75	4	2,331
Retroactivity	11,804	5,910	1,256	0	168	45	4,425

SOURCE: Cost of Living Council computer printout, May 24, 1974.

the Committee were not audited so that the audited cases are a partial sample (but quite possibly a representative sample); (2) the vast majority of audited cases—where action was requested—were approved in full by the Committee mainly because they were within the standards set by the Pay Board; (3) the partial denial and denial in full[73] columns indicate positive definitive actions by the Committee; and (4) the retroactivity line verifies that this was a concern and tool of the Committee. Thus, these data show that many of the cases reviewed by the Committee were within the standards set by the Cost of Living Council. This may be evidence to the point mentioned before—that the existence of the Committee (and Cost of Living Council) may in itself have produced a stabilizing effect on wage settlements. (That so many cases were within the standard is especially noteworthy considering the inflation that was experienced during 1973–1974.)

Tables IV-3 through IV-5 contain data on average hourly earnings by industry for certain time periods. Before discussing the tables, we shall look at the data in them.

Average hourly earnings, as reported by the Bureau of Labor Statistics, are based on "establishment data." They are derived from reports of payrolls and manhours for production and related workers. The hourly earnings differ from wage rates since the earnings are the actual return to a worker (including overtime and premium pay) for a stated period of time whereas rates are the amounts stipulated for a given unit of work or time.[74]

For purposes of this chapter, wage rates and benefit schedules would definitely be preferable to these earnings data. The earnings data are not adjusted for the delay that was inherent in the control program and are therefore biased downward (higher rates than those in effect had been negotiated especially during the early months of the Stabilization Program). Furthermore, the earnings data are sensitive to hours worked as well as to wage rate changes.[75] Wage rates, as explained above, however, are not available by industry. Hence these earnings data are the best approximation to wage rate data and are likely to pick up basic wage changes across industries at any one point in time. (Furthermore, to the extent that the control programs were designed to moderate labor costs, these earnings data are appropriate tools to measure the success of the programs.)

Table IV-3 presents the average hourly earnings by industry for the years 1969–1975. The industrial breakdowns contained in Table IV-3 (and the following tables) were chosen to highlight the Committee's activities and to offer relevant comparisons. Of note in the table is the fact that the average hourly earnings figure for retail food stores remained below the "low wage figure" until some time in 1974. This average reflects the fact that a large number of employees in the food industry were not subject to controls during the Committee's existence. Besides giving a broad picture of hourly earnings throughout the economy during this period, the table demonstrates that from

TABLE IV-3.   AVERAGE HOURLY EARNINGS, BY INDUSTRY, 1969-1975

| Year | Total Private | Manufacturing | | | | Wholesale and Retail Trade | Wholesale Trade | Retail Trade | Retail Trade | |
		Manufacturing	Nondurable	Nondurable Food and Kindred Products	Nondurable Food and Kindred Products, Bakery				General Merchandise	Food Stores
1969	$3.04	$3.19	$2.91	$2.96	$3.00	$2.56	$3.23	$2.30	$2.24	$2.55
1970	3.22	3.36	3.08	3.16	3.22	2.71	3.44	2.44	2.38	2.71
1971	3.44	3.56	3.26	3.38	3.47	2.87	3.67	2.57	2.48	2.91
1972	3.67	3.81	3.47	3.59	3.72	3.02	3.88	2.70	2.60	3.09
1973	3.92	4.07	3.68	3.82	3.97	3.20	4.12	2.87	2.73	3.27
1974	4.22	4.40	3.98	4.15	4.29	3.47	4.49	3.10	2.97	3.60
1975	4.54	4.81	4.35	4.57	4.70	3.75	4.89	3.34	3.21	3.95

SOURCE: EMPLOYMENT AND EARNINGS TABLE C-2, BUREAU OF LABOR STATISTICS, U.S. DEPARTMENT OF LABOR.

1970 to 1972—the years immediately preceding the Committee's existence—the two categories of cases, bakery manufacturing and retail food stores, that appeared to occupy most of the Committee's attention also had had as large or larger percentage increases in hourly earnings as any other industrial classification contained in Table IV-3. Retail trade food stores increased average hourly earnings by 14% ($2.71 to $3.09) while retail trade general merchandise increased by 9.2% and bakery manufacturing increased by 15.5% while nondurable manufacturing increased by 12.7%.

Since the various control periods did not parallel calendar years, Tables IV-4 and IV-5, which focus on average hourly earnings (and changes therein) at key dates during and after these periods are probably more useful than Table IV-3. These tables, taken together, add further evidence that the existence of the Committee had some impact on hourly earnings (and hence probably wage rates) in the food industry.

Table IV-4 shows that from January 1973 to April 1973 the average hourly earnings of retail food stores increased by only one cent whereas general merchandise stores increased by nine cents. As mentioned earlier, this was a period during which few cases were processed by the Committee and food wages were effectively frozen from March 29 until April 20, 1973.

Table IV-5, which is based on data contained in Table IV-4, is even more persuasive. This table presents annualized percentage increases by industry for three time periods: August 1971–January 1973 (Phases I and II); January 1973–April 1974 (the Committee's existence and Phases III and IV); and April 1974–April 1975 (the first postcontrol year). This table shows that in all cases annualized percentage changes in hourly earnings were much lower during control periods than during the first postcontrol year. (It is true that prices climbed faster during the postcontrol year—although not significantly higher than the final months of the Committee's existence—but so did the unemployment rate.)

Table IV-5 also indicates that the annualized percentage increase in retail food stores (6.5%) was identical during the Committee's existence (despite much faster price increases) to the increase during Phase I and Phase II and significantly below the postcontrol increase (12.4%) and the increase for retail trade general merchandise (8.2%) and wholesale trade (7.6%) during the same time period. This suggests that the Committee had some possible moderating influence. The increase for wholesale and retail trade—including retail food stores—from January 1973 to April 1974 was, however, in excess of the increase for total private industry and manufacturing. This may reflect supply and demand factors or the relatively low-wage status of retail and wholesale trade.

The results for food manufacturing are more mixed but are not inconsistent with the Committee's having had an impact. Food and

TABLE IV-4.   AVERAGE HOURLY EARNINGS, BY INDUSTRY, ON VARIOUS DATES BETWEEN AUGUST 1971 AND APRIL 1975

| Date | Total Private | Manufacturing | | | | Wholesale and Retail Trade | Wholesale Trade | Retail Trade | Retail Trade | |
		Manufacturing	Nondurable	Nondurable Food and Kindred Products	Nondurable Food and Kindred Products, Bakery				General Merchandise	Food Stores
August 1971	$3.46	$3.59	$3.27	$3.35	$3.51	$2.89	$3.70	$2.57	$2.49	$2.93
January 1972	3.55	3.70	3.39	3.53	3.60	2.97	3.82	2.66	2.57	3.02
August 1972	3.66	3.80	3.47	3.57	3.74	3.01	3.86	2.70	2.60	3.09
January 1973	3.77	3.98	3.61	3.75	3.81	3.11	3.99	2.78	2.61	3.20
April 1973	3.83	4.01	3.63	3.78	3.85	3.16	4.07	2.83	2.70	3.21
January 1974	4.02	4.21	3.83	4.00	4.15	3.35	4.29	2.99	2.82	3.43
April 1974	4.07	4.25	3.87	4.08	4.16	3.38	4.37	3.01	2.88	3.46
May 1974	4.14	4.33	3.91	4.12	4.18	3.44	4.41	3.08	2.95	3.54
July 1974	4.21	4.41	4.03	4.19	4.32	3.49	4.48	3.12	3.02	3.62
January 1975	4.39	4.65	4.22	4.40	4.48	3.65	4.73	3.24	3.11	3.83
April 1975	4.44	4.71	4.27	4.48	4.55	3.70	4.80	3.29	3.20	3.89

SOURCE: Employment and Earnings Table C-2, Bureau of Labor Statistics, U.S. Department of Labor.

TABLE IV-5.   ANNUAL PERCENTAGE INCREASES IN AVERAGE HOURLY EARNINGS, BY INDUSTRY, FOR SELECTED TIME PERIODS

Time Period	Total Private	Manufacturing	Nondurable	Manufacturing Nondurable Food and Kindred Products	Manufacturing Nondurable Food and Kindred Products, Bakery	Wholesale and Retail Trade	Wholesale Trade	Retail Trade	Retail Trade General Merchandise	Retail Trade Food Stores
August 1971 to January 1973 (Phases I and II)	6.3%	7.7%	7.3%	8.4%	6.0%	5.4%	5.5%	5.8%	3.4%	6.5%
January 1973 to April 1974 (food committee)	6.4	5.4	5.8	7.0	7.4	7.0	7.6	6.6	8.2	6.5
April 1974 to April 1975 (post controls)	9.0	10.8	10.3	9.8	9.4	9.5	9.8	9.3	11.1	12.4

SOURCE: Employment and Earnings Table C-2, Bureau of Labor Statistics, U.S. Department of Labor.

kindred products and its subcomponent, bakery, had higher percentage increases in hourly earnings during the Committee's existence than did nondurable manufacturing in general. However, both rates were significantly lower than the corresponding rates for the postcontrol year. Furthermore, the food and kindred products increase (7.0%) during the Committee's existence was lower than the increase (8.4%) during the prior control periods.

Other examples could undoubtedly be given. The data are rough, but in the author's viewpoint are in general consistent with the proposition that the Cost of Living Council had an impact on labor costs from January 1971 to April 1974 and that the Food Wage Committee processed cases and had an impact on dispute settlement and labor costs in the food industry during the time period January 1973–April 1974.

We now turn to the concluding section of this chapter.

Costs and Benefits, Lessons Learned, and Open Questions

A brief assessment is in order. What can clearly be stated is that the Committee did its best to carry out the assignments given to it. Obstacles which it had to surmount included its short duration, its limited staff, problems caused by the nature of the food industry and the prior phases of stabilization, and the inflationary state of the economy. What cannot be so definitively appraised is the success of this effort and the relevance of the Committee's experience to any future stabilization program.

The food industry, especially on the price side, was a major target of controls. Because food wages were to be controlled, it is probably true that the costs of controls were lower and the benefits higher given the existence of the Committee than they would have been if they had been administered in another manner. Costs associated with wage controls affect different groups: the food industry, the government, and workers not receiving increases agreed to in collective bargaining or those proposed by management alone. Also to be considered are the effects on collective bargaining itself.

Certainly controls entailed substantial costs to the industry. There was considerable expense involved in forms, records, legal fees, new administrative requirements, and the like. Further, there were costs associated with delayed implementation of decisions. Also, since the food industry was probably under more strict controls than most other industries, it may have acted as a deterrent for individuals or firms entering it or a discouragement to new investment during the controls period. The magnitude of these costs to the industry will never fully be measured. Suffice it to recognize that they were substantial.

The cost to the government was also great. A staff had to be assembled and additional people were hired for the program. Again, there is no doubt that the government made every effort to minimize this cost (perhaps with some detrimental effects to the program).

There were also the costs that manifested themselves in the bargaining process. These did not appear to be numerous. There is a feeling that due to the Regulations, higher fringe benefits—especially pension and health and welfare—may have been negotiated than would have been the case in a no-control economy.[76] Also, there is some evidence that the general wage and salary standard became the minimum amount that was negotiated. In some situations this may have added to the cost of the contract. As a consequence of controls, contracts became shorter in duration and resulted in additional costs to the industry.[77]

On the positive side the following points should be made. First, the Committee's policies probably did not affect the industry adversely. The wage level at the time the program ended was almost certainly no higher and most probably lower than it would have been without the Committee's efforts. Furthermore, the Committee achieved some progress in rationalizing the wage structure in a number of labor markets with the result that the wage-over-wage comparisons that followed the Committee's work were probably less inflationary than otherwise.

Second, the Committee provided a vehicle for sustained and productive interaction of top level labor and management in the industry. It certainly fostered a better appreciation of problems of mutual concern which carried over to the post-controls period.[78]

Third, the Committee served as the nucleus for the formation of the Joint Labor-Management Committee chaired by Wayne Horvitz.

Fourth, the Committee, with the help of the Cost of Living Council, administered the wage and salary stabilization policy flexibly without adherence to a single number. Rigid rules and formulas were kept to a minimum, thus eliminating many of the worst problems and abuses of Phase II.

Fifth, the Cost of Living Council and the Committee managed to keep labor actively participating for the entire program. This occurred at a time when the AFL-CIO was increasing its attacks on the Administration and its economic policies.

Sixth, the Committee managed to process a lot of cases and follow through on its assignments. The absence of law suits and front-page publicity, which had characterized its predecessor stabilization agencies, would appear to testify to the Committee's ability to reach consensus.

Seventh, the Committee's involvement in dispute settlement, however infrequent, emphasized that wage and benefit stabilization can fruitfully be linked to dispute settlement. The Federal Mediation and Conciliation Service was closely associated with the Committee. These activities and contacts should also prove helpful to the food industry in the future.

As a necessary adjunct to its mission, the Committee had to concern itself with collective bargaining in the food industry. Many people learned about this structure by working on the Committee, with the Committee, or for the Committee. The Committee bent over backwards to avoid instituting any policy that might cause long-run distortions or seriously disrupt the collective bargaining process in the industry.

The Phase II stabilization period and the Tripartite Committee stage did educate the food industry to the costs associated with wage settlements. The submission forms forced the parties to "cost out" their settlements. In the writer's opinion, this cost consciousness should prove beneficial to labor and management in the industry.

Weighing the costs or benefits of the program, it is reasonable to conclude that, given the necessity of wage stabilization, its administration by the Tripartite Committee was more effective, in cost-benefit terms, than under other forms of administrative arrangements.

We now turn to a discussion of some of the lessons learned from the Committee's experience.

Lessons Learned from the Committee's Operation

The following are some of the lessons to be learned from the Committee's experience with wage stabilization.

Perhaps the major lesson learned, or relearned, is that wage stabilization entails hard work and is both complicated and delicate. Such a program should not be entered into lightly. A short-run stabilization program may produce results that would be destabilizing in the long run, if wages are arbitrarily reduced or distortions created or allowed to develop by application of mechanical rules.[79] Moreover, a program of stabilization once put in place may develop a life of its own and its duration is unpredictable.

Another lesson is that advance preparation might seem to alleviate some of the problems that were experienced under stabilization. The existence of data bases (perhaps on an industry-by-industry basis), suitable forms, a system to receive, process, and return these forms, and a working computer program or process to aid the effort are administrative prerequisites. These tools would eliminate much of the delay and would provide the information on which to make decisions. Any inflation monitoring agency should include in its responsibilities the development of suitable data for a stabilization agency should the need arise.

The Committee's experience also suggests that a meaningful program requires adequate staffing. The food wage stabilization effort directly involved over 50 full-time civil servants and many more on a part-time basis in support services for an industry with many millions of employees and several hundred thousand enterprises. Understaffing seriously risks the success of a program as well as heightens the possibilities of long-term destabilization. While self-implementation and a single standard may minimize staff, it docs not, at least in the conditions of 1972–1974, create effective and constructive wage stabilization.

Another lesson is that a stabilization effort needs time to work and such time is very hard to secure. Stabilization often requires in the short run large adjustments for those who have lagged behind or are at the low end of a sequence of adjustments before meaningful stabilization efforts can become effective. Also, inflationary periods when controls are most likely to be applied create wage distortions as units fight to catch up and diverse escalation formulas produce varying wage adjustments. Time is needed for contracts to expire and for new settlements to come before the stabilization agency. However, the luxury of time may not be available. Labor's response to any control program is often hostile. Hence time, which may be so critical to the program's success, is hard to guarantee as patience wears thin and irritation with contraints grows.

Any stabilization program to continue must have a degree of cooperation from the affected parties. Without this support a combination of legislative investigations, lawsuits, attacks in the press, amendments to the program (low wage, hearing requirement, open meetings), widespread violations, and strikes is likely seriously to weaken, if not destroy, the program.[80] In the Committee experience labor and management could have seriously crippled the program.

The entire control experience, especially where regulations and rules were so important, emphasized the importance of knowing the rules of the game. The experience also suggested that labor unions were, on the whole, better equipped with offices or representatives in Washington and with their preoccupation with collective bargaining to learn the rules than were many companies. The size and financial condition of a company, and union, often determined how well one played the stabilization regulation game. These consequences, while perhaps somewhat inevitable, emphasized the importance of issuing and promulgating widely stabilization rules which were simply stated and easily comprehensible. The Committee, reflecting its composition and as a matter of deliberate policy, was a significant means of communication and education of the parties.

Another lesson, based both on the Phase II and on the Committee's experience, is that a single number or "general wage and salary standard," whether stated in percentage or dollar terms, will not lead to stabilization. Such a standard may buy time, but sooner or later a more flexibly administered program must take place either de facto or de jure, or the end result will be distortions or widespread noncompliance.

The experience also suggests that industry-by-industry stabilization is complicated and hard work but is probably still the only way to accomplish long-term structural objectives as well as short-term wage control objectives. Industry definition is complex, and overlapping union jurisdictions and business enterprises complicate the task. Also each industry requires supporting staffs. Still, industry focus allows knowledgeable parties, with vested interests and careers at stake, to focus on the problems and insures that the participants have a professional and personal interest in the solution to these problems.

Another lesson to be learned from the Committee's experience is that should stabilizing agencies not adopt reasonable or responsive rules, Congress and the courts will impose specific rules. This principle is well illustrated in the handling of the low wage exemption.

A further lesson can be derived from the Cost of Living Council's experience, reinforced by the Committee's experience. Stabilization carried out by a tripartite body, whose members can freely discuss problems of mutual concern based on mutual respect acquired by day-to-day problem solving, can serve as a vehicle or catalyst to consider reforms in bargaining structure or other practices which it is hoped may yield long-term effects surviving the stabilization period. The view of the Cost of Living Council after January 1973 was that since controls were in effect it was appropriate to seek to achieve some longer-term objectives; indeed securing labor-management cooperation on such longer-term objectives tends to facilitate short-term stabilization.

Another lesson is that tripartitism is the best vehicle to administer a stabilization program which contains both short-run and long-run objectives. A tripartite program insures involvement of the affected parties, brings expertise to the decision-making process, and tends to encourage acceptance of decisions. These factors are desirable, if not essential, for any stabilization program.

In summary, this chapter has argued that the total experience of the Committee suggests that a future wage stabilization program, at least in circumstances akin to those existing in 1971–1974, should include or consider the following ingredients: no reliance on a single standard; a good data base; a tripartite committee; strong liaison with the Federal Mediation and Conciliation Service and, at least peripherally, dispute settlement; no employee unit size cut-offs; consideration of the impact of work rule changes on the stabilization effort; coverage of both union and nonunion sectors; a parallel price program; serious consideration of the low wage question; recognition that rigid regulations encourage gamesmanship by the parties; provision of a decontrol strategy; and, if constituted on an industry basis and all industries are not controlled, some genuine and readily explainable reason for this difference in treatment.[81]

Food Wage Stabilization—Some Open Questions

It is fitting to close this chapter with some of the unresolved questions growing out of the food wage stabilization experience in 1972–

1974 that merit study. Like the lessons outlined above, these issues are based mainly on the author's experience.

Any economic stabilization program involving restraints on wages and prices operates within a given economic and political climate which may be critical in determining both organizational structure and basic policies and procedures. After widespread public and interest group support for controls in 1971, the Cost of Living Council and the Committee in 1973–1974 operated in a generally hostile political and economic environment. The assessment of the Committee's results and effectiveness must reflect the distinctive characteristics of the 1973–1974 period. Similarly, future stabilization strategies must take into account the economic and political conditions of the time. One question then is how much the experience would have differed in another time period under different political and economic events.[82]

A second issue is whether price control necessitates correlative wage control. This question involves issues of equity, practicality, and economics.[83] If it is decided that price controls and wage and benefit controls must be simutaneously imposed, the question arises as to how closely and with what administrative and policy means should the two programs be coordinated.

A third question is whether a wage control program needs a strong compliance program. The Cost of Living Council experience offers little guidance. During Phase II and the period of the Committee's existence there was no strong compliance program; voluntary compliance was relied upon and was seemingly forthcoming. Whether this would be true in future programs is an open question.

Closely related to the compliance issue is whether the Internal Revenue Service should have been involved in the wage stabilization program. IRS involvement did prevent the development of a new federal agency with field offices, and one that could be readily terminated, but it is questionable whether IRS participation furthered wage stabilization goals or worked to the long-run advantage of the Service. The IRS was looked upon with deep suspicion by labor and management in collective bargaining affairs, more so among labor, and the IRS often felt that stabilization was keeping it from its regular activities. A broader but related question is whether any existing agency should be converted to a stabilization agency if the need arose.[84]

Although the author believes, based on the Committee's experience, that a wage stabilization agency should also have dispute settlement responsibilities, there are differences of views on this matter as illustrated by the strong views of those in charge of Phase II. The degree of attention and involvement of a stabilization program in dispute settlement may be listed as a fourth question.

A fifth issue, and a repetitive one from earlier stabilization periods, concerns whether sectoral or industry wage stabilization is preferable to a single economy-wide stabilization program administered without specialization. A single program may appear to be more equitable and to preclude special rules; on the other hand, a sectoral program can probably secure greater participation of the parties and deal with the most complex areas. In the past some combination of the two approaches has been used. In addition to an evaluation of the basic economic forces present which suggest the desirability of wage stabilization, consideration should be given to such factors as to whether the underlying imbalances in the wage structure are industry-wide, regional-wide, or economy-wide and to the expected duration of the stabilization program. Certainly in 1973 it appeared that certain sectors of the economy needed much more attention than others. This question also is linked to the question of whether wage and price controls must accompany each other.

A sixth question involves whether wage controls can be (should be) administered responsibly again by the government without widespread support of the parties or under conditions in which the affected parties strongly objected to them. In the author's mind it is doubtful that the government alone could administer an effective and substantial stabilization program if the affected parties seriously objected to it and decided to be noncooperative.[85]

A seventh question concerns the time frame of the stabilization program. Is it conceived to last a few months, a year, or a number of years? The appropriate policies and administrative devices should be expected to be quite different. The 1971 program was intended to be short in duration, and the general wage standard self-administration and the smallest possible bureaucracy were decisions related to this view of duration. But events turned out differently, and some of these policies were inappropriate. The uncertainty of duration is an issue for all planning for stabilization.

CHAPTER V

International Food Policy Issues

GLENN L. NELSON

GLENN L. NELSON

Glenn L. Nelson is associate professor in the Department of Agricultural and Applied Economics, University of Minnesota. He was formerly assistant professor in the Department of Agricultural Economics, Purdue University. He served with the Cost of Living Council as branch chief of the Analytic Branch, Policy Analysis Division, Office of Food where his duties included supervising economic and statistical analyses related to food and agricultural policy. His governmental experience also includes positions as economist of the Policy Research Division, Office of Economic Opportunity, and as a consultant for higher education with the Bureau of Higher Education, Michigan Department of Education.

Professor Nelson is the author of two reports on the impact of price controls, prepared under contract with the U.S. Department of the Treasury; he was also a consultant for a study of shortages in the livestock-feed grain sector which was funded by the National Commission on Supplies and Shortages.

He was a member of a task force jointly sponsored by the Economic Statistics Committee of the American Agricultural Economics Association and by the Economic Research Service of the U.S. Department of Agriculture which reported in January 1976 on Review and Evaluation of Price Spread Data for Foods.

CHAPTER V

International Food Policy Issues

THE U.S. AGRICULTURAL SECTOR is greatly affected by international events and institutions.[1] And conversely, U.S. policies have important impacts on other countries because of the nation's importance in world production and trade.

The value of agricultural exports reached a record $22 billion in 1974, an amount equal to 23% of total U.S. exports (Figure V-1). Agricultural exports have played an important role in offsetting the increased cost of imports resulting in large part from higher petroleum prices. From 1972 to 1974 agricultural exports more than doubled in value, a growth rate slightly in excess of that for nonagricultural exports.

Exports absorb a large proportion of total U.S. production of major field crops (Table V-1). In recent years exports equaled over half of wheat production, nearly half of soybeans and their products, over one-fifth of feed grain production (principally corn), and over one-third of cotton production. Although always significant, foreign demand has varied greatly with a destabilizing impact on U.S. markets.

The resolution of international food policy issues is clearly relevant to domestic food price stability. At a minimum, domestic policies designed to reduce the rise in domestic prices must recognize the potential for large exports in response to differentials between domestic and foreign prices. Increased exports would, of course, exacerbate the domestic problems of limited supplies and upward pressures on prices. On the other hand, since the United States is a major exporter of agricultural products, the possibility of dampening domestic price increases by restricting exports is very real. The brief soybean embargo and export restrictions in 1973 are examples of the use of export controls. U.S. exports of the major field crops are

FIGURE V-1.   U.S. MERCHANDISE TRADE BY COMMODITY GROUP, 1962–1974[a]

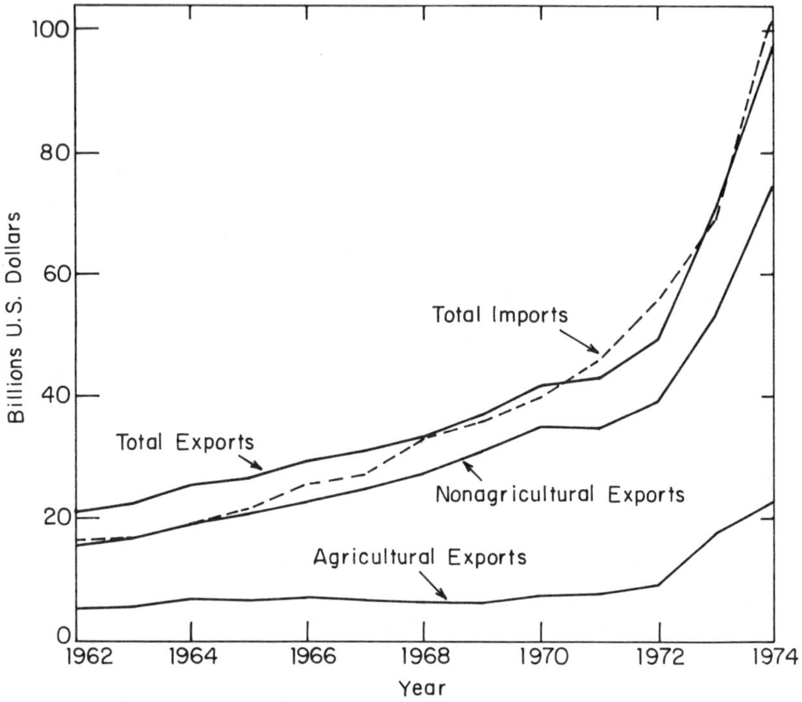

a Data are on a balance-of-payments basis and exclude military shipments.

SOURCE: USDA, *World Monetary Conditions in Relation to Agricultural Trade,* WMC-8, May 1975, p. 27.

sufficiently large so that a relatively small reduction in exports can have a substantial impact on domestic supplies and prices. The outstanding example is wheat. A decision to reduce exports by only 5% in 1973–1974 when wheat stocks were tight and prices rose to record levels would have increased supplies available for domestic food, working stocks, and other uses by 57 million bushels or 6%—with a substantially larger percentage impact on domestic prices. Many other examples of the interrelationships of international food policy issues and domestic price stability could be cited here, but they will be left until later when the issues are discussed in more detail.

The purpose of this chapter is to examine international policy issues primarily from the perspective of their impacts on domestic food price stability. The record of recent years will be examined for lessons which might be applicable in future periods of shortage. Of particular interest are the degree to which international policies are (1) mandated by domestic price controls, (2) complements to domestic stabilization policy, or (3) substitutes for direct controls on prices.

This chapter consists of three major sections. First, the goal of domestic price stabilization is briefly discussed. Second, the principal features of the international environment which have a destabilizing impact on the domestic scene are examined. Third, the major policy options and their implications are treated.

DOMESTIC PRICE STABILIZATION

Stability in an economic context may have a variety of meanings. Some people refer to stability relative to a constant price while others use a trend line as a base. Still others use the term to describe the rate

TABLE V-1.   U.S. PRODUCTION AND EXPORTS OF MAJOR FIELD CROPS, 1971-1972 THROUGH 1974-1975

Commodity and Marketing Year	Production	Exports	Exports/Production (in percentages)
Wheat (millions of bushels)			
1971-1972	1618	633	39%
1972-1973	1545	1186	77
1973-1974	1705	1148	67
1974-1975[a]	1793	1050	59
Soybeans (millions of bushels)			
1971-1972	1176	417[b]	35[b]
1972-1973	1271	479[b]	38[b]
1973-1974	1547	539[b]	35[b]
1974-1975[a]	1233	400[b]	32[b]
Corn (millions of bushels)			
1971-1972	5641	796	14
1972-1973	5573	1258	23
1973-1974	5647	1243	22
1974-1975[a]	4651	1075	23
Total feed grains[c] (millions of tons)			
1971-1972	208	27	13
1972-1973	200	43	22
1973-1974	205	44	21
1974-1975[a]	165	37	22
Cotton (millions of bales)			
1971-1972	10.5	3.4	32
1972-1973	13.7	5.3	39
1973-1974	13.2	6.1	46
1974-1975[a]	11.5	3.9	34

[a] Forecast.

[b] Beans only; a portion of the oil and meal produced domestically are exported— 16% and 28%, respectively, in 1973-1974. Thus, nearly half of all soybeans and related products are typically exported.

[c] Corn, sorghum, oats, and barley.

SOURCES: USDA, *Agricultural Supply & Demand Estimates,* No. 27, June 11, 1975; *Wheat Situation,* WS-232, May 1975; *Fats and Oils Situation,* FOS-277, April 1975; *Feed Situation,* FDS-257, May 1975; *Cotton Situation,* CS-270, April 1975.

at which an economic system attains equilibrium prices, which may shift markedly over time.

In this chapter stability pertains to the reduction of variation around a long-term trend. The trend of prices is determined by such factors as population growth, income growth, climatic shifts, production technology, and the opportunity cost of resources devoted to food production and processing. Thus, shifts in these causal variables cause shifts in food prices which are not addressed here. The definition of "long term" may vary among commodities and time periods, but in general several years should be considered. Thus, this study is primarily concerned with means of reducing above-trend prices and raising below-trend prices when the deviation from the long-term trend is expected to persist for a year or more. Very little attention will be devoted to reducing seasonal variations within a year or to changing basic trends.

As has been stated, the present perspective is the role of international food policies in achieving stabilization of domestic food prices. This should *not* be taken as an indication that other policy goals are irrelevant or of lower priority. Other goals that should be taken into consideration include adequate returns to producers, public versus private dominance in selected areas of economic decision making, economic growth, humanitarianism, and social and political stability.[2] However, domestic price stabilization does appear to be a very important consideration. When inflation became very rapid in 1972–1974, domestic stabilization policy often dominated other interests. Overseas food aid programs were cut back, exports were embargoed or strongly discouraged, available government-held reserves were poured into commercial markets, barriers to dairy imports were lowered, and so on. Cries of anguish rose from both foreign nations and special interests in the United States, but price increases in the United States were certainly dampened to some degree. The nature of these international policy tools and the problems of their implementation, which are not well understood, warrant careful examination.

Most of this presentation focuses on grains and oilseeds, but it is very important not to lose sight of the implications for the livestock and poultry sectors. Although meat and poultry producers were not directly affected by the extensive agricultural programs of the 1950's and 1960's, the stability in feed prices caused by large grain reserves appears to have increased stability in livestock prices. The results of a study by the Council of Economic Advisers, given in Table V-2, show a correspondence of more stability in corn and soybean prices with greater stability in beef cattle and hog prices. Since feed is a major cost of livestock producers, there is a clear and convincing rationale for a causal relationship.

Recent events confirm the linkage between instability in grain prices and livestock and poultry prices. These events have been discussed in some detail in Chapter I, but a brief review here may be helpful. High

TABLE V-2. INDICATORS OF THE VARIANCE OF SELECTED FARM PRICES
IN CONSTANT DOLLARS, SELECTED PERIODS, 1910-1971

Commodity and Period	Mean[a]	Variance	Coefficient of Variation
Corn			
1910-1949	1.73	.227	.276
1950-1971	1.31	.072	.206
Soybeans			
1910-1949	3.08	.914	.311
1950-1971	2.56	.091	.118
Beef cattle			
1910-1949	16.43	17.9	.258
1950-1971	22.36	13.2	.162
Hogs			
1910-1949	19.88	23.7	.245
1950-1971	19.13	8.7	.154

[a] Annual averages: Dollars per bushel for corn and soybeans; dollars per hundred pounds for beef cattle and hogs.

SOURCE: Council of Economic Advisers, *Annual Report* transmitted with the *Economic Report of the President,* Washington: Government Printing Office, 1975, p. 176.

prices of corn have been a significant factor in plummeting hog production and escalating pork prices. Births of pigs from December 1974 through May 1975 were down 22% from the preceding year and were the lowest since the depression year of 1935.[3] This is merely another turn in a series of gyrations related to the blighted corn corp of 1970, the large crop in 1971, and unprecedented export demand beginning in 1972. Since the full cycle of expanding production by withholding females for breeding requires at least two years, the disruption of hog production will affect pork prices through at least 1977—and probably longer.

The impact of high feed prices has a similar destabilizing effect on other commodities. The number of cattle in feedlots on April 1, 1975, was the lowest for that date since 1963.[4] Beef prices were at very high levels, and in addition, the premium paid for grain-fed beef widened considerably over the price of grass-fed beef. The number of egg-laying hens dropped 12% from 1971 to 1975, after trending upward in the 1960's.[5] Broiler production stagnated after 1972 following a strong uptrend for many years.[6] Milk production in 1975 was 4% below the 1972 level; one must go all the way back to the Korean War years of 1951-1952, when feed prices were also high, to find a period of lower milk production than in 1973-1975.[7] Factors other than varying feed prices, such as government price controls and fluctuations in consumer income, have also led to instability in livestock and poultry production and prices. However, there can be no doubt that greater variation in grain and oilseed prices are reflected in the prices of animal product sectors. The relationships are complicated by varying time lags which may cause instability to persist long after the original shock to the system occurred.

IMPACTS OF INTERNATIONAL EVENTS AND INSTITUTIONS ON U.S. MARKETS

Before moving to a discussion focusing directly on international food policy issues facing the United States, it is useful to examine the world context. The events and institutions in foreign countries impose constraints on, and present opportunities for, U.S. stabilization policies. Three general topics are covered in this section: (1) natural phenomena, (2) social and political institutions, and (3) projected trends.

Natural Phenomena

Weather is a primary source of instability in food production throughout the world. Droughts, floods, frosts, and other weather factors occur frequently but unpredictably. In addition to weather, production often varies as a result of disease, insect infestations, and even shifting ocean currents.

Appendix Tables V-1 through V-9 contain data on production and consumption of wheat, rice, feed grains, and protein meals from 1960–1961 through 1975–1976 for the United States, three other major exporters (Canada, Australia, and Argentina), and the remainder of the world. Production trends were computed, and instability was then measured by calculating the deviations of actual figures from trend values (Appendix Tables V-10 and V-11).[8]

World production of the major food grains, wheat and rice, trended upward at a rate of 17 million metric tons per year in the period 1960–1961—1974–1975. Production in the United States grew at an average of 1.2 million tons per year, and the U.S. contribution to world production remained quite constant at about 7%. The average deviation from the trend line of growth was 12 million tons or slightly over 2% of production. The extremes ranged from a positive 21 million tons in 1968–1969 to a negative 21 million tons in 1972–1973 (about 4% of trend line production). In the 1960's year-end stocks of wheat were usually equal to 12% to 16% of food grain consumption (stocks of rice are so small and constant that they are not a significant factor). This level of stocks provided a sufficient margin of flexibility or insurance so that production shortfalls were absorbed without drastic price changes. Hardship, even to the point of starvation, was of course evident in some poorer countries but higher income nations such as the United States experienced few troubles—or even net benefits as farm price support subsidies declined. The food grain problems of the 1960's tended to be those of distribution of available supplies and not of world-wide scarcity.

Wheat stocks relative to food grain consumption declined from 14% to 18% in the late 1960's to 7% to 8% in 1975 and 1976. When stocks reach such low levels, shortfalls from trend line production tend to create severe hardship in low income countries and raise prices in developed countries such as the United States. Requirements for ending stocks reflect a variety of factors such as (1) the need for minimal working inventories, i.e., the "pipeline" cannot become completely empty, (2) a lack of perfect correspondence between the end of the designated crop year and the actual transition from old to new crop supplies, and (3) an economic and physical inability to balance surplus and shortage areas completely in any one year through transport of grain. Thus, ending stocks can never reach zero. Based on events in recent years, wheat stocks of 7% to 8% of world food grain consumption are at near minimal levels. Production shortfalls in this environment must be dealt with primarily by cutting consumption rather than stocks. The instability evident in historical food grain production clearly should be cause for concern.

The United States contributed 9% of the instability in world food grain production in 1960–1961—1974–1975, approximately equaling its contribution of 7% to production. The nature of the instability of production, however, has been quite different in the principal exporting and rest-of-world countries. Instability in Canada, Australia, Argentina, and the United States has been primarily a result of instability of acreage harvested while instability in the rest-of-world is primarily a function of yield variability. Since government policies in exporting countries have been a major cause of fluctuations in acreage, there is some reason to believe that acreage—and thus production—instability could be reduced somewhat from historical levels if exporting countries deemed it desirable. Examination of the 1960–1961—1974–1975 period does reveal that the four major exporting countries tended to show positive deviations from trend in acreage when beginning stocks tended to be low. This is encouraging. Statistics on instability developed from historical series on production only would appear to overstate the degree of the problem in times of scarcity *if* one asumes that governments will not restrict acreage in such circumstances.

The importance of instability of production is that it leads to marked variation in U.S. exports—and prices if stocks are low (Figure V-2). Deviations of wheat and rice production from trend in the rest-of-world countries ranged from a negative 23 million tons to a positive 18 million tons in the 1960–1961 to the 1974–1975 period. During this same period U.S. exports of wheat varied from 15 to 32 million tons per year; as is to be expected, U.S. exports tend to be directly related to shortfalls in world production. Variability of export demand has been a much more important factor in causing instability

FIGURE V-2.   WHEAT EXPORTS FROM THE U.S. AND OTHER MAJOR EXPORTERS
RELATIVE TO PRODUCTION OF WHEAT AND RICE IN REST-OF-WORLD,
1960-1961—1974-1975

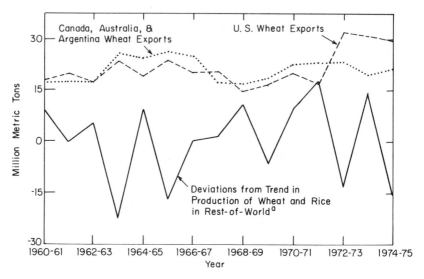

[a] World less Canada, Australia, Argentina, and U.S.

SOURCES: Appendix Table V-11; USDA, *Foreign Agriculture Circular*, FG 9-76, May 1976.

of prices than fluctuations in domestic demand. Exports rose from an average of 18 million tons in 1969-1970 through 1971-1972 to an average of 31 million tons in 1972-1973 through 1974-1975, while domestic consumption averaged 22 and 20 million tons, respectively.

The willingness of the United States to hold wheat stocks was undoubtedly a stabilizing influence in the period examined. The United States held about 32% of world wheat stocks, a proportion considerably greater than its share of production (13%) or contribution to instability (6%). In 1974 and 1975 U.S. stocks at the end of the marketing year fell to 12% and 14%, respectively, of world stocks.

World production of coarse grains, used primarily for animal feed, rose at an average rate of 14.3 million metric tons per year in 1960-1961 through 1974-1975. U.S. production increased at a trend rate of 3.5 million tons per year; U.S. production as a fraction of world production declined slightly over this period. The average deviation of world production from its trend was 13 million tons which equaled about 3% of production. The extremes were a positive 32 million tons in 1973-1974 and a negative 24 million tons in 1974-1975 which equaled 4% and 6%, respectively, of trend line production. As was the case for food grains, the fluctuations did not lead to major impacts during the 1960's when year-end stocks usually equaled 14% to 20%

of consumption. However, year-end stocks in 1974–1975 equaled only 8% of consumption, and fluctuations of up to 6% of trend in production had a major destabilizing impact on world—and in turn—U.S. prices.

The U.S. contribution to world instability of coarse grain production in 1960–1961 through 1974–1975 was 64%, much greater than its 31% share of world production. Relative to other countries, the United States was a major destabilizing factor in world coarse grain production; but during the 15-year period the United States held about 65% of world stocks, roughly in line with its contribution to production instability. The percentage of U.S. to world stocks fell to 38% and 30% in 1974 and 1975, respectively. As in the case of food grains, government policies in the United States contributed to fluctuations in acreage, so that historical series may overstate the degree of production instability in periods when no acreage was being withheld from production.

The impact of fluctuations in coarse grain production in other countries on U.S. exports is illustrated in Figure V-3. Deviations from trend in all other countries varied from a negative 18 million tons in 1965–1966 to a positive 19 million tons in 1973–1974 (6% and 5% of trend line production, respectively). The average deviation was 6.5 million tons or about 2% of production. U.S. exports ranged from 12 to 41 million tons per year. Exports were inversely related to de-

FIGURE V-3. COARSE GRAIN EXPORTS FROM THE U.S. RELATIVE TO PRODUCTION IN REST-OF-WORLD, 1960-1961—1974-1975

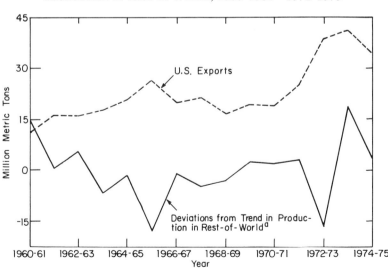

a World less U.S.

SOURCES: Appendix Table V-11; USDA, *Foreign Agriculture Circular*, FG 9–76, May 1976.

viations from production trends in other countries as a general pattern, altough a significant exception occurred in 1973–1974. Other countries raised ending stocks by 7 million tons and increased consumption by 36 million tons during 1973–1974, while the United States lowered stocks by 10 million tons and reduced consumption by 2 million tons under the influence of prices over 50% higher than in 1972–1973. Some possible reasons for these disparate developments will be discussed in the next section on foreign social and political institutions.

World production of protein meal, used primarily for animal feed, rose at an average rate of 5% per year in 1960–1961 through 1974–1975. Production in the United States grew slightly faster, 6% per year; the U.S. fraction of production moved up from 43% to 52% over the 15-year period. The average deviation of world production from its trend was 1.2 million metric tons or about 2.6%. The range of deviations was a plus 3.3 million tons in 1974–1975 and a negative 3.4 million tons in 1973–1974, about 5.5% of trend production. The United States accounted for 67% of world instability of production over the period, a proportion significantly higher than its contribution to production. Some of the U.S. instability reflects government agricultural programs, as in the cases of food grains and coarse grains. The marked slow-down of the rate of world growth in protein meal production from 1970–1971 through 1973–1974 was a major factor underlying the large foreign demand for U.S. supplies and the extreme rise in prices; actual world production rose only 3.6 million tons from 1970–1971 to 1973–1974 as compared with the 7.0 million tons which would have been consistent with trend growth.

Social and Political Institutions

Foreign social and political insitutions often add to, or even accentuate, the natural sources of instability discussed above. These institutions had major impacts on U.S. stabilization policy in 1971–1974, and they can be expected to play an important role in future world and U.S. price trends. Four topics will be examined in this section: (1) cycles of economic growth and recession, (2) shifting exchange rates, (3) foreign agricultural and food policies which insulate producers and consumers from market forces, and (4) state-trading arrangements.

Cycles of Economic Growth and Recession. The rate of growth in consumers' purchasing power is a factor whose variability adds significantly to the instability of food demand—and thus food prices. More rapid economic growth leads to greater increases in food demand while recessions result in little or no increase in demand. In 1972 and 1973 the economies of the Western nations were in a strong expansion phase; the OECD countries registered gains of about 6% in real gross product in these two years, as compared with about 4% in

TABLE V-3. ANNUAL GROWTH RATES OF REAL GROSS PRODUCT
IN SELECTED WESTERN COUNTRIES, 1969-1974

| | Percent Change From Previous Year | | |
	U.S.	EC	OECD
1969	2.7	6.0	4.8
1970	−0.4	5.0	3.2
1971	3.3	3.3	3.8
1972	6.2	4.0	5.7
1973	5.9	5.6	6.1
1974	−2.2	2.0	−0.2

SOURCES: Organization for Economic Co-Operation and Development, *Main Economic Indicators,* Paris, France: OECD, May 1975; Council of Economic Advisers, *Annual Report* transmitted with the *Economic Report of the President,* Washington: Government Printing Office, 1975.

the preceding years (Table V-3). This was partially responsible for the very strong demand for U.S. agricultural exports and high agricultural prices. A recession dominated the Western world in 1974, which was a factor in limiting the increases in grain prices in 1974–1975 to rather small amounts despite a drop of 61 million tons in world grain and rice production which forced a 38-million ton drop in consumption.

The impact of changes in income varies by both commodity and income level. The relationship between changes in income and consumption is measured by the income elasticity, i.e., the percentage change in quantity demanded resulting from a 1% change in income. As incomes rise, most consumers tend to shift from cereals and starches to relatively more meats, vegetables, fruits, fats, and other foods with a higher cost per calorie. People on a virtually subsistence diet will first increase their calorie intake before moving to more costly foods. The resulting picture is shown in Table V-4.

In developing market economies, such as India, consumption of virtually all major food categories is directly related to income. The direct consumption of cereals is included in this pattern, with the exception of coarse grains. Increased expenditures for calories are given equal priority with added expenditures for protein, although both trail fats. On a calorie basis, food purchases rise about 0.24% for every 1% change in income in all developing market economies; in India's case the income elasticity is estimated to be 0.43%.

Consumers in more developed economies place much less emphasis on buying additional calories as income rises. The total quantity of cereals consumed is actually inversely related to income; when the reverse occurs for a specific type, such as rice in the United States, the food is typically not a primary staple in that country—despite its status

TABLE V-4.   ESTIMATED INCOME ELASTICITIES
FOR SELECTED COMMODITIES AND COUNTRIES (IN PERCENTAGES)

| | Developed Market Economies | | | Developing Market Economies | | Centrally Planned Economies | | World |
| | U.S. | EC | Total | India | Total | USSR | Total | Total |
Commodity								
Cereals	−.24	−.29	−.24	.25	.13	−.30	−.10	−.02
Wheat	−.30	−.32	−.26	.50	.23	−.30	−.27	−.24
Rice	.20	.11	−.21	.40	.20	.30	.14	.23
Coarse grains	−.06	−.13	−.15	−.17	−.08	−.32	−.07	−.03
Vegetables	.10	.30	.46	.70	.45	.40	.25	.35
Fruits	.25	.58	.54	.80	.62	.72	.56	.55
Meat	.24	.48	.35	1.17	.56	.50	.39	.32
Whole milk	−.50	.08	−.03	.80	.79	.30	.15	.08
Fats and oils	.01	.13	.14	.92	.55	.64	.38	.22
Total food								
Calories	−.01	.08	.07	.43	.24	.01	.04	.10
Proteins	−.01	.13	.12	.40	.24	.04	.06	.11
Fats	.05	.22	.19	.72	.47	.51	.31	.22
Farm value	.04	.25	.25	.57	.41	.27	.19	.19

SOURCE: Food and Agriculture Organization of the United Nations, *Agricultural Commodity Projections, 1970–1980,* Rome, 1971, Volume II, Table B.

as a cereal. The marginal consumption of fats is most likely to continue to increase as income rises, but protein purchases also show a clear tendency to rise in most cases. Income elasticities of nearly all food groups are lower than those for developing countries, reflecting a shift of priorities from food to nonfood items.

The aggregate figures for the world are a blend of the results for the developing and developed countries. Changes in income lead to little or no change in direct consumption of cereals, all other causal factors being assumed constant, but purchases of fruits, vegetables, meat, and fats and oils move in the same direction as income changes.

In conclusion, cycles of economic growth and recession create different sorts of instability for different countries and commodities. Consumption of nearly all commodities in lower income nations responds positively to economic growth and negatively to recessions. In developed countries, on the other hand, an economic slump such as the 1974–1975 recession may actually *increase* the demand for direct consumption of cereals and starches and decrease the demand for meat, fruits, vegetables, fats, and other higher cost foods; the reverse would be true in periods of economic growth such as 1972–1973. These patterns are reflected in the composition of U.S. export sales; shifts in the world demand for meat often affect the United States most directly through the sale of feed grains. The rapidly rising incomes in 1972 and 1973 were certainly a major factor underlying the rapid escalation of meat, poultry, feed grain, and protein meal prices.

Shifting Exchange Rates. A second destabilizing influence of major importance was the shifting exchange rate of the dollar. In August 1971, when the President announced Freeze I, he also suspended the convertibility of the dollar into gold—which had the immediate effect of devaluing the dollar. By the end of 1971 the value of the dollar had fallen 6% relative to the currencies of U.S. major overseas agricultural customers (Figure V-4). In other words, the cost faced by foreign buyers of U.S. agricultural products was 6% lower in late 1971 than it would have been in the absence of a currency realignment. Exports of grains increased very little in 1971–1972 relative to 1970–1971, only 3 million metric tons, and—in any case—beginning U.S. stocks of 51 million tons in 1971–1972 appeared to provide a more than adequate cushion for increased foreign demand. The exchange value of the dollar relative to major agricultural customers maintained a rather constant level through 1972.

FIGURE V-4. EXCHANGE VALUE OF DOLLAR RELATIVE TO CURRENCIES OF MAJOR AGRICULTURAL CUSTOMERS,[a] APRIL 1971—DECEMBER 1974

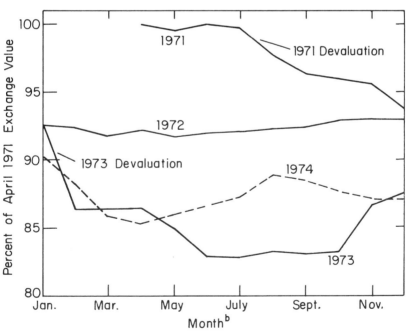

[a] An average weighted by 1971 value of U.S. commercial exports of agricultural products to 14 major markets.

[b] Exchange rate as of last trading day of each month.

SOURCE: Personal communication with ERS, USDA. A similar chart of these figures appears in USDA, *World Monetary Conditions in Relation to Agricultural Trade.*

The dollar was devalued a second time in February 1973 and subsequently allowed to fall further in a system of floating exchange rates. The economic environment of this second devaluation was much different from that in August 1971. As noted above, the Western world was experiencing a strong economic expansion in 1972 and 1973 which was leading to soaring consumer demand, in contrast to 1971 when countries were immersed in a slow-down or the early stages of recovery. By early 1973 wheat prices were 57% above a year earlier, corn prices were up 28%, and soybean meal prices were up 135%. Although grain reserves remained substantial, they were clearly declining. It was in this setting that the exchange value of the dollar fell 7% in February and then floated down another four percentage points by mid-1973. The cumulative devaluation of the dollar by June–July 1973 relative to early 1971 was 17%.

The realignment of currencies meant that foreign purchasers of U.S. farm products were faced with a significantly smaller price increase than U.S. customers. The devaluations were designed to encourage exports in order to remedy balance of payment problems, so the above price shifts are not surprising. The important point is that the very success of the policy led to larger exports and higher domestic prices than would otherwise have occurred. The persistence of substantial exports in 1973–1974 despite a rebound in production in other countries is partially explained by the devaluations, as well as by economic cycles and other factors to be discussed below.

Changes in the relative value of currencies will continue to be an important variable in explaining price fluctuations. Most major exchange rates are now "floating", i.e., subject to continuous change as a result of a combination of private and governmental actions. It would be surprising, however, if future changes would be as swift and large as the 1971 and 1973 shifts. After mid-1973 the dollar strengthened in the second half of the year, weakened in early 1974, strengthened again in the spring and summer, and then slowly trended downward in late 1974.

Foreign Agricultural and Food Policies. The third institutional factor consists of foreign agricultural and food policies which insulate producers and consumers from market forces. These policies obscure and distort price signals regarding the relative scarcity of goods. Producers and consumers, in turn, do not adjust their production plans or consumption in a manner consistent with the world situation. People in those countries that are wholly or largely subject to market forces, such as in the United States, are forced to make disproportionate adjustments in order to equilibrate world supply and demand. These larger adjustments are typically accomplished through greater price fluctuations, which is the central concern of this chapter.

The policies of the following important customers of the United States will be discussed first: the European Community (EC), Japan, developing countries, and centrally planned countries. This will be followed by a brief examination of the stabilization policy of Canada, an important competitor of the United States in world wheat trade. The policies of these countries serve as good illustrations of programs found elsewhere, as well as being important in themselves.

EC food and agricultural policies are, for the most part, designed to insulate EC producers and consumers from world prices while allowing freely functioning markets within the EC.[9] The principal policy instruments are illustrated in Figure V-5. *Target prices* are selected for individual products; these prices represent the desired level of prices received by EC producers. *Intervention prices* are set below target prices and are those prices at which EC agencies must buy all of the commodities offered to them. Intervention prices are analogous to the loan rates defined in U.S. policies. Actual market prices typically vary within a range bounded by the intervention and target prices.

The target and intervention prices were almost invariably set above world market prices until recent years (see Figure V-6, to be discussed in more detail later). The resulting price differentials encourage imports and discourage exports—tendencies which must be offset by appropriate trade policies. Lower priced imports are not allowed to enter at prices below *threshold prices,* which are prices at ports established at levels consistent with interior target prices. The difference between the world price and the threshold price is the *import levy*; the levy is collected by the EC and may be changed as often as daily in order to offset fluctuations in world prices. When surpluses collect within the EC and exports are desired, *restitution payments* are made to exporters which equal the difference between EC and world prices.

FIGURE V-5. EC PRICE SUPPORT AND STABILIZATION SYSTEM

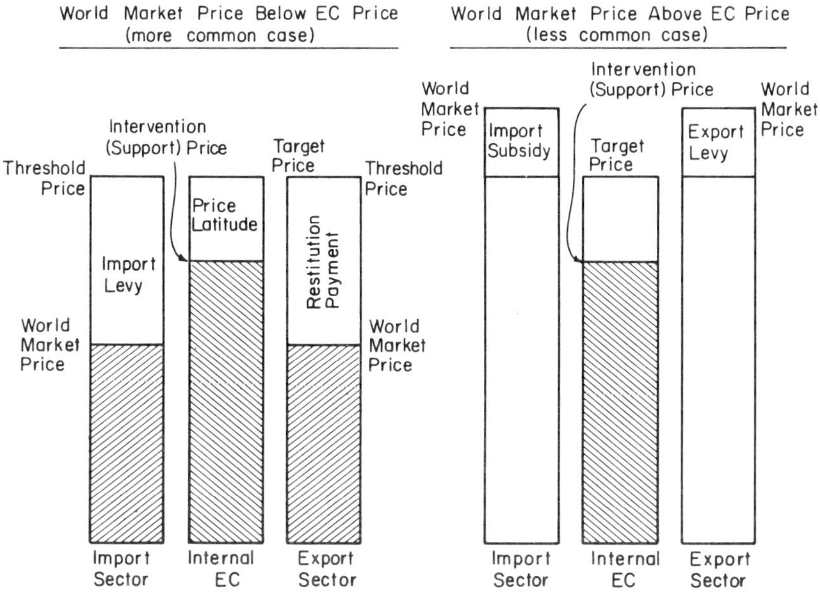

FIGURE V-6.   EC AND WORLD MARKET PRICES FOR SELECTED AGRICULTURAL
PRODUCTS, 1968–1969—1972–1973

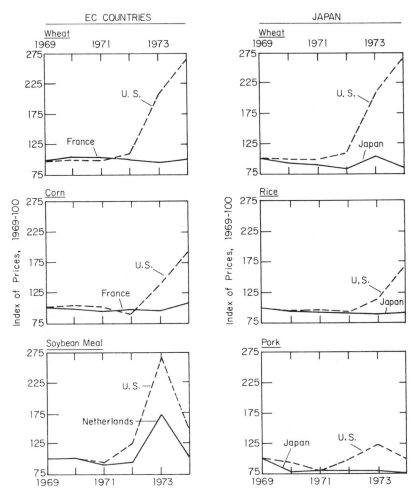

SOURCE: See Appendix Table V-12 for data and sources.

The rapid rise in prices of commodities traded internationally has resulted in the unusual situation of world prices exceeding EC target prices in several instances. Trade restrictions are also used in these circumstances to insure adequate supplies at stable prices, i.e., to prevent unwanted exports and facilitate needed imports. The most important policy instrument is the *export levy*. When commodities are being exported, the levy is set at a level sufficient to cover the difference between world prices and desired EC prices. The incentive to export thus disappears so long as the difference between EC and world prices does not exceed the levy. Export levies were applied to rice and grains in 1973 and 1974. In cases where the commodity is imported, the EC will occasionally pay import subsidies to importers so that the EC price can be maintained below the world price. Sugar is a good example of this practice.

The results of the EC price support and stabilization system are illustrated in Figure V-6 for several important commodities. EC policies have clearly tended to stabilize internal prices relative to world prices. Changes in prices of internationally traded goods were often absorbed in changed import and export levies rather than reflected in EC prices.

As mentioned earlier, policies of foreign nations which insulate their citizens from price fluctuations—such as the policies of the EC—are a destabilizing influence on other nations. For example, when the economic system was signaling a growing scarcity of wheat supply relative to demand in 1972–1973—1973–1974 through higher prices, EC policies shut out these signals. EC users of wheat continued to use wheat as before, rather than cutting back as did U.S. users. The unwillingness of other countries to subject themselves to the rigors of price rationing was clearly a factor in the high level of exports from the United States and the consequent explosion of prices.

The comparison of changes in selected prices in the EC and the United States is made more directly in Figure V-7. It must be emphasized that the price indexes represent merely changes over time within countries and not relative price levels between countries. The price series have been adjusted for differing rates of inflation in the countries. Thus, the price indexes in Figure V-7 indicate how selected agricultural prices changed over time relative to other prices facing producers and consumers. Prices are of course the market's means of transmitting information on the relative availability of products; a higher relative price leads to more production and less consumption and vice versa for lower relative prices.

In the three comparisons of EC and U.S. prices the United States consistently showed more price response to world scarcity in 1973 and 1974. In the cases of wheat and corn EC prices in real terms increased by little or nothing from 1969 to 1974 while U.S. prices were doubling for corn and more than doubling for wheat. EC consumers were clearly not subjected to the same degree of adjustment and disruption experienced by U.S. consumers.

The charts in Figure V-7 reflect the impacts of devaluation as well as EC policies. The distinction is illustrated well by a contrast of wheat and corn prices with soybean meal prices. Soybeans and soybean meal are not subject to import levies, and their EC prices normally follow world prices. Wheat and corn prices, on the other hand, are heavily influenced by EC trade restrictions as well as currency realignments. The devaluation of the dollar had the expected impact on soybean meal prices. The U.S. price declined slightly less than the Netherland's price in 1971 because the August devaluation had a small impact on the annual average. The U.S. price increased considerably

FIGURE V-7.   INDEXES OF REAL PRICES OF SELECTED AGRICULTURAL PRODUCTS IN EC COUNTRIES, JAPAN, AND THE UNITED STATES, 1969–1974

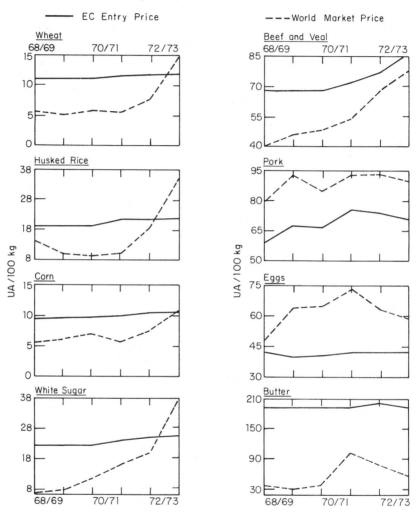

SOURCES: USDA, *Agricultural Prices: Annual Summary 1974,* Pr 1–3 (75), June 1975. Council of Economic Advisers, *Annual Report* transmitted with the *Economic Report of the President,* 1975, p. 252. Statistical Office of the European Communities, *Agricultural Statistics,* 1974–1, September 1974. Commission of the European Communities, *The Economic Situation in the Community,* 1975–1, March 1975. OECD, *Agricultural Policy in Japan,* 1974, Table 20, p. 52.

more than the Netherland's price in 1972 and 1973 as the relative value of the dollar continued to fall. The percentage changes in each country from 1973 to 1974 were again quite comparable as the exchange value of the dollar became relatively stable at a lower level. The devaluation shifted some of the burden of high prices associated with scarcity from other countries to the United States, but it did not prevent the economic system from correctly transmitting price signals regarding year-to-year changes in commodity availability. EC trade policies with respect to wheat and corn, on the other hand, effectively obliterated nearly all price signals originating in international markets. EC citizens shared in the burdens of adjusting to increased scarcity of soybean meal but not of wheat and corn.

Japan, another very important foreign customer, engages in price stabilization policies which have an impact on the United States in a manner similar to those of the EC.[10] The Japanese institutions, however, are quite different from those of the EC. The regulatory systems vary among commodities, but a few general tendencies can be noted. The Japanese government supports producer prices of many products—including rice, wheat, and milk—at levels exceeding those paid by domestic users (Table V-5). In some cases, such as milk, the price differential is paid as a deficiency payment to producers. In the case of cereals much of the production is purchased by the government or its designated agencies and subsequently sold at lower prices. In 1974 the government selling prices of rice and wheat equaled only 74% and 34%, respectively, of purchase prices.

Imports and exports of cereals are directly controlled by the government, e.g., all imports of grains are purchased by the government. For some commodities, such as pork, the government restricts price fluctuations within a prespecified range through a combination of (1) domestic purchases for storage or sales from government storage and (2) regulation of imports. As a general conclusion, the Japanese government seeks to stabilize producer returns and consumer costs through extensive government involvement in the marketing system.

A comparison of Japanese and U.S. prices for wheat, rice, and pork is presented in Figure V-7. The contrast is dramatic in the case of the cereals, a result similar to that for EC and U.S. cereal prices. Internal Japanese selling prices for wheat and rice showed little or no response to increased world scarcity in 1973 and 1974, while U.S. prices soared. Although the differences were less pronounced for pork, here too Japanese prices were more stable than U.S. prices and showed no response to the 1973 short supply of meat relative to demand. Devaluation of the dollar was an important factor in these results, but the differential price changes were sufficiently large that Japanese policies must also have had a substantial impact. Japanese consumers, like those in the EC, were not forced to adjust to changing world supply and demand conditions to as large an extent as U.S. consumers.

A 1975 USDA survey of over 50 developing countries indicates that restrictive pricing and trade policies were common in these nations as well as developed countries.[11] Controls on consumer prices were found in 35 countries; 38 countries controlled producer prices. Export controls or taxes were utilized by 32 nations, and import subsidies were paid in 17 countries. These policies distort the price signals generated in a market system of free exchange. A common objective appears to be one of reducing the fluctuations in consumer

TABLE V-5.   JAPANESE GOVERNMENT INTERVENTION PRICES OF SELECTED AGRICULTURAL PRODUCTS, 1967–1974 (IN YEN)

Product	1967	1968	1969	1970	1971	1972	1973	1974
Rice (brown/150 kilograms)								
Government purchase price	19,492	20,640	20,640	20,681	21,305	22,384	25,752	35,038[a]
Government selling price	15,023	17,343	18,742	18,604	18,442	18,291	19,288	25,760
Mill price[b]	19,000	20,541	20,541	20,541	20,541	20,541	21,578	n.a.
Wheat (standard grade/60 kilograms)								
Government purchase price	3,155	3,388	3,291	3,552	3,788	3,931	4,466	7,685[c]
Government selling price	1,941	1,941	1,935	1,940	1,944	1,895	2,620	2,589
Milk for manufacturing (per kilogram)								
Guaranteed producer price	40.39	42.52	43.52	43.73	44.48	45.48	48.51	70.02
Standard sales price	34.79	36.58	37.03	37.10	37.42	37.78	40.49	53.41
Butter (per kilogram)								
Target stabilization price	612	647	647	647	647	647	698	914
Pork (carcass, per kilogram)								
Upper limit price	390	390	410	422	434	440	465	620
Lower limit price	320	320	335	345	355	360	380	507

n.a. Data not available.
[a] Includes a special incentive payment of 1,000 yen.
[b] Price paid by mills; labeled as "consumer price" in cited source.
[c] Includes a special incentive payment of 2,000 yen.
SOURCES: Organization for Economic Co-Operation and Development, Agricultural Policy in Japan, Paris, France: OECD, 1974, Table 20, p. 52; Personal communication with ERS, USDA.

food prices. To the degree that this objective is fulfilled, utilization of commodities tends to be more stable than warranted by supply conditions; once again, a portion of the burden of adjustment is shifted to economies with freer markets, such as the United States.

State Trading Arrangements. Prices in the centrally planned economies are probably more stable than prices in any other grouping of countries. The USSR, a major importer of U.S. grains in recent years, provides a useful and important example. Prices of meat and bread in state retail stores have been stable since mid-1962, including the 1973–1974 period; almost all bread is sold in these stores, but meat which is sold elsewhere may have undergone price changes.[12] Although nonprice rationing such as shortages and waiting lines may have been important at times, the Soviet government clearly attempts to stabilize prices of staple foods while maintaining their availability. In past years the government has been willing to absorb large deficits in order to achieve this goal. Thus, in this case too, the conclusion emerges that a significant proportion of the necessary consumption and price adjustments required by fluctuations in world supply and demand is shifted to countries with freer markets.

The problems of instability in open economies are accentuated by the lack of information they possess regarding the current situation and plans in some centrally planned economies. The principal example of the damaging potential of such circumstances is the Soviet purchase of grain from the United States in 1972. This has been discussed elsewhere in some detail, and the material will not be repeated here. The most important point in this context is that more adequate information on the part of U.S. market participants would undoubtedly have led to an earlier price rise, probably a slightly more rapid shift in U.S. export policy, and possibly a somewhat smaller Soviet purchase. The shock of the 1972 Soviet grain deal has resulted in a greater awareness of the need to analyze carefully all available information on supplies and utilization in centrally planned economies, which is a partial solution to the problem. However, the basic problem of a lack of information persists. Until the centrally planned economies reveal their current estimates of stocks, production, utilization, and anticipated net trade position, the instability in relatively open economies will be enhanced—beyond that associated with the impacts of a system such as the EC or Japan which ward off adjustment but provide information.

The above examples are drawn from countries which tend to be net importers of foodstuffs. Since these countries are direct purchasers of U.S. products, the manner in which their policies increase the volatility of U.S. exports and prices is easily discerned. However, it is important to note that stabilization policies in other exporting nations can also be a destabilizing influence on U.S. markets. Canada, a major exporter of wheat, is a good illustration. Canadian millers purchase wheat for use in domestic flour at a price set by the government; the price has generally been lower than that received for exported wheat, especially in recent years. The government provides a payment to producers, through the Canadian Wheat Board, which equals the difference between the guaranteed and the export price. Canadian consumers can thus be protected from an increase in flour and bread prices, so long as they are willing to bear the taxes needed to finance the wheat subsidies. While the U.S. retail price of flour rose 71% from 1971 to 1974, the Canadian price increased only 46%.[13] The decision of the Canadian government to dampen domestic prices of wheat-related products tended to lessen the incentives for Canadian consumers to cut back consumption of such products. This, in turn, led to slightly lower quantities available for export and thus increased pressure on U.S. supplies. While the impact of the policies of a single country such as Canada should not be exaggerated, the cumulative effect of many such policies was considerable.

A wide spectrum of countries encompassing developed and underdeveloped as well as centrally and privately planned have adopted policies which insulate them from market forces. These policies tended to create greater instability in the remaining countries with freer markets, principally the United States, in recent years. Eventually, of course, the United States also took actions to mitigate the rise in commodity prices, such as price controls and export restrictions. The advantages and disadvantages of alternative policy responses by the United States will be examined later, after a brief discussion of future trends.

Future Trends

Forecasts related to food supplies, demands and balances are uncertain in most circumstances, and especially so in the current environment. The range of possible situations is extremely broad in the short run because of vagaries of weather, energy prices, and world economic growth. However, a dominant view appears to be emerging with regard to probable trends over the decade 1975–1985. The views expressed below are certainly not universally held, but they are the result of considerable effort by a variety of analysts.

Major studies of world food supplies and demands have been completed in recent years by (1) the Food and Agriculture Organization of the United Nations,[14] (2) Iowa State University,[15] (3) the University of California,[16] and (4) USDA.[17] Although the coverage and the assumptions differ somewhat, the analyses deal with the same fundamental variables and concerns. All four efforts present projections for 1985 which facilitate comparisons. The following conclusions apply to expected trends in the 1975–1985 period.

Aggregate world production of food is expected to increase slightly faster than demand. World food demand is expected to grow at an annual rate of approximately 2.5%, of which about 2% represents population increase and the remainder higher incomes. The annual rate of increase in production is expected to be only marginally higher, perhaps 0.1% or 0.2% above that of demand. There exists significant concern that new technological advances will not be forthcoming as rapidly as in the past, but much of this concern focuses on the period after 1985.[18] The price of agricultural products relative to other goods and services is expected to decline from the high levels of 1974–1975 but probably not to the levels of the 1960's.

Since production is quite variable from year to year and the margin of production over demand is narrow, shortages and high prices are very likely in some years. This is especially probable in the next few years since reserve stocks are at very low levels relative to consumption. In the latter part of the 1970's and during the 1980's fluctuations in total supplies (production plus beginning stocks) and prices will depend heavily on domestic and international policies, especially with regard to reserve stocks. If stocks remain at low or modest levels, prices are likely to be more unstable than if reserve stocks are available in years of low production.

Of the principal agricultural products, feed grains, protein meals, meats, and poultry will experience the fastest rates of gain in demand. As per capita incomes rise, consumers tend to eat more meat and poultry which in turn gives rise to increased demand for animal feeds. The consumption of food grains (principally wheat and rice) per capita responds much less to gains in income; in high income countries the per capita demand for the principal food grain often *declines* as income rises, e.g., wheat in the United States and EC and rice in Japan. However, aggregate food grain consumption in less developed countries (LDC's) will probably rise at an annual rate exceeding 3% due to rapid population growth (over 2.5% per year) and a positive response to income change.

All four of the studies concluded that the developing nations of the world will need increasingly large imports of cereals from the developed, exporting nations such as the United States. The basis for the expected shortfalls in LDC's and surpluses in developed countries is found in differences in growth rates of demand, rather than supply. Food production in the developing countries has grown as fast as production in developed countries. However, population in the developing countries has grown much faster than elsewhere. The result is that production per capita has been relatively constant over the last two decades in the developing countries while increasing in the developed nations. Demand per capita has increased steadily in both groups, so that transfers from the developed to the developing countries have risen. These general trends are expected to continue.

The ability of developing countries to purchase the needed cereals is in serious question, especially in view of the current and expected financial drain as a result of high petroleum prices. The realistic alternatives appear to be: (1) massive aid programs to assist the development of LDC's so that their food production increases more rapidly and their ability to finance needed food imports improves markedly; (2) moderate aid programs in consort with moderate to large food imports on concessional terms; (3) massive concessional food sales; or (4) periodic food shortages in developing nations— potentially catastrophic in the poorest countries such as Bangladesh, India, and Sri Lanka.

Another important conclusion of the FAO and USDA studies is that the sporadic nature of purchases and sales by centrally planned economies, especially the USSR and People's Republic of China, is likely to continue. Prior to the 1960's the USSR absorbed much or all of production shortfalls by stock depletion, livestock slaughter, and lower human consumption. However, the USSR and China have exhibited an increasing tendency to enter the world market to alleviate domestic shortages. Their influence has proved very disruptive on several occasions since they do not release information on domestic production prospects and thus potential needs.

Several very important conclusions flow from this discussion of future trends. First, uncertainties abound. Second, the trend in total world production relative to demand is not so likely to be a major problem as is the distribution of supplies. Third, the developing nations are likely to require larger transfers of aid from the developed countries. Fourth, while its exact nature is uncertain, instability of production, trade, and prices is almost certain to exist.

These probable trends, considered in combination with the natural and institutional sources of instability discussed earlier, have important implications for U.S. price stabilization policy.

Policy Options and Implications

A review of past experience and an analysis of projections lead to several interrelated conclusions. First, the world-wide balance of supply and demand of agricultural commodities, especially cereals, is subject to major instabilities. The most important causes are rooted in natural events, both domestically and in other countries, which lead to large fluctuations in production. Government policies of diverting varying amounts of land from production have also played a significant role in production variability. The balance of supply and demand is also upset by unstable demand as economic growth is interrupted by periodic recessions.

Second, these shocks to the supply-demand balance will have large impacts on countries with freely fluctuating prices in the next few years because grain stocks are very low relative to consumption. If stocks are not rebuilt during years of above-average production, fluctuations in production and demand will lead to major shifts in prices in such economies for the indefinite future.

Third, the United States will bear a disproportionate share of the burdens of adjustment if current policies continue. Many countries are unwilling to let prices vary to the extent that world supply and demand conditions dictate as necessary to equate quantities available and consumption. When some countries refuse to change their prices and consumption, the others that rely on a system of price rationing find that they are subject to more extreme instability—on both the upside *and* downside—than if adjustments were more equally shared.

Fourth, U.S. consumers, producers, and policy makers will object strenuously to any precipitous change in food and agricultural prices—and probably adopt additional stabilization policies beyond those currently in effect. Producers are concerned that large price declines lead to lower incomes. Federal programs consisting of income supplements and price guarantees for producers have partially alleviated this concern, but as of mid-1975 the guarantees were significantly below costs of production. The anger of consumers as food costs rise is of course a reflection of the strain placed on their household budgets. Policy makers responding to rising food prices are in part reacting to the feelings of consumers. However, they are also aware that any price increase with a major impact on the Consumer Price Index (CPI) quickly leads to a multitude of inflationary pressures throughout the economy as the result of automatic escalator clauses tied to the CPI and pressures for more expansionary monetary and fiscal policies to counter recessionary tendencies. A policy maker can no longer "sit tight" while food prices rise, knowing that the pressure is likely to subside with the next production cycle—leaving little or no impact on other sectors. In the current environment inflationary pressures originating in a single sector can indirectly set off a new round of wage and price increases throughout much of the economy.

If the four points noted above are accepted, the choice facing the United States is not *whether* to have a stabilization policy in the food and agricultural sector but rather *what kind* of policy is appropriate. A decision to leave food and agricultural matters totally to the free market, both domestically and internationally, might be sustained for a few months or even a few years in the present international context. However, it seems inevitable that the concentration of adjustment within U.S. markets would eventually lead to precipitous price changes and a revision of policy. In recognition of such forces federal programs have been developed to limit price declines, as noted above, but there are no well-developed policies for limiting price rises. With no additional forethought, the policy response to the next round of food price increases would probably be a rather ad hoc set of measures such as occurred in 1971–1974. As the political pressures to "do something" became irresistible, it is very conceivable that the United States would again turn to direct price controls—including ceilings, abrupt restrictions on commercial and concessional exports, and sudden relaxations of import restraints. In view of the degree to which U.S. agricultural prices are influenced by international events, virtually any effective domestic stabilization program of more than a few months' duration would necessitate measures to insulate U.S. prices and markets from foreign pressures.

The alternative course of action is to recognize the vulnerability of U.S. markets to instability and to formulate stabilization policies. These policies would probably consist of a mix of measures designed (1) to create more stability of U.S. prices while not restricting the access of any customer to U.S. supplies and (2) to provide for an orderly manner of insuring that an adequate supply of agricultural commodities is retained in domestic markets even in times of extreme world-wide shortage and high prices. It is in this spirit that this section of the chapter has been written. The potential problems and benefits of using international food policies as a means of stabilizing domestic prices are explored. Trade policies are considered first. This is followed by a discussion of grain reserves.

Trade Policy

Trade policy consists primarily of the conditions imposed upon exports and imports. It is widely used by other countries to stabilize domestic prices, as has been discussed earlier. In times of relatively high world prices, export quotas and taxes and import subsidies can be used to maintain lower domestic price levels. When world prices are relatively low, domestic prices can be maintained at a higher level through export subsidies and import quotas and taxes.

The United States has often found it essential to insulate higher, government supported domestic prices from lower world prices. Export subsidies, import quotas, and import taxes have a long history in the United States. All were in operation in 1971 when the Economic Stabilization Program was initiated.

The logical policy response to rapidly rising domestic prices is to reduce export subsidies and remove import restrictions. These policy changes will ordinarily increase domestic supplies and decrease foreign availabilities; domestic prices should rise less than if the restrictive trade policies remained while foreign prices will tend to rise more. As described in Chapter I, the United States did respond in the expected fashion. Subsidies on commercial grain exports were removed, and restrictions on imports of beef and dairy products were eased—to cite the most important cases among commercial trade. However, there were major problems in using trade measures as elements of discretionary policies.

The major problem was the lag between the perception of a need for changes and the implementation of policy changes. The subsidy on wheat exports was allowed for the total Soviet wheat sale, plus other foreign purchases for a brief time *after* the Soviet sale. Terminating the subsidy at an earlier date might have reduced foreign purchases; it certainly would have led to lower costs for U.S. taxpayers and greater foreign exchange earnings. The increased import quotas for dairy products were consistently enacted weeks or even months after the action should have been taken. The result was greater fluctuations in consumer prices and more disruption of domestic production and processing than was necessary. The political and administrative clearance process for a major shift in trade policy almost inevitably seems to consume such a long time that the use of trade policy to attain short-term goals is highly inefficient.

The most successful case of reduced subsidies, those on concessional sales, i.e., foreign food aid, was also one of the most controversial. The level of concessional sales is almost totally under the administrative control of the Executive Branch and can be quickly adjusted. Concessional exports of wheat and flour declined to 151 and 64 million bushels in 1972–1973 and 1973–1974, respectively, in contrast to an annual average of 425 million bushels in the 1960's. Exports of feed grains and rice on concessional terms also declined significantly in 1973–1974 from prior levels. The pattern of recent years is indicative of the nature of the program since its inception. Concessional shipments have tended to be greatest when U.S. stocks were high and prices low. The objective of lowering government storage costs, and thus the total costs of farm price support programs, was an important consideration. The pattern is also consistent with the goal of domestic price stabilization—exports are reduced when supplies are tight. Thus, the U.S. food aid program has in the past been responsive to domestic price stabilization and could be conducted similarly in the future.

The controversy arises because U.S. food aid to foreign nations has been lowest when food supplies were tightest—as it was most generous when stocks seemed a liability rather than an asset. A true "food aid" program would tend to show exactly the reverse pattern; i.e., aid shipments would increase in times of scarcity and high prices when needs in low-income countries were greatest. It is little wonder that other nations are critical of the U.S. food aid posture when officials describe it solely as a reflection of our charitable nature. While not surprising, we should recognize that our willingness to share has been related to our own welfare as well as to the suffering of people in foreign nations.

Another related point is that many concessional sales have been made for foreign policy reasons not directly related to widespread hunger or malnutrition. Some examples would be large shipments to South Korea, South Viet Nam, Pakistan, and Israel accounting for 19%, 16%, 9%, 6%, respectively, of total government financed exports of grains and preparations in fiscal year 1973.[19] Reducing food aid shipments made for national security purposes in times of scarcity may be disruptive to U.S. foreign policy objectives, but such reductions do not necessarily entail a significant increase in human nutritional problems.

The place of concessional sales in the foreign policy of the United States will depend upon how two central issues are resolved. In view of the expected need of the developing nations for aid in future years (as reviewed in the preceding section), this component of U.S. policy will demand careful consideration. The first issue, not to be dealt with in detail here, is the proportion of food and nonfood aid. The use of food aid is discouraged by some because it may lower prices in receiving countries, discourage their production, and leave developing countries more dependent on food imports; these people urge that aid be given as technical help or cash. The second issue is the relative priority to be given to domestic price stabilization versus humanitarian and national security goals. Food aid exports can be varied so as to yield greater domestic price stability, as in the past, but continuation of this approach will infringe upon the other goals.

Restrictions on exports have been much less common than export subsidies in U.S. history, but these were tried during the ESP with limited success. The Constitution prohibits the levying of export taxes (although there is some legal debate concerning how broadly this should be applied), so that the most promising avenue of export controls was quotas. Export controls were abruptly placed on shipments of soybeans, cottonseed, and related products on June 27, 1973, and continued through September 21, 1973, as described more fully in Chapter I. Neither the U.S. Department of State nor foreign countries were consulted in advance of the decision—and foreign customers were irate. The rise in domestic soybean and soybean meal prices was halted, satisfying the prime objective of the policy, but the lateness of the controls relative to the marketing year (September–August) and the arbitrary nature of the quotas (a fixed percentage of unshipped contracts, with exceptions) left nearly all parties angry.

Systems of less formal export controls based on consultations and unwritten agreements played an important role on two occasions. The first was in early 1974 and focused on wheat, prices of which were soaring to unprecedented highs. Foreign buyers and U.S. exporters were urged to defer shipments until new crop wheat could be substituted for old crop; the major positive response came from the Soviet Union. This response and other developments led to lower wheat prices. The chosen policy, although risky, was generally regarded as successful—and certainly preferable to formal export controls. Informal arrangements were again made in the winter months of 1974–1975 in an attempt to limit feed grain exports. The U.S. crop was down sharply because of adverse weather, and prices were rapidly rising. The Soviets were again responsive in limiting their purchases. The system of extensive consultation and negotiation with actual and potential customers, with a substantial role played by the Department of State, was more acceptable to foreign nations than the formal controls. Despite the high feed prices and consequent cutbacks in livestock production, the policy of informal controls was apparently viewed as a success by most federal officials. Neither domestic producers nor consumers were highly upset, and the U.S. free trade posture underwent little additional erosion.

Reliance on informal export controls in times of shortage does, however, contain significant risks. First, the informal action may not prove a sufficient remedy, and it may make the subsequent enactment of formal controls less effective or more difficult to implement. The informal action is a clear signal of the U.S. government's concern about supplies. Foreign customers may increase their efforts to insulate themselves from the impacts of potential export controls by accelerating delivery schedules and raising their contractual commitments, and thus aggravate the domestic supply-demand balance. Second, the uncertainties inherent in informal agreements leave farmers and private traders in a very poor position for planning in a rational manner. The resulting indecision and "gamblers' psychology" may result in poor selling and buying choices and inefficient resource allocation. Third, some countries may prefer the give-and-take of open market competition for exportable supplies rather than that of secluded diplomatic negotiation and compromise. Fourth, if the informal policy does fail, the time expended in its trial and evaluation may lead to a need for a more severe formal policy later, as compared with formal controls adopted at an earlier date. Assuming that a given quantity must be shifted from foreign to domestic utilization, waiting until later in the marketing year to impose export controls will require a larger adjustment relative to remaining supplies. The soybean experience is a good illustration of the dangers of waiting until late in the marketing year to act.

Sporadic purchases by centrally planned economies with little or no advance information are an important destabilizing influence on prices in open economies, as noted earlier in this chapter. A system of export controls, more stringent than informal negotiations, designed to deal with sporadic purchases might be attempted. One approach would be to identify certain countries, such as the Soviet Union, as unstable customers whose purchases must receive government approval before the sales contracts are valid. However, the formal delineation of some countries for unique, adverse treatment would lead to numerous, and potentially serious, diplomatic problems. An alternative which might prove slightly more feasible, at least diplomatically, would be a legislated policy which defined "sporadic purchases" and made them subject to government approval. For example, desired purchases which exceeded the average of the last few years' actual purchases of a country by more than some percentage (say 30%) would automatically be submitted for government review and consent prior to becoming valid contracts. The regulation would apply to *all* countries, but it would affect only sporadic purchasers.

Regular customers, such as the EC and Japan, would feel no impact since their regular history of purchases would guarantee them access to current U.S. supplies.

While superficially appealing because the policy attacks a specific problem, export controls focused on a country or subset of countries encounter substantial difficulties. Those countries barred from making purchases of U.S. commodities would ordinarily be expected to buy elsewhere, such as from Canada, Argentina, Australia, South Africa, Thailand, or EC. The importing countries which might normally have made purchases in non-U.S. markets would find it advantageous, or even necessary, to turn to the United States if they were not barred from doing so. Resale of export contracts would also increase; i.e., U.S. sales to uncontrolled countries would rise and these countries would in turn make increased sales to nations barred from U.S. markets. Through these devices and others the shortages existing in countries barred from making U.S. purchases would quickly have an impact on the United States despite attempts to insulate ourselves. The situation would be analogous to that of the Arab embargo on exports of petroleum to selected countries; substitutions and resales led to a world-wide sharing of the burdens rather than a concentration in a few embargoed countries such as the Netherlands and the United States. As the policy focusing on a few specific countries showed increasing signs of failure, there would be pressures to shift to a more comprehensive export control policy. The major hope for avoiding such a failure would probably stem from faith in a large diplomatic effort to impress upon other countries the need to refrain from resales or other actions which would dissipate the impact of the shortage in the "sporadic purchasing" nation to the remainder of the world. The chances of success for such a diplomatic effort are probably better if the shortage situation is of a shorter duration, such as a few months, rather than nearly a year or longer.

When the dual problems of the pressure for comprehensive export controls and the need for providing supplies to steady customers are recognized, an overall limit on exports could be set and simultaneously allocated to countries. The allocations would take into consideration the buying patterns of recent years, in order to favor steady customers at the expense of sporadic purchasers. Since total exports would be fixed, any resales would not affect supplies or prices in U.S. domestic markets. There would be a problem of determining who received the windfall gain made possible by a difference between U.S. and world prices. The gain could be captured by the government, i.e., taxpayers, if export licenses were sold; if not, whoever succeeded in winning the export business would reap the gains.

Several conclusions flow from this examination of trade policy and domestic price stabilization. Comprehensive export controls could easily lead to a substantial lowering of domestic agricultural prices, but domestic and foreign interests would vehemently object. The protests of other nations could probably be lessened to the degree that the policy was announced well before its effective date, thus leaving sufficient time for other countries to plan accordingly. Export controls focused on a few countries, presumably those with sporadic purchase patterns, are not likely to be successful in terms of significantly affecting domestic prices unless the controls are of a short duration and an intense diplomatic effort accompanies the trade controls. Changing levels of import quotas, import duties, export subsidies, and export quotas in order to achieve more stable domestic prices has proved a clumsy policy in the U.S. context; policy changes are made too late and are rarely of the correct magnitude. A major exception to this general pattern is subsidized food aid exports. These have responded rather appropriately and quickly to the needs of domestic price stabilization, but the resulting pattern of "aid" implies that the needs of foreign recipients deserve a low priority in policy decisions.

Grain Reserves

The basic principles employed in using grain reserves to stabilize prices are very simple.[20] Stocks are accumulated in years when prices are below average because of large supplies or depressed demand; this action raises prices above the level which would exist in the absence of stock building. Stocks are drawn down in years when prices are above average as the result of small supplies or strong demand, which causes prices to be lower than they would be if stocks were not available or used. Thus, price variation would be reduced; the impact of a reserve stock policy on the average price level is heatedly disputed.

A reserves policy can, at least in principle, temper the major problems related to instability of commodity markets. Shifts in supply and demand, either domestic or foreign, could be buffered by appropriate stock policy—as outlined above—and price fluctuations could thereby be reduced. The maintenance of reserves would moderate both downswings and upswings in prices; its dual nature should make it more acceptable to producers *and* consumers than one-sided measures such as existing minimum price guarantees or proposed export controls. Producers would be receiving protection from consumers (taxpayers) against extremely low prices, and consumers would be insured against high prices at the expense of producers.* Exports to sporadic purchasers could be met wholly or partially from reserve stocks. The United States could reap the benefits of the resulting foreign exchange earnings which flow from increased exports while

---

* Since producers now enjoy a program which sets minimum but not maximum prices, they may be politically reluctant to support a shift to a reserve program. Any impetus for change will in all likelihood come from consumers.

avoiding a portion of the price rise normally accompanying increased demands on current production. Food aid shipments during periods of relative scarcity could also be made wholly or partially from reserve stocks. Such a procedure would leave a greater proportion of current production in commercial channels and thus reduce upward pressure on prices—while maintaining the U.S. commitment to foreign food aid. In summary, reserves can contribute to greater price stability in the context of fluctuating demand and production, sporadic purchases by a few countries, and a continuing commitment to food aid programs.

The level of reserves will in large part determine the probability of avoiding recourse to other stabilization policies, such as direct price controls and trade restrictions. A larger reserve will be adequate for offsetting more extreme imbalances in supply and demand, while a smaller reserve makes it more likely that price fluctuations will be sufficiently large so that producers or consumers will demand a policy response. As stated at the outset of this section, the present international context which focuses adjustment problems into open economies such as the United States virtually insures that some stabilization policy will be required in the food and agricultural sector. The trade-offs among the alternatives are the relevant decision variables. No conceivable level of reserves will eliminate all probability of the need for direct controls on prices and trade, just as no system of U.S. price and trade controls could eliminate any need for reserves. The critical need is to weigh the costs and benefits of each policy and to choose the appropriate mix accordingly. The United States cannot, and should not expect to, carry the full burden of stabilizing *world prices* through a system of *U.S. financed reserves*. The task is too massive, and the benefits too dispersed among the citizens of all nations. The United States must decide to what extent it will contribute to world price stability—and beyond which it will be subject to world market fluctuations and possible recourse to trade restrictions.

Reserves of commodities have been accumulated by the U.S. government on many occasions in the past. This experience reveals several significant problems which must be recognized. The budgetary costs of acquisition and storage in years of reserve building can be very large. A large portion of these costs may be recouped in years of stock depletion, but the historical record shows significant net costs to the government, i.e., the taxpayers. Federal outlays for farm income stabilization (including items not directly related to reserves but which affect their formation, such as land retirement) peaked at $5.3 billion in 1968–1969, averaged $4.4 billion in 1967–1968 through 1971–1972, and fell to $0.9 billion in 1974–1975.[21]

Another major problem has been the tendency of reserve stock programs which were originally justified in large part as price *stabilization* policies to evolve into price *support* schemes. Acquisition and release prices were established at such high levels that government stocks grew without apparent limit—until land retirement programs limited production. Stock disposal efforts concentrated on procedures designed *not* to affect prices in commercial markets (i.e., domestic and foreign food aid), rather than on moderating upward fluctuations in prices. Government costs escalated to very high levels with this type of program.

The final major problem is a widespread feeling among farmers and some analysts that a reserve stock depresses average prices and returns in addition to reducing instability—as opposed to those who argue that reserve stocks reduce price fluctuations with little or no impact on average prices and returns. The arguments rest on hypotheses concerning the shape of the demand curves for various commodities, shifts in demand and supply—both here and abroad—resulting from price fluctuations in previous periods, the relevant alternative policy for purposes of analysis, the operating rules of the stabilization agency, and other related variables.[22] At this stage of the debate, no conclusion with applicability to the real world, as opposed to simplified theoretical systems, appears possible.

If the major issues are resolved in favor of some scale of reserve program, a host of related questions arise. Among the most important are the matters of (1) determination of acquisition and release prices, (2) who will hold reserve stocks, and (3) where reserve stocks should be located. The guidelines for when stocks should be accumulated or depleted are of course crucial to the success of the program. The determination of the "trend" price around which short-term price fluctuations should be stabilized is a source of much controversy— witness the current disagreements as to whether the world is entering an era of increased food shortages or is merely experiencing a temporary reduction of supply relative to demand as the result of unusual, random weather patterns. If acquisition and release prices are set too high, stocks and program costs will escalate—as noted earlier. On the other hand, setting prices at levels too low will lead to little or no protection from upward aberrations of prices. The level of stocks would provide a useful check against extreme errors. When stock levels reached a stipulated high level, this could trigger a cessation of government purchases and/or a lowering of the acquisition price (the latter would be very difficult to implement politically). At the other extreme, a lack of accumulation of stocks of a specified size over a certain time period could trigger higher acquisition and release prices. Since costs of production depend heavily on land values, which in turn depend on commodity prices, adjustment formulas based on costs are subject to major errors unless derived so as to avoid a self-induced downward or upward spiral. The decision as to the width of the desired price range, i.e., the difference between acquisition and release prices, would have an important bearing on the scale and likelihood of government action. A wider price range would leave more latitude for unrestricted market forces and reduce the level of required stocks than a narrower range.

Mistakes will be made in the selection of price bounds, as is true of all stabilization policies, and the final choice of a stabilization strategy should include an evaluation of the probability and costs of errors. A reasonable point of departure for the discussion would seem to be a granting of broad administrative discretion on the use of reserves for food aid purposes but more stringent rules on the release of stocks into commercial channels. Such operating rules would contribute modestly to price stability in most periods and would have a much greater impact in years of more extreme scarcity, while somewhat allaying producers' fears of prices being depressed by government sales.

The issues of who will hold the stocks and where they should be located are interrelated. From the viewpoint of domestic price stabilization, as well as other vantage points, the United States should clearly retain control of the reserve stocks it finances rather than transferring them to an international agency. Any other resolution seems very unlikely with the possible exception of relatively small quantities donated to an international agency for the express purpose of emergency famine relief. The other important aspect of the ownership issue is the public-private trade-off. At one extreme are those who desire no governmental commitment to reserve stocks; i.e., all U.S. stocks should be financed and held by private firms, farm and nonfarm. At the opposite end of the spectrum are those who argue that the federal government should assume full responsibility for holding reserve stocks. The options of public subsidies to the private sector for storage make the issues of control and financing matters of degree rather than bipolar alternatives. The best location for reserve stocks depends in part on the anticipated contingency. In the case of wheat, the export market is very large and is the major source of instability. A significant proportion of wheat reserves should have ready access to export terminals; farm-stored wheat may be impossible to move quickly, as occurred in the massive transportation tie-up in late 1972 and 1973. A high proportion of feed grains, on the other hand, is fed to livestock near the place of grain production. Extensive reliance on farm storage might work well in this case.

SUMMARY OF POLICY OPTIONS

The primary concerns of this chapter were stated in the introduction, namely, the degree to which international policies are (1) mandated by domestic price controls, (2) complements to domestic stabilization policy, or (3) substitutes for direct controls on prices.

A commitment to a completely free market policy both domestically and internationally is not likely to stand the test of time. The current international environment focuses too much of the world's adjustment to changes in the supply-demand balance into the few open economies such as the United States. If a substantial reduction of agricultural trade barriers could be accomplished in the current trade negotiations, the chances of success for a free market approach would improve markedly. Barring this unlikely development, the domestic price fluctuations seemingly inherent in free U.S. markets will prove unacceptable to producers or consumers—as they have in the past.

The existing policy of providing a low level of protection for producers when prices fall but relying on free markets when prices are rising will probably falter. If prices drop precipitously, producers will demand more protection through government purchases or some other form of price protection; the system of increased support prices might lead to import embargoes and export subsidies to insulate U.S. prices from world forces. If food and agricultural prices rise steeply, consumers will demand price controls and export restrictions. While attempts to remove all or most interference in agricultural markets can succeed for intervals of time, there will probably be intermittent periods of intense and abrupt government action in response to especially wide price swings.

Recourse to direct price controls will almost inevitably lead to trade restrictions in order to insulate controlled domestic prices from the prices of commodities in international markets.

While trade restrictions are virtually mandated by direct price controls, the reverse is not true. Trade restrictions in the form of export taxes or quotas might be substituted for direct price controls as a means of limiting price rises. An Administration might find it politically difficult, however, to impose formal export controls outside of a general system of direct price and wage controls. Export subsidies and import quotas might be wholly or partially substituted for other means of preventing extremely low prices in domestic markets. In view of the random fluctuations in supply and demand and the aversion of people to price fluctuations, there can be no guarantee that trade restrictions will not be required. Those who dislike such restrictions because of their divisive economic and political impacts can only hope to minimize the likelihood of having to turn to this policy. Utilization of trade policy levers as discretionary measures is fraught with difficulties because of political and administrative lags. The major model of success in the trade area, *as viewed strictly from a domestic price stabilization posture,* is the operation of the foreign food aid program; food aid exports have consistently been inversely related to domestic concern with high and rising food prices.

A grain reserve policy is a means of stabilization which may be partially substituted for a system of trade controls or domestic price controls. No reserve system of practical scale will completely ward off the need for trade restrictions, but the probability of being forced to resort to restrictions can be reduced. A grain reserves policy is not a necessary complement to direct price controls, especially in the context of high prices. Government-held stocks of grain may increase as a result of government purchases designed to support prices about certain levels. The typical historical pattern has been for government stock building to be based almost entirely on the goal of raising farm prices, with little or no official articulation of using the stocks to moderate price advances in future periods. However, the accumulated stocks have often served as a cushion in times of relative scarcity, such as in 1972 and 1973. This logical, if not always well defined, sequence of events has led some observers to show little concern for the explicitness of U.S. reserves policy so long as the government is willing and able to accumulate reserves in periods of depressed prices.

The resolution of international food policy is clearly relevant to domestic food price stability.

CHAPTER VI

Lessons of Food Controls, 1971–1974

John T. Dunlop

JOHN T. DUNLOP

John T. Dunlop is Lamont University Professor, Harvard University. His experience includes over nine years with the administration of controls programs. He was director of the Cost of Living Council from January 11, 1973, with the start of Phase III to the end of statutory authority for controls on April 30, 1974. He was also chairman of the Construction Industry Stabilization Committee, 1971–1974, the agency responsible for wage controls in construction.

Professor Dunlop was a Public Member of the Wage Stabilization Board during the Korean War period of controls; he was on the staff of the War Labor Board and a vice-chairman of the Boston Regional Board in World War II and later a member of the staff of the director of Economic Stabilization.

Professor Dunlop was Secretary of Labor in the period March 1975 through January 1976.

His writings on the 1971–1974 controls program include "Inflation and Incomes Policies: The Political Economy of Recent U.S. Experience," The Eighth Monash Economics Lecture, 1974, and "Wage and Price Controls As Seen By a Controller," 1975.

CHAPTER VI

Lessons of Food Controls, 1971–1974

THE PRECEDING REVIEW of agricultural developments, and the operation of price and wage controls at the manufacturing, wholesale and retail levels, provides the essential setting in which to bring together in summary the lessons of direct food controls.

The extraordinary events of the period 1971–1974 prompt the question whether these developments, including the political context of controls, were so peculiar as to provide any reliable guidance for future programs. World grain production in 1972 declined by 36 million metric tons (3.2%) in contrast to an annual average increase of 34 million metric tons in the period 1961–1971.*[1] The sudden disappearance of Peruvian anchovies helped to create a shortage of animal feeds. A simultaneous boom in Japan, Western Europe, and the United States for the first time in the era since World War II appreciably increased disposable income and particularly the demand for feed grains and red meats. The oil embargo substantially accelerated the unprecedented world-wide inflation and had a direct effect on fertilizer prices. The controls program of August 15, 1971, had been imposed as part of a "new economic policy" that included the devaluation of the dollar relative to other currencies and the adoption of floating exchange rates that increased the attractiveness of U.S. agricultural exports abroad and raised the price of imports at home. The first peacetime controls program emerged in the setting of a presidential election and operated under a divided government in the gathering storm of Watergate. These were hardly ideal economic and political circumstances in which to operate a direct controls program,

---

* World grain stocks declined from 148 million tons at the start of the 1972–1973 season to 108 million tons at the end of the season.

and they created a setting in which controllers could have only a minor impact at best on food prices to consumers.

The discussion of this chapter is divided into two parts; the first comments on the controls program of 1971–1974 given the major characteristics of the period, and the second part is devoted to more general inferences about future controls programs. The first part might be described as a summary commentary on the policy design and administration of food controls in the early 1970's, and the second part is concerned with general lessons for the future. This distinction is essential if future policy makers in a planning or action mode are to avoid simply refighting the last controls battles, on the presumption that the setting and the issues are the same as the early 1970's. It is not always possible or desirable to separate sharply in these discussions considerations applicable to the food industry alone and those related to controls in the economy generally since the policy design of a controls program is seldom entirely specialized to a single sector.

THE POLICY DESIGN AND ADMINISTRATION OF FOOD CONTROLS, 1971–1974

Margin Controls Without Ceilings on Primary Agricultural Products

Food controls in 1971–1974 were essentially controls over the cost-justification used by food manufacturers, gross margins used by wholesalers and retailers, and profit margin limitations relative to a base period used for all enterprises without any direct controls over the prices of primary agricultural products. Controls were confined to the least volatile parts of the food and agriculture sector. Retail and wholesale food prices basically rode up with the rise in primary agricultural prices which were dictated primarily by world demand and supply conditions.

Although statutory authority existed for direct controls on primary agricultural prices, the President never delegated such authority to the stabilization authorities: "The provisions . . . shall not apply to the prices charged for raw agricultural products."[2] The rationale for this decision was that "attempts to repress price increases might cause shortages and lead to black markets or rationing."[3] As world prices for primary agricultural products rose sharply in late 1972 and 1973, an attempt to impose direct controls restraining such prices in the United States would also have accelerated exports, already enhanced by devaluation, tending further to reduce domestic stocks and to increase domestic prices.

The only tools that could have been used to restrain prices of domestic raw agricultural products significantly in the circumstances of 1972–1973 were a comprehensive set of export controls, domestic rationing, and food subsidies for which there was no legislative authorization.* These extreme measures used in World War II were not likely to have secured the requisite support for their enactment and administration in the setting of 1971–1974. Price ceilings on raw agricultural products or a requirement of exclusive purchase and sale of raw products had not been utilized in World War II.[4] The flavor of the policy atmosphere in late 1971 and 1972 was described by Price Commissioners Lanzillotti and Hamilton:

> The Price Commission tried hard from February through early summer of 1972 to impress on [the Department of] Agriculture the importance of reevaluating agricultural policy, especially the acreage set-aside program. It received in return the impression that departmental policy was directed instead toward raising farm income and that, if higher food prices were the result, this was the commission's problem. As on many other questions about controls, such administration views prevailed, and actions relevant to increasing supply had to await the presidential election in November.[5]

Controls over margins at wholesale and retail levels, in the setting of rapid increases in raw agricultural prices, could be expected to have imperceptible effects on retail food prices.[6]

Creditability of Controls Under Conditions of Large Agricultural Price Increases

With the detachment of hindsight, it is easy to see, and it is now widely recognized, that the rise in retail food prices in the period was very largely the consequence of the rapid rise in primary agricultural prices reflecting world-wide factors. Despite the repeated statement of the Cost of Living Council to this effect,[7] the popular perception of 1972 and 1973, widely held at the time by press and media, was that retail food price increases reflected profits in the food industry, a softness in controls or lack of conviction of controllers, and a shift in controls organization and policies made on January 11, 1973. The fact is that controls in the food industry were basically unaltered from Phase II and to Phase III. Editorial, media, and the press comments widely held that more restrictive controls were required to prevent price increases.** The political process engendered widespread Congressional demands for a freeze, and the Senate Democratic caucus voted unanimously on June 5, 1973, for a stringent freeze on all prices. In this climate of opinion, President Nixon imposed ceilings on

---

* The earlier elimination of acreage set-asides, the removal of the subsidy for wheat exports, and the provision of incentives to increase production and to increase imports could have been helpful.

** See *Business Week*, Editorial of March 10, 1973: "Like it or not, the Administration should also expand its price controls to include farm prices—raw agricultural products changing hands for the first time." Editorial of May 12, 1973: "Price controls should apply to all farm and food products. . . ." These editorials were reproduced in advertisements by *Business Week* in many newspapers.

meat prices on March 29, 1973, and, against the advice of all his economic advisers, imposed a second general freeze on June 13, 1973.

It would be hard to exaggerate the impact of a drum fire of editorial opinion, press, and media on controls decisions in the first half of 1973, placing pressure on the President and the Congress for more "stringent" controls in the face of rising prices, particularly food and meat prices. (Food prices in the Consumer Price Index rose 9% from January to June 1973 and 18% from January to December 1973.) Stringent ceiling prices on domestic raw agricultural prices, in the face of a world-wide inflation, would have encouraged an even greater rate of agricultural exports from the country or required a massive export control system and further complicated the role of the dollar in international markets. In addition, editorial and press opinion also focused on wage policy and the very large number of major negotiations in 1973. It was argued that the wage guideline of 5.5% had been undermined by Phase III and that wage inflation and serious industrial conflicts were likely, exacerbated by the food inflation.[8] Despite these unsettling influences, wages and industrial relations remained stable and constructive.

These developments illustrate that stabilization authorities are no less required to deal with widespread beliefs, political pressures, and popular convictions about inflation and controls than with economic forces of demands, supplies, and prices. The surge of political and press pressures for more stringent controls in the face of food inflation in the first half of 1973 underscores the central importance of public explanation, widespread creditability, and political leadership in any controls program. The period further illustrates how difficult it is for administrators to follow a course designed to deal with economic dimensions when strong public views and pressures dictate an opposing policy, no matter how erroneous or misguided that policy may be in the judgment of administrators or how much a blunder it may be seen to be in the judgment of history.

It may well be that no controls program can ever be expected to be creditable and sustain public support at a time when food prices, as measured by the food component of the Consumer Price Index, increase at the rates they did in 1972–1974: 20.1% from December 1972 to December 1973 and 11.2% from December 1973 to December 1974. These rates of increase were so unprecedented, particularly in peacetime, that public creditability in controls could not be maintained. The viability of controls is undermined in circumstances under which raw agricultural prices increase so rapidly.

Consequences of the Failure of Forecasting

One of the major features of the controls period was the unexpected rate of food price increases. Stabilization authorities and public opinion were totally unprepared for increases of the order of magnitude of 1973 and 1974. In the late fall of 1972, for instance, the Department of Agriculture estimated that retail food prices for 1973 would average 4% to 4.5% over 1972. In February 1973 the estimate was raised to 5% to 5.5%.[9] These estimates were raised throughout the spring and summer; in the end, the year-over-year change in retail food prices was 14.5%.* A threefold order of magnitude in error of estimation of food price increases undermines any basis for confidence in policy making. Although predictions were a little more realistic, the actual year-over-year change for 1973–1974 was almost identical to that of 1972–1973, 14.4%. Most private forecasters did little better than the Department of Agriculture in 1972–1973.

The unprecedented and unexpected rates of retail food price increases were further destructive of confidence when placed in the setting of the rates of inflation held out as goals to the country. The interim objective of the Economic Stabilization Program was to reduce the rate of inflation that prevailed before August 15, 1971, by half, to a rate of 2% to 3% by the end of 1972. The Consumer Price Index as a whole had increased 3.9% and the food component had increased 5.6% in the period January to August 1971. In the year December 1971–December 1972, all items increased 3.4% and food 4.7%. The Council of Economic Advisers stated that "the President has established a goal of getting the rate of inflation down to 2.5% or less by the end of 1973."[10] The subsequent rates of increase were so large and unexpected* as to undermine confidence in the program no matter what might have been the extenuating circumstances.

The developments underscore the central importance of agricultural forecasting, quantities, and prices in food controls. The major reason for the gross errors in forecasting food prices was the failure to relate the economy of the United States to the rest of the world. For many years previously, large stockpiles had moderated the effects of changes in world demand and supply on domestic prices. "No U.S. agency has an adequate model of the world economy, or even an adequate conceptual framework in which to discuss interactions among the food, agricultural, and other sectors in the world economy."[11] The effects of further devaluation of the dollar from the

---

* The experience of the Price Commission with agricultural forecasts for 1971–1972 is described as follows: ". . . The Department of Agriculture provided the Commission with forecasts and outlook papers. . . . Unfortunately, their analysis did not prove to be especially helpful in anticipating the problems of food prices. . . . Over time, reports from the department became increasingly inaccurate and heavily influenced by department policy and 'official outlook' and few persons on the Commission placed much faith in them." Lanzillotti, Hamilton, and Roberts, *Phase II in Review,* p. 20.

* "Instead of prices rising at year's end by 2½ to 3%, I'd put my guess at 4%." Paul Samuelson, "What's Wrong," *Newsweek,* March 19, 1973, p. 81. The increase of the Consumer Price Index in the last three months of 1973 over the last three months of 1972 was 10.3%.

Smithsonian levels and the organization of forecasting in the Department of Agriculture also played a role.

Had the order of magnitude of the agricultural supply-demand imbalances, the disappearance of stockpiles, and price increases been appreciated in advance, it might have been possible to prepare the public for these developments in a more creditable way; supplies could have been increased somewhat and prices constrained to a degree by removing acreage limitations, increasing imports, and other measures if done early enough. But the absence of good forecasting precluded appropriate limited action and led to despair and disillusionment by controllers and the public alike. The American people have reacted well to genuine emergencies, but in 1973 the definition of the magnitude of problems was not perceived in time to take constructive policy and administrative steps. It is always difficult to forecast the future, but the events of 1972–1973 were indeed peculiar in their order of magnitude.

Ceilings by Enterprise Rather than by Product and Industry

One of the basic decisions underlying price controls in the 1971–1974 period was to frame price restraints on a firm-by-firm basis in terms of cost-justification used for food manufacturers, gross margins used for food retailers, and profit-margin limitations used for all enterprises, relative to some base period. This approach is in contrast to the setting of explicit ceiling prices by product and market as was done under controls in World War II and the Korean period. The cost-justification, gross-margin, and profit-margin limitations were thought to be more appropriate in an economy with slack and to permit individual establishments or pricing units to adjust prices on the basis of individual situations and to permit a large degree of self-administration of controls. Little consideration was given to industry price and cost patterns.[12] Variations in prices of individual items could more readily be adjusted by private pricing decision makers. It was also felt that explicit ceiling prices would encourage enterprises to raise prices to the ceilings, because in 1972 many realized or actual prices were below quoted prices. Ceiling prices, it was felt, would also require a much larger stabilization bureaucracy.

However, the cost-justification, gross-margin, and profit-margin limitation rules tended to work hardship among enterprises in which the base periods reflected quite different experiences. For some the specified base period proved to be generous and for others most restrictive. Many enterprises could readily argue that their experience in the base period was unusual and inappropriate for purposes of limiting profit margins. As the economy recovered and profits expanded, the profit-margin rules for firms approaching these limits tended to result in uneconomic expenditures and to create other distortions. In genuinely tight markets the margin control rules would have resulted in quite different prices in the same market, skewing the allocation of resources in an inefficient manner. Moreover, cost-justification, gross-margin, and profit-margin rules resulted in prices at retail that it was difficult, if not impossible, for a consumer to check.

Changing Stages in the Controls Program

The controls period 1971–1974 was characterized by frequent changes in policies, in administrative arrangements, and in designations of programs—two freezes and three other phases in 32.5 months. These comprehensive changes in a controls program were sometimes held to reflect indecision and to confuse business and labor organizations which had to conform with regulations. Consumers, who were expected to play a pivotal role in compliance, were likewise confused by so frequent and rapid changes.

But every stabilization program confronts a delicate balance between maintaining continuity and adapting to changing circumstances.[13] Controls wear out and those under regulations find ways to exploit loopholes and to develop practices which reduce their effectiveness. Particular regulations may begin to have significant adverse effects on output or on quality of production. The objective circumstances of the domestic economy and of each sector change, often dramatically. It may be necessary to reorganize administrative agencies and to make changes in personnel. History suggests that getting out of controls is a difficult, and always treacherous, undertaking in its administrative arrangements and impact upon prices and wages. Every major controls program in U.S. history has reflected various subperiods and policies, although the 1971–1974 period used labels (phases, freezes, and stages) in public discourse in a unique way as a means of making transitions in general policies. The phase designations probably tended to obscure the continuity in some basic policies through the whole period including such elements as the pass-through of costs, profit margin comparisons with base periods, and industry and size-of-firm approaches to coverage. Wage policy and administration remained unchanged from January 1973 through April 1974.

Stabilization programs inherently tend to change some policies during the course of controls. These changes were not always made in the 1971–1974 period so as to portray firm direction and central policy. A sense of discreetness overcame a view of coherence. Undoubtedly an awareness of continuity was difficult to establish in a setting in which the real world of economics and politics was changing so dramatically in ways not generally understood or appreciated.

Difficulty of Getting Out of Controls

The controls program, beginning with the Freeze of August 15, 1971, was intended to be of limited duration, and the original view of getting out was simply to drop wage and price controls in a matter of months or no later than after the elections in November 1972. But, for one thing, controls proved surprisingly popular with the public and, for another, significant inflationary pressures were emerging notably in the food and agricultural sector; they continued strong in medical care; the economy seemed headed for a major expansion in production; there were stirrings in petroleum prices; and the year 1973 was to be a major period in collective bargaining negotiations. What had seemed so simple in August 1971—merely to drop all controls no later than the end of 1972—now turned out to be most complicated and perhaps unwise.

In these circumstances the plan (Phase III) was to keep the general regulations but to introduce a substantial degree of self-administration, save in three sectors where inflationary pressures were adjudged to be most serious—in food, medical care, and construction—and where the regulations, somewhat tightened, would continue to be administered in virtually the same manner. As a means to exit from controls, the plan was to introduce more self-administration except in these critical sectors, and any others which should become evident, and then gradually to move from self-administration to the elimination of controls formally as inflationary pressures permitted. This approach to decontrol had collapsed before the second freeze on June 13, 1973, and a new design for getting out of controls had to be created.

There were three main elements to the decontrol policy from June 1973 to April 1974:

(1) Controls should be removed on a sector-by-sector basis beginning with those sectors, insofar as possible, where controls could be shown to be doing the most harm to output and particularly to decisions to expand plant and equipment.

(2) Price and wage controls should be removed at the same time for a sector identically defined in product and labor markets, except that the general executive compensation regulations should continue to apply.

(3) In removing price and wage controls for a sector the stabilization authorities sought, depending on the problems of each sector, various commitments from individual companies for periods after controls to enhance the short-term and long-term stability of the sector and the economy. These commitments included such assurance as stability in prices for a specified period; limitations on increases in prices to a given amount or to a specified level; increases in plant capacity; informal limitations on exports; improvement of price and other statistical information furnished to the government; revisions in compensation provisions of collective bargaining agreements, and improved machinery for labor-management consultation and problem-solving.[14] The record of the period is that these various commitments, in exchange for decontrol, were very largely kept.

On June 1, 1973, 42.6% of the Consumer Price Index and 73.9% of the Wholesale Price Index were subject to controls. As a consequence of the gradual sector-by-sector decontrol policy, by the end of April 1974, when stabilization authority expired, only 12.2% of the Consumer Price Index and 31.5% of the Wholesale Price Index remained under controls.[15]

Gradual decontrol was not applied to the food sector; controls on retail food prices were retained until near the end when, in mid-April 1974, announcement was made of the establishment of a Joint Labor-Management Committee to seek to improve procedures for settlement of disputes over the terms of collective agreements, to consider the structure of bargaining among crafts and localities, and to address productivity and other common problems.[16] Controls on prices at the processor level in the food industry were retained until the end except for canned fruits and vegetables where price decontrol was instituted in exchange for a commitment to increase the size of the 1974 pack and to limit price increases in the next crop year.

Despite extensive discussion and proposals within the Food Advisory Committee, comprised of representatives of business, labor, consumer, and academic interests, as to decontrol among retail, wholesale, and manufacturing sectors within the food industry, strong hostility existed to such an approach among the labor unions in the food industry. It was clear that partial decontrol in the retail food sector made little sense since the major retail outlets handled the full range of products; moreover, wage controls had to apply to all retail operations or none. The unions were fearful that because of the political sensitivity to prices in supermarkets an attempt might be made, administratively or in Congress, to continue wage and price controls on retail food operations after all other controls had lapsed, and accordingly they opposed separating wholesale and manufacturing operations from retail food operations for decontrol. Since the establishment of the Joint Labor-Management Committee in retail food was judged to be more significant, partial decontrol within the food manufacturing sector was not accomplished except for canned fruits and vegetables where an overriding consideration of output in the 1974 pack was compelling.

Export Controls

Export controls on raw agricultural products involve the same balancing of effects on current supply and future production compared with price and wage responses involved in more direct controls. In addition, such controls involve complex issues of commercial relations with U.S. trading partners and effects on exchange rates. From the early spring of 1973 the stabilization authorities had sought, over the firm opposition of the Department of Agriculture, to secure a monitoring system which reported agricultural export commitments each week and their destination. The specter of the political consequences of the Russian grain sales of 1972 and the rise in primary agricultural prices were forces supporting a monitoring system. A system of export reporting and export controls was in effect on ferrous scrap.

But it was not until mid-June 1973 that a reporting system was instituted; such a system is complex and time should have been taken to perfect the information and reporting procedures. Cash soybean prices, which had been $5 to $6 a bushel earlier in the year, moved up dramatically until they peaked at $12.27 a bushel on June 5. They were in the neighborhood of $11.50 when the Secretary of Commerce imposed an embargo on exports of soybeans, cottonseed, and related products on June 27. Prices fell dramatically to $6.15-$6.25 during July 6 to 9. A licensing system replaced the embargo on July 2; allocations as a percentage of unshipped contracts were as follows: soybeans, 50%; soybean meal, 40%; cottonseed and related products, 100%. On August 1 all allocations were increased to 100%, and on September 21 these export restrictions were terminated with the harvesting of the new crop.

The stabilization authorities were concerned with the squeeze induced by the sharp rise in feed costs on producers of poultry, eggs, hogs, and other users of soybeans. They interpreted the surge of soybean prices to mean that export commitments had been made in excess of remaining stocks from the old (1972) crop or that stocks were likely to be dangerously low as the old crop year came to an end. The hastily imposed monitoring system could not be so reliable as one that had been operational for a period. If such emergencies arise in the future, proven reporting sources are required. Moreover, had the crisis been foreseen, various measures, including genuine consultation with foreign customers, should have been undertaken.

Although the center of concern was soybeans, it was necessary, even for the brief period of a month or so, to impose export limitations on more than 100 different related items, including soybean meal and various types of oil and substitutes. Export controls are complex, and to deal with the full range of agricultural products would be an enormous undertaking. Substitutions are very widely possible among basic agricultural products, so that restraints on one commodity lead to enhanced demands for others.

One of the principal issues to be raised with export controls is their impact on relations with foreign customers who are concerned about the reliability of supply. These considerations were extensively discussed in the Food Committee of the Cost of Living Council and with those in the State Department charged with trade responsibilities. The President emphasized restraints on the use of export controls when the second freeze was relaxed on food prices on July 18, 1973.

> But permanent control of exports is not the policy of this government .... To a considerable degree, export controls are self-defeating as an anti-inflation measure. Limiting our exports reduces our foreign earnings, depresses the value of the dollar, and increases the cost of things we import .... Moreover, limiting our agricultural

exports runs counter to our basic policy of building up our agricultural markets abroad . . . . However, reports of export orders for agricultural commodities will continue to be required. Our policy must be guided by the fundamental importance of maintaining adequate supplies of food at home.[17]

Authority for export controls was not a part of the stabilization legislation but was authorized under continuing authority (Export Administration Act of 1969) to control exports in the event of "abnormal foreign demand" and that the commodity is a "scarce material." Export controls were used for an extended time in the stabilization period to restrain the price of ferrous scrap and to reduce the pressures on steel prices. In general, export controls are a complex and double-edged tool to be used after other measures have been exhausted and to be resorted to with great restraint.

Controls on Wages and Benefits

The retail food sector posed some of the more complex questions of wage stabilization in the period 1971–1974. Phase II exacerbated subsequent problems for both controllers and for labor and managements. Self-administration of smaller units permitted some crafts to move ahead of other crafts or localities which were restrained by having to submit applications, thereby accentuating distortions. The units permitted self-administration were often artificial as compared with the realities of industrial relations and collective bargaining. Fringe benefit valuation on a cost basis was often arbitrary and permitted distortions in relative benefits with different age and composition of units. The substitution between fringes and wages in the compensation package created serious pressures for subsequent increases. The provision for advanced approval of larger units with self-administration of smaller units by craft and locality resulted in serious distortions.

The Pay Board apparently took inconsistent actions on similar cases in the same locality. It had no internal mechanism to achieve consistency in case handling nor did it have a compilation of wage data and benefits to provide a reference base for relative wages and benefits. The few cases in which previously negotiated increases were reduced appear to have been selected quite arbitrarily. Staff or representatives of labor and management familiar with the industry had not participated in the administration of the regulations or case handling.

The unions in the retail food industry were extremely hostile to the notion in January 1973 that mandatory controls should continue on their sector and that most others should be allowed a high degree of self-administration. The large backlog of cases would be certain to grow, and while other sectors could put increases into effect promptly, the food industry was required to wait for long periods for case decisions. The problems rehearsed above are designed to illuminate the wage control system and the set of attitudes engendered in the labor and management leaders of the industry by early 1973.

In this setting, in order to preserve a wage controls program it seemed essential to secure the full cooperation of labor and management in the food industry. A Tripartite Food Industry Wage and Salary Committee was established, subject to the Director of the Cost of Living Council, to administer the wage controls, to facilitate the resolution of collective bargaining disputes over the terms of agreements, and to explore means of improving the structure of bargaining and productivity for the long term.*

The most urgent lesson to emerge from this experience with wage controls in the food industry is that the general formula or guidepost sort of regulation executed by staff or self-administered can be applied for only a very limited period—measured in months—to a sector with complex industrial relations, wage structure, and fringe benefit relationships and a large number of agreements. Only a tripartite group, considering individual cases, can achieve over a longer period a degree of continuing stabilization and requisite industrial peace. Only if national leaders on both sides of an industry, in which collective bargaining is dominant, are prepared to participate and support a program of wage restraint (and price restraint) can the program survive for long and avoid strikes directed against the controls program.

The Economic Costs of Controls

The effect of controls upon economic efficiency and shortages was a persistent concern of controllers in the 1971–1974 period, as in earlier periods of stabilization. The longer controls are in effect and the greater the degree to which prices are held below market levels, and relative price relationships are altered, and the tighter the economy, the greater the potential effects upon resource allocations.

In the food area examples of such distortion can readily be identified in the period: the meat ceilings imposed on March 29, 1973, and continued until September 10, 1973, resulted in some withholding from the market for a period. The custom slaughtering by food chains to assure meat supplies at retail distorted traditional marketing arrangements and squeezed retailers' margins. The second freeze of June 13, 1973, unlike the August 15, 1971, freeze, had adverse effects on food production as in the case of poultry, dramatized by drowning baby chicks. Restraining domestic prices below world prices encouraged exports of hides, fertilizers, and meats. In the case of some fruits and vegetables and sugar, vertically integrated firms that experienced little cost increases as an aggregrate were compelled by the regu-

---

* The work of the Committee for the duration of the controls program is described and appraised in Chapter IV.

lations to price below less-integrated firms purchasing raw agricultural products and passing on their increased costs through higher prices. The mix of products at retail food outlets and their relative prices were perhaps altered by price controls as retailers, wholesalers, and manufacturers sought to adjust to the changing regulations instead of to price signals.

Reference should be made to the substantial private costs of complying with the regulations, including accounting records, forms, and specialized personnel to deal with the detailed regulations prescribing pricing rules.[18]

It should be observed that in the main there was widespread compliance with the regulations; indeed violations were relatively rare, particularly among larger enterprises.

In general, as Marvin H. Kosters has concluded, in the stabilization period the short-run costs of controls were not enormous. "Evidence of adverse effects during the period of controls is generally not readily apparent in broad measures of production or other indicators either of individual industries or for the overall economy."[19] But the costs were nonetheless real and the frustrations substantial.

Profits Under Controls

An important measure of price controls in the retail and wholesale food industries is to assess the consequences on profits as a percentage return on stockholders' equity and as a percentage return on sales during the controls period.[20]

Retail food chains showed profits as a percentage of stockholders' equity of 5.2% in 1972 and 8.2% in 1973 compared with 10.9% for the period 1963–1970. They showed profits as a percentage return on sales of 0.5% in 1972, 0.7% in 1973, and 0.9% in 1974, compared with an average of 1.2% for the period 1963–1970. Thus, profits by either measure were reduced in the controls period, relative to the preceding years, despite the enormous rise in food prices at retail and the temptation to blame such increases on widening profits. No attempt was made to assess whether the reduction in profits was a simple consequence of controls or whether in the absence of controls profits would not have been compressed to a degree by rising costs.

Food manufacturers taken as a group (SIC 20) showed rates of return on stockholders' equity of 11.2% in 1972 and 12.8% in 1973, compared with an average of 10.6% in the period 1963–1970. They showed profits as a percentage return on sales of 2.6% in 1972, 2.6% in 1973, and 2.8% in 1974 compared with an average of 2.6% in the period 1963–1970. Thus, profits of food manufacturers as return on equity were slightly higher in the controls period but profits as a percentage return on sales were essentially unchanged. Both rose with the elimination of controls after April 30, 1974.

These profit figures are consonant with the view that under the regulations retail and manufacturing food prices simply rode up with the increase in raw agricultural prices during the controls period. As Chapter III concludes, ". . . the food price inflation which characterized the 1972–1974 period was caused principally by rapidly rising agricultural prices which direct controls on prices were unable to prevent from being passed-through eventually to the consumer."*

Implications for Future Controls Programs

This section, or indeed the volume itself, is not to be regarded as advocating or predicting that another era of comprehensive wage and price controls, including direct food controls, is likely to be imposed in the near future. Nonetheless each period of inflationary price pressures seems to revive interest and political support for direct controls. As Lloyd Ulman enunciates in his principle of the Catnip Effect, ". . . incomes policy is well-nigh irresistible to politicians in office."[21] The resort to incomes policies, a term which ordinarily encompasses direct governmental limitations on prices and wages, has become widespread among Western economies in recent years.[22]

This second part constitutes a listing of some of the major implications for future public and private policies, particularly in the food and agricultural sector, derived from the preceding review of the experience in the 1971–1974 period and from earlier wartime controls.

The Central Role of Food Prices to a Controls Program

Food prices at retail in inflationary periods are a central focus of political and economic policy if past periods of direct controls are any guide. Food prices have a direct impact on every household; food is the largest component of family expenditures and is relatively larger for the poorest families. Food prices, dependent in large part on agricultural prices, are volatile, and their movements are highly visible. Food purchases each day and week repetitively dramatize retail food price increases to the public irrespective of the source or reasons for the increases. The supermarket is the forum in which the consumer and the controls program come recurrently face to face. The political process, the Congress, the press and the media, administrative procedures, and the courts are subsequent encounters.

The acceptability of a comprehensive direct controls program to the public has been perceived by stabilization authorities historically to be uniquely dependent on the course of food prices. Even though

---

* It is not appropriate to use various measures of farm-retail spread to infer directly the profits of retailers or manufacturers because significant changes in product mix occur, the geographical mix of activities changes, and other factors become operative.

For a technical discussion, see Council on Wage and Price Stability, Staff Report, *Marketing Spreads for Food Products,* May 1975, pp. 25–48.

controls on food prices may prove ineffectual in keeping food prices from rising, a total controls program to be creditable publicly has been thought to require direct controls on retail food prices, and wage controls in the sector are thought essential if prices are under direct controls. Price Commissioners Lanzillotti and Hamilton reported that a diverse group of experienced economists on November 3, 1971, reached a consensus that after the freeze scheduled to end in mid-November, retail food, rents, and services probably should not be controlled.[23] But the pivotal role of food prices in shaping the public and political acceptability of controls, combined with the judgment that the slack in the economy likely to prevail in the short period envisaged for controls would prevent serious damage, was decisive in the decision to institute a comprehensive program of controls at wholesale and retail in November 1971. As it turned out, food prices were again *"le bête noir*, the biggest single bugbear, of the entire price control program."[24]

The retail and wholesale food sectors present a fundamental enigma to governmental controls policies and to these private sectors no less. Below these sectors raw agricultural prices may increase; indeed it may be desirable that they do increase, in order to bring forth additional domestic production and to respond to increased international demand, relative to supplies. Above these sectors are households and workers who adjudge a controls program largely on the basis of what happens to food prices at retail. It may well be that a comprehensive direct controls program may impose hardship on the wholesale and retail food sectors, and even reduce agricultural supplies, in order to achieve the political support thought necessary to restrain other sectors in which controls may have more significant restraining effects. It may be that a future controls program might consider concentrating on nonfood items, explaining and accepting the inflation inherent in the relatively competitive food and agricultural markets, while seeking to enhance agricultural supplies in the domestic market.

Food Prices and Wage Decisions

There is one further pivotal reason for the decisive importance of wholesale and retail food prices to any direct controls program and that is the impact of food prices on collective bargaining settlements and compensation movements. Food price increases and higher consumer prices beyond small amounts generally have a direct effect on wage rate increases, under collective bargaining settlements, on the size of wage-rate increases under cost-of-living escalator clauses,* and even on wage setting in the absence of unions.

---

* In 1970, 26% of major collective bargaining agreements contained cost-of-living escalator clauses while in 1977 as a consequence of the inflationary experience such clauses were contained in 60% of major agreements. Wage changes may be related in a great variety of ways to a given change in the cost-of-living index.

While food prices in the market place may come down as well as go up, in the modern Western world money wages are not reduced; they only increase. Thus, a temporary rise in food prices of a significant size is likely to result in a permanent increase in the level of money wages, with continuing effects on prices of finished goods and services and on international competitive positions at given exchange rates.

Programs of direct controls accordingly are likely to give special attention to retail food prices, apart from the sensitivity of households, because of their special significance to the wage determination process. Again, a food controls program may present the enigma that it may be of marginal value or even adverse in its effects in the food sector, but it may be instituted and maintained because of its central importance to the political viability of the controls program generally and to the creditability of imposed wage restraints more specifically. Such a state of affairs makes cooperation from the food and agriculture sector the more difficult.

The Political and Economic Setting and Purposes of Controls

The operations of any direct controls program will be decisively influenced by the economic and political environment in which the program is developed and the way in which this context changes during the life of the program.[25] A food direct controls program, in addition, will be influenced decisively by the pre-existing agricultural policies and production or marketing controls, as Chapter II stresses. Not all inflationary periods are the same, and the relations among various interest groups and the legislature and executive branches of government also vary appreciably. Inflation may arise in wartime or in peace. Price increases may be engendered largely from abroad or as a consequence of domestic policies. Inflation may have its roots in government fiscal policy, agricultural shortages from poor weather or large export demands, or a rapid build-up of investment expenditures. Wage structures may be balanced or involve considerable distortion generating further inflationary pressures. A controls period may commence with a constructive industrial relations climate or may start in industrial strife. A controls period may begin with substantial unused capacity and resources or at a time of growing shortages of capacity and skilled labor. The program may be instituted in a period of seasonal food price declines, as was the freeze on August 15, 1971, when the harvest led to seasonal price declines below the price ceilings, thereby materially facilitating controls, or a freeze may be instituted when agricultural supplies are seasonally low before the harvest, as on June 13, 1973, thereby adversely affecting agricultural output in some products. The size of the cattle and hog population and the extent of agricultural stockpiles may be important to the results of a controls program.

The point is that the economic and political setting of controls is likely to have a decisive effect on their performance. The design of the controls program cannot simply be lifted from past models or general purpose planning; to be workable, wage and price controls need to be congruent with the specific economic and political environments and their development. Indeed, the purposes of direct controls programs may vary a great deal and contain quite different elements. Thus, controls may be designed as an attack on administered prices, or on inflationary collective bargaining structures and wage push inflation, or they may be designed to facilitate redistribution of income toward the low wage earners, or to restrain the consequence of agricultural shortages, or to facilitate a transfer of resources to wartime purposes. A perceptive analysis and appraisal of the initial and the evolving economic, legislative, and political setting are essential to the design and continuing redesign of any direct controls program. The absence of data and the intrusion of political elements into forecasting make hard analysis the more difficult.

The Priority of Supply-Enhancing Measures at an Early Date

Even though controllers seek to regulate price directly, it is essential that close attention be directed at all times to the underlying demand and supply conditions in policy making and administration of a program. This injunction is particularly significant in the food sector where a continuous monitoring of stocks, production, and usage at home and abroad by top economic policy makers is imperative. A world-wide perspective is essential, particularly in food and feed grains. Indeed, the more that requisite adjustments can be made through the underlying demand and supply conditions the less will be the strain and adverse effects on the direct controls mechanism. In constraining agricultural price inflation, a variety of governmental actions have been taken to increase domestic supply[26]—to eliminate acreage set-asides, to eliminate direct subsidies on export of farm products, to sell government-owned stocks, to eliminate quotas on imports, to assure fertilizer supplies and transportation, and to eliminate the restrictive features of marketing orders,[27] among others.

Experience suggests that one of the great difficulties in taking such supply actions in times of food price inflation, with or without direct controls, is to initiate such measures early enough. Thus, the Price Commission sought to have acreage set-asides eliminated in the spring of 1972, but it was not until the end of 1972 that set-asides were reduced and not until the spring of 1973 that they were eliminated in the vital food and feed grains. Indeed, if such supply-enhancing measures are taken early enough, direct controls may be avoided or their impact may be less onerous. The political process has its own calender, but so does nature. The winter wheat crop is planted in the fall to be harvested in the following summer, and corn is planted in the spring to be harvested in the fall; it takes 24 months to raise beef for market. These processes cannot be constrained by political fiat and may not fit the political calendar.

These supply-enhancing activities of government are to be given first priority at a timely date in the food and agricultural sector if the alternative of the imposition of direct controls in the face of rapid price increases is to be avoided or their effects mitigated.

The Need for Economic and Political Accommodation Among Agriculture, Industry, Workers, and Consumers

One of the indelible lessons of direct control periods is the sharp conflicts of interest that develop between farm groups and others in the community. Higher farm prices mean higher incomes to farmers no less than they tend to mean higher costs to food manufacturers, to wholesalers, to retailers, and to workers and consumers. Net income of farm operators more than doubled in the price inflation of 1972–1973.[28] Moreover, many farmers feel that their prices have been historically too low, and they particularly resent interference with market forces on occasions when they would otherwise at long last "make up" for low prices or the vagaries of nature. Agricultural interests, of course, are not entirely homogeneous. Short-term increases in feed grain prices work adversely to the interests of producers of cattle, hogs, and chickens who are quite sensitive to their margins between feed costs and selling price. In each stabilization or controls period there have been sharp conflicts, reflecting these different interests, between the stabilization agencies and farm groups and agricultural committees of the Congress.

The simple fact is that agricultural policy in the large, both in legislative and in administrative decisions, has necessarily become an integral part of general economic policy and foreign policy—with or without direct controls. Food prices are decisive to living costs of the whole population and to the rachet process of wage setting. Agricultural prices are decisive to farm income and to relative incomes of other groups. Agricultural products are a major component of international trade and trade negotiations, and large and sudden bulk purchases by totalitarian governments where demands are difficult to anticipate may have decisive effects on price and agricultural output; agricultural technology may be a significant item in international negotiations with developing countries and the communist bloc. Agricultural issues deeply involve the Congress and have an impact on many other questions. Decisions in these areas, with or without controls, cannot simply be left to the Department of Agriculture. They are an essential element of general economic policy making; they are central to direct controls if they are in effect.

A cabinet-level Food Committee of the Cost of Living Council was established in January 1973 with primary responsibility for agricultural and food policy under controls. The Secretary of Agriculture, as a matter of course, was a member along with those charged with economic policy making and stabilization responsibility. This committee was continued after controls expired in 1974 as a food committee of the Economic Policy Board.

The location of the review of economic analysis of agriculture and food, a check on forecasts, the relation to international economic and foreign policy, and the monitoring of the interaction between agricultural decisions and general economic policy, with or without controls, is one of the major structural decisions of the executive branch of the federal government.

In a controls program, particularly of longer duration, one of the most difficult and central problems relates to the establishment, if possible, of a continuing equilibrium or relatively stable relationship among agricultural prices, industrial prices, and wages and services. If one of these elements moves beyond a narrow range, it tends to upset the relationships with the others. Perhaps the only stabilization program in this country which achieved a modicum of stability and acceptability in these relationships was accomplished by the hold-the-line executive order on April 8, 1943, in World War II. The President vetoed the Bankhead bill which would have increased agricultural prices by prohibiting the deduction of subsidies paid to farmers in the computation of parity prices, and at the same time he tightened wage and price controls appreciably. Some food prices were rolled back and subsidies to processors were introduced to prevent adverse effects on production. A new coordinating Office of Economic Stabilization was established.[29] These actions provided the basis for relative stability in wage rates, industrial prices, and agricultural and food prices at the height of the war effort. This relative stability and accommodation was maintained for more than two years until the end of hostilities which was followed by the immediate postwar explosion in prices and wages.

A controls program of considerable duration needs to establish a sense of accommodation among major interest groups and relative stability among agricultural and food prices, industrial prices, and wages, or to establish an acceptable means of making periodic adjustments.

The Duration of Controls

One of the critical features in the design of any controls program is the duration contemplated at the outset. A short program need be less concerned with the frustrations and hostilities which inherently build up over time; any controls program tends to wear out as conflicts become more entrenched and as many parties develop means to get around rules and regulations and to discover loopholes. A longer period of controls must confront and give greater attention to relative wage relationships. More detailed legislation and more directions by congressional oversight committees tend to develop and court litigation compels more and more detailed specification of regulations. A program of short duration may probably choose more self-administration and a lesser degree of administrative machinery than a program expected to last a number of years.

The fact is, of course, that historically in each controls period there has been uncertainty over the duration of controls. The designers of the 1971 controls expected a period of a few months, or no longer than a year, that is, until immediately after the elections of 1972. But direct controls sometimes develop a life of their own and unexpected events arise as they did in late 1972 and 1973 when the difficulties of getting out of controls came to be more fully appreciated. While the intended duration of controls may be expected to influence the character of the program and its administration, controllers need to be aware that any projected termination date may be extended.

It is far easier to get into wage and price controls than it is to get out of them, at least gracefully. The end-game of controls is most difficult. Historically, controls were abandoned at the end of the World War II and Korean programs in a rout. There tends to be a post-controls bulge in prices and wages which may undo or counteract the restraint period; the administrative machinery tends to be demoralized and is difficult to manage; and the tendency to ignore or to flout regulations is enhanced. A strong tendency develops in the business community and among consumers to blame all problems on government controls; if only controls would go away, all problems would be solved.* The respect for governmental rules and the preservation of a very scarce resource, direct wage and price controls, for a future period of genuine emergency are values which a conscientious controller should rate highly.

The Lessons of Wage Controls

A brief summary of lessons growing out of wage stabilization programs in food and in the economy generally is in order.[30] The Pay Board in Phase II (November 14, 1971–January 10, 1973) eschewed any role in the settlement of labor-management disputes.

> As a body, the Board has adhered to the view that the acceptance of the goal of disputes settlement would be inconsistent with the economic premises underlying the stabilization program and with standards of equity . . . . Acceptance of disputes settlement as a goal also would reward the strong while controlling the weak, who have only a limited capacity to inflict harm on the community.[31]

The Pay Board felt that its record indicated that stabilization responsibilities could be carried out independently of concerns with industrial relations.

---

* In the spring of 1976 I met in an airport a business executive whose company had had considerable conflict with the Cost of Living Council over allowable price increases in 1973–1974. After discussion about the general business situation, I asked about prices in his company. "Lousy" he said, "but I can't blame that on you now."

This Phase II view was consistent with its short-term expectations as to the duration of the controls program, the reliance upon a formula for a single and uniform wage standard, the related commitment to a relatively small staff, and the absence of industrial relations experience among many of the public members of the tripartite board.[32] As described by Vaughn in Chapter IV, the Tripartite Food Industry Wage and Salary Committee in Phases III and IV, on the other hand, was much involved in dispute resolution and maintained a close working relationship with the Federal Mediation and Conciliation Service. This view toward disputes is associated with a concern over acceptable wage structures and differentials, the rejection of a single standard for achieving wage stabilization, and an interest in assisting the parties to improve the structure of collective bargaining and productivity and thereby to reduce the potential for inflation over the long term. Moreover, the members of the Tripartite Committee were experienced in industrial relations and considered cases individually. The distortion which the formula approach of Phase II inflicted on the wage and benefit structure of the industry and the industrial relations consequences of such arbitrary dislocation of wage relationships had to be corrected if a wage controls program was to be maintained after January 1973 in the food sector.

The basic character of wage inflation, at least in the United States, is that it distorts historical or emerging wage relationships, among occupations, industries, and localities that are particularly related to one another by market or industrial relations forces. The task of a wage stabilization program, then, is to restore these relationships in order to permit longer-term stability rather than the continuation of efforts of closely related groups to outdo one another. Thus, a single wage standard of 5.5% is a peculiarly inappropriate approach to wage stabilization; a single figure will only continue, and widen in absolute figures, the extent of distortions. Some groups of employees need to be given more and others less in order to reduce the extent of distortion and to move toward wage and benefit stability.[33]

In summary, the procedural fundamental of wage controls is the necessity for sympathetic involvement of labor and management leaders. The substantive fundamental is the objective of the gradual restoration of historical and emerging wage, salary, and benefit relativities, correcting the distortions which are the essence of compensation inflation.[34]

Stabilization and Other Functions

Periods of direct wage and price controls are characterized by very substantial and unusual grants of authority to the stabilization agencies. There arise in the legislative process and in administration considerable pressures and opportunities to use these powers for purposes only indirectly related to stabilization, but to achieve various forms of social and economic change under the rubric of controls over prices and wages.

For instance, other government agencies or various organized groups had been seeking for years to secure and to use publicly statistical data by product line or by a detailed firm and industry breakdown that had been regarded as confidential or proprietary and had not been publicly available. The stabilization agencies were regarded as the ideal means to use their extraordinary powers to secure these data and to make them available, directly, or through committees of the Congress. Or, the movement for unit pricing, pricing on a standard of weight or measurement rather than by container, sought to advance its cause by having the stabilization agencies adopt rules requiring such pricing on the grounds that price stability and information to consumers should be enhanced. Or, repeatedly stabilization authorities confronted the question as to what extent they should accept prevailing or conventional systems of accounting and to what extent they should require separate records, at times designed to achieve longer-term reforms in accounting procedures. Or, wage controls in legislation may be explicitly designed to be redistributive in favor of low incomes. Indeed, European incomes policies, unlike those in this country, have ordinarily been so intended.[35]

This range of issues involves complex and troubling problems. Stabilization authorities have sufficient to do and more than enough difficulties without courting others gratuitously, but many a decision may be seen as—and in fact may be—taking a position on such a long-standing issue. Short-term stabilization policies may in fact have longer-term or "reform" effects. Those subject to controls, as well as controllers, will have much on their minds concerning the post-controls consequences of regulations or policies. There may be a very fine line between policies necessitated by stabilization and those viewed as intended to achieve reforms in information reporting, competitive positions, and market structures.

In principle, experience suggests that stabilization agencies had best concentrate on the controls assignment rather than allowing the agency to be used as a means of imposing controversial reforms tangential to its main purposes. A concern with longer-term stability and policies or practices which reduce the continuing potential for inflation, however, particularly if developed cooperatively with affected groups, may prove to be a major contribution of a stabilization era. Indeed, the mobilization of concern over long-term problems may be essential to achieve respect and compliance with short-term controls. Thus, a controls period may prove appropriate in eliminating restrictive policies of government affecting agricultural production and in working to change the structure of collective bargaining in certain industries.[36] Such changes have an impact both immediately on the rate of inflation and on longer-term price and wage stability.

Impact on Controls on Monetary and Fiscal Policy

One of the persistent problems of periods of direct wage and price controls is their effect in turn upon monetary and fiscal policy. It is inappropriate to presume that the level of federal expenditures and tax receipts and monetary policy of the Federal Reserve Board are unaffected by the presence of direct controls. Indeed, there is every reason to expect that controls are to some degree a substitute for more stringent fiscal and monetary policy. As George P. Shultz has written:

> It seems almost inevitable that the proclaimed existence of controls or an incomes policy sends through the political process the feeling that this policy is dealing, at least in some fashion, with the problem of inflation. It follows that the government can be more forthcoming in stimulating the economy.[37]

Attempts to measure the quantitative effects of controls on prices inappropriately treat monetary and fiscal policy as given and unaffected by controls. The resort to controls almost necessarily leads to a less stringent fiscal and monetary policy to constrain inflation. Monetary policy was expansionary throughout most of the controls period; the most rapid rate of increase in money supply took place in the latter part of 1972.

It is no accident that the Federal Reserve Board and its chairman, Arthur F. Burns, have become a persistent advocate of some form of incomes policy, although not for a program of comprehensive or mandatory wage and price controls.[38] The monetary authorities feel that they are shouldering an unduly large share of the burden of restraining inflation and seek help from all quarters: government fiscal policy, antitrust policy, structural reform in labor and product markets, and restraint on wages and prices.

Monetary and fiscal policy is not likely to be unaffected by the imposition of controls. Controls programs affect the will and determination with which the stringencies of fiscal and monetary policies are perceived and pursued.

Controls in an International Emergency

In contemplating how to deal with food price inflation, or in the execution of actual programs, the lesson is that increasing supply (or restricting demand) is the first consideration. A related lesson is that supply-enhancing measures do not respond in political time; each activity requires a relatively fixed time frame to secure responses. It will take several years to build fertilizer plants, a planting and harvesting season to increase acreage and production, and several years to increase current output of beef by increasing the stock of cattle, while a matter of months is adequate for chickens, and the time required to increase imports will vary with stocks abroad and the time of the year. The time frame for supply responses places great premium on more accurate and current information on agricultural and food supplies, production, consumption, imports and exports, prices, and so on. Government data systems leave much to be desired. The time frame of supply responses also places great emphasis on the need for analysis and integration of food policy into general economic policy, international and domestic. Agricultural and food policy is too significant to be left to the Department of Agriculture, although it should be involved in the general economic councils on these and other issues.

The imposition of margin controls at wholesale and retail price levels, except for very short periods measured in weeks under unusual circumstances, can be expected simply to lead to prices to consumers which rise or fall with the underlying producers' prices or raw agricultural prices.* Variations in margins make relatively minor differences in final consumer food prices as a group. Accordingly, attention is again forced back upon the underlying domestic and world prices of agricultural products.

In a true emergency, such as in international conflict, direct restraints on food prices to be effective cannot be confined to margin controls at manufacturing, retail, or wholesale prices or even to specific ceilings. A system of controls which involves raw agricultural products would be necessary including a complex of import and export controls, controls over stock, production stimulus subsidies, or other measures that could only be justified by a true international emergency.

Summary

In general, wage and price controls applied across the U.S. economy in the effort to constrain inflation are a limited and special purpose tool in peace time. On balance they can be expected to have only a relatively small effect on inflation for a limited period to keep the rate of price and wage increases below the rates that might otherwise prevail. In some periods they may even exacerbate the rate of inflation by restricting and distorting supply and collective bargaining. There is serious danger that direct controls may encourage lax fiscal and monetary policies.

Such controls, however, may have a more constructive effect on some particular sectors if imaginatively and cooperatively applied. They may also be used as a means of encouraging and placing in effect private and public measures to increase supplies or to eliminate governmental policies which keep down output and supplies, thereby constraining the rate of price increase.

---

* There may also be some distortions in production and relative prices.

In many, if not most, circumstances, food prices are at the center of the concerns of any stabilization or incomes policy. Food prices have proved to be very difficult to control at retail or wholesale levels because of the close relationship with volatile agricultural prices fundamentally determined by international forces. But food prices are decisive to the extent of wage increases, and once wage and benefit rates increase they do not decline to old levels.

The best way to affect food prices is through supplies coming on the domestic market, relative to demand. But it takes considerable time to stimulate supplies through higher prices, greater productivity, greater imports, and lower inducements to export or to withhold from the market through marketing orders. Agriculture has been the subject for a long time of a network of governmental controls through price supports, acreage restrictions, import controls, marketing orders, and the like. (See Chapter II.) Agricultural prices are influenced by world-wide developments. (See Chapter V.) A premium is thus placed in stabilization programs on economic and agricultural forecasting and early measures to modify the existing government regulations in order to increase supply.

If direct controls are applied to the agriculture and food sector as a last resort, it is essential to see that the adverse effects of price controls on production and output are held to a minimum, that distortions in product-mix and distribution are kept tolerable, and that wage controls do not distort wage relationships or increase industrial strife materially. If supplies are very short, relative to demand, direct price controls will prove ineffectual; only the strong measures of export controls, subsidies to enhance production, and rationing are likely to prove effective for even a short period. These are extreme measures which have been used in the United States only at the height of wartime mobilization.

Any resort to direct controls must involve the participation of representatives of a broad spectrum of industry and agriculture for prices and labor and management representatives for wage and benefit controls if they are to be effective. The consent of the controlled is essential if wage and price regulations are to persist for a considerable period and to reflect the least amount of distortions and post-controls dislocations.

APPENDIXES

APPENDIX I

The appendix for Chapter I consists of 14 tables. There is no accompanying text. See Chapter I for references and detailed explanations.

APPENDIX TABLE I-1.   CORN: ACREAGE, YIELD, PRODUCTION, AND PRICES, 1969–1970 THROUGH 1974–1975[a]

	1969–1970	1970–1971	1971–1972	1972–1973	1973–1974	1974–1975[b]
			(raw data)			
Acreage (millions)						
Set-aside	27.2	26.1	14.1	24.4	6.0	—
Harvested for grain	54.6	57.4	64.0	57.4	61.9	65.2
Yield (bushel/acre)	85.9	72.4	88.1	97.1	91.2	71.3
Production (millions of bushels)	4,687	4,152	5,641	5,573	5,647	4,651
Ending stocks (millions of bushels)	1,005	667	1,126	709	483	295
Price (per bushel)[c]	$1.16	$1.33	$1.08	$1.57	$2.55	$2.95
			(percentage change from year earlier)			
Acreage						
Set-aside	—	−4	−46	+73	−75	−100
Harvested	—	+5	+12	−10	+8	+5
Yield	—	−16	+22	+10	−6	−22
Production	—	−11	+36	−1	+1	−18
Ending stocks	—	−34	+69	−37	−32	−39
Price[c]	—	+15	−19	+45	+62	+16

[a] Marketing year beginning October 1.
[b] Preliminary.
[c] Received by farmers; excludes support payment.
SOURCES: USDA, *Feed Situation*, FdS-255, November 1974, and FdS-258, September 1975. USDA, *Agricultural Supply & Demand Estimates*, No. 32, October 14, 1975.

APPENDIX TABLE I-2. HOGS AND PIGS ON FARMS,
TEN CORN BELT STATES, 1969-1975[a]

Year	March 1	June 1	September 1	December 1
		(million head)		
1969	40.4	44.5	44.6	43.1
1970	40.2	49.1	51.0	50.4
1971	44.4	48.6	47.6	46.4
1972	41.7	45.4	45.6	44.6
1973	41.5	45.3	45.9	46.7
1974	42.7	45.0	44.4	41.6
1975	35.4	36.2	36.7	
		(percentage change from year earlier)		
1970	−0.5	+10.3	+14.4	+16.9
1971	+10.4	−1.0	−6.7	−7.9
1972	−6.1	−6.6	−4.2	−3.9
1973	−0.5	−0.2	+0.7	+4.7
1974	+2.9	−0.7	−3.3	−10.9
1975	−17.1	−19.6	−17.3	

[a] Ohio, Indiana, Illinois, Wisconsin, Minnesota, Iowa, Missouri, South Dakota, Nebraska, Kansas.

SOURCES: USDA, *Hogs and Pigs,* December 1972 through September 1975. USDA, *Hogs and Pigs: Revised Estimates, 1965-69,* Statistical Bulletin No. 496, November 1972.

APPENDIX TABLE I-3. BEEF COWS AND BEEF COW REPLACEMENTS,
JANUARY 1, 1965-1975

	Beef Cows[a]		Beef Cow Replacements[b]	
Year	Millions of Head	Percent Change	Millions of Head	Percent Change
1965	33.4	—	5.70	—
1966	33.5	0.3	5.76	1.0
1967	33.8	0.9	5.90	2.4
1968	34.6	2.4	6.11	3.6
1969	35.5	2.6	6.15	0.7
1970	36.7	3.4	6.43	4.6
1971	37.9	3.3	6.66	3.6
1972	38.8	2.4	6.99	5.0
1973	40.9	5.4	7.44	6.4
1974	43.0	5.1	8.23	10.6
1975	45.4	5.6	8.88	7.9

[a] Beef cows and heifers that have calved.
[b] Heifers 500 pounds and over being held for beef cow replacements.
SOURCE: USDA, *Cattle.*

APPENDIX TABLE I-4.   PRICES RECEIVED BY FARMERS IN THE UNITED STATES,
JANUARY 1970—DECEMBER 1974 (1967 = 100)

Month	1970	1971	1972	1973	1974
January	113	107	120	145	198
February	114	112	122	149	202
March	114	112	120	159	194
April	111	111	120	158	183
May	110	112	123	163	175
June	110	112	125	172	165
July	112	111	127	173	175
August	109	111	128	208	181
September	110	111	130	191	178
October	109	112	129	184	185
November	106	114	130	181	182
December	105	117	137	185	177
Annual Average	110	112	126	172	183

SOURCE: USDA, *Agricultural Prices,* Supplement No. 1 to May 1974, and selected
more recent issues.

APPENDIX TABLE I-5.   CONSUMER PRICE INDEX,
JANUARY 1970—DECEMBER 1974 (1967 = 100)

Month	1970	1971	1972	1973	1974
January	113.3	119.2	123.2	127.7	139.7
February	113.9	119.4	123.8	128.6	141.5
March	114.5	119.8	124.0	129.8	143.1
April	115.2	120.2	124.3	130.7	143.9
May	115.7	120.8	124.7	131.5	145.5
June	116.3	121.5	125.0	132.4	146.9
July	116.7	121.8	125.5	132.7	148.0
August	116.9	122.1	125.7	135.1	149.9
September	117.5	122.2	126.2	135.5	151.7
October	118.1	122.4	126.6	136.6	153.0
November	118.5	122.6	126.9	137.6	154.3
December	119.1	123.1	127.3	138.5	155.4
Annual Average	116.3	121.3	125.3	133.1	147.7

SOURCE: Council of Economic Advisers, *Economic Report of the President,* 1972–1975.

APPENDIX TABLE I-6. CONSUMER PRICE INDEX FOR FOOD,
JANUARY 1970—DECEMBER 1974 (1967 = 100)

Month	1970	1971	1972	1973	1974
January	113.5	115.5	120.3	128.6	153.7
February	114.1	115.9	122.2	131.1	157.6
March	114.2	117.0	122.4	134.5	159.1
April	114.6	117.8	122.4	136.5	158.6
May	114.9	118.2	122.3	137.9	159.7
June	115.2	119.2	123.0	139.8	160.3
July	115.8	119.8	124.2	140.9	160.5
August	115.9	120.0	124.6	149.4	162.8
September	115.7	119.1	124.8	148.3	165.0
October	115.5	118.9	124.9	148.4	166.1
November	114.9	119.0	125.4	150.0	167.8
December	115.3	120.3	126.0	151.3	169.7
Annual Average	114.9	118.4	123.5	141.4	161.7

SOURCE: Council of Economic Advisers, *Economic Report of the President,* 1972–1975.

APPENDIX TABLE I-7. CONSUMER PRICE INDEX FOR ALL ITEMS LESS FOOD,
JANUARY 1970—DECEMBER 1974 (1967 = 100)

Month	1970	1971	1972	1973	1974
January	113.3	120.3	124.0	127.5	135.6
February	113.9	120.4	124.2	127.9	136.8
March	114.6	120.6	124.5	128.4	138.4
April	115.4	120.9	124.9	129.1	139.6
May	116.0	121.6	125.4	129.7	141.3
June	116.5	122.2	125.7	130.3	142.9
July	117.0	122.4	125.9	130.4	144.4
August	117.2	122.7	126.1	130.9	146.1
September	118.0	123.1	126.7	131.8	147.8
October	118.9	123.5	127.1	133.1	149.1
November	119.6	123.7	127.4	134.0	150.4
December	120.2	123.9	127.6	134.8	151.3
Annual Average	116.7	122.1	125.8	130.7	143.6

SOURCE: Council of Economic Advisers, *Economic Report of the President,* 1972–1975.

APPENDIX TABLE I-8.   MEAT IMPORTS SUBJECT TO U.S. IMPORT QUOTA
RESTRICTIONS, JANUARY 1970—DECEMBER 1974 (IN MILLIONS OF POUNDS,
PRODUCT WEIGHT)

Month	1970	1971	1972	1973	1974
January	124.5	83.4	86.9	106.2	118.0
February	100.7	65.1	80.8	98.4	82.3
March	112.0	88.3	75.4	88.3	104.9
April	88.7	86.2	105.4	97.9	91.4
May	62.1	76.8	107.9	113.1	80.6
June	93.4	101.0	106.4	91.5	78.6
July	110.0	94.4	106.8	105.9	59.4
August	113.0	104.9	164.6	153.7	101.4
September	107.6	158.6	163.8	110.3	91.8
October	89.3	80.4	145.1	150.0	72.3
November	79.3	63.2	119.0	130.0	93.2
December	89.8	130.3	93.4	109.1	105.2
Total	1,170.4	1,132.6	1,355.5	1,354.4	1,079.1

NOTE: Rejections for calendar year 1969 equaled 13.5 million pounds, 17.4 million pounds for 1970, 21.0 million pounds for 1971, 17.8 million pounds for 1972, 18.4 million pounds for 1973, and 9.6 million pounds for 1974.

SOURCE: USDA, *Livestock and Meat Situation,* No. 205, October 1975.

APPENDIX TABLE I-9. SOYBEANS: SUPPLY, DISPOSITION, AND PRICES, 1965–1974 (YEAR BEGINNING IN SEPTEMBER)

	1965	1966	1967	1968	1969	1970	1971	1972	1973	1974[a]
Acreage harvested for beans (in millions)	34.4	36.5	39.8	41.4	41.3	42.2	42.7	45.7	55.8	52.5
Yield (bushels/acre)	24.5	25.4	24.5	26.7	27.4	26.7	27.5	27.8	27.7	23.5
Supply (millions of bushels)										
Stocks, September 1	30	36	90	166	327	230	99	72	60	171
Production	845	928	976	1107	1133	1127	1176	1271	1547	1233
TOTAL	875	964	1066	1273	1460	1357	1275	1343	1607	1404
Disposition (millions of bushels)										
Domestic[b]	589	612	633	660	797	824	786	804	897	797
Exports	251	262	267	287	433	434	417	479	539	421
TOTAL	840	874	900	947	1230	1258	1203	1283	1436	1218
Stocks, August 31 (millions of bushels)	36	90	166	327	230	99	72	60	171	186
Price received by farmers (per bushel)	$2.54	$2.75	$2.49	$2.43	$2.35	$2.85	$3.03	$4.37	$5.68	$6.50[c]

[a] Preliminary.
[b] Includes crushings which are exported.
[c] ERS estimate.
SOURCE: USDA, Fats and Oils Situation, FOS-275, November 1974, and FOS-280, October 1975.

APPENDIX TABLE I-10. SELECTED RETAIL DAIRY PRODUCT PRICES AND MARGARINE PRICES, JULY 1971—DECEMBER 1974 (IN CENTS)

Year and Month	Dairy Products Index (1967 = 100)	Fresh Milk, Grocery (per half gallon)	American Cheese (per half pound)	Ice Cream (per half gallon)	Butter (per pound)	Margarine, Colored (per pound)
1971						
July	116.0	59.2	53.2	86.2	87.5	32.6
August	116.0	59.2	53.1	85.7	87.5	32.8
September	116.1	59.3	53.0	85.9	87.6	33.2
October	116.0	59.2	53.2	85.3	87.6	33.3
November	115.9	59.2	53.3	85.6	87.5	33.2
December	116.1	59.2	53.2	86.2	87.3	33.2
1972						
January	116.4	59.5	53.3	85.9	87.5	33.0
February	116.9	59.8	53.8	85.5	87.5	33.3
March	117.3	60.1	53.8	86.2	87.5	33.4
April	117.4	60.1	54.1	85.9	87.4	33.3
May	117.3	60.0	54.1	85.8	87.1	33.2
June	117.0	59.8	54.2	85.9	86.7	33.3
July	116.8	59.6	54.3	85.8	86.6	33.0
August	116.6	59.4	54.4	85.4	86.5	33.0
September	116.9	59.4	54.7	86.0	86.6	33.1
October	117.1	59.5	54.6	85.6	87.2	33.0
November	117.7	59.8	55.1	85.9	87.3	32.9
December	118.3	60.1	55.6	85.5	87.2	32.9

1973						
January	119.1	60.6	55.9	86.3	87.4	32.6
February	121.0	61.9	56.5	86.7	87.4	32.7
March	121.5	61.9	56.9	87.8	87.7	32.9
April	121.8	61.9	57.6	88.0	85.4	33.5
May	123.2	62.7	58.7	88.6	85.3	34.0
June	124.1	63.1	59.2	89.1	85.0	35.1
July	124.1	63.2	59.4	88.8	85.0	35.2
August	126.6	64.7	59.9	89.7	88.7	36.8
September	130.3	66.3	60.7	92.7	99.9	41.2
October	137.3	70.3	63.5	96.3	106.0	44.3
November	141.2	73.1	66.8	98.6	100.2	45.1
December	144.9	75.3	69.1	99.6	101.5	45.1
1974						
January	146.3	75.9	70.5	100.3	100.1	45.9
February	149.3	77.6	73.1	100.9	97.1	48.2
March	151.5	78.9	74.3	101.1	95.4	51.3
April	153.7	80.0	75.5	102.9	95.8	53.3
May	154.6	80.4	75.7	105.2	94.1	53.8
June	153.8	79.9	74.6	107.4	91.0	54.7
July	151.6	78.4	72.3	108.4	90.3	54.5
August	150.7	77.5	70.9	108.6	90.5	57.5
September	151.1	77.3	71.0	109.9	93.5	63.7
October	151.7	77.5	71.4	112.3	94.4	66.4
November	152.7	77.6	72.9	114.6	95.9	69.3
December	155.3	79.2	73.0	119.8	96.4	70.7

SOURCE: USDA, *Dairy Situation*, DS-339, March 1972, through DS-357, September 1975.

APPENDIX TABLE I-11.　SELECTED WHOLESALE DAIRY PRODUCT PRICES, JULY 1971—DECEMBER 1974 (IN CENTS PER POUND)

Year and Month	Butter[a]	American Cheese[b]	Nonfat Dry Milk
1971			
July	67.8	56.0	31.8
August	67.8	56.0	31.9
September	68.1	56.0	32.0
October	68.0	56.0	32.0
November	67.9	56.1	32.1
December	68.0	58.2	31.9
1972			
January	67.8	58.5	31.8
February	67.8	58.7	32.0
March	67.8	59.6	31.9
April	67.7	57.9	32.2
May	67.7	57.8	31.8
June	67.7	58.0	32.0
July	67.8	59.3	32.1
August	69.5	60.1	32.2
September	70.2	60.0	33.0
October	69.4	61.1	34.2
November	69.2	63.0	35.9
December	70.5	63.8	37.6
1973			
January	67.7	63.8	39.4
February	67.7	63.8	39.8
March	64.2	65.2	42.4

APPENDIX TABLE I-11 (CONTINUED)

Year and Month	Butter[a]	American Cheese[b]	Nonfat Dry Milk
1973 (continued)			
April	61.6	65.8	44.1
May	61.0	66.2	44.6
June	61.0	67.8	44.9
July	63.4	68.4	46.1
August	78.2	71.3	48.4
September	85.9	80.8	50.0
October	79.3	84.2	51.8
November	75.0	86.3	52.0
December	72.0	88.2	53.1
1974			
January	68.5	89.9	54.0
February	64.1	91.1	57.8
March	68.1	91.2	62.2
April	68.2	88.4	67.0
May	60.5	77.9	62.1
June	60.6	71.1	57.5
July	60.8	71.2	56.9
August	67.1	72.5	57.2
September	67.7	76.5	57.4
October	68.8	78.5	57.7
November	68.9	77.8	57.0
December	65.3	72.6	56.8

[a] 92-score, Chicago.
[b] 40-pound blocks, f.o.b. Wisconsin assembling plants.
SOURCE: USDA, *Dairy Situation*, DS-339, March 1972, through DS-352, September 1974.

APPENDIX TABLE I-12.   MILK PRICES RECEIVED BY FARMERS,
ALL MILK SOLD TO PLANTS, JANUARY 1972—DECEMBER 1974

	Price (dollars per hundredweight)			Change From Year Earlier (percent)		
	1972	*1973*	*1974*	*1972*	*1973*	*1974*
January	6.12	6.56	8.89	2.2	7.2	35.5
February	6.13	6.60	8.92	2.9	7.7	35.2
March	6.02	6.54	8.96	2.7	8.6	37.0
April	5.86	6.43	8.84	2.3	9.7	37.5
May	5.79	6.40	8.25	3.4	10.5	28.9
June	5.72	6.40	7.69	3.6	11.9	20.2
July	5.80	6.57	7.61	3.0	13.3	15.8
August	5.99	7.19	7.74	4.2	20.0	7.6
September	6.21	7.87	8.07	3.8	26.7	2.5
October	6.38	8.32	8.34	4.8	30.4	0.2
November	6.52	8.66	8.48	5.5	32.8	−2.1
December	6.54	8.80	8.25	6.0	34.6	−6.2
Average	6.07	7.14	8.32	3.4	17.6	16.5

SOURCE: USDA, *Dairy Situation,* DS-353, November 1974 and DS-357, September 1975.

APPENDIX TABLE I-13.   U.S. MILK PRODUCTION,
JANUARY 1972—DECEMBER 1974

	Production (billions of pounds)			Change From Year Earlier (percent)		
	1972	1973	1974	1972	1973	1974
January	9.72	9.52	9.29	1.5	−2.0	−2.5
February	9.39	8.93	8.76	4.4	−4.9	−1.9
March	10.45	10.18	9.99	2.3	−2.6	−1.8
April	10.57	10.30	10.12	1.4	−2.5	−1.7
May	11.27	10.95	10.84	1.0	−2.8	−1.0
June	10.95	10.53	10.56	1.2	−3.8	+0.3
July	10.44	10.01	10.14	1.5	−4.1	+1.2
August	9.98	9.49	9.69	1.2	−4.9	+2.1
September	9.43	8.88	9.14	1.1	−5.9	+3.0
October	9.44	8.95	9.13	−0.1	−5.2	+2.0
November	8.91	8.59	8.67	−1.0	−3.6	+0.9
December	9.36	9.05	9.09	−0.7	−3.3	+0.4
Total	119.90	115.38	115.42	1.2	−3.8	[a]

[a] Less than 0.05%.

SOURCES: USDA, *Dairy Situation*, DS-354, March 1975 and DS-357, September 1975.

APPENDIX TABLE I-14. CALIFORNIA-ARIZONA NAVEL ORANGES, 1972–1973 AND 1973–1974 SEASONS, PRORATES, SHIPMENTS, AND PRICES

Week Ended	Prorate[a] (carlot equivalent)		Fresh Weekly Shipments (carlot equivalent)		Total Weekly Shipments[b] (carlot equivalent)		Fresh/Total Weekly Shipments (in percent)		California F.O.B. Price (dollars/carton)	
	1972–1973	1973–1974	1972–1973	1973–1974	1972–1973	1973–1974	1972–1973	1973–1974	1972–1973	1973–1974
Pre-December	4106	2912	4495	2772	6046	3490	74	79	3.34	4.36
December 6	1703	1220	1670	1254	2366	1616	71	78	3.11	3.66
13	1708	1395	1666	1507	2134	1928	78	78	3.25	3.70
20	950	900	1067	919	1748	1369	61	67	3.71	3.77
27	750	700	632	666	1168	912	54	73	3.87	3.71
January 3	750	825	702	878	1328	1165	53	75	3.59	3.72
10	950	800	964	938	1693	1302	57	72	3.52	3.71
17	1100	850	1070	960	1709	1311	63	73	3.53	3.64
24	1125	1050	1080	1182	1746	1535	62	77	3.58	3.68
31	1100	1350	1172	1537	2000	1989	59	77	3.65	3.77
February 7	1100	1350	1132	1747	1884	2311	60	76	3.59	3.86
14	1100	1550	956	1623	1447	2164	66	75	3.55	3.85
21	1100	1750	954	1614	1626	2151	59	75	3.56	3.77
28	1100	1850	1119	1586	1896	2106	59	75	3.62	3.67

March	7	1310	1850	979	1634	1617	2170	61	75	3.67	3.43
	14	1299	1750	799	1647	1470	2223	54	74	3.75	3.36
	21	1250	1600	974	1682	1874	2336	52	72	3.87	3.31
	28	1280	1550	747	1676	1357	2354	55	71	3.86	3.26
April	4	1145	1400	720	1427	1632	1932	44	74	3.87	3.25
	11	1026	1400	651	1508	1292	2118	50	71	3.98	3.53
	18	455	1500	415	1273	872	1817	48	70	4.05	3.78
	25	—	1350	245	1108	561	1591	44	70	4.08	3.71
Post-April		—	2300	298	2108	779	3175	38	66	3.70	3.53
Season Total		26,407	33,202	24,507	33,246	40,245	45,065	61	74	3.59	3.65

[a] The volume prorates that are indicated on the table do not necessarily establish an absolute limit due to the many varied provisions of the order. These include such things as allowances for overshipments and undershipments and carryover of credits, loans among handlers, and loans of credits between districts.

[b] Total includes fresh shipments, exports, processed and eliminated as too damaged for human consumption; those eliminated equaled 4% and 2% in 1972–1973 and 1973–1974, respectively.

[c] Frost damage significantly limited total production and affected quality.

SOURCE: *Annual Report of Navel Orange Administrative Committee*, supplied by Fruit and Vegetable Division, Agricultural Marketing Service, USDA, 1973–1974.

APPENDIX II-1

Statement of Bertram C. Tackeff, President, Boxed Beef Distributors, July 5, 1973 (Press Release)

Boxed Beef Distributors of Boston, New England's largest distributor of beef-in-a-box is advising all of its customers that effective this date they intend to dramatically slow down or terminate their beef distribution facilities in Boston for an indeterminate period of time. Temporarily, operations in the company's Maine and Connecticut divisions will remain open, but on a limited basis.

Boxed Beef Distributors, with headquarters in Boston, is responsible for the distribution of approximately the equivalent of 2500 head of cattle per week in the New England area. The company produces no beef of its own; but acts as a low cost distributor of beef cuts to retailers and purveyors throughout the six state region. Hundreds of accounts are in part or in total dependent upon Boxed Beef Distributors for their main sources of beef supply.

Boxed Beef accounts for approximately 7% of the total beef consumed in the New England area. The company handles approximately 700,000 pounds per week of pre-fabricated cuts of beef.

Mr. Bertram C. Tackeff, President of the company, is advising his accounts that the situation in the beef industry is nearly chaotic. The company has been faced with ceilings on their selling prices which are lower than the costs which it would have to incur to replace the product at present cost levels. The company believes that it is typical of a large segment of the beef industry, and that disastrous consequences will occur in the nation's distribution network unless the Government allows beef prices to respond to the natural laws of supply and demand. At the present time, the situation is analogous to trying to put a cover on a steaming kettle of water. Something will have to give. Currently, the company finds that it cannot secure sufficient product as shortages are developing.

Mr. Tackeff believes that far more harm is being done by the present status of the price regulations, than the possible good they can achieve. The current situation will remedy itself if the unevenly imposed shackles are dismantled. *In the final analysis, the only method possible to bring about eventually lower prices is dependent on the ability to encourage increased production.* The freeing of the market place may be painful to consumers and users in the short run; but it remains the only practical way of dramatically increasing the supply of product.

The company will request a hearing by the Price Commission in Washington unless it appears that the intention of that commission is to return the beef industry to the free market place.

APPENDIX II-2

Cost Council Extends Current Price Freeze To Commodity Futures

Ruling Effective Next Wednesday, But Raw Agricultural Products Will Continue to Be Exempt

WASHINGTON—The Cost of Living Council extended the price freeze to commodity futures contracts, starting next Wednesday.

Contracts for raw agricultural products will continue to be exempt, but contracts for other commodities, such as soybean meal and silver, will be subject to a ceiling price set by the exchange on which the contract is traded.

The ceiling will be the highest at which at least 10% of the volume of the commodity was traded in the nearest future between June 1 and June 8, the base period of the freeze. The nearest future will generally be the contract maturing in July, but if an exchange didn't have a July future in a certain commodity, the nearest could be August, for example.

The ceiling price for a commodity could differ among the various exchanges.

The council said its current regulations had resulted in "significant disparities" in several commodities between the spot, or cash, price—which is subject to the freeze—and the futures price—which has been exempt. The council specifically mentioned crude soybean oil, soybean meal, iced broilers, frozen pork bellies, platinum, palladium, silver, gold, copper, silver coins and propane.

The council said that if futures prices had been allowed to rise well above cash prices, "the effect would have been to artificially increase demand which, in turn, would have tended to drive all cash prices for the commodities under discussion to 100% of the freeze prices and would have perhaps encouraged widespread violation of the rule requiring any delivery on a futures contract to be made at the freeze prices."

In addition, the council said, traders who normally rely on futures trading as a hedge against price declines in volatile markets could suffer "substantial losses" if the cost of buying a futures contract to cover an earlier hedge rises significantly. Furthermore, the council said, trading by market speculators is encouraged when futures prices are out of line with cash prices. "New speculation in futures is particularly undesirable at a time when the council is fully engaged in efforts to stem inflation and reduce prices," the council said.

SOURCE: *The Wall Street Journal,* June 28, 1973.

APPENDIX III-1

Economic Stabilization Program (ESP) Food Sector Developments—Regulatory Provisions

This appendix is based almost exclusively on an unpublished paper written by Dale S. Bowen entitled, "Condensed Summary of Progressive Changes in Price Controls," Touche Ross and Company, August 31, 1974. Mr. Bowen was chairman of the Rules and Regulations Task Force of the Food Advisory Committee.

Summary of general ESP stages:

Phase I (Freeze I)	90-day price freeze, August 15 to November 13, 1971.
Phase II	Cost pass-through controls, November 14, 1971, to January 10, 1973.
Phase III	Voluntary cost pass-through controls, except for food, January 11 to June 12, 1973.
Meat Ceiling	Mandatory ceilings on processed meat, March 19 to September 8, 1973.
Freeze II	60-day price freeze, all sectors, June 13 to August 11, 1973.
Phase IV	Cost pass-through controls, two stages of implementation for food, August 12, 1973, to April 30, 1974.

Stage A–transition from freeze to margin control: August 12 to September 8, 1973.

Stage B–food margin control for food: September 9, 1973 to April 30, 1974.

Termination of ESP: April 30, 1974.

Key provisions applicable to food industry, by stage. . . .

Phase I: August 15 to November 14, 1971

- Mandatory controls;

- Ceiling prices calculated on the basis of prices in effect during the 30-day period from July 16 to August 14, 1971;

- Raw agricultural products exempt; and

- The price calculation permitted the use of the highest prices charged for at least 10% of the sales by class of purchases. Temporary special offerings were included in the calculation.

Phase II: November 14, 1971 to January 10, 1973

GENERAL PROVISIONS

Mandatory Participation—With the exception of exempted industries, participation by business and labor was required by law, between November 14, 1971 and January 10, 1973.

Categories—To facilitate the administration of controls, business firms were classified by size on the basis of annual revenues into three groups; Tier 1 firms had revenues in excess of $100 million, Tier II firms from $50 to $100 million, and Tier III was under $50 million.

Base Price—"The base price of a product or service was that price charged by a seller to a particular class of purchaser within a particular span of time defined by Program regulations." The Phase II Base Price was the same as that for Phase I, which permitted the use of the highest prices charged for at least 10% of the sales by class of purchases during the 30-day period from July 16 to August 14, 1971.

Price Adjustments on the basis of Allowable Cost Increases—Firms were permitted to adjust their prices upward above base prices to account for increases in certain allowed costs which had occurred in some specified time interval, since those base prices were established. In some cases firms were required to provide notification of intent to raise prices in advance, along with appropriate documentation that costs had increased. In all cases, reports were required substantiating that firms had complied with pricing rules. All cost increases considered by the firm to be valid were not necessarily allowed. Distinctions were recognized between differing types of industries.

Exemptions—Certain types of products were not subjected to these price regulations. Raw agricultural products, exports, and imports were exempt.

Term Limit Pricing—Some firms found that they would prefer to raise their prices more in line with market forces than with the dictates of allowable cost increases. The Price Commission was willing to negotiate an across-the-board average price increase of 2.0% or less in exchange for pricing flexibility on individual products. The simultaneous occurrence of Volatile Pricing Authority and Term Limit Pricing posed administrative difficulties.

SPECIAL RULES FOR RETAILERS AND WHOLESALERS

Customary Initial Percentage Markup—Retailers were expected not to exceed their customary initial percentage markups over the cost of goods purchased for resale.

Item Control—Normally retailers were expected not to exceed their markups on an item-by-item basis. However, provisions existed whereby certain firms could qualify for control by category or group of products, in which case the average markup for the year was used.

LIMITATIONS ON PROFIT MARGIN APPLICATIONS

Parent Firms—Application was on a firm-wide basis; parent firms were defined to include directly or indirectly controlled subsidiaries.

Certain Types of Activities were Exempt—In keeping with the general exemptions, farming, insurance, foreign entities, and public utilities were not subject to profit margin limitations.

Method for Calculating Profit Margin—The calculation of profit was based upon profits before taxes and long-term interest.

Loss/Low Profit Exemptions—Firms that could demonstrate that they were operating at a loss or very low profit position based upon capital turnover ratios could seek relief from these pricing rules on request.

Profit Margin Limitations—In addition to the specific price limitations imposed by allowable cost increases, firms were also required to keep within historical profit margins; those based on any two of the three fiscal years prior to August 15, 1971. This requirement was imposed on a firm-wide basis and also served to restrain price behavior.

SPECIAL RULES FOR THE MANUFACTURING AND SERVICE SECTOR

Allowable Cost Increases by Product Line—For this industry costs and prices were controlled by product line, normally based upon the Standard Industrial Classification Code. These cost increases were measured from the last price change before August 15, 1971. A product line encompassed a group of several individual products. The distribution of cost increases among the several products was within the discretion of the firm.

Individual Items Subject to Maximum Increases—Even though price controls were applied to product lines, individual products within the product line were also limited to maximum amounts.

Volatile Pricing—Because some raw material costs fluctuated in very unpredictable patterns, many firms found it impossible to live with a requirement to provide notification and justification for price increases in advance. Tier I firms were required to prenotify 30 days in advance. To account for this problem a special exemption from prenotification requirements was granted to Tier I firms that demonstrated that their cost increases were substantially based upon volatile raw materials. If granted volatile pricing authority, these firms could only pass through their volatile costs on a dollar and cents basis.

Penalty—Violators of these rules were subjected to a penalty of three times the amount of the lesser of either price increase average or the profit margin average.

Phase III: January 11 to June 12, 1973

GENERAL PROVISIONS APPLICABLE TO ALL FIRMS

Voluntary Participation—With the exception of the food, health, and construction sectors, participation in the Economic Stabilization Program was voluntary during the period January 11 through June 12, 1973. Those sectors under mandatory controls continued to be regulated by the main features of the Phase II program. Those firms in the voluntary sector which had over $250 million per year in revenues were asked to continue reporting. Any firm under 60 employees, in the voluntary or mandatory sector, was exempted from controls. The rationale for a voluntary program for the bulk of the economy was predicated partially upon the relative success experienced with Phase II.

Prenotification—In May 1973 the voluntary sector was required to begin providing notification in advance of price increases exceeding 1.5%.

Change in Base Price—For all firms, including food, the base price from which price increases were to be measured was changed to those prices authorized or legally in effect on January 10, 1973. This change recognized the authority adjustments that had occurred since Phase I.

Cost Increases—Along with the new base prices, the period for measuring cost increases also had to be changed. Cost increases were measured cumulatively from those established as of the last price change before January 11, 1973.

RETAIL AND WHOLESALE (INCLUDING FOOD FIRMS)

Item Control Relaxed—The Phase II item-by-item control was relaxed to give these firms a choice of item or category control. Categories were defined as specified aggregations of items.

New Base Periods—For reporting purposes the base periods were altered to allow the use of any four consecutive quarters ending before February 5, 1972, or the fiscal year ending before August 15, 1971. Changing base periods had the effect of changing base prices and base costs, from which changes were measured.

Provisions for Seasonality—The seasonal nature of many retail and wholesale activities was frequently not taken into account by the allowable choices of base periods, adversely affecting the firms involved. The Phase III rules provided for firms to take into account seasonal fluctuations as well as government mandated increases in calculating base prices and costs.

Definition of Parent Firm—The definition of "Parent Firms" used in Phase II was clarified to include consolidated entities. Unconsolidated entities with revenues in excess of $10 million per year were also made subject to profit margin limitations. Accordingly, the applicability of this rule was expanded.

New Base Period—Again, the base period for determining profit margins was expanded to include any completed fiscal years after August 15, 1971.

Meat Ceilings: March 19 to September 8, 1973

MEAT CEILING PRICES

Mandatory Control at Processor, Wholesale and Retail Levels—March 19 to September 8, 1973.

Applicable to fresh cuts of red meat, edible by-products, and food products containing 65% meat.

Base Period—30 days prior to March 28 or nearest preceding 30-day period.

The base price was the highest price for 10% of sales by class of purchaser excluding temporary (four days) special deals and allowances.

Not applicable to food service organizations selling direct to consumer.

Cost increases for imported meat were restricted to pass-through on a dollar-for-dollar basis.

For those firms that were permitted to exercise volatile pricing authority because of their inability to account properly for frequently fluctuating raw material price changes, a system of Gross Margin Control was devised. This system was also useful in coping with the problem of changing raw material and product mix. These gross margins were also subject to ceiling limits.

Pork and lamb removed from ceiling prices on July 18.

Freeze II: June 13 to August 11, 1973

GENERAL PROVISIONS

Sixty Days—June 13 to August 11, 1973.

Food 90 days to September 8, 1973, subject to dollar-for-dollar pass-through on raw agricultural products beginning July 18.

Not applicable to raw (unprocessed) agricultural products, meat under ceiling prices, and imports resold without a change in form.

Base Period—June 1 to June 8 or nearest preceding 7-day period.

Base Price—highest price for 10% of shipments by class of purchaser without excluding temporary special deals and allowances.

Phase IV, Stage A: August 12 to September 8, 1973

GENERAL PROVISIONS

Termination of the Freeze on nonbeef agricultural products.

Price increases were permitted, based on the pass-through of increases in raw agricultural costs on a dollar-for-dollar basis.

A system of invoice certification was established to provide a means of regulating price increases above ceiling levels.

Phase IV, Stage B: September 9, 1973 to April 30, 1974

GENERAL PROVISIONS

Categories—Return to three Tiers, over $100 million, $50 to $100 million, and under $50 million, based on total firm sales for most recently completed fiscal year.

Exemptions—Continuing exemption of raw agricultural products, exports, and imports from pricing regulations. Firms under 60 employees were also exempt.

FOOD MANUFACTURING

Volatile Pricing—Automatic volatile pricing for all food manufacturing where raw agricultural costs could be passed through without prenotification.

Cost Increases for Food Raw Material—Dollar-for-dollar pass-through of cost increases and decreases in "food material" (raw, semiprocessed and processed agricultural and marine products including by-products). Base cost period is the base period.

Cost Increases for Items Other than Food Raw Materials—Other cost increases were subject to prenotification (Tier I) and regular Phase IV rules, except that the base cost period was the fiscal quarter following the base period.

Measurements of Food Raw Material—Food raw material *units* on an input basis (purchases adjusted for inventories) or an output basis (sales).

Use of Product Lines—Products continued to be grouped and controlled on a product line basis (any price for any item within a four digit Standard Industry Classification Code was subject to the pricing regulations).

Base Period for Establishing Price—The same base period for all product lines of any four consecutive fiscal quarters of the eight fiscal quarters ended prior to May 11, 1973, except for meat products where a separate base period extending the choice of four consecutive fiscal quarters back to May 25, 1970, is applicable.

Hedging—Special rules for hedging transactions were provided to permit an accounting of gains and losses due to hedging.

Product Mix and Seasonality—Provisions were made by which firms could account for the impact that changes in the mix of products within a product line could impose. These changes may affect costs and revenues, producing apparent violations of the revenue limit for a product line. Excess revenues that were attributable to seasonal fluctuations in costs or revenues could also be excused upon proper justification.

Permission to Use Non-Food Rules—Firms with less than $50 million sales in food manufacturing may elect to use regular Phase IV rules (Subpart E of the regulations).

Food Retailing

Firms with 75% of total sales in retail food had two special options in recognition of low base period earnings for the industry:

Expanded Period from Which to Choose a Base Period—Either one of the last *two* fiscal years ended prior to February 5, 1973, or the most recent four consecutive fiscal quarters ended before February 5, 1973.

Option to Use One Storewide Category for Control Purposes—May treat all sales under one merchandise category.

Food Service

Subject to regular Phase IV rules for manufacturers (Subpart E).

Profit Margin

Continued to be subject to profit margin limitations on a firm-wide basis.

APPENDIX III-2

Double Counting When Base Cost Period and Base Period Overlap

Double counting of costs means counting prior cost increases that have already been implemented as price increases in the calculation of permissible revenues. The cost increase that occurs in the base period is reflected both in the base period average price and in the net allowable cost increase used to adjust that price. It is not the same problem as that of windfall, which is simply a wider margin between current period price and costs that result because "base period" costs are greater than "base cost period" costs from which cost increases are measured.

Double counting does occur if the "input method" of measuring cost increases is used. Demonstration:

$$R_0 = \sum_{t=1}^{4} R_t = \sum_{t=1}^{4} P_t V_t \qquad C_{mt} = \text{Constant}$$

$$\pi = \text{Constant}$$

$$t = 5 = \text{Current Period} \qquad V_t = \text{Constant}$$

$$C_{d1} = C_{d2} < C_{d3} = C_{d4} \qquad C_{d5} = C_{d4}$$

$$C_{d3} - C_{d2} = a$$

$$P_1 = P_2 < P_3 = P_4 \qquad P_3 - P_2 = a$$

$$R_0 = V_t \sum_{t=1}^{4} P_t = V(P_1 + P_2) + V(P_3 + P_4)$$

$$= 2VP_1 + 2VP_3$$

$$= 2VP_1 + 2VP_1 + 2Va$$

$$= 4P_1 V + 2Va$$

where

R_0 = base period revenues

R_t = revenues for time period "t"

t = quarterly time periods

t=1, ... 4 = base period quarters

t=5 = current quarter

P_t = average price during time period "t"

V_t = volume during time period "t"

C_{mt} = raw material cost in period "t"

π = profit

C_{dt} = non-raw material costs during time period "t"

If the input method is used and the base cost period = base period, the firm may measure cost increases from the first day of base cost period to the first day of the current period. It may use costs at C_{d1}.

$$C = \frac{C_{d5} - C_{d1}}{C_{d1}} \left(\frac{C_{d1}}{P_1}\right) = \frac{a}{P_1}$$

$$\frac{R_5}{V_5} = \frac{R_o}{4V}\left(C + 1\right) = \frac{4P_1V + 2aV}{4V}\left(\frac{a}{P} + 1\right)$$

$$= \left(\frac{P}{2} + \frac{4}{2}\right)\left(\frac{4}{P} + 1\right)$$

$$= \frac{\cancel{P}a}{2\cancel{P}} + \frac{a^2}{2P_1} + \frac{\cancel{P}a}{2\cancel{P}} + \frac{a}{2}$$

$$= \frac{5a}{2} + \frac{a^2}{2P_1}$$

Using the output method, measuring cost increases from the average level of cost during the base period, no double counting occurs. Average cost from the foregoing = $C_{d1} + a/2$

$$\text{Average Revenue} = \frac{4P_1V + 2aV}{4V} = P_1 + \frac{a}{2}$$

$$C = \frac{C_{d5} - \text{Avg. Cost}}{\text{Avg. Cost}}\left(\frac{\text{Average Cost}}{\text{Average Revenue}}\right)$$

$$\frac{(C_{d1} + a) - \left(C_{d1} + \frac{a}{2}\right)}{\left(\cancel{C_{d1} + \frac{a}{2}}\right)}\left(\frac{\cancel{C_{d1} + \frac{a}{2}}}{P_1 + \frac{a}{2}}\right) = \frac{a}{2P_1 + a}$$

$$\frac{R_5}{V_5} = \frac{(4PV + 2aV)}{4V}\left(\frac{a}{2P + 2}\right) + 1 = \underline{\underline{a + P}}$$

ILLUSTRATION OF DOUBLE COUNTING OF "a"

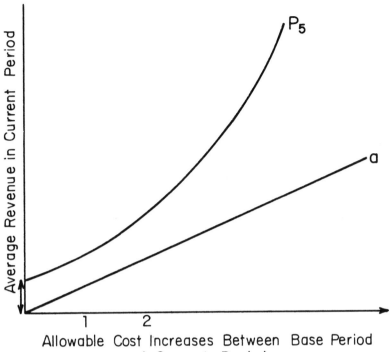

APPENDIX V

The appendix for Chapter V consists of 19 tables. There is no accompanying text. See Chapter V for references and detailed explanations.

APPENDIX TABLE V-1.   WORLD RICE AND WHEAT SUPPLY AND CONSUMPTION, MARKETING YEARS 1960-1961—1975-1976[a] (IN MILLIONS OF METRIC TONS)

Year	Rice Production[b]	Wheat Production	Consumption[c]	Ending Stocks[d]	Stocks (percent of consumption)
1960-1961	226.9	240.5	237.4	76.9	32.4
1961-1962	238.0	226.6	238.4	65.1	27.3
1962-1963	234.7	256.5	251.1	70.5	28.1
1963-1964	250.3	238.3	246.8	62.0	25.1
1964-1965	264.3	275.6	265.5	72.1	27.2
1965-1966	256.8	265.8	284.6	53.3	18.7
1966-1967	259.1	307.5	282.7	78.1	27.6
1967-1968	282.8	295.8	292.0	81.9	28.0
1968-1969	284.1	328.4	303.2	107.1	35.3
1969-1970	295.1	309.5	322.8	93.8	29.1
1970-1971	305.2	313.8	335.3	72.3	21.6
1971-1972	310.5	346.2	345.1	73.4	21.3
1972-1973	298.2	339.9	361.8	51.5	14.2
1973-1974	324.5	368.4	363.2	56.7	15.6
1974-1975[e]	327.9	350.3	352.6	54.4	15.4
1975-1976[f]	341.0	359.0	361.0	52.4	14.5

[a] Data are based on an aggregate of differing local marketing years.

[b] Rice consumption is assumed to be approximately equal to rice production, and few countries maintain appreciable stocks.

[c] For countries for which stocks data are not available, or for which no adjustments have been made for year-to-year changes, consumption estimates assume a constant stocks level.

[d] Stocks data are only for selected countries and exclude such important countries as the USSR, the People's Republic of China, and part of Eastern Europe for which stocks data are not available; the aggregate stocks level have, however, been adjusted for estimated year-to-year changes in USSR grain stocks.

[e] Preliminary.

[f] Projection.

SOURCES: USDA, *Foreign Agriculture Circular*, FG 12-75, October 7, 1975. Personal communication with FAS, USDA.

APPENDIX TABLE V-2.   WORLD TOTAL WHEAT AND RICE SUPPLY
AND CONSUMPTION, MARKETING YEARS 1960-1961—1975-1976[a]
(IN MILLIONS OF METRIC TONS)

Year	Total Wheat[b] and Rice[c]		Ending Wheat Stocks[d]	Wheat Stocks (percent of total wheat and rice consumption)
	Production	Consumption		
1960-1961	467.4	464.3	76.9	16.6
1961-1962	464.6	476.4	65.1	13.7
1962-1963	491.2	485.8	70.5	14.5
1963-1964	488.6	497.1	62.0	12.5
1964-1965	539.9	529.8	72.1	13.6
1965-1966	522.6	541.4	53.3	9.8
1966-1967	566.6	541.8	78.1	14.4
1967-1968	578.6	574.8	81.9	14.2
1968-1969	612.5	587.3	107.1	18.2
1969-1970	604.6	617.9	93.8	15.2
1970-1971	619.0	640.5	72.3	11.3
1971-1972	656.7	655.6	73.4	11.2
1972-1973	638.1	660.0	51.5	7.8
1973-1974	692.9	687.7	56.7	8.2
1974-1975[e]	678.2	680.5	54.4	8.0
1975-1976[f]	700.0	702.0	52.4	7.5

[a] Data are based on an aggregate of differing local marketing years.

[b] For countries for which stocks data are not available, or for which no adjustments have been made for year-to-year changes, consumption estimates assume a constant stocks level.

[c] Rice consumption is assumed to be approximately equal to rice production, and few countries maintain appreciable stocks.

[d] Stocks data are only for selected countries and exclude such important countries as the USSR, the People's Republic of China and part of Eastern Europe for which stocks data are not available; the aggregate stocks level have, however, been adjusted for estimated year-to-year changes in USSR grain stocks.

[e] Preliminary.

[f] Projection.

SOURCES: USDA, *Foreign Agriculture Circular*, FG 12-75, October 7, 1975. Personal communication with FAS, USDA.

APPENDIX TABLE V-3.   WORLD COARSE GRAINS SUPPLY AND CONSUMPTION, MARKETING YEARS 1960–1961—1975–1976[a] (MILLIONS OF METRIC TONS)

Year	Production	Consumption[b]	Ending Stocks[c]	Stocks (percent of consumption)
1960–1961	416.0	406.4	99.8	24.6
1961–1962	397.1	412.0	84.9	20.6
1962–1963	417.2	419.4	82.7	19.7
1963–1964	425.8	422.5	86.0	20.4
1964–1965	427.9	434.7	79.2	18.2
1965–1966	443.4	460.3	62.3	13.5
1966–1967	474.6	470.4	66.5	14.1
1967–1968	495.7	484.7	77.5	16.0
1968–1969	501.1	497.6	81.0	16.3
1969–1970	522.6	529.2	74.4	14.1
1970–1971	518.9	535.1	58.2	10.9
1971–1972	573.8	557.7	74.3	13.3
1972–1973	559.4	577.1	56.6	9.8
1973–1974	608.2	611.5	53.3	8.7
1974–1975[d]	570.6	578.2	45.7	7.9
1975–1976[e]	592.4	590.4	47.7	8.1

[a] Data are based on an aggregate of differing local marketing years.

[b] For countries for which stocks data are not available, or for which no adjustments have been made for year-to-year changes, consumption estimates assume a constant stocks level.

[c] Stocks data are only for selected countries and exclude such important countries as the USSR, the People's Republic of China and part of Eastern Europe for which stocks data are not available; the aggregate stocks level have, however, been adjusted for estimated year-to-year changes in USSR grain stocks.

[d] Preliminary.

[e] Projection.

SOURCE: USDA, *Foreign Agriculture Circular,* FG 12-75, October 7, 1975.

APPENDIX TABLE V-4.   WORLD GRAINS AND RICE SUPPLY AND CONSUMPTION,
MARKETING YEARS 1960-1961—1975-1976[a] (MILLIONS OF METRIC TONS)

Year	Production	Consumption[b]	Ending Stocks, Omitting Rice[c]	Stocks, Omitting Rice (percentage of consumption)
1960–1961	883.4	870.7	176.7	20.3
1961–1962	861.7	888.4	150.0	16.9
1962–1963	908.4	905.2	153.2	16.9
1963–1964	914.4	919.6	148.0	16.1
1964–1965	967.8	964.5	151.3	15.7
1965–1966	966.0	1001.7	115.6	11.5
1966–1967	1041.2	1012.2	144.6	14.3
1967–1968	1074.3	1059.5	159.4	15.0
1968–1969	1113.6	1084.9	188.1	17.3
1969–1970	1127.2	1147.1	168.2	14.7
1970–1971	1137.9	1175.6	130.5	11.1
1971–1972	1230.5	1213.3	147.7	12.2
1972–1973	1197.5	1237.1	108.1	8.7
1973–1974	1301.1	1299.2	110.0	8.5
1974–1975[d]	1248.8	1258.7	100.1	8.0
1975–1976[e]	1292.4	1292.4	100.1	7.7

[a] Data are based on an aggregate of differing local marketing years.

[b] For countries for which stocks data are not available, or for which no adjustments have been made for year-to-year changes, consumption estimates assume a constant stocks level. Rice consumption is assumed to be equal to rice production.

[c] Stocks data are only for selected countries and exclude such important countries as the USSR, the People's Republic of China and part of Eastern Europe for which stocks data are not available; the aggregate stocks level have, however, been adjusted for estimated year-to-year changes in USSR grain stocks. Few countries maintain appreciable stocks of rice.

[d] Preliminary.

[e] Projection.

SOURCES: USDA, *Foreign Agriculture Circular,* FG 12-75, October 7, 1975. Personal communication with FAS, USDA.

Appendix Table V-5. Wheat: Area,[a] Yield, and Production in Specified Countries and World Total, 1960-1961—1975-1976[b]

Year	United States Area (millions of hectares)	Yield (quintals/ hectare)	Production (millions of metric tons)	Canada, Australia and Argentina Area (millions of hectares)	Yield (quintals/ hectare)	Production (millions of metric tons)	Rest-of-World Area (millions of hectares)	Yield (quintals/ hectare)	Production (millions of metric tons)	World Total Area (millions of hectares)	Yield (quintals/ hectare)	Production (millions of metric tons)
1960–1961	21.0	17.6	36.9	19.0	13.6	25.8	164.0	10.8	177.8	204.0	11.8	240.5
1961–1962	20.9	16.0	33.5	20.6	9.8	20.2	161.6	10.7	172.9	203.1	11.2	226.6
1962–1963	17.7	16.8	29.7	21.3	13.8	29.4	169.2	11.7	197.4	208.2	12.3	256.5
1963–1964	18.4	17.0	31.2	23.5	16.0	37.6	166.0	10.2	169.5	207.9	11.5	238.3
1964–1965	20.2	17.3	34.9	25.4	14.8	37.6	171.4	11.8	203.1	217.0	12.7	275.6
1965–1966	20.1	17.8	35.8	23.1	13.3	30.8	173.6	11.5	199.2	216.8	12.3	265.3
1966–1967	20.2	17.6	35.5	25.7	16.2	41.5	168.9	13.6	230.5	214.8	14.3	307.5
1967–1968	23.8	17.2	41.0	27.1	11.4	31.0	168.5	13.3	223.8	219.4	13.5	295.3
1968–1969	22.4	18.9	42.4	28.6	13.4	38.2	173.7	14.3	247.8	224.7	14.6	328.4
1969–1970	19.3	20.4	39.3	24.8	14.5	35.8	173.6	13.5	234.4	217.7	14.2	309.5
1970–1971	17.6	20.9	36.8	15.2	14.3	21.8	173.2	14.7	255.2	206.0	15.2	313.8
1971–1972	19.3	22.8	44.0	19.3	14.8	28.6	173.0	15.8	273.6	211.6	16.4	346.2
1972–1973	19.1	22.0	42.0	21.2	13.1	27.8	168.7	16.0	270.1	209.0	16.3	339.9
1973–1974	21.8	21.3	46.4	22.7	15.3	34.6	172.2	16.7	287.4	216.7	17.0	368.4
1974–1975[c]	26.5	18.4	48.8	21.2	14.3	30.3	172.0	15.8	271.2	219.7	15.9	350.3
1975–1976[d]	27.9	20.8	58.1	22.9	15.6	35.7	172.6	15.4	265.2	223.4	16.0	359.0

[a] All data for area represent harvested rather than planted area, wherever possible.
[b] Includes grain harvest occurring within July–June of the year, except that crops from the early-harvesting Northern Hemisphere areas are "moved forward"; i.e., the May 1974 harvests in areas such as India, North Africa, and southern USA are actually included in the 1974–1975 accounting period which begins July 1, 1974.   [c] Preliminary.   [d] Projection.

Sources: USDA, *Foreign Agriculture Circular,* FG 10-74, April 1974, and FG 12-75, October 7, 1975.

APPENDIX TABLE V-6. RICE (ROUGH): AREA,[a] YIELD AND PRODUCTION IN SPECIFIED COUNTRIES AND WORLD TOTAL, 1960-1961—1974-1975[b]

Year	United States Area (millions of hectares)	United States Yield (quintals/ hectare)	United States Production (millions of metric tons)	Canada,[c] Australia and Argentina Area (millions of hectares)	Canada,[c] Australia and Argentina Yield (quintals/ hectare)	Canada,[c] Australia and Argentina Production (millions of metric tons)	Rest-of-World Area (millions of hectares)	Rest-of-World Yield (quintals/ hectare)	Rest-of-World Production (millions of metric tons)	World Total Area (millions of hectares)	World Total Yield (quintals/ hectare)	World Total Production (millions of metric tons)
1960–1961	0.6	38.4	2.5	0.1	40.5	0.3	117.4	19.1	224.1	118.1	19.2	226.9
1961–1962	0.6	38.2	2.5	0.1	43.3	0.3	118.3	19.9	235.2	119.0	20.0	238.0
1962–1963	0.7	42.0	3.0	0.1	42.4	0.3	119.7	19.3	231.4	120.5	19.5	234.7
1963–1964	0.7	44.4	3.2	0.1	42.6	0.3	120.0	20.6	246.8	120.8	20.7	250.3
1964–1965	0.7	45.9	3.3	0.1	45.3	0.4	123.7	21.1	260.6	124.5	21.2	264.3
1965–1966	0.7	47.7	3.5	0.1	47.5	0.3	122.6	20.6	253.0	123.4	20.8	256.8
1966–1967	0.8	48.4	3.9	0.1	46.8	0.4	125.3	20.3	254.8	126.2	20.5	259.1
1967–1968	0.8	50.9	4.1	0.1	49.4	0.5	127.2	21.9	278.2	128.1	22.1	282.8
1968–1969	1.0	49.6	4.7	0.1	49.3	0.6	128.7	21.7	278.8	129.8	21.9	284.1
1969–1970	0.9	48.1	4.1	0.1	46.1	0.7	129.4	22.4	290.3	130.4	22.6	295.1
1970–1971	0.7	51.1	3.8	0.1	48.1	0.6	128.9	23.3	300.8	129.7	23.5	305.2
1971–1972	0.7	52.9	3.9	0.1	44.1	0.5	132.7	23.1	306.1	133.5	23.3	310.5
1972–1973	0.7	52.6	3.9	0.1	44.5	0.6	128.5	22.9	293.7	129.3	23.1	298.2
1973–1974	0.9	47.9	4.2	0.2	47.9	0.7	132.2	24.2	319.6	133.3	24.3	324.5
1974–1975[d]	1.0	49.8	5.2	0.2	46.5	0.8	133.0	24.2	321.9	134.2	24.4	327.9

[a] Harvested area as far as possible.

[b] The world rice harvest stretches over 6 to 8 months. Thus 1974–1975 production represents the crop harvested in late 1974 and early 1975 in the Northern Hemisphere, and the crop harvested in early 1975 in the Southern Hemisphere.   [d] Preliminary.

[c] For purposes of aggregation with data for wheat and coarse grains, note that Canada produces no rice.

SOURCES: USDA, *Foreign Agriculture Circular*, FG 12-73, October 26, 1973; FG 23-74, November 1, 1974; and FG 12-75, October 7, 1975; *Rice Situation*, RS-25, April 1975; *World Agricultural Production and Trade*, June 1973, June 1974, and June 1975; *Review of World Rice Markets and Major Suppliers*, FAS-M-246, August 1972. Personal communication with FAS, USDA.

APPENDIX TABLE V-7. COARSE GRAINS[a]: AREA,[b] YIELD, AND PRODUCTION IN SPECIFIED COUNTRIES AND WORLD TOTAL, 1960-1961—1975-1976[c]

Year	United States Area (millions of hectares)	United States Yield (quintals/ hectare)	United States Production (millions of metric tons)	Canada, Australia and Argentina Area (millions of hectares)	Canada, Australia and Argentina Yield (quintals/ hectare)	Canada, Australia and Argentina Production (millions of metric tons)	Rest-of-World Area (millions of hectares)	Rest-of-World Yield (quintals/ hectare)	Rest-of-World Production (millions of metric tons)	World Total Area (millions of hectares)	World Total Yield (quintals/ hectare)	World Total Production (millions of metric tons)
1960–1961	52.3	27.1	141.9	15.4	14.8	22.8	201.8	12.5	251.3	269.5	15.4	416.0
1961–1962	43.2	29.5	127.5	14.0	13.4	18.8	205.4	12.2	250.8	262.6	15.1	397.1
1962–1963	42.0	30.8	129.6	13.5	15.8	21.3	205.3	13.0	266.3	260.8	16.0	417.2
1963–1964	43.2	32.5	140.3	15.0	16.5	24.7	208.9	12.5	260.8	267.1	15.9	425.8
1964–1965	40.0	30.6	122.5	14.1	15.5	21.8	210.8	13.5	283.6	264.9	16.1	427.9
1965–1966	39.5	36.5	144.2	14.5	17.7	25.7	206.3	13.3	273.5	260.3	17.0	443.4
1966–1967	40.2	36.1	144.9	15.4	18.8	29.0	207.1	14.5	300.7	262.7	18.1	474.6
1967–1968	41.3	39.5	162.9	15.7	15.6	24.5	209.0	14.8	308.3	266.0	18.6	495.7
1968–1969	39.8	39.0	155.3	16.9	17.6	29.7	210.0	15.1	316.1	266.7	18.8	501.1
1969–1970	39.2	41.3	161.7	18.3	18.8	34.4	211.9	15.4	326.5	269.4	19.4	522.6
1970–1971	40.8	35.9	146.1	19.4	19.9	38.7	210.3	15.9	334.1	270.5	19.2	518.9
1971–1972	43.7	43.4	189.6	19.8	18.9	37.5	209.1	16.6	346.7	272.6	21.0	573.8
1972–1973	38.4	47.4	182.0	19.7	19.3	38.1	214.2	15.8	339.3	272.3	20.5	559.4
1973–1974	41.8	44.6	186.6	19.7	20.4	40.1	222.4	17.2	381.5	283.9	21.4	608.2
1974–1975[d]	40.8	36.8	150.3	18.1	18.4	33.3	228.2	17.0	387.0	287.1	19.9	570.6
1975–1976[e]	42.1	43.4	182.9	19.3	19.9	38.5	230.8	16.1	371.0	292.2	20.3	592.4

[a] Rye, corn, barley, oats, and sorghum.   [b] All data for area represent harvested rather than planted area, wherever possible.
[c] Includes grain harvests occurring within July–June of the year, except that crops from the early-harvesting Northern Hemisphere areas are "moved forward"; i.e., the May 1974 harvests in areas such as India, North Africa, and southern USA are actually included in the 1974–1975 accounting period which begins July 1, 1974.
[d] Preliminary.   [e] Projection.
SOURCES: USDA, *Foreign Agriculture Circular*, FG 10-74, April 1974; FG 5-75, March 1975; and FG 12-75, October 7, 1975; *World Agricultural Production and Trade*, March 1973, June 1973, June 1974, September 1974, and October 1975; *Trends in World Grain Production: 1960 to 1972*, FAS M-249, February 1973.

APPENDIX TABLE V-8. WHEAT AND RICE (ROUGH): AREA,[a] YIELD AND PRODUCTION IN SPECIFIED COUNTRIES AND WORLD TOTAL, 1960-1961—1974-1975[bc]

Year	United States			Canada, Australia and Argentina			Rest-of-World			World Total		
	Area (millions of hectares)	Yield (quintals/hectare)	Production (millions of metric tons)	Area (millions of hectares)	Yield (quintals/hectare)	Production (millions of metric tons)	Area (millions of hectares)	Yield (quintals/hectare)	Production (millions of metric tons)	Area (millions of hectares)	Yield (quintals/hectare)	Production (millions of metric tons)
1960-1961	21.6	18.2	39.4	19.1	13.7	26.1	281.4	14.3	401.9	322.1	14.5	467.4
1961-1962	21.5	16.7	36.0	20.7	9.9	20.5	279.9	14.6	408.1	322.1	14.4	464.6
1962-1963	18.4	17.8	32.7	21.4	13.9	29.7	288.9	14.8	428.8	328.8	14.9	491.2
1963-1964	19.1	18.0	34.4	23.6	16.1	37.9	286.0	14.6	416.3	328.7	14.9	488.6
1964-1965	20.9	18.3	38.2	25.5	14.9	38.0	295.1	15.7	463.7	341.5	15.8	539.9
1965-1966	20.8	18.9	39.3	23.2	13.4	31.1	296.2	15.3	452.2	340.2	15.4	522.6
1966-1967	21.0	18.8	39.4	25.8	16.2	41.9	294.2	16.5	485.3	341.0	16.6	566.6
1967-1968	24.6	18.3	45.1	27.2	11.6	31.5	295.7	17.0	502.0	347.5	16.7	578.6
1968-1969	23.4	20.1	47.1	28.7	13.5	38.8	302.4	17.4	526.6	354.5	17.3	612.5
1969-1970	20.2	21.5	43.4	24.9	14.7	36.5	303.0	17.3	524.7	348.1	17.4	604.6
1970-1971	18.3	22.2	40.6	15.3	14.6	22.4	302.1	18.4	556.0	335.7	18.4	619.0
1971-1972	20.0	24.0	47.9	19.4	15.0	29.1	305.7	19.0	579.7	345.1	19.0	656.7
1972-1973	19.8	23.2	45.9	21.3	13.3	28.4	297.2	19.0	563.8	338.3	18.9	638.1
1973-1974	22.7	22.3	50.6	22.9	15.4	35.3	304.4	19.9	607.0	350.0	19.8	692.9
1974-1975[d]	27.5	19.6	54.0	21.4	14.5	31.1	305.0	19.4	593.1	353.9	19.2	678.2

[a] Harvested area as far as possible.

[b] The world rice harvest stretches over 6 to 8 months. Thus 1974–1975 production represents the crop harvested in late 1974 and early 1975 in the Northern Hemisphere, and the crop harvested in early 1975 in the Southern Hemisphere.

[c] Includes grain harvests occurring within July–June of the year, except that crops from the early-harvesting Northern Hemisphere areas are "moved forward"; i.e., the May 1974 harvests in areas such as India, North Africa, and southern USA are actually included the 1974–1975 accounting period which begins July 1, 1974.   [d] Preliminary.

SOURCES: USDA, Foreign Agriculture Circular, FG 12-73, October 26, 1973; FG 10-74, April 1974; FG 23-74, November 1, 1974; and FG 12-75, October 7, 1975; Rice Situation, RS-25, April 1975; World Agricultural Production and Trade, June 1973 and June 1974; Review of World Rice Markets and Major Suppliers, FAS-M-246, August 1972. Personal communication with FAS, USDA.

APPENDIX TABLE V-9. WORLD PROTEIN MEAL PRODUCTION
AND U.S. SOYBEAN AREA, YIELD AND PRODUCTION, 1960–1975

Year	U.S. Soybeans Area[b] (millions of acres)	Yield (bushels/acre)	Production (millions of bushels)	Meal Production[a] (millions of metric tons) U.S.	Rest-of-World	Total
1960	22.6	23.5	533	13.6	17.9	31.5
1961	23.7	23.5	555	14.1	18.9	33.0
1962	27.0	25.1	679	16.6	19.9	36.5
1963	27.6	24.2	669	16.5	20.1	36.6
1964	28.6	24.4	699	17.1	21.0	38.1
1965	30.8	22.8	701	17.1	22.7	39.8
1966	34.4	24.5	846	20.1	23.3	43.4
1967	36.5	25.4	928	20.9	24.9	45.8
1968	39.8	24.5	976	21.7	25.7	47.4
1969	41.4	26.7	1107	24.9	25.0	49.9
1970	41.3	27.4	1133	25.7	26.8	52.5
1971	42.2	26.7	1127	25.5	28.1	53.6
1972	42.7	27.5	1176	26.4	28.1	54.5
1973	45.7	27.8	1271	28.8	27.3	56.1
1974	55.8	27.7	1547	34.3	31.4	65.7
1975	52.5[c]	23.5[c]	1233[c]	27.8[c]	33.6[d]	61.4[d]

[a] Meal production estimated on the basis of average assumed extraction rates and crushing and therefore represents potential rather than actual meal production. Expressed on a soybean meal equivalent basis at 44% protein.

[b] Harvested.

[c] Preliminary.

[d] Forecast.

SOURCES: USDA, *Foreign Agriculture Circular,* FFO 7-74, June 1974, and FOP 2-75, April 1975; *Fats and Oils Situation,* FOS-277, April 1975.

APPENDIX TABLE V-10. TIME TRENDS[a] FOR THE PRODUCTION OF GRAINS, RICE AND PROTEIN MEALS BASED UPON 1960–1961 THROUGH 1974–1975

| | Intercept | | Time Trend | | |
	Coefficient	Standard Error	Coefficient	Standard Error	R^2
Wheat					
World	221	8	9.28	0.84	0.91
U.S.	30.1	1.6	1.05	0.18	0.72
Canada, Australia, and Argentina	30.2	3.5	0.16	0.38	0.01
Rest-of-world	161	7	8.08	0.72	0.91
Rice					
World	220	4	7.17	0.42	0.96
Wheat and rice					
World	440	8	16.78	0.89	0.96
U.S.	32.8	1.7	1.19	0.19	0.76
Canada, Australia, and Argentina	30.4	3.5	0.19	0.38	0.02
Rest-of-world	377	7	15.4	0.78	0.97
Coarse grains					
World	372	10	14.31	1.09	0.93
U.S	124	8	3.52	0.84	0.57
Canada, Australia, and Argentina	17.7	1.7	1.47	0.18	0.83
Rest-of-world	230	5	9.33	0.58	0.95
Grains and rice					
World	813	15	31.46	1.68	0.96
U.S.	156	8	4.71	0.91	0.67
Canada, Australia, and Argentina	48.1	3.5	1.66	0.39	0.58
Rest-of-world	609	11	5.09	1.18	0.97
Protein meal					
World	1.48	0.01	0.021	0.001	0.98
U.S.	1.11	0.01	0.026	0.001	0.97
Rest-of-world	1.25	0.01	0.016	0.001	0.96
Soybeans					
U.S.	2.70	0.01	0.031	0.002	0.97

[a] Linear regression was performed on the data using a functional form of

$$W_t = \alpha_0 + \alpha_1 t + \epsilon_t,$$

where

W_t is production in year t

α_0 is the intercept

α_1 is the coefficient of time

t is time, i.e., 1, 2,..., 15

ϵ is the residual remaining after the time trend has been removed.

In the case of protein meal and soybeans, log W_t was used in place of W_t.

UNITS: All commodity quantities are million metric tons, with the exception of U.S. soybean production which is million bushels.

SOURCES: See Appendix Tables V-1–V-9. Minor revisions of data have occurred since this regression analysis was performed; these revisions have been incorporated into Tables V-1–V-9, but the regressions were not up-dated since the results would change very little—if at all.

APPENDIX TABLE V-11.   INSTABILITY OF PRODUCTION (AS MEASURED BY DEVIATIONS FROM TREND) FOR SELECTED COMMODITIES AND AREAS, 1960–1961 THROUGH 1974–1975 (IN MILLIONS OF METRIC TONS)

	Wheat				Rice		Wheat and Rice			
Year	United States	Canada, Australia, Argentina	Rest-of-World	World	United States	World	United States	Canada, Australia, Argentina	Rest-of-World	World
1960–1961	5.7	−4.6	9.9	11.0		−0.1	5.5	−4.5	9.2	10.1
1961–1962	1.2	−10.4	−3.3	−12.4		3.8	0.9	−10.3	0.0	−9.5
1962–1963	−3.6	−1.3	12.9	8.0		−6.7	−3.6	−1.3	5.3	0.4
1963–1964	−3.2	6.7	−24.1	−20.6		1.8	−3.1	6.7	−22.6	−19.0
1964–1965	−0.5	6.6	0.4	6.4		8.6	−0.5	6.6	9.4	15.5
1965–1966	−0.7	−0.4	−12.3	−13.3		−6.1	−0.6	−0.5	−17.5	−18.6
1966–1967	−2.0	10.1	9.8	18.0		−11.0	−1.7	10.1	0.2	8.6
1967–1968	2.5	−0.5	−3.8	−1.8		5.6	2.8	−0.5	1.5	3.8
1968–1969	2.8	6.5	11.4	20.7		−0.3	3.6	6.6	10.7	20.9
1969–1970	−1.3	4.0	−10.2	−7.6		3.5	−1.2	4.1	−6.6	−3.7
1970–1971	−4.9	−10.2	1.5	−13.6		6.5	−5.2	−10.2	9.3	−6.1
1971–1972	1.3	−3.6	11.7	9.5		4.6	0.9	−3.7	17.6	14.8
1972–1973	−1.8	−4.5	−0.4	−6.7		−14.9	−2.3	−4.6	−13.7	−20.6
1973–1974	1.6	2.6	11.7	15.9		4.2	1.2	2.6	13.6	17.4
1974–1975	2.9	−1.1	−15.2	−13.4		0.5	3.4	−1.1	−16.4	−14.1
Contribution to world instability[a]										
Absolute	10.6	32.7	135.6	178.9		78.2	16.3	31.8	135.0	183.1
Percent	6	18	76	100		100	9	17	74	100
Contribution to world production										
Percent	13	11	76	100		100	7	6	87	100

(continued on next page)

APPENDIX TABLE V-11. (CONTINUED)

Year	Coarse Grains				Grains and Rice				Protein Meal		
	United States	Canada, Australia, Argentina	Rest-of-World	World	United States	Canada, Australia, Argentina	Rest-of-World	World	United States	Rest-of-World	World
1960–1961	14.9	3.7	11.4	29.9	20.3	-0.9	19.3	38.7	-0.1	-0.5	-0.5
1961–1962	-3.8	-1.8	2.5	-3.0	-2.9	-12.1	0.6	-14.5	-0.4	-0.2	-0.5
1962–1963	-5.5	-0.8	6.2	0.0	-9.1	-2.1	12.0	0.8	1.2	0.1	1.3
1963–1964	2.0	1.2	-7.7	-4.6	-1.1	7.8	-31.4	-24.7	0.1	-0.4	-0.3
1964–1965	-19.4	-3.2	1.8	-20.8	-19.9	3.4	13.8	-2.7	-0.3	-0.3	-0.6
1965–1966	-1.2	-0.8	-17.0	-19.0	-1.8	-1.3	-32.9	-36.0	-1.4	0.6	-0.8
1966–1967	-3.8	1.1	-1.8	-4.6	-5.5	11.1	2.1	7.7	0.5	0.4	0.8
1967–1968	10.6	-4.9	0.3	6.0	13.5	-5.4	1.3	9.4	0.1	1.1	1.1
1968–1969	-0.5	-1.2	-1.7	-3.3	3.2	5.4	8.6	17.2	-0.4	1.0	0.6
1969–1970	2.1	2.1	0.6	4.8	0.9	6.2	-7.7	-0.6	1.4	-0.6	0.8
1970–1971	-16.9	4.9	-2.8	-14.8	-22.1	-5.3	6.0	-21.4	0.8	0.3	1.0
1971–1972	22.7	2.2	0.9	25.8	23.6	-1.5	17.6	39.7	-1.0	0.6	-0.4
1972–1973	12.1	1.3	-17.9	-4.5	9.8	-3.2	-31.3	-24.7	-1.7	-0.4	-2.2
1973–1974	13.1	1.8	17.0	31.9	14.3	4.4	28.6	47.4	-1.1	-2.3	-3.4
1974–1975	-26.5	-5.5	8.2	-23.8	-23.1	-6.5	-6.7	-36.4	2.6	0.7	3.3
Contribution to world instability[a]											
Absolute	126.9	9.7	60.4	196.8	120.5	22.0	179.1	321.9	12.1	5.9	17.6
Percent	64	5	31	100	37	7	56	100	67	33	100
Contribution to world production											
Percent	31	6	63	100	18	6	76	100	47	53	100

[a] Sum of the absolute values of deviations with the same sign as the world deviation minus the sum of the absolute values of deviations with the opposite sign as the world deviation.

SOURCE: See Appendix Table V-10.

APPENDIX TABLE V-12.   EXCHANGE VALUE OF DOLLAR
RELATIVE TO CURRENCIES OF MAJOR AGRICULTURAL CUSTOMERS,[a]
APRIL 1971—MARCH 1975 (PERCENT OF APRIL 1971 EXCHANGE VALUE)

Month[b]	1971	1972	1973	1974	1975
January		92.6	92.6	90.3	86.2
February		92.4	86.3	88.3	84.5
March		91.8	86.4	85.8	85.9
April	100.0	92.2	86.5	85.3	
May	99.6	91.7	85.0	86.0	
June	100.0	92.0	82.8	86.6	
July	99.8	92.1	82.7	87.3	
August	97.7	92.3	83.2	88.9	
September	96.4	92.4	83.1	88.5	
October	95.9	92.9	83.2	87.7	
November	95.6	93.0	86.7	87.1	
December	93.8	92.9	87.5	87.1	

[a] An average weighted by 1971 value of U.S. commercial exports of agricultural products to 14 major markets.

[b] Exchange rate as of last trading day of each month.

SOURCE: Personal communication with ERS, USDA. A chart of these figures appears in USDA, *World Monetary Conditions in Relation to Agricultural Trade.*

APPENDIX TABLE V-13.   EC AND WORLD MARKET PRICES
FOR SELECTED AGRICULTURAL PRODUCTS, 1968-1969—1973-1974

Product	Season[a]	EC Entry Price (UA/100 kilograms)	World Market Price[b] (UA/100 kilograms)	Ratio (percent)
Wheat[c]	1968–1969	10.95	5.61	195
	1969–1970	10.95	5.11	214
	1970–1971	10.95	5.79	189
	1971–1972	11.28	5.39	209
	1972–1973	11.74	7.67	153
	1973–1974	11.86	14.94	79
Husked rice	1968–1969	19.04	13.79	138
	1969–1970	19.06	10.27	186
	1970–1971	19.06	9.07	210
	1971–1972	20.91	10.22	205
	1972–1973	21.31	18.58	115
	1973–1974	21.47	35.49	60
Corn	1968–1969	9.59	5.39	178
	1969–1970	9.69	6.09	159
	1970–1971	9.69	6.88	141
	1971–1972	9.81	5.58	176
	1972–1973	10.32	7.24	143
	1973–1974	10.43	10.68	98

(continued on next page)

Appendix Table V-13.   (Continued)

Product	Season[a]	EC Entry Price (UA/100 kilograms)	World Market Price[b] (UA/100 kilograms)	Ratio (percent)
White sugar	1968–1969	22.35	6.29	355
	1969–1970	22.35	7.51	298
	1970–1971	22.35	10.99	203
	1971–1972	23.80	15.75	186
	1972–1973	24.55	19.30	127
	1973–1974	24.80	37.52	66
Beef and veal	1968–1969	68.00	40.24	169
	1969–1970	68.00	46.18	147
	1970–1971	68.00	48.51	140
	1971–1972	72.00	53.96	133
	1972–1973	76.63	68.26	112
	1973–1974	86.20	77.50	111
Pork	1968	74.03	55.01	135
	1969	70.82	51.56	137
	1970	69.47	52.03	134
	1971	78.50	60.14	131
	1972	77.46	52.69	147
	1973	85.82	65.59	131
Eggs	1968	63.20	46.00	137
	1969	63.43	42.00	151
	1970	63.30	31.50	201
	1971	64.76	40.00	162
	1972	65.25	41.00	159
	1973	63.27	57.00	111
Butter	1968–1969	190.93	37.90	504
	1969–1970	191.25	31.18	613
	1970–1971	191.25	39.80	481
	1971–1972	195.80	114.35	171
	1972–1973	201.15	80.82	249
	1973–1974	192.33	60.08	320

[a] Varies with products.

[b] EC entry price, excluding levies or aids.

[c] "Soft" wheat in EC terms, which more closely corresponds to dominant U.S. types than "hard" wheat which is a durum type.

Sources: Statistical Office of the European Communities, *Yearbook of Agricultural Statistics: 1974*, October 1974, Table F4, p. 254; Organisation for Economic Co-Operation and Development, *Agricultural Policy of the European Economic Community*, (Paris, France: OECD, 1974), Table 6, p. 24.

APPENDIX TABLE V-14.   WHEAT PRICE IN FRANCE AND THE UNITED STATES,
1969–1974

	France			United States		
Year	Current (French francs/ 100 kilograms)	1970 Currency[a]	Index (1969 = 100)	Current (dollars/ bushel)	1970 Currency[a] (dollars/ bushel)	Index (1969 = 100)
1969	42.96	45.3	100	1.26	1.33	100
1970	46.94	46.9	104	1.33	1.33	100
1971	49.02	46.5	103	1.36	1.30	98
1972	49.85	44.7	99	1.57	1.45	109
1973	52.23	43.7	96	3.16	2.77	208
1974	59.04	45.1	99	4.48	3.56	268

[a] Deflated with implicit GNP deflator.

SOURCES: U.S. wheat price (simple average of monthly price received by farmers for all wheat)—USDA, *Agricultural Prices: Annual Summary 1974,* Pr 1-3(75), June 1975.

U.S. implicit GNP deflator—Council of Economic Advisers, *Annual Report* transmitted with the *Economic Report of the President,* Washington: Government Printing Office, 1975, p. 252.

French wheat price (blé tendre, qualité moyenne standard, correspondant au décret P.S. 75 franco organisme stockeur, vrac)—Statistical Office of the European Communities, *Agricultural Statistics,* 1974–1, September 1974; Personal communication with ERS, USDA.

French current and real gross domestic product—Commission of the European Communities, *The Economic Situation in the Community,* 1975–1, March 1975; Organisation for Economic Co-Operation and Development, *National Accounts of OECD Countries,* 1961–1972.

APPENDIX TABLE V-15.   CORN PRICE IN FRANCE AND THE UNITED STATES,
1969–1974

	France			United States		
Year	Current (French francs/ 100 kilograms)	1970 Currency[a] (French francs/ 100 kilograms)	Index (1969 = 100)	Current (dollars/ bushel)	1970 Currency[a] (dollars/ bushel)	Index (1969 = 100)
1969	45.34	47.8	100	1.13	1.19	100
1970	46.43	46.4	97	1.23	1.23	104
1971	48.03	45.6	95	1.27	1.21	102
1972	51.77	46.5	97	1.17	1.08	91
1973	54.30	45.4	95	1.89	1.66	140
1974	67.56	51.6	108	2.92	2.32	195

[a] Deflated with implicit GNP deflator.

SOURCES: U.S. corn price (simple average of monthly price received by farmers)—USDA, *Agricultural Prices: Annual Summary 1974,* Pr 1-3(75), June 1975.

U.S. implicit GNP deflator—Council of Economic Advisers, *Annual Report* transmitted with the *Economic Report of the President,* Washington: Government Printing Office, 1975, p. 252.

French corn price (mais, moyenne des qualités commercialisées départ organisme stockeur, vrac)—Statistical Office of the European Communities, *Agricultural Statistics,* 1974–1, September 1974; Personal communication with ERS, USDA.

French current and real gross domestic product—Commission of the European Communities, *The Economic Situation in the Community,* 1975–1, March 1975; Organisation for Economic Co-Operation and Development, *National Accounts of OECD Countries,* 1961–1972.

APPENDIX TABLE V-16.   SOYBEAN MEAL PRICE IN THE NETHERLANDS AND
UNITED STATES, 1969–1974

| | Netherlands | | | United States | | |
Year	Current (Fl/100 kilograms)	1970 Currency[a] (Fl/100 kilograms)	Index (1969 = 100)	Current (dollars/ ton)	1970 Currency[a] (dollars/ ton)	Index (1969 = 100)
1969	36.4	38.4	100	74.5	78.6	100
1970	39.0	39.0	102	79.2	79.2	101
1971	37.5	34.6	90	77.8	74.5	95
1972	43.2	36.5	95	105	97	124
1973	85.3	66.8	174	238	209	266
1974	50.9	36.6	95	141	112	142

[a] Deflated with implicit GNP deflator.

SOURCES: U.S. soybean meal price (44% protein, bulk, Decatur)—USDA, *Fats and Oils Situation,* FOS-275, November 1974, and FOS-278, June 1975.

U.S. implicit GNP deflator—Council of Economic Advisers, *Annual Report* transmitted with the *Economic Report of the President,* Washington: Government Printing Office, 1975, p. 252.

Netherlands soybean meal price (toasted extracted, ruw eiwit 50%, ruwe celst. 5%, Boordvrij/disponibel Rotterdam)—Statistical Office of the European Communities, *Agricultural Statistics,* 1974–1, September 1974; Personal communication with EC Information Service, Washington, D.C.

Netherlands current and real gross domestic product—Commission of the European Communities, *The Economic Situation in the Community,* 1975–1, March 1975; Organisation for Economic Co-Operation and Development, *National Accounts of OECD Countries,* 1962–1973, Volume I.

Appendix Table V-17.   Wheat Price in Japan and the United States,
1969–1974

	Japan			United States		
Year	Current (yen/150 kilograms)	1970 Currency[a] (yen/150 kilograms)	Index (1969 = 100)	Current (dollars/ bushel)	1970 Currency[a] (dollars/ bushel)	Index (1969 = 100)
1969	1935	2063	100	1.26	1.33	100
1970	1940	1940	94	1.33	1.33	100
1971	1944	1860	90	1.36	1.30	98
1972	1895	1729	84	1.57	1.45	109
1973	2620	2144	104	3.16	2.77	208
1974	2589	1754	85	4.48	3.56	268

[a] Deflated with implicit GNP deflator.

Sources: U.S. wheat price (simple average of monthly price received by farmers for all wheat)—USDA, *Agricultural Prices: Annual Summary 1974*, Pr 1-3(75), June 1975.

U.S. implicit GNP deflator—Council of Economic Advisers, *Annual Report* transmitted with the *Economic Report of the President*, Washington: Government Printing Office, 1975, p. 252.

Japanese wheat price (standard grade, government selling price)—Organisation for Economic Co-Operation and Development, *Agricultural Policy in Japan*, Paris, France: OECD, 1974, Table 20, p. 52; Personal communication with ERS, USDA.

Japanese implicit GNP deflator—Organisation for Economic Co-Operation and Development (OECD), *Main Economic Indicators*, April 1975; OECD, *Main Economic Indicators: Historical Statistics, 1955–1971*, March 1973.

APPENDIX TABLE V-18. CONSUMER RICE PRICE IN JAPAN
AND THE UNITED STATES, 1967-1974

Year	Japan			United States		
	Current (CPI index)	1970 Currency[a] (CPI index)	Index (1969 = 100)	Current (CPI index)	1970 Currency[a] (CPI index)	Index (1969 = 100)
1967	83.9	96.7	92	100.0	115.0	105
1968	92.3	102.4	98	101.8	112.6	103
1969	98.2	104.7	100	103.7	109.4	100
1970	100.0	100.0	96	106.2	106.2	97
1971	102.8	98.4	94	109.4	104.7	96
1972	106.7	97.4	93	109.9	101.7	93
1973	115.9	94.8	91	141.9	124.4	114
1974	143.6	97.3	93	237.7	188.9	173

[a] Deflated with implicit GNP deflator.

SOURCES: U.S. rice price (CPI index, 1967 = 100)—U.S. Department of Labor, *Monthly Labor Review,* July 1975; USDA, *Food Consumption, Prices and Expenditures,* Supplement for 1973 to Agricultural Economic Report No. 138, December 1974, Table 97, p. 70.

U.S. implicit GNP deflator—Council of Economic Advisers, *Annual Report* transmitted with the *Economic Report of the President,* Washington: Government Printing Office, 1975, p. 252.

Japanese rice price (index for *all* cereals consumed directly by people which is heavily dominated by rice, 1970 = 100)—Personal communication with ERS, USDA.

Japanese implicit GNP deflator—Organisation for Economic Co-Operation and Development (OECD), *Main Economic Indicators,* April 1975; OECD, *Main Economic Indicators: Historical Statistics, 1955-1971,* March 1973.

APPENDIX TABLE V-19.   PORK PRICE IN JAPAN AND THE UNITED STATES,
1967–1974

	Japan			United States		
Year	Current Index	1970 Currency[a] Index	Index (1969 = 100)	Current (in cents)	1970 Currency[a] (in cents)	Index (1969 = 100)
1967	91.0	104.8	81	51.5	59.2	96
1968	110.1	122.2	95	51.7	57.2	93
1969	121.0	129.0	100	58.5	61.7	100
1970	100.0	100.0	78	58.8	58.8	95
1971	109.5	104.8	81	52.1	49.8	81
1972	115.0	104.9	81	65.3	60.4	98
1973	125.1	102.4	79	87.3	76.5	124
1974	142.9	96.8	75	77.4	61.5	100

[a] Deflated with implicit GNP deflator.

SOURCES: U.S. pork price (wholesale cuts, cents per retail pound)—USDA, *Marketing & Transportation System,* MTS-197, May 1975, pp. 9, 17, and 22.

U.S. implicit GNP deflator—Council of Economic Advisers, *Annual Report* transmitted with the *Economic Report of the President,* Washington: Government Printing Office, 1975, p. 252.

Japanese pork price (wholesale index, 1970 = 100)—Personal communication with ERS, USDA.

Japanese implicit GNP deflator—Organisation for Economic Co-Operation and Development (OECD), *Main Economic Indicators,* April 1975; OECD, *Main Economic Indicators: Historical Statistics, 1955–1971,* March 1973.

ENDNOTES

CHAPTER I

1. The material in this chapter draws heavily upon research supported by the Office of Economic Stabilization, Department of the Treasury, and reported in *Food and Agricultural Policy in 1971–1974: Reflections on Controls and Their Impact*, December 1974, by Glenn L. Nelson. The points of view and opinions in this chapter do not necessarily represent the official position or policy of the Department of the Treasury.

2. For a more detailed description of these policies and their context see Council of Economic Advisers, *Economic Report of the President* (Washington: Government Printing Office, 1972).

3. Executive Order 11615 of August 15, 1971, by President Richard M. Nixon as reproduced in Office of Emergency Preparedness, *Stemming Inflation: The Office of Emergency Preparedness and the 90-Day Freeze* (Washington: Government Printing Office, 1972), pp. 229–230.

4. Class 1–5 farms; omits those having a value of products sold of less than $2,500, except for farms which normally would have had sales of at least $2,500.

5. The weighting of prices is an important factor in reaching this conclusion. The retail market basket weights used in Figure I-2 show "farm value" declining 3% from August to September while the USDA index of prices received by farmers (Appendix Table I-4) shows no change from August to September. Farm prices, as measured by the USDA index, were higher in October and November than in August.

6. *The Wall Street Journal*, December 3, 1971, p. 11.

7. For additional information see USDA, *Feed Situation*, No. 241, November 1971, pp. 12–14.

8. USDA, *Feed Situation*, No. 242, February 1972, pp. 3–5, and No. 243, April 1972, p. 3.

9. *The Wall Street Journal*, March 27, 1972, p. 4.

10. *The Wall Street Journal*, March 30, 1972.

11. The following two reports contain reviews of the data on farm-retail spreads: Council on Wage and Price Stability, *Marketing Spreads for Food Products*, staff report prepared by Charles Handy and Richard King, May 1975; and USDA, *Review and*

Evaluation of Price Spread Data for Foods, report of task force jointly sponsored by the American Agricultural Economics Association and the USDA, January 1976.

12. C. Jackson Grayson, Jr., with Louis Neeb, *Confessions of a Price Controller* (Homewood, Ill.: Dow Jones-Irwin, Inc., 1974), pp. 126–127.

13. The Russian wheat deal has generated a large amount of discussion and writing. A sampling of the different versions can be found in:
Joseph Albright, "Some Deal," *New York Times Magazine,* November 26, 1973.
Martha M. Hamilton, *The Great American Grain Robbery & Other Stories* (Washington: Agribusiness Accountability Project, 1972).
Dale E. Hathaway, "Food Prices and Inflation," *Brookings Papers on Economic Activity,* 1:1974, especially pp. 85–90.
John A. Schnittker, "The 1972–1973 Food Price Spiral," *Brookings Papers on Economic Activity,* 2:1973, pp. 498–506.
James Trager, *Amber Waves of Grain* (New York: Arthur Fields Books, 1973).

14. *The Wall Street Journal,* May 26, 1972, p. 5; May 30, 1972, pp. 2, 22; and July 10, 1972, p. 4.

15. USDA, *Wheat Situation,* WS-221, August 1972.

16. *The Wall Street Journal,* July 10, 1972, p. 4.

17. Albright, "Some Deal," p. 98.

18. Marvin H. Kosters in association with J. Dawson Ahalt, *Controls and Inflation: The Economic Stabilization Program in Retrospect,* Domestic Affairs Study 37 (Washington: American Enterprise Institute, December 1975), p. 65.

19. Albright, "Some Deal."

20. *Ibid.* and Schnittker, "The 1972–1973 Food Price Spiral," p. 500.

21. For additional details, see USDA, *Wheat Situation,* WS-221, August 1972, pp. 9–11.

22. The other members of the Food Industry Advisory Committee were: James M. Beggs, Consultant to the Department of Transportation and formerly Under Secretary to the Department of Transportation; Charles E. Bishop, Chancellor of the University of Maryland, College Park; Clifton B. Cox, President and Chief Executive Officer of Armour Food Company; William D. Farr, President of the Farr Farms Company; Mary T. Hamilton, Associate Professor of Finance at Loyola University of Chicago and former member of the Price Commission; Terrance Hanold, Chairman of the Executive Committee of the Pillsbury Company; Eunice P. Howe, Chairman of the Consumer Advisory Council, Massachusetts Consumer Council; William J. Kuhfuss, President of the American Farm Bureau Federation; Morris E. Lewis, Jr., Chairman of the Board and Chairman of the Management Committee, Super Valu Stores, Inc.; H. Wesley McAden, Vice President of Cook Industries, Inc.; William S. Mitchell, President of Safeway Stores, Inc.; Andrall E. Pearson, President and member of the Executive Committee of Pepsi-Cola, Inc.; Harry Ralston Poole, Executive Vice President, Amalgamated Meat Cutters and Butcher Workmen of North America, AFL-CIO; Martin Sorkin, private consultant on economics; Harvey T. Stephens, Director and Executive Vice President of ARA Service, Inc.; and Abraham Weiss, Chief Economist and Director of Research of the International Brotherhood of Teamsters.

23. *The Wall Street Journal,* March 13, 1973, p. 33.

24. USDA, *Feed Situation,* FDS-247, February 1973, p. 3.

25. A brief description of federal marketing orders for milk and other products is available in USDA, *Price Impacts of Federal Market Order Programs,* report of the Interagency Task Force, Special Report 12, Farmer Cooperative Service, January 7, 1975.

26. USDA, *Dairy Situation*, DS-344, March 1973, p. 20.

27. USDA, *Dairy Situation*, DS-346, July 1973, p. 21.

28. *The Wall Street Journal*, July 29, 1974, p. 14.

29. Council of Economic Advisers, *Economic Report of the President* (Washington: Government Printing Office, 1976), p. 268.

30. USDA, *1975 Handbook of Agricultural Charts*, Agriculture Handbook No. 491, October 1975, p. 5.

31. Cost of Living Council, *Economic Stabilization Program Quarterly Report: April 1, 1973 through June 30, 1973* (Washington: Government Printing Office, 1973), p. 24.

32. Cost of Living Council, *Economic Stabilization Program Quarterly Report: July 1, 1973 through September 30, 1973* (Washington: Government Printing Office, 1973), pp. 29–30.

33. A significant proportion of the problems derived from the manner in which freeze prices were computed. For a discussion of these problems, see Chapters III and IV on the food regulations.

34. For a more complete discussion of this action see USDA, *Fats and Oils Situation*, FOS-269, October 1973, pp. 11–12.

35. Karl A. Fox, "An Appraisal of Deficiencies in Food Price Forecasting for 1973, and Recommendations for Improvement," Iowa State University, Ames, Iowa, November 29, 1973.

36. These points are documented in a series of court cases challenging the legality of maintaining beef ceiling prices. Both the CLC position and opposing arguments are presented. The most complete presentations of the economic arguments are found in: (1) U.S. District Court, Northern District of California, *Pacific Coast Meat Jobbers Association, et al.* vs. *Cost of Living Council, et al.*, August 1–2, 1973; Willard Williams, Professor at Texas Tech University, was an expert witness for the plaintiffs, and Glenn Nelson, CLC economist at the time, was an expert witness for the defense. (2) U.S. District Court, District of Nebraska, *Minden Beef Co. and Greater New York Association of Meat and Poultry Dealers, Inc.* vs. *Cost of Living Council*, August 8, 1973; Everett Pederson, Professor at the University of Nebraska, was an expert witness for the plaintiffs, and Nelson was again an expert witness for the defense.

37. The survey of prices for the CPI is conducted on the first Tuesday, Wednesday, and Thursday of the earliest week which contains a Tuesday of each month.

38. See references in endnote 11 of this chapter.

39. *The Wall Street Journal*, July 29, 1974, p. 14.

40. USDA, *Wheat Situation*, WS-224, May 1973, p. 2.

41. USDA, *Wheat Situation*, WS-225, August 1973, p. 2.

42. Remaining exports of 700 million bushels (1,100 less 400) implied exports of 233 million bushels per quarter, or a drop of 167 bushels per quarter; the ratio of 167 to 400 is 0.4175.

43. USDA, *Wheat Situation*, WS-226, November 1973, p. 29.

44. USDA, *Wheat Situation*, WS-229, August 1974, pp. 6, 10.

45. USDA, *Dairy Situation*, DS-347, September 1973, pp. 11–12.

46. *Ibid.*, p. 19; USDA, *Dairy Situation*, DS-350, March 1974, pp. 24–25; DS-351, July 1974, pp. 20–24.

47. USDA, *Dairy Situation*, DS-349, March 1974, p. 24; DS-350, May 1974, pp. 24–25.

48. USDA, *Dairy Situation*, DS-348, November 1973, p. 28; DS-349, March 1974, p. 24.

49. This section relies heavily on staff work by Paul Christ and William Hand, Office of Food, CLC; the authors are, of course, solely responsible for the interpretation presented here.

50. For other published descriptions of these events see James T. Bonnen, "The 1973 Economic Report of the President: Implications for Agricultural Policy," *American Journal of Agricultural Economics*, 55:3, August 1973, pp. 391–398; Allen Grommet, "Enactment of the Agriculture and Consumer Protection Act of 1973: A Case Study in Agricultural Policy Formation in an Urban-Industrial Society," presented at the American Agricultural Economics Association meeting, College Station, Texas, August 18–21, 1974; Mary Russell, "Confusion Marks Passage of Farm Bill," *The Washington Post*, July 23, 1973, p. A8.

CHAPTER II

1. A number of reviewers contributed to the clarification and focus of this chapter as well as to the statistical consistency of various sources of data. I am grateful for their help but at the same time I take full reponsibility for the material and views contained in the chapter. The reviewers include Professor Henry B. Arthur, Harvard Business School; Dr. Otto C. Doering III, USDA; Dr. Lawrence A. Duewer, USDA; Dr. Peter M. Emerson, USDA; Dr. Kenneth R. Farrell, USDA; Dr. Kenneth J. Fedor, Vice President, Quaker Oats Co.; Professor Glenn L. Nelson, Purdue University; Donald S. Perkins, Chairman of the Board, Jewel Companies, Inc.; Dr. Mark J. Powers, CFTC; Dr. Gary Seevers, CFTC; and Ms. Laurie Hall and Kenneth C. McCorkle, Research Assistants, Harvard Business School.

2. Three excellent articles provide a concise historical perspective of U.S. food control policies. They are as follows: George B. Rogers, *Price Control Programs, 1917–71*, USDA Agricultural Report #223, April 1972; George B. Rogers, "Farm Price Controls—Help or Hindrance?" *Journal of Northeastern Agricultural Economics Council*, Vol. II, No. 1, June 1973; A. D. Rasmussen, G. L. Baker, and J. S. Ward, *A Short History of Agricultural Adjustment 1933–75*, USDA Agricultural Information Bulletin #391, March 1976.

3. Rasmussen, Baker, and Ward, p. 9.

4. Rogers, *Price Control Programs 1917–71*, p. 23.

5. Ray A. Goldberg, *The Soybean Industry* (Minneapolis: University of Minnesota Press, 1952), pp. 84 and 111.

6. *Ibid.*, p. 114.

7. Rogers, *Price Control Programs, 1917–71*, p. 3.

8. USDA, *Livestock and Meat Situation*, December 1974.

9. USDA, *Marketing and Transportation Situation*, November 1974.

10. Albert J. Eckstein and Dale M. Heien, *A Study of Shortages in the U.S. Livestock-Feed Grains Economy During 1971–74*, prepared for the National Commission on Supplies and Shortages, May 31, 1976, pp. 91–92 (in draft form).

11. *Ibid.*

12. *Ibid.*, p. 94.

13. *Ibid.*

CHAPTER III

1. See Chapter I.

2. See Chapter I.

3. Kenneth J. Fedor, Cost of Living Council memorandum, "Food Price Regulations," January 8, 1973.

4. John T. Dunlop, statement before the Subcommittee on Production and Stabilization of the Senate Committee on Banking, Housing and Urban Affairs, February 6, 1974, p. 20.

5. USDA, "Price Impacts of Federal Market Order Programs," January 7, 1975.

6. Executive Order 11695, January 11, 1973.

7. Office of Economic Stabilization, Department of the Treasury, "Historical Working Papers on the Economic Stabilization Program, August 15, 1971 through April 30, 1974" (Washington: Government Printing Office), Part I, p. 8.

8. These points are also made in the "Working Papers," *ibid,* pp. 20–23.

9. *Ibid,* p. 35.

10. Council on Wage and Price Stability, "Marketing Spreads for Food Products," Staff Report, May 1975, p. 25.

11. USDA, Economic Research Service, "Developments in Marketing Spreads for Agricultural Products in 1975," Report No. 328, p. 7.

CHAPTER IV

1. The author is especially indebted to John T. Dunlop for the chance to participate in this experience. Valuable comments on this manuscript were made by Mr. Dunlop and by Robert O. Aders, Robert Dorsher, Kenneth J. Fedor, Wayne L. Horvitz, D. Quinn Mills, and Abraham Weiss. The author greatly benefited by such comments but retains sole responsibility for any errors or omissions in this chapter. Finally, the author tried to write this chapter from the personal viewpoint of a professional economist who was very involved in the Economic Stabilization Program. Statements made in this chapter are from this perspective and experience and do not necessarily reflect the views of other individuals or institutions with whom the author worked before, during, and after this period.

2. See, for instance:
Daniel J. B. Mitchell, "Phase II Wage Controls," *Industrial and Labor Relations Review,* April 1974, pp. 351–375.
Daniel Quinn Mills, *Government, Labor and Inflation* (Chicago: The University of Chicago Press, 1975).
John T. Dunlop, "Fundamentals of Wage Stabilization," *Daily Labor Reports,* Bureau of National Affairs, Washington, D.C., February 4, 1974, Section F.
John T. Dunlop, "Wage and Price Controls as Seen by a Controller," Industrial Relations Research Association, *Proceedings of the 1975 Annual Spring Meeting, May 8–10, 1975,* pp. 457–463.
Arnold Weber, "Making Controls Work," *The Public Interest,* Winter 1973, pp. 28–40.
Albert Rees, "Tripartite Wage Stabilizing in the Food Industry," *Industrial Relations,* May 1975, pp. 250–258.
Pay Board Portrait (Washington: Government Printing Office, 1973).

John T. Dunlop, "An Appraisal of Wage Stabilization Policies," in *Problems and Policies of Dispute Settlement and Wage Stabilization During World War II* (Washington: U.S. Department of Labor, 1950), pp. 155–186.

3. Others may prefer the term "pay stabilization" or "compensation stabilization." The issue of what constitutes wage or pay stabilization will be discussed later.

4. National Association of Food Chains Executive Bulletin which quoted Cornell University's "Operating Results of Food Chains 1974–75."

5. "Wholesaling," *Progressive Grocer*, April 1975, p. 136.

6. *Ibid.* I could not find comparable figures for retail firms.

7. Internal Pay Board Memorandum, 1973, entitled "Retail Food Stores."

8. 1967 Enterprise Statistics, Part 1; U.S. Department of Commerce, Bureau of the Census (Series ES 67–1), January 1972.

9. *Employment and Earnings*, Volume 19, No. 10, April 1973, and *Employment and Earnings*, Volume 22, No. 3, September 1975 (Washington: U.S. Department of Labor, Bureau of Labor Statistics).

10. Super Market Institute, "The Super Market Industry Speaks," Sixteenth Annual Report, 1964, in Herbert R. Northrup et al., *Restrictive Labor Practices in the Supermarket Industry* (Philadelphia: University of Pennsylvania Press, 1967), p. 34.

11. Independents in Milwaukee, Chicago, Dallas, and St. Louis are some examples that came to the Committee's attention.

12. "Wholesaling," *Progressive Grocer*, April 1975, p. 159.

13. Both examples have been greatly simplified in the text. They are illustrative, however, of some of the automation issues concerning employees, unions, and employers in the retail food industry.

14. While there are also a Phase III Stage A, Phase III Stage B, and Phase IV, the differences in these phases had substantive implications only for price regulation. Hence, Phase III will be used to indicate all of these phases.

15. Further elaboration on all phases can be found in *Historical Working Papers on the Economic Stabilization Program August 15, 1971 to April 30, 1974* (Washington: Office of Economic Stabilization, Department of the Treasury, 1974). Note especially the Wage Stabilization Policies found on pp. 325–427. The Regulations themselves can be found in *Code of Federal Regulations 6* (Washington: Government Printing Office, 1974).

16. The memorandum is named after George Meany, President of the AFL-CIO. Labor insisted on the assurance when the possibility arose that the Cost of Living Council would oversee and possibly reverse Pay Board actions.

17. See Henry H. Perritt, Jr., and Robert C. Dresser, "Policy Planning," pp. 20–28, in *Historical Working Papers on the Economic Stabilization Program August 15, 1971 to April 30, 1974.*

18. Labor costs can be held, let us say, to an increase of 5.5% by giving all workers just 5.5%. This will not necessarily lead to wage stabilization, especially in the long run, unless the underlying wage structure is roughly in balance and workers view as equitable "percentage differences" in wage rates.

19. John T. Dunlop, *Wage and Price Controls as Seen by a Controller*, p. 460. Also see Dunlop's "Fundamentals of Wage Stabilization," in *Daily Labor Reports* and D. Quinn Mills, *Government, Labor and Inflation*, p. 102. For complete citations see note 2 above.

20. The points essentially come from Dunlop, "Fundamentals of Wage Stabilization," p. F-1, 2.

21. Forms will be discussed below. The experience with the mail was personal but not unique. Pay Board staff often requested parties to mail correspondence to their homes for fear it would be lost or delayed if official channels were used. The first computer printout examined by the author contained erroneous information about the firm the author previously worked for. Also, the Great Atlantic and Pacific Tea Company was listed as A&P, Great A&P, Atlantic and Pacific Tea Company, etc., making any computer sorting and grouping process impossible. These situations severely hampered the Committee's operations, especially during the early days of its existence.

22. Inconsistently, this policy was never extended to the largest units (above 5,000 employees). This exacerbated the delay problems and created some inequities.

23. The 5.5% and 0.7% for qualified benefits also allowed some automatic exceptions, usually capped at 7%. This does not alter the argument. See also Daniel J. B. Mitchell, "Phase II Wage Controls," pp. 353–354, for a good summary of the exception policy of the Pay Board.

24. A Miami, Florida-New York City relationship was argued because the "facts" fitted the rules. Retirement migration was cited as a causal link. The argument, of course, was not accepted by the Committee. The fact that it was used illustrates the problem with a regulation approach.

25. In collective bargaining situations, the appropriate unit is the bargaining unit. Again, "benefit units" often extend beyond local bargaining units. Furthermore, in nonunion and exempt situations there are often company-wide benefit plans with local or smaller wage setting units. There were methods for dealing with these situations but they involved further delays and some opportunities for ingenuity.

26. The PB-3A was designed to be a simpler form. It was analogous to the short form for income tax purposes. It could only be used for units with fewer than 5,000 employees. In the early days of the Pay Board, there were no forms. The first forms PB-1 and PB-2 appeared in early 1972 and were succeeded by PB-3 in the spring of 1973. All forms used during the program can be found in "Data Appendix," *Historical Working Papers on the Economic Stabilization Program August 15, 1971 to April 30, 1974*, pp. 483–501.

27. No attempt was made, *per se*, to control or evaluate occupational wage rates. Contracts or wage plans were required with submissions but the requirement was never enforced.

28. The added costs of previously existing fringe benefits due to wage increases.

29. The Pay Board used the phrase "cows in the barn" to refer to contracts that had expired or that presented no problems with deferred increases. It implied that as soon as all the old contracts expired, effective stabilization could begin. The Pay Board expired before this happened.

30. Dunlop in "An Appraisal of Wage Stabilization Policies," pp. 160–161, makes an interesting distinction between delays resulting in slower wage increases because of slowness in changing of basic policy as opposed to slower wage increases as a result of delays in processing cases. The latter, which seemed prevalent during Phase II, is much more injurious to effective wage stabilization since faith in the process will soon be eroded and the desire to break the rules will become very powerful.

31. The IRS, under Pay Board rules, could not approve large percentage increases unless such power was specifically delegated to it in specific cases or classes of cases. When confronted with these nondelegated large increase cases, the IRS would deny them, creating expectations in many employers' minds of a "finality" and "deliberateness" that was simply not the case. This especially caused problems when these "final" decisions were eventually reversed to restore traditional relationships.

32. The court case successfully challenging the $1.90 level was *Jennings v. Connally*, 347 F. Supp. 409 (D.D.C. 1972). In *Jennings v. Shultz*, 355 F. Supp. 1198 (D.D.C. 1972) the court upheld the $2.75 level. The issues surrounding the low wage level were difficult for the stabilization agencies to resolve. They had to recognize the Congressional mandate to pay "low wage employees special attention." However, a high rate, in 1972, might have undermined the Administration's opposition to a minimum wage bill. Also, a wage level of $3.35 would exempt roughly half of the labor force, and with such a large proportion exempt the equity and "equality of sacrifice" so necessary for a wage stabilization program would have been damaged. Furthermore, once the program began to change the figures retroactively special problems arose since employers would have financial difficulty with long retroactive payments and, further, collective bargaining could not be expected to renegotiate contracts. Other problems including disputes between the Council and the Pay Board surrounded the low wage issue. The whole subject is discussed in Thomas R. Goin, "Phase II Wage Stabilization Policies & Concepts," pp. 345–347, in *Historical Working Papers on the Economic Stabilization Program August 15, 1971 to April 30, 1974*. One final point, the low wage exemption hit the food industry particularly hard partly because of the numerous part-time employees. It is interesting that to the author's best knowledge, at no point did the food industry—or any other industry—apply for "relief" by asking that part-timers be exempt from the low wage exemption.

33. Full elaboration is beyond the scope of this chapter. Implementation of the policy meant literally calculating increases on an individual-by-individual basis which was costly. Furthermore, since percentage increases were the allowed norms, crossovers had to be identified—persons starting below the low wage level and with the increase going above to determine the allowed percentage implementation, but in order to calculate the percentage the crossovers had to be known. Furthermore, if wage rates had been the focus and not the percentage, many complications would have been alleviated. The low wage regulation was contained in Section 201.19, *Code of Federal Regulations 6*.

34. Essentially, this meant a continuation of Phase II controls for food.

35. The definition is substantively discussed in another section below. The definition itself can be found in *Code of Federal Regulations 6*, subpart L, see "Food" and "Food Operations."

36. All these problems could be overcome but they put substantial burdens on the sophistication of the wage review process and of course involved delay.

37. The appeals for reconsideration of Phase II decisions added support to this statement.

38. "All the local bargaining problems were the consequences of the people in Washington not knowing what they were doing" would be a harder statement for a local Federal Mediation official to make with a representative of FMCS actively working with the Committee.

39. All cases are referred to by their generic committee names. No specific references are available. All case files may be found in the Archives.

40. For all practical purposes, they remained operationally separate until the decontrol phase.

41. The original public members were Wayne L. Horvitz, Albert Rees, chairman and Laurence E. Seibel. The two additional public members were Marten Estey and Father Leo Brown.

The original management members were Robert O. Aders, Kroger Company; Robert E. Palenchar, Swift and Company; Darrell Stiffler, The Great Atlantic and Pacific Tea Company; and Herman Weber, Safeway Stores. Mr. Weber was later replaced by Ernest Boyce, Colonial Food Stores. Robert K. Fox, Food Employers Council, Inc., was added as an alternate employer member.

The original labor members were Daniel E. Conway, Bakery and Confectionery Workers International Union; Richard C. McAllister, Retail Clerks International Association; Harry R. Poole, Amalgamated Meat Cutters and Butcher Workmen; and Abraham Weiss, International Brotherhood of Teamsters. Mr. Weiss was later replaced as representative of the Teamsters by John J. Greeley. Alvin E. Heaps, Retail, Wholesale and Department Store Union, was added as an alternate labor member.

42. Later, by delegation to the Administrator of the Office of Wage Stabilization.

43. The Cost of Living staff, which essentially worked for the Committee, did not report to the Director of the Committee but rather to the Director for Controlled Industries until July 1973. After this date, the staff that worked primarily on food wage cases reported to the Director of the Committee.

44. Had the Committee lasted longer, the problems of confidentiality of information certainly woould have increased. Management and the public, as well as the people that submitted nonunion cases, feared that such information might be used as tools for organizing. Yet not to process these cases would cause problems, especially in strong nonunion areas. The author believes that had the Committee's life been longer an all-public committee would have made recommendations in these cases.

45. This "Interim Decision and Order" was not final and hence could be issued before a hearing. The parties themselves could make it "final" by accepting it or they could appeal (and stay execution) by requesting a hearing (which was always granted) or by written appeal, tacitly waiving the hearing. Thus, cases could continue to be processed before the hearing. (The hearing requirement put added burdens on parties, especially small units, geographically distant from Washington, D.C.).

46. Initially, the public attended the meetings but seldom, if ever, remained for a long period of time. The case decided by Judge Green, before the United States District Court for the District of Columbia was *Ralph Nader, et al. v. John T. Dunlop, et al.*, Civil Action No. 769–73.

47. See *Pay Board Portrait*, p. 20. Part of the reason for the large volume is the fact that the Committee required more cases to be submitted. This is discussed below.

48. Of the 31 cases remaining in mid-June 1974, decisions had been reached in 17 and were in the process of being typed.

49. The clearest case of the latter point arose early in the Committee's existence. One company in very bad economic condition as the result of an extended strike sought wage relief after signing a contract identical to those of other companies in the area. These other companies were paying (with Council approval) the higher rates. The Committee, however, felt it had to approve the other contract to be consistent with stabilization since that is what the parties had negotiated and submitted.

50. It has often been felt that delay was a deliberate policy instrument used by the stabilization agencies during Phase II. As noted in footnote 30, delays arising from case processing can severely undermine the stabilization effort.

51. The Committee reviewed lists of all cases that met the various criteria and voted acceptance of the lists before any recommendations were forwarded to the Director of the Cost of Living Council. All cases passed through the Committee.

52. The subcommittee, unlike the task force, was composed of members of the full Committee. Hence cases that could not be resolved at the subcommittee level were seldom readily resolved at the full Committee level. It was subsequently decided to eliminate the subcommittee and send cases directly to the full Committee.

53. The task force would often forward cases with "new" issues directly to the Committee for policy guidance. The bakery consecutive workweek was such an issue.

54. Toward the end of controls, the Committee was very conscious of discrepancies between "contract rates" and rates actually being paid as the result of past decisions.

55. There were four such lawsuits. It is the author's opinion that tripartitism was a prime reason for the relatively small number because if feelings ran so strongly about a case as to result in a lawsuit, the case probably would have been deadlocked in Committee. Also, as stated above, the procedural aspects of case processing by the Committee protected the affected parties' rights and insured their involvement (hearing requirement) more than was the case during Phase II.

56. At the time of the fact finding, he was on leave from the Committee for some months.

57. Even percentage comparisons became impossible because of the PB-3 and PB-3A forms being used, the treatment of qualified benefits, and low wage calculations.

58. See, for example, *Pay Board Portrait,* p. 20; and Mitchell, "Phase II Wage Controls," pp. 361–365.
No useful, consistent data are available, or can be constructed from the records of the stabilization program to judge directly the effectiveness of the 1971–1974 experience with wage controls. The main reasons for this conclusion follow.
Wage data were never collected; all submissions were in percentage terms. Since different forms could be used, PB-3 or PB-3A, by most units and since the forms would usually give different percentages for the same wage adjustments, comparable data are not available. Until June 1972 PB-1 and PB-2 forms were used with still different results. Because of the treatment of qualified benefits, the fact that wages below $3.50 could be increased without approval, and as a consequence of "nonchargeable" adjustments such as increases resulting from promotions, payments for longevity, or automatic in-grade progression, and increases in payments for qualified benefits necessary to maintain existing benefit levels, the final percentages recorded often deviated from what actually happened. Some data never reached the Pay Board because small units could be processed by the IRS.

59. During Phase III the Office of Wage Stabilization abandoned the quantitative approach to recording effects of Committee actions in favor of a qualitative recording as to whether it was approved in full, in part, or denied. Even this information was not systematically entered into the computer.

60. To the author's knowledge, no unit ever was held to a zero increase.

61. Labor vehemently objected to this practice during Phase II. Technically, the Committee recommended that this Phase II rule be disallowed and the Director of the Cost of Living Council approved the recommendation.

62. Exemption of part-timers from the low wage rules would have alleviated this problem, but it was never proposed to Congress.

63. It lasted one-half a work day and was resolved by a discussion with the Director of the Cost of Living Council. The issue was whether strictly to limit retroactive payments to a maximum length of time—say, one year.

64. It appeared that companies could not accrue money from one tax year to the next once a decision (final or not) had been rendered by the Pay Board or Cost of Living Council.

65. The Construction Committee often held front runners and those with distorted rates on the high side to increases below 5.5%. The Pay Board never did.

66. The Committee's experience amply documented that size of unit was no criterion for special treatment. Many small units—say, mechanics—are affected by and

affect larger units—say, warehousemen and truckers. Larger units are more visible but are not always more significant in the wage-setting process.

67. It is interesting that these regulations were little noticed by the press and their importance has almost entirely been overlooked by other writers on stabilization. It is probably true that much of the food industry was unaware of either the Regulations or their significance.

68. Many came in on company (usually small company) letterheads stating that "such and such wanted permission to give 'John Doe' an x percent raise."

69. It is always possible that other causes besides the Committee's efforts produced the results contained in the aggregate data.

70. Strikes and lockouts involving six workers or more and lasting a full shift or more. For a more elaborate description of the data and their limitations, see "Appendix B. Scope Definition and Methods," *Analysis of Work Stoppages* (Washington: Bureau of Labor Statistics.)

71. Both 1971 and 1974 were partial control years. The periods January 1, 1971— August 14, 1971 and May 1, 1974—December 31, 1974 were without controls for the entire economy. During most of 1973 and 1974, however, as explained earlier in the text, most of the economy except food, health, and construction were under voluntary controls. Data availability prevented including a later year than 1974 and during the years 1971 and 1974 wages were predominantly noncontrolled. These years were also the years surrounding the Committee's activity. Hence, these were the years chosen for comparison.

72. These data are based on an audit undertaken by the Council staff in 1974. (The audit was attempted as a recognition that the quantitative percentage data—as explained in the text—were not reliable, consistent, or comparable.) Because of the limit of staff availability, the audit, as the data indicate, was never completed.

73. To the author's knowledge, no wage case was "denied in full." These cases probably represented appeals of initial decisions where all that was under consideration was the wage adjustment partially denied in the earlier decision or a submission for the second increase within a "control year" where the first increase was above the standard.

74. This paragraph is paraphrased from the discussion of Establishment Data in "Explanatory Notes," *Employment and Earnings*, Bureau of Labor Statistics, U.S. Department of Labor.

75. Weekly hours for private industry for the control periods were as follows: 1971—37.0 hours; 1972—37.1 hours; 1973—37.1 hours; 1974—36.6 hours. Source: Table C-1, *Employment and Earnings*, April 1975.

76. Because of the nature of the forms and the use of the computer during Phase II, no such information is available for the control period. Also, the absence of data collection for the food industry in the precontrol period (or thereafter, for that matter) precluded comparison.

77. Shorter contracts, of course, also added somewhat to the Committee's work load.

78. In at least one case, as an adjunct to the Committee's activity, the top executive of one supermarket chain for the first time met the International President of one of the unions that represented a large number of the company's employees.

79. The Committee certainly encountered many destabilized situations directly resulting from Phase II stabilization action.

80. John T. Dunlop makes these points in "Wage and Price Controls as Seen by a Controller," *loc. cit.*, pp. 458–459.

81. Many of these points come from a list the author found in his files. The author of the list was not identified, but the list was probably prepared by the staff of the Office of Wage Stabilization.

82. The world food price increases, the Russian grain sale, the oil embargo, and "Watergate" are obvious aspects of the 1973–1974 environment.

83. If the answer to this question is positive, the related question—raised elsewhere in this volume—becomes more important. Can food prices be controlled without controlling prices of primary agricultural commodities, at least in times of rapid price increases?

84. The Committee's experience did illustrate another fact; once the IRS became involved it was difficult to remove it from the wage picture. Reasons for this were communications, the IRS's continued involvement in price matters and the public's association—accurate during Phases I and II—of the IRS with all aspects of stabilization, including wages in the food industry. In earlier stabilization periods the Wage and Hour local offices were used to receive applications.

85. Admittedly, the public sector would need governmental involvement. Failure to control any one sector might generate feelings of discrimination and perceived inequities.

CHAPTER V

1. The material in this chapter draws heavily upon research supported by the Office of Raw Materials, Department of the Treasury, and reported in *International Food Policy Issues and Domestic Price Stabilization*, July 1975, by Glenn L. Nelson. The points of view and opinions in this chapter do not necessarily represent the official position or policy of the Department of the Treasury.

2. The listing was influenced by that in Dale E. Hathaway, *Government and Agriculture: Public Policy in a Democratic Society* (New York: Macmillan Company, 1963), Chapter 1.

3. USDA, *Hogs and Pigs*, June 23, 1975.

4. USDA, *Livestock and Meat Situation*, LMS-203, June 1975, p. 7.

5. USDA, *Poultry and Egg Situation*, PES-290, June 1977, p. 17.

6. *Ibid.*, p. 23.

7. USDA, *Dairy Situation*, DS-355, p. 9; USDA, *Agricultural Statistics 1972*, p. 436.

8. Trends were calculated with equations linear in both time and the dependent variable, with one exception noted below. Equations with the dependent variable in log form, which would be appropriate if the variable changed at a constant *percentage* rate over time, were explored but did not yield uniformly or markedly superior results with the exception of protein meal and soybean production.

9. This discussion is based largely upon the description found in Organization for Economic Co-Operation and Development, *Agricultural Policy of the European Economic Community* (Paris, France: OECD, 1974).

10. This discussion is based largely upon the description found in *Agricultural Policy in Japan* (Paris, France: OECD, 1974).

11. Abdullah A. Saleh, "Disincentives to Agricultural Production in Developing Countries: A Policy Survey," *Foreign Agriculture*, FAS, USDA, March 1975 Supplement.

12. USDA, *The World Food Situation and Prospects to 1985*, Foreign Agricultural Economic Report No. 98, ERS, December 1974, p. 30.

13. U.S. Department of Labor, *Monthly Labor Review*, and Statistics Canada, *Prices and Price Indexes*.

14. A major study with much detail was completed in 1971: Food and Agriculture Organization of the United Nations, *Agricultural Commodity Projections*, 1970–1980, Volumes I and II, CCP 71/20, Rome, 1971. These projections were extended to 1985 and otherwise modified in a report for the United Nations World Food Conference in 1974: United Nations, *Assessment of the World Food Situation: Present and Future*, Item 8 of the Provisional Agenda, E/CONF/ .65/3, November 1974. The FAO projections discussed in the text are those in the latter report, unless specifically stated otherwise.

15. Leroy L. Blakeslee, Earl O. Heady and Charles R. Framingham, *World Food Production, Demand, and Trade* (Ames, Iowa: Iowa State University Press, 1973).

16. University of California Food Task Force, *A Hungry World: The Challenge to Agriculture, Summary Report and General Report* (Berkeley: Division of Agricultural Sciences, University of California, 1974).

17. USDA, *World Food Situation, op. cit.*

18. For example, see National Academy of Sciences, *Agricultural Production Efficiency*, report of the Committee on Agricultural Production Efficiency, Washington, D.C., 1975.

19. USDA, *U.S. Agricultural Exports Under Public Law 480*, ERS-Foreign 395, October 1974, pp. 57 and 59.

20. The issue of grain reserves has been addressed by many other writers. The following sources are interesting starting points for additional reading:

W. R. Bailey, F. A. Kutish, and A. S. Rojko, *Grain Stocks Issues and Alternatives–A Progress Report*, Agricultural Economic Research Report, ERS, USDA, February 1974.

Willard W. Cochrane, *Feast or Famine: The Uncertain World of Food and Agriculture and Its Policy Implications for the United States*, (Washington: National Planning Association, February 1974). The dissenting opinions appearing in the footnotes to the "Statement by the NPA Agriculture Committee" should be noted.

Timothy Josling, *An International Grain Reserve Policy*, British-North American Committee, sponsored in part by the National Planning Association, Washington, D.C., 1973.

USDA, *World Food Situation, op. cit.*, pp. 40–47.

Frederick V. Waugh, "Reserve Stocks of Farm Products" in *Agricultural Policy: A Review of Programs and Needs, Volume V*, Technical Papers, National Advisory Commission on Food and Fiber, August 1967.

21. U.S. Office of Management and Budget, *The Budget of the United States Government, Fiscal Year 1976* (Washington: Government Printing Office, 1975).

22. For an analytic argument that a reserves policy may decrease producers' income see Roger Gray, "Grain Reserves Issues," presented at the National Agricultural Outlook Conference sponsored by the USDA, Washington, D.C., December 9–12, 1974; reproduced in *1975 U.S. Agricultural Outlook,* committee print prepared for the Committee on Agriculture and Forestry, Senate, 93rd Congress, 2nd Session, December 23, 1974, pp. 40–46.

CHAPTER VI

1. John A. Schnittker, "The 1972–1973 Food Price Spiral," *Brookings Papers on Economic Activity* (2: 1973), pp. 498–499.

2. Executive Order 11615, August 17, 1971, and Executive Order 11627, October 16, 1971. Section 1 (C).

3. Robert F. Lanzillotti, Mary T. Hamilton, and R. Blaine Roberts, *Phase II in Review, The Price Commission Experience* (Washington: The Brookings Institution, 1975), pp. 56–57. The first two authors were members of the Price Commission and the third was a staff economist.

4. In World War I a Food Administration Grain Corporation centralized all purchasing of grain and flour for overseas, eliminating all competitive bidding by overseas buyers. The Lever Act also permitted a single price at which all wheat was purchased by the Grain Corporation from farmers. Charles O. Hardy, *Wartime Control of Prices* (Washington: The Brookings Institution, 1940), p. 150.

5. *Phase II in Review*, p. 65.

6. Prices received by farmers in the United States rose 87.4% in the period from August 1971 to August 1973 while the food component of the Consumer Price Index rose 24.5% in the same period. The figures for the period August 1971–August 1974 are 63.1% and 35.7% respectively.

7. See report prepared by the Cost of Living Council Committee on Food and released on March 20, 1973, *Economic Stabilization Program Quarterly Report*, covering the period January 11, 1973, through March 31, 1973, pp. 69–76.

8. "Labor and Phase Three," Editorial, *Washington Star*, January 18, 1973; "Befogged Guideline," *New York Times*, February 27, 1973; "Phase Three's Unused Stick in the Closet," *Wall Street Journal*, May 30, 1973, p. 16.

9. USDA, Economic Research Service, *Quarterly Situation and Outlook Memorandum*, November 3, 1972, and February 6, 1973.

10. *Economic Report of the President*, Transmitted to the Congress, January 1973, p. 81.

11. Karl A. Fox, "An Appraisal of Deficiencies in Food Price Forecasting for 1973, and Recommendations for Improvement," Council of Economic Advisers, November 29, 1973.

12. Marvin H. Kosters, In Association with J. Dawson Ahalt, *Controls and Inflation, the Economic Stabilization Program in Retrospect* (Washington: American Enterprise Institute for Public Policy Research, 1975), p. 19.

13. George P. Schultz, "Foreword" in Kosters, *ibid.*

14. For a substantial discussion, see, Office of Economic Stabilization, Department of the Treasury, *Historical Working Papers on the Economic Stabilization Program*, August 15, 1971 to April 30, 1974, Part II, "Removing Controls: The Policy of Selective Decontrol," pp. 859–948. Also see, D. Quinn Mills, "Some Lessons of Price Controls in 1971–1973," *Bell Journal of Economics*, Spring 1975, pp. 3–49.

15. *Economic Stabilization Program Quarterly Report*, January 1, 1974, through May 1, 1974, Cost of Living Council, pp. 62–65.

16. Wayne L. Horvitz, "The Joint Labor-Management Committee in Retail Food—A Preliminary Report," *Proceedings of the National Academy of Arbitrators*, April 1976, pp. 142–215.

17. *Economic Stabilization Program Quarterly Report*, July 1, 1973 through September 30, 1973, Cost of Living Council, pp. 87–88.
The Commission on the organization of the government for the conduct of Foreign Policy in its June 1975 Report (in seven volumes) includes in Appendix H, Case Study I, pp. 18–32 entitled, "Commodity Export Controls: The Soybean Case, 1973," by Edward F. Graziano (November 1974). The case study provides a very partial and inadequate view of the events. It fails to mention the discussions in theFood Committee of

the Cost of Living Council which included the Secretary of Agriculture that were begun in the early spring of 1973 on this subject. It grossly misstates the view of participants. Its assessment of the outcome cannot be accepted in many particulars.

18. For an estimate of costs, see, *Statement of John T. Dunlop, Director, Cost of Living Council, Before the House Banking and Currency Committee*, March 6, 1974, A-106–A-109.

19. *Controls and Inflation*, p. 100.

20. Council on Wage and Price Stability, Staff Report, *Marketing Spreads for Food Products*, May 1975, pp. 22–24.

21. Lloyd Ulman, "Phase II in Contest: Towards an Incomes Policy for Conservatives," in Walter Galenson, ed., *Incomes Policy: What Can We Learn from Europe?*, (Ithaca: New York State School of Industrial and Labor Relations, 1973), p. 89.

22. For a useful summary, see, Anne Romanis Braun, "The Role of Incomes Policy in Industrial Countries Since World War II," *Staff Papers*, International Monetary Fund, March 1975, pp. 1–36.

23. Lanzillotti, Hamilton, and Roberts, *Phase II in Review*, pp. 30–31. The group included Gardner Ackley, Arthur F. Burns, David L. Grove, Richard B. Heflebower, and Walter W. Heller.

24. *Ibid.*, p. 56. Compare this statement with the views of Chester Bowles, Administrator of Price Controls in World War II: "This gradual public acceptance of the need to close legislative gaps was due in large measure to Henderson's constant reiteration of the fact that price controls without wage controls were bound to fail, and that without firm control over food prices wage controls were impossible," Chester Bowles, *Promises to Keep: My Years in Public Life, 1941–1969* (New York: Harper and Row, 1971), p. 37.

25. For a comparative discussion of various programs to restrain wages and prices in the United States, see, Craufurd D. Goodwin, Ed., *Exhortation and Controls, The Search for Wage-Price Policy 1945–1971* (Washington: The Brookings Institution, 1975); D. Quinn Mills, *Government, Labor and Inflation, Wage Stabilization in the United States* (Chicago: The University of Chicago Press, 1975).

26. *Statement of Dr. John T. Dunlop, Director, Cost of Living Council Before the House Banking and Currency Committee, March 6, 1974*, p. 43; A-16-18, *Hearings Before the Committee on Banking and Currency, House of Representatives*, 93 Cong., 2nd Ses. on H. R. 13206, March 6, 7, 8, 1974, pp. 8–368.

27. *Price Impacts of Federal Market Order Programs*, Report of Interagency Task Force, January 7, 1975, Special Report 12, USDA, Farmer Cooperative Service.

28. Net income to farm operators, excluding net inventory change, increased from a level of around $12 billion in the decade before 1972 to $17.3 billion in 1972 and $29.5 billion in 1973; including net inventory change the figure was $18.2 billion in 1972 and $33.1 billion in 1973.

29. *The United States At War*, prepared under the auspices of the Committee of Records of War Administration by the War Records Section, Bureau of the Budget, 1946, pp. 385–391. U.S. Department of Labor, *The Termination Report, National War Labor Board*, Vol. 1, 1946, pp. 240–259.

30. See, John T. Dunlop, *Inflation and Incomes Policies: The Political Economy of Recent U.S. Experience*, The Eighth Monash Economics Lecture, 1974 (Australia: Monash University, Australia, September 9, 1974). John T. Dunlop, "Wage and Price Controls as Seen by a Controller," Industrial Relations Research Association, *Proceedings of the 1975 Annual Spring Meeting*, May 8–10, 1975, pp. 457–463.

31. Arnold R. Weber, "Making Wage Controls Work," *The Public Interest*, Winter 1973, p. 32.

32. Among the early major cases of the Pay Board, the public members were out-voted by labor and management members approving higher adjustments in the railroad and coal cases; the courts set aside the decision in the aerospace cases.

33. "If Phase II and the Pay Board had any salutary effect, it was to preside over the restabilization of the national wage structure in the wake of dislocations induced by unusually large settlements in the construction, transportation, and retail food industries." Arnold R. Weber in *Exhortations and Controls*, p. 381. This retrospective view is ironical in that the restoration of wage relationships was nowhere the stated policy of the board.

34. John T. Dunlop, "Wage and Price Controls as Seen by a Controller," p. 463.

35. Lloyd Ulman and Robert J. Flanagan, *Wage Restraint: A study of Incomes Policies in Western Europe* (Berkeley: University of California Press, 1971), pp. 224–232.

36. See, John T. Dunlop, "Toward a Less Inflationary Economy," remarks to the Society of American Business Writers, San Francisco, May 6, 1974, Cost of Living Council Release, May 6, 1974.

37. George P. Shultz, "Reflections and Wage and Price Controls," Janeway Lectures, Princeton University, November 4–5, 1975 (manuscript), p. 25.

38. See, for example, Statement by Arthur F. Burns, Chairman, Board of Governors of the Federal Reserve System before the Committee on the Budget, U.S. Senate, March 22, 1976.

Index

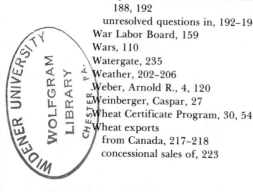